RATIONALITY AND DYNAMIC CHOICE

RATIONALITY
AND
DYNAMIC CHOICE

Foundational explorations

EDWARD F. McCLENNEN

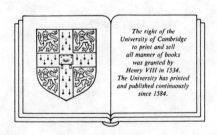

The right of the
University of Cambridge
to print and sell
all manner of books
was granted by
Henry VIII in 1534.
The University has printed
and published continuously
since 1584.

CAMBRIDGE UNIVERSITY PRESS
Cambridge
New York   Port Chester   Melbourne   Sydney

Published by the Press Syndicate of the University of Cambridge
The Pitt Building, Trumpington Street, Cambridge CB2 1RP
40 West 20th Street, New York, NY 10011, USA
10 Stamford Road, Oakleigh, Melbourne 3166, Australia

First published 1990

Printed in Canada

Library of Congress Cataloging-in-Publication Data
McClennen, Edward F. (Edward Francis), 1936–
Rationality and dynamic choice : foundational explorations / by
Edward F. McClennen.
p. cm.
ISBN 0-521-36047-1
1. Reasoning. 2. Decision-making. I. Title.
BC177.M224 1990   89-17392
128′.3 – dc20   CIP

British Library Cataloguing in Publication Data
McClennen, Edward F.
Rationality and dynamic choice : foundational explorations.
1. Rationality
I. Title
153.4′3

ISBN 0-521-36047-1 hardback

. . . 'tis only in two senses, that any affection can be call'd unreasonable. First, When a passion, such as hope or fear, grief or joy, despair or security, is founded on the supposition of the existence of objects, which really do not exist. Secondly, When in exerting any passion in action, we chuse means insufficient for the design'd end, and deceive ourselves in our judgment of causes and effects. Where a passion is neither founded on false supposition, nor chuses means insufficient for the end, the understanding can neither justify it nor condemn it.

David Hume, *Treatise*,
Bk. II, Pt. III, Sec. III

Contents

Conditions on orderings and acceptable-set functions

Alpha An acceptable-set function $D(\cdot)$ [$= C(\cdot)$] defined on X satisfies Alpha just in case for all x in S, and all S^* such that S^* is a superset of S, if x is not in $D(S)$, then x is not in $D(S^*)$ (p. 23).

Beta An acceptable-set function $D(\cdot)$ [$=C(\cdot)$] defined on X satisfies Beta just in case for all x and y in S, and all S^* such that S^* is a superset of S, if both x and y are in $D(S)$, then either x and y are both in $D(S^*)$ or neither is in $D(S^*)$ (p. 23).

CF (context-free choice) An acceptable-set function $D(\cdot)$ [$= C(\cdot)$] satisfies CF just in case $D(\cdot)$ satisfies both Alpha and Beta (p. 23).

CFO (context-free ordering) The ordering R defined over any set of alternatives X is not changed by adding new alternatives, that is, by expanding X to some superset Y (p. 29).

CIND (independence for choice) Let g_1, g_2, and g_3 be any three gambles, let $g_{13} = [g_1, p; g_3, 1 - p]$ be a gamble over g_1 and g_3 such that one stands to confront the gamble g_1 with probability p and the gamble g_3 with probability $1 - p$, and let $g_{23} = [g_2, p; g_3, 1 - p]$ be similarly defined. Then g_1 is in $D(\{g_1, g_2\})$ iff for $0 < p \leq 1$, g_{13} is in $D(\{g_{13}, g_{23}\})$ (pp. 57–8).

CIND-E (equivalent choice independence) For any g_1, g_2, and g_3, and $0 < p \leq 1$, if both g_1 and g_2 are in $D(\{g_1, g_2\})$ then both g_{13} and g_{23} are in $D(\{g_{13}, g_{23}\})$, where $g_{13} = [g_1, p; g_3, 1 - p]$ and $g_{23} = [g_2, p; g_3, 1 - p]$ (p. 137).

CIND-S (strict choice independence) For any g_1, g_2, and g_3, and $0 < p \leq 1$, if g_2 is not in $D(\{g_1, g_2\})$ then g_{23} is not in $D(\{g_{13}, g_{23}\})$, where $g_{23} = [g_2, p; g_3, 1 - p]$ and $g_{13} = [g_1, p; g_3, 1 - p]$ (p. 139).

DC (dynamic consistency) For any choice point n_i in a decision tree T, if $D(S)(n_i)$ is not empty and $s(n_i)$ is in $D(S(n_i))$, then $s(n_i)$ is in $D(S)(n_i)$; and if $s(n_i)$ is in $D(S)(n_i)$, then $s(n_i)$ is in $D(S(n_i))$ (p. 120).

DC-EXC (exclusion) For any choice point n_i in a decision tree T, if $s(n_i)$ is defined and $s(n_i)$ is not in $D(S(n_i))$, then s is not in $D(S)$ (p. 119).

DC-INC (inclusion) For any choice point n_i in a decision tree T, if $D(S)(n_i)$ is nonempty and $s(n_i)$ is in $D(S(n_i))$, then there is some plan s^* in $D(S)$ such that $s(n_i) = s^*(n_i)$ is the plan continuation of s^* at n_i, and hence such that $s(n_i) = s^*(n_i)$ is in $D(S)(n_i)$ (pp. 118–19).

DF (dynamic feasibility) To assess plan p at a choice node n_i, anticipate how you will choose at its (potential) "future" choice nodes n_j and declare infeasible all future alternatives under p that are inadmissible at n_j (p. 174).

DSO (dominance in terms of sure outcomes) For $g = [o_1, E_1; \ldots; o_n, E_n]$ and $g^* = [o_1^*, E_1; \ldots; o_n^*, E_n]$, if $o_i R o_i^*$ for all i, then $g R g^*$; and if, in addition, $o_j P o_j^*$ for some j, then $g P g^*$ (p. 50).

D-SUB (dynamic substitution) If plans s and r differ solely by a substitution of indifferents at some choice point, then s and r are indifferent (p. 176).

FSD (principle of first-order stochastic dominance) For any two gambles g_1 and g_2 defined over the same set of sure outcomes, if g_1 first-order stochastically dominates g_2, then $g_1 P g_2$ (p. 54).

GDE (general dominance for a fixed partition of events) For $g = [g_1, E_1; \ldots; g_n, E_n]$ and $g^* = [g_1^*, E_1; \ldots; g_n^*, E_n]$ if $g_i R g_i^*$ for all i, then $g R g^*$; and if, in addition, $g_j P g_j^*$ for some j, then $g P g^*$ (p. 49).

GDP (general dominance for fixed probabilities) For $g = [g_1, p_1; \ldots; g_n, p_n]$ and $g^* = [g_1^*, p_1; \ldots; g_n^*, p_n]$, if $g_i R g_i^*$ for all i, then $g R g^*$; and if, in addition, $g_j P g_j^*$ for some j, then $g P g^*$ (p. 49).

ICO (independence for constant outcomes) For any $0 < p \le 1$ and any four gambles g_1, g_2, g_3, and g_4, $g_{13} = [g_1, p; g_3, 1 - p] R g_{23} = [g_2, p; g_3, 1 - p]$ iff $g_{14} = [g_1, p; g_4, 1 - p] R g_{24} = [g_2, p; g_4, 1 - p]$ (p. 45).

IND (independence) Let g_1, g_2, and g_3 be any three alternative gambles. Then $g_1 R g_2$ iff $g_{13} = [g_1, p; g_3, 1 - p] R g_{23} = [g_2, p; g_3, 1 - p]$, where $g_{ij} = [g_i, p; g_j, 1 - p]$ is a complex gamble in which there is p probability of being exposed to the gamble g_i and $1 - p$ probability of being exposed to g_j and $0 < p \le 1$ (p. 44).

ISO (independence for sure outcomes) Let o_1, o_2, and o_3 be any three sure outcomes (monetary prizes, etc.). Then $o_1 R o_2$ iff, for $0 < p \le 1$, $[o_1, p; o_3, 1 - p] R [o_2, p; o_3, 1 - p]$ (p. 44).

MIC (minimal intelligible choice) The evaluative method must be such that it generates a nonempty acceptable set for each subset of X, that is, such that there exists an acceptable-set function $D(\cdot)$ defined over X (pp. 39–40).

MD (mixture dominance) If each of two lotteries g_1 and g_2 is preferred (or dispreferred) to a third gamble g_3, then so too is any convex combination of g_1 and g_2 (p. 173).

MO (monotonicity) If o_1 and o_2 are two sure (nonrisky) prizes such that $o_1 P o_2$, then for any two gambles of the form $g_p = [o_1, p; o_2, 1 - p]$ and $g_q = [o_1, q; o_2, 1 - q]$, $g_p P g_q$ iff $p > q$ (p. 53).

NEC (normal-form/extensive-form coincidence) Let T be any decision tree with associated set of plans S, and let T^n be the decision problem that results by converting each s in S into its normal form, so that each s in S is mapped into s^n in S^n. Then for any plan s in S, s is in $D(S)$ iff s^n is in $D(S^n)$ (p. 115).

PR (plan reduction) Let T be any decision tree with associated set of plans S, and let G_S be the set of prospects associated with such plans. Then for any plan s in S and associated prospect g_s in G_S, s is in $D(S)$ iff g_s is in $D(G_S)$ (p. 114).

RD (reduction) Any compound gamble is indifferent to a simple gamble with $o_1, \ldots, o_r$ as outcomes, their probabilities being computed according to the ordinary probability calculus. In particular, if $g^{(i)} = [o_1, p_1^{(i)}; o_2, p_2^{(i)}; \ldots; o_r, p_r^{(i)}]$ for $i = 1, \ldots, s$, then $[g^{(1)}, q_1; g^{(2)}, q_2; \ldots; g^{(s)}, q_s] I [o_1, p_1; o_2, p_2; \ldots; o_r, p_r]$, where $p_i = q_1 p_i^{(1)} + \ldots + q_s p_i^{(s)}$ (p. 47).

RF (restricted feasibility) A plan s is feasible iff $s(n_i)$ is in $D(S(n_i))$ for every choice point n_i, $i \neq 0$, for which s is defined (p. 134).

RPR (restricted plan reduction) For any plan s, such that s satisfies SF, s is in $D(S)$ iff g_s is in $D(G_S)$ (p. 135).

SEP (separability) For any tree T and any node n_i within T, let $T(n_i)^d$ be a separate tree that begins at a node that corresponds to n_i but otherwise coincides with $T(n_i)$, and let $S(n_i)^d$ be the set of plans available in $T(n_i)^d$ that correspond one to one with the set of truncated plans $S(n_i)$ available in $T(n_i)$. Then $s(n_i)$ is in $D(S(n_i))$ iff $s(n_i)^d$ is in $D(S(n_i)^d)$ (p. 122).

SF (separable feasibility) A plan s is feasible iff $s(n_i)^d$ is in $D(S(n_i)^d)$ for every *choice* point n_i, $i \neq 0$, for which s is defined (p. 134).

SI (Savage independence) Let E and $-E$ be mutually exclusive and exhaustive events conditioning the various components of four gambles g_{13}, g_{23}, g_{14}, g_{24}, and let the schedule of consequences be as follows:

	E	$-E$
g_{13}	g_1	g_3
g_{23}	g_2	g_3
g_{14}	g_1	g_4
g_{24}	g_2	g_4

Then $g_{13} \, R \, g_{23}$ iff $g_{14} \, R \, g_{24}$ (p. 45).

SR (simple reduction)   Let T be any decision tree with associated set of plans S such that each plan s in S requires for its implementation a single choice "up front" by the agent, and let G_S be the set of prospects associated with such plans. Then for any plan s in S and associated prospect g_s in G_S, s is in $D(S)$ iff g_s is in $D(G_S)$ (p. 113).

SUB (substitution)   Let $g_{1x} = [\ldots g_1 \ldots]$ and $g_{2x} = [\ldots g_2 \ldots]$ be two complex gambles that are alike in every respect except that in one or more places where g_{1x} has g_1 as a component outcome, g_{2x} substitutes g_2. Then $g_1 \, I \, g_2$ iff $g_{1x} \, I \, g_{2x}$ (p. 45).

TR (truncated plan reduction)   Let n_i be any node in a decision tree T, and let $S(n_i)$ be the set of truncated plans that can be associated with $T(n_i)$. Then $s(n_i)$ is in $D(S(n_i))$ iff $g_{s(n_i)}$ is in $D(G_{S(n_i)})$ (p. 121).

VRPR (very restricted plan reduction)   For any plan s in any tree T, such that s satisfies VSF, s is in $D(S)$ iff g_s is in $D(G_S)$ (p. 136).

VSF (very separable feasibility)   If s and r are such that both satisfy the "only if" part of SF but there exists some n_i, $i \neq 0$, such that both s and r are defined at n_i, then neither s nor r itself is a feasible plan; what is feasible are (1) a modified version of s that is just like s except that at n_i it calls for choosing either $s(n_i)$ or $r(n_i)$ and (2) a modified version of r that is just like r except that at n_i it calls for choosing either $s(n_i)$ or $r(n_i)$ (p. 136).

WO (weak ordering)   An agent's preference ordering R of X constitutes a weak ordering R of X just in case R is connected, is fully transitive, and satisfies CFO (p. 30).

Acknowledgments

I am deeply indebted to the following people for provocative thoughts, useful suggestions, and hardheaded criticisms – all of which have helped, over a period of many years, to shape both the form and the substance of this book: Maurice Allais, Kenneth Arrow, John Bennett, Daniel Ellsberg, Ed Freeman, David Gauthier, Peter Hammond, Bengt Hansson, John Harsanyi, Mark Kaplan, Henry Kyburg, Isaac Levi, R. Duncan Luce, Paul Lyon, Hanan Polansky, Mark Machina, Frederic Schick, and last of all (but only alphabetically) Teddy Seidenfeld. I am also indebted to Mary Nevader for her editing.

1

Introduction and
sketch of the main argument

1.1 Two principles of rationality

The theory of rational choice and preference, as it has been developed in the past few decades by economists and decision theorists, rests on a pair of principles. The first, the *weak ordering principle* (WO), as it is usually formulated, takes rational choice to consist in the maximization of a weak preference ordering defined over the set of feasible alternatives. Adopting the usual terminology of speaking of x as weakly preferred to y when x is either (strictly) preferred to y or x and y are indifferent, a preference relation weakly orders a feasible set X just in case it is (1) *connected* – if x and y are any two alternatives in X, then either x is weakly preferred to y or y is weakly preferred to x (possibly both), and (2) *fully transitive* – for any three alternatives x, y, and z in X, if x is weakly preferred to y, and y is weakly preferred to z, then x is weakly preferred to z. Correspondingly, choice can be said to maximize such an ordering on X when the alternative x chosen satisfies the condition that there be no other alternative y in X such that y is (strictly) preferred to x. As it turns out, however, there is a quite distinct condition that is also presupposed – albeit usually only implicitly – in the weak ordering principle, namely, that the ordering is context free. To say that an ordering is context free is to say that the ordering on any set X can be built up piecewise, by combining information concerning how the agent preferentially orders pair sets of alternatives in X when they are presented in isolation from any of the other alternatives in X.

The second principle, the *independence principle* (IND), applies to a special set of options. It requires that rational choice among risky options – those involving chance-conditioned outcomes – satisfy an independence condition with respect to component gambles or payoffs. On one frequently employed version of this principle, the requirement is that for any three gambles g_1, g_2, and g_3, g_1 is weakly preferred to g_2 iff a (compound) gamble that yields g_1 with probability p, and g_3 with probability $1 - p$, is weakly preferred to a gamble that yields g_2 with the same probability p, and g_3 with probability $1 - p$, for any $p > 0$.

It is a familiar enough result that if an agent's preference and choice behavior satisfies these two principles, as well as certain other somewhat more technical postulates, and if various structural assumptions are satisfied, then his behavior can be represented by a utility function defined over payoffs and well-defined gambles that satisfies the expected utility hypothesis.[1] That is, there exist numbers $u(g_1)$, $u(g_2)$, and so on that can be assigned to component gambles, g_1, g_2, and so on, such that

(1) the magnitudes of the numbers reflect the agent's preferences, that is, $u(g_1) \geq u(g_2)$ iff g_1 is weakly preferred to g_2,

and

(2) the utility to the agent of any gamble is equivalent to its *expected* utility: that is, for any gamble of the form $g = [g_1, p_1; g_2, p_2; \ldots; g_n, p_n]$, such that $p_1 + p_2 + \cdots + p_n = 1$, $u(g) = p_1 u(g_1) + p_2 u(g_2) + \cdots + p_n u(g_n)$.

It is also well known that if the agent's preference and choice behavior satisfies these two principles, together with a somewhat more extended set of additional postulates and structural assumptions, then his beliefs about the likelihood of various events can be represented by a well-defined subjective probability measure over sets of mutually exclusive and jointly exhaustive events. That is, they imply that his subjective "degrees of belief" about the occurrence of such events will be representable as *point* probabilities that satisfy the usual axioms of a probability measure.[2] Finally, these two constructive results can be logically integrated to yield an even more powerful theorem to the effect that the agent's preferences over consequences and actions, and degrees of belief with regard to conditioning events, can be represented respectively by a utility measure and and a subjective probability measure, such that the utility of any action whose possible outcomes are conditioned by various mutually exclusive and exhaustive events is equivalent to the subjective expected utility of that action.[3] In very general terms, then, the weak ordering principle and the strong independence axiom are cornerstones for the modern theory of rational choice and subjective probability.

1.2 The focus of the book

The two principles in question, together with their implications, are subject to both a descriptive and a normative interpretation. That is, they can be taken as descriptive of the preference and choice behavior of actual agents, or as prescriptive – as specifying conditions that should be satisfied by any agent. On the usual account, the sense of "should" to which appeal is made in such a case is *nonmoral*: The notion is not that agents have a moral obligation to satisfy such conditions, but simply that these conditions can be understood as constitutive of ideally rational behavior and, hence, as setting normative standards by appeal to which the agent's choice behavior can be criticized.

It is customary, in the study of such principles, to distinguish between logical and justificatory issues. On the one hand, there is the logical question of what theorems can be proved, given that one assumes this or that set of principles of rationality. For example, many have been preoccupied with the question of what set of principles are necessary, or sufficient, for the existence of utility indicators that satisfy the expected utility property or the existence of well-defined subjective probabilities. On the other hand, there is the quite distinct question of how such principles themselves can be defended or established when they are taken either as descriptive or as normative for preference and choice.

The focus of this book is on normative and justificatory issues. I shall be concerned with the weak ordering and independence principles as normative for, rather than descriptive of, preference and choice behavior; and I shall be preoccupied with the question of how one might justify these principles when they are so interpreted, rather than with the question of their logical implications. That is, my concern will be with the question of how one might justify the claim that a thoughtful, rational decision maker ought (in some nonmoral sense of that term) to avoid violating these two principles.

1.3 The problem of justification

When the principles in question are taken as descriptive of preference and choice behavior, whether they do in fact describe the behavior of actual agents need not raise a special methodological issue. That is, they are then ordinary empirical hypotheses subject to the usual canons of empirical verification. If, however, they are taken as normative for preference and choice, this does seem to pose a methodological problem.

Recent discussions of justification suggest that one might adopt either a foundationalist approach, and seek to ground these principles in other, even more fundamental principles (which are themselves unquestionable), or a coherentist approach, and argue that the principles are normatively valid because they explicate or codify the way in which we are in fact disposed to think about evaluating and choosing among alternatives.[4] Some foundationalists have even suggested that the principles themselves are intuitively secure – and thus that there is no need to appeal to even more fundamental principles. It is true, of course, that any foundationalist account will have to appeal eventually to something that is itself taken to be intuitively secure. What one hopes for, however, are starting points that command nearly unanimous acceptance, at least among thoughtful and knowledgeable researchers. Unfortunately, the above-mentioned principles do not appear to meet this test. Both have been the subject of sustained, spirited, and thoughtful questioning by a number of decision theorists.[5] Thus, they appear to be unsuitable starting points. But this last consideration would also seem to work against any "coherentist" argument as well. The principles in question do not codify the choice behavior of competent or even expert decision makers.

1.4 An alternative approach to justification

There is, however, a quite distinct and more promising approach to the justification of these principles. It can be argued that if the agent's preference and choice behavior fails to satisfy one or the other of these principles, it will be possible to place him in a situation in which he will choose in a pragmatically indefensible manner. More specifically, the argument is that the agent will fail to achieve his intended objective or will fail to maximize with regard to his own preferences with respect to outcomes.

The appeal to such a pragmatic test for determining what is and is not rational finds an early and unusually clear expression in Hume's *Treatise* – particularly the passage I have taken as the epigraph for this work, in which Hume argues that rationality requires choice of means that are appropriate to the realization of one's ends.[6] If this is adapted to the present context, a principle of choice is valid if failure to adhere to it would result in choice of means insufficient to desired ends – in the agent pursuing his objectives less effectively than he could have under the circumstances in question.

Such an appeal to pragmatic considerations is also implicit in the way in which the independence axiom is defended in an important early article by Milton Friedman and Leonard J. Savage.[7] They argue that the independence assumption can be secured by appeal to what they term the "sure-thing" (or dominance) principle. This principle requires choice of action x over y if, for each of a set of mutually exclusive and exhaustive conditioning events, the outcome of having chosen x is always at least as good as the outcome of having chosen y and in at least one case better. So formulated, the principle captures neatly the spirit of Hume's requirement that choice of means be sufficient to desired ends: The agent who violates the sure-thing principle ends up having to settle, regardless of the turn of events, for something no more, and under certain circumstances even less, desirable than what he could have secured had he chosen differently.

The pragmatic approach also finds expression in an argument to the effect that by failure to abide by this or that principle of choice the agent can be turned into a "money pump." The suggestion is that an entrepreneur can offer such an agent a sequence of trades, each of which, in turn, he will be disposed to accept even though, as a result of accepting all of the trades, he will end up facing the same prospect he did at the outset – except that he will be poorer, and the entrepreneur richer, by some amount of money. And since it seems possible for the entrepreneur to exploit the agent repeatedly in this fashion, the implication is that he can be "pumped" for all the money he has.[8] The money-pump argument is related, in turn, to the "dutch-book" argument appealed to by Ramsey, de Finetti, and others in defense of the claim that rational agents should have well-defined subjective probabilities satisfying the usual constraints on probability measures.[9] Briefly put, this argument purports to show that an agent who fails to have such well-defined subjective probabilities can be manipulated into accepting a combination of money bets such that, regardless of how events turn out, he must end up losing money – that is to say, he will end up violating the dominance principle.

1.5 Hammond's consequentialist argument

More recently, the economist Hammond has offered a somewhat related, although much more formal and complex, argument in defense of both the weak ordering and the strong independence principles.[10] Hammond's argument shares with the ones mentioned in the preceding section an orientation to pragmatic considerations about outcomes or consequences, and it also shares with the money-pump argument the appeal to a dynamic, or sequential, choice framework. Indeed, in Hammond's case, this dynamic framework is explicitly developed in a very systematic manner, the thrust of the argument being that acceptance of certain principles of dynamic choice requires a commitment to the two principles of expected utility theory.

In the original version of his argument, the agent who violates one or the other of these two principles can be placed in a dynamic choice situation in which, roughly speaking, what he would now prefer that he choose at some later point in the decision tree is not what he would then prefer to choose (when he arrives at that later point). That is, violations of the ordering or independence principles with regard to preferences for outcomes and gambles over outcomes can induce a "dynamically inconsistent" shift from one temporal point to another in the agent's preferences. The suggestion, in turn, is that such shifts cannot be squared with the assumption that the agent always chooses to maximize with respect to his preferences for consequences. More recently, Hammond has reformulated this point and argued that on a suitable axiomatic formalization of such a principle of consequences within a dynamic choice framework, the weak ordering and independence principles can be shown to follow logically, that is, to be recoverable as theorems.

I find myself unpersuaded by Hammond's argument. I believe that if his argument is construed axiomatically (as he himself intends), it is subject to a number of objections. One can discern in his argument implicit appeal to at least three distinct rationality conditions the conjunction of which, though sufficient to yield the intended theorems, can be questioned. Among other things, it can be argued that the theorem goes through only on condition that one make a rather strong presupposition about what plans are feasible for the decision maker. Given an appropriate reformulation of the criterion of feasibility and an adjustment of the rationality conditions to this new criterion, the theorems do not go through. Hammond can, of course, insist that the feasibility presupposition is acceptable, but the problem is simply that his formal construction provides no leverage one way or the other. Moreover, even if one were to resolve this issue in his favor, it remains an open question whether the consequentialist principle to which he appeals really can ground all three of the factored conditions. My sense is that on a plausible construal of his consequentialist principle, one of the requisite conditions cannot be defended.

1.6 Pragmatism and dynamic choice

Hammond's dynamic choice framework, however, makes possible a much more precise formulation of the pragmatic arguments mentioned in Section 1.4. In particular, it can be shown that agents who are prepared to relax either the weak ordering or the independence principle do face certain potential shifts over time in their preferences. The existence of such shifts makes the agent liable to end up implementing a plan that is strictly dominated, with respect to preferences for outcomes, by another plan that is also available to him. That is, it appears that the agent will end up failing to do as well as he could, given his own preferences for outcomes.

This point can be illustrated by a very simple example. Consider the following prospects:

$$g_1 = [\$2400, 1],$$
$$g_2 = [\$2500, {}^{33}/_{34}; \$0, {}^{1}/_{34}],$$
$$g_3 = [\$2400, {}^{34}/_{100}; \$0, {}^{66}/_{100}],$$
$$g_4 = [\$2500, {}^{33}/_{100}; \$0, {}^{67}/_{100}],$$

where [\$2400, 1] is to be read as "The agent will get \$2400 with probability 1," that is, with certainty, and [\$x, p; \$y, 1−p] is to be read as "The agent will get \$x with probability p, and \$y with probability 1 − p." Suppose, now, the agent prefers the prospect g_1 to g_2, but also prefers g_4 to g_3. In the presence of certain other seemingly uncontroversial assumptions, such a preference pattern can be shown to violate the independence principle.[11] Consider also a prospect $g_3+ = [\$2401, {}^{34}/_{100}; \$1, {}^{66}/_{100}]$, in which the very same events that condition the payoffs in g_3 condition marginally larger payoffs. It is plausible to suppose that the agent in question will prefer g_4 to g_3+ and g_3+ to g_3.[12] Finally, suppose that the agent is exposed to these various prospects in virtue of being confronted by the sequential decision problem shown in Figure 1.1, where squares designate choice points and circles designate chance happenings. At the first

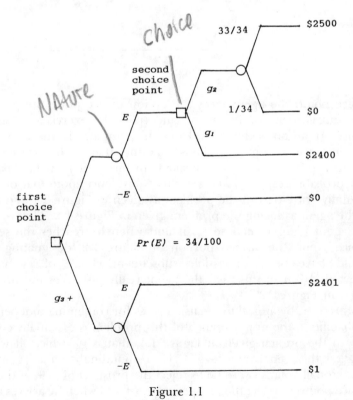

Figure 1.1

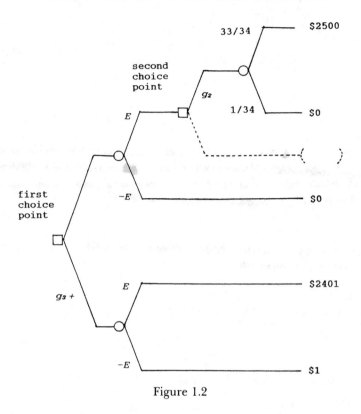

Figure 1.2

choice point, the agent faces the option of accepting the prospect g_3+ outright or continuing on and (possibly) exercising a second choice. If he takes the second option, planning, in the event that circumstances permit it, to choose g_2 rather than g_1, he exposes himself to a prospect that is equivalent (in terms of monetary payoffs and probabilities) to g_4. To see this equivalence, note that one can mentally erase part of the problem as given in Figure 1.1 and think of the agent as facing the problem given in Figure 1.2. That is, since the agent plans to choose g_2, if and when he reaches the second choice point, the dashed portion of Figure 1.2, designating what would have been a possible subsequent choice of g_1, is not relevant.[13] But in this case, the agent really just faces the problem given in Figure 1.3.

Moreover, by appeal to the usual rules for combining independent probabilities, the upper branch of this problem is essentially equivalent to the branch given in Figure 1.4, that is g_4, which, it will be recalled, the agent prefers to g_3+. Correspondingly, for an agent who conditionally plans (were he to reject the prospect of g_3+ at the first choice point) to reject the prospect of g_1 (if and when he arrives at the

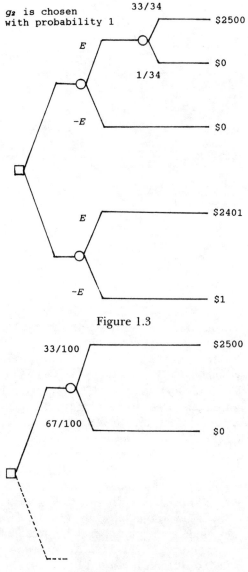

Figure 1.3

Figure 1.4

second choice point), the problem presented in Figure 1.1 is essentially equivalent to the one given in Figure 1.5.

Moreover, since it is plausible to suppose that he will choose g_4 over g_3+ in the problem given in Figure 1.5, we may infer that for the problem given in Figure 1.1, he will choose to reject g_3+ and head toward the second choice point.

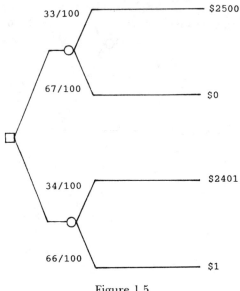

Figure 1.5

Now suppose the agent does just this. If chance operates so that he does not arrive at the second choice point (event $-E$ takes place), he gets \$0 – which is less than the \$1 he would have received, *under the very same chance condition,* had he accepted g_3+ at the outset. Suppose, however, that chance favors him (event E takes place), and he arrives at the second choice point. Despite the plan he formulated to himself at the first choice point, what he now faces is a choice between prospect g_1 and prospect g_2. That is, in terms of the "dashed-line" notation employed earlier, what he now faces is simply the "undotted" portion of the problem given in Figure 1.6. But *by hypothesis,* he prefers g_1 to g_2, and thus it is plausible to suppose that he will, in fact, end up choosing g_1. Notice, however, that what he then gets is \$2400, which is less than the \$2401 he would have received, *under the very same chance condition* (event E takes place), had he accepted g_3+ at the outset. Thus, he loses either way. That is, no matter how chance works (E or $-E$), he does worse than he would have done had he initially chosen g_3+.

Here, then, is an example of a carefully formulated pragmatic argument. Moreover, given the continuing controversy over the status of the weak ordering and the independence principles as normative for choice, it would seem to mark out a very promising justificatory approach. If anything is likely to command universal assent among thoughtful people, it is just the notion that effective choice of means to ends is (at the very least) *a* criterion of rationality. Any argument that succeeded in grounding the weak ordering and independence

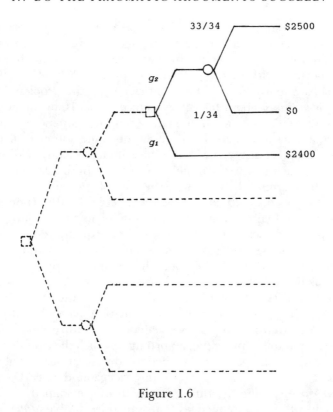

Figure 1.6

principles in such explicitly pragmatic considerations would come as close as one might hope to being dispositive.[14]

1.7 Do the pragmatic arguments succeed?

Once again, however, I am unpersuaded. Failure to abide by either the weak ordering or the independence principle does not unavoidably expose the agent to being "pumped" or to the choosing of means insufficient to his ends. Agents who choose not to conform to these principles are in fact liable to preference shifts, but they can employ strategies that will frustrate those who seek to trap them in any sort of pragmatic difficulty. Thus, whatever merit there is to the two principles in question, support for them is not readily forthcoming from a theory of rationality whose basic principle is that choice of means be sufficient to one's ends.

   The notion that there are strategies available to a rational agent that can protect him from pragmatic difficulties is not new. Such a thesis is at least implicit in the work of a number of economists and finds very explicit expression in a recent argument by the philosopher Schick.[15] Briefly put, the reply runs as follows: The agent gets into pragmatic difficulty as a result of choosing in a *myopic* manner – by treating the choice to be made at each point in the decision tree as if it were an isolated choice, unconnected not only with what came before but, even more important, with anything that can be projected about the choices he will subsequently make. The agent can avoid the problem by becoming *sophisticated* about his future choices – that is, by anticipating how he will be disposed to choose later on in the sequence of choices to be made. He can project that if he accepts some option available to him early in the sequence, the choices he will subsequently be disposed to make will frustrate what he hopes to accomplish by that earlier choice. Bearing that in mind, he must take the feasibility of any plan as conditioned by how his "subsequent" self will be disposed to choose and limit himself to deliberation over just those plans that he judges are feasible in this sense. In terms of the example discussed earlier, the sophisticated chooser projects that he will not choose g_2 if and when he comes to the second choice point and, hence, that the prospects effectively available to him at the first choice node reduce to g_3+ and g_3. Since, by hypothesis, the former is preferred to the latter, the agent will choose g_3+ outright and thereby avoid any pragmatic difficulty.

This way of approaching the problem of one's future choices tacitly invokes a separability principle, according to which the agent's future preferences among options are shaped by considerations that abstract from, and thus are separable from, the background of earlier preferences. More specifically, future preferences are shaped by a concern for just those consequences that remain realizable *at that future time*.[16] As the example discussed earlier suggests, preferences that are separable in this sense turn out to have significant implications for how one can cope with pragmatic problems. The sophisticated chooser, of course, can control to some degree the options of the future self, but his control does not extend, except under special, exogenously specified conditions, to shaping the preferences of that future self. On this model, the present self views its problem as essentially one of making accurate predictions concerning the behavior of its own future self in various hypothetical situations and then using that information as a parameter in a function, the value of which the chooser seeks to maximize. In effect, the sophisticated chooser faces a situation in which the best he can expect to do is come into a *reactive equilibrium* with his own future self.[17] He must choose a plan that maximizes his own preferences against the projected *independent* maximizing behavior of his future self.

1.8 Resolute choice

There is, however, a very different way to deal with the pragmatic problems that can attend preference shifts. There are circumstances under which it is both possible and rational for an agent to choose deliberately to violate the separability principle. Imagine, for example, an agent who is inclined to adopt a particular course of action – a plan calling for a sequence of choices to be made in the future – but who, in the manner of the sophisticated chooser, reflects that the plan calls upon him to make some choice in the future that he projects he would not otherwise be disposed to make. Now suppose that the agent does in fact adopt this plan and then proceeds to implement it. In particular, suppose that he proceeds, against the background of his decision to adopt a particular plan, to do what the plan calls upon him to do, even though it is true (and he knows it to be true) that were he not committed to choosing in accordance with that plan, he would now be disposed to do something quite distinct from what the plan calls upon him to do. I propose to describe such an agent as a *resolute* chooser.

To return once again to the example given earlier, a resolute chooser will reject g_3+ at the first choice point and, in the event that he arrives at the second choice point, select g_2 rather than g_1. He will do so for the reason that he thereby executes the plan to which he is committed, namely, to expose himself to the prospect g_4. In this respect, a resolute chooser could be said to look not only to the future but also to the past – to the way the options now open to him relate to plans already adopted and partially executed. In so doing, however, he violates the separability condition. That is, his choice at the second choice point is different from the choice he would make were he to face the options there de novo, that is, with no occasion to settle on the plan of exposing himself to the prospect of g_4.

As the example suggests, those who have the capacity for resolute choice also avoid the pragmatic difficulties to which the myopic chooser falls victim. Thus, the capacity for resolute choice, like the capacity for sophisticated choice, has important implications for the pragmatic case that some have sought to make in favor of the two principles of the modern theory of rational choice. Those who adopt evaluation procedures that fail to satisfy either the weak ordering or the independence principle have in fact two distinct strategies for avoiding the pragmatic difficulties to which preference shifts make them liable.

I shall also argue, however, that a resolute approach is pragmatically superior to a sophisticated approach.[18] There are situations in which those who resort to a sophisticated strategy fail to realize certain gains that can be realized by those who are capable of being resolute. To be sure, what emerges from this is *not* an argument for being resolute in general, nor for a general abandonment of the separability condition. It is an argument for the value of being resolute, and the value of relaxing the separability condition, in a specific class of situations.

1.9 The issue of feasibility

Those accustomed to thinking in terms of sophisticated choice have a
standard retort. They argue that a resolute approach calls upon the
agent to pursue a plan that is simply not feasible. Thus, on this view,
any pragmatic advantage that might be alleged for a resolute approach is chimerical. I am prepared to acknowledge the force of this
line of reasoning, but I hope to persuade the reader that it is subject
to a serious flaw. What is feasible for a rational agent can be fixed only
by reference to a theory of rationality. If the separability condition is
a constraint on rational choice, this may indeed have implications for
what is feasible for a rational agent. But one central issue is precisely
whether the separability principle is a rationality condition. Thus, to
argue *from* separability *to* the infeasibility of resolute choice is to beg
an important issue.

By contrast, to argue from pragmatic considerations *against* unqualified acceptance of the separability principle as a rationality principle
does not involve such a question-begging step. If the separability principle can be shown to be pragmatically questionable, this has definite
implications for what, at least in principle, is feasible for a rational
agent. That is, if there are circumstances under which a resolute
approach is more rational than a sophisticated approach, then under
those circumstances a course of action that otherwise would have to be
regarded as not feasible may in fact be feasible. The argument to be
constructed, then, is not undermined by considerations of feasibility.
What rationalizes a certain course of action can also motivate the
agent and thus undercut a presumption against that course of action
being feasible.

If this establishes the real possibility of resolute choice, still it is
necessary to reflect further on the conditions under which the capacity for resolute choice might plausibly be exercised. Here it will prove
useful to appeal to the concept of an *intra*personal choice problem.
One can think of the agent as "decomposable" into a sequence of
time-defined selves, each with its own set of preferences and interests.
Within that sort of interpretive framework, a necessary condition for
an agent actually employing a resolute approach is a sense that the
cost to him of failing to be resolute is that each of his own time-
defined selves will judge itself to be worse off, as compared with the
outcomes of the successful execution of a resolute approach.[19] Of
course, it cannot be denied that being resolute requires something
akin to what is called "strength of will" or "willpower." Those who are
steeped in more philosophical traditions will recognize in all of this a
familiar set of problems, including that of weakness of will. Since
weakness of will seems to be a ubiquitous feature of the human con-

dition, I shall offer some thoughts concerning the larger set of limitations within which real (as distinct from ideally rational) agents must operate.

1.10 Other implications of resolute choice

The exploration of resolute choice opens the door to a much more liberal conception of rational sequential choice. In this respect, the present book is at best merely a prolegomena to a more general theory of pragmatic choice. Bratman has made an important contribution to such a general theory, in which the notion of a plan is given a central place, and in Chapter 13 I shall have something to say about how the thesis of this book relates to his work.[20]

Consideration of the possibility of resolute choice also puts one in mind of the deeper presuppositions of the modern theory of rationality. One concerns how the choice behavior of one's own future self is to be conceptualized. In the account given by the modern theory, the behavior of the future self sets a problem for the present self, since the present self must reckon with the fact that the final outcome is not simply a function of how it chooses but also how its own future self chooses, where that future self is presumed to make that choice from its own independently defined perspective.[21] In this respect, the presuppositions of the modern theory in the case of the isolated decision maker choosing against nature simply reflect presuppositions that are central to the modern theory of interdependent, interactive situations involving more than one agent – the type of situation addressed by game theory. To take the simplest example, the normative model of the sophisticated chooser, which I propose to reject, has as its *inter* personal counterpart a model in which two players are to make choices in sequence. On the usual account, the player who chooses first should determine the preference-maximizing responses of the second player to each of the possible moves that he, the first player, could make, and then choose a course of action with maximum expected return, given a maximizing response by the second player.

The model of sophisticated choice, then, views the individual in the intertemporal, intrapersonal problem as constrained by an ontological separation of selves that is as deep as that which obtains in the case of interpersonal choice involving separate individuals. That is, an agent's future self is to be conceptualized as an independent entity that is no more beholden to the present self, in principle, than is any one person to another person with a distinct set of preferences or interests. It is always possible, of course, to posit preferences of later selves that are responsive to the preferences of earlier selves (just as one can, for example, posit that an individual has preferences that reflect interests in the well-being of other distinct individuals), but on the usual account, and from the perspective of a general theory of rational sequential choice, these must be treated as purely ad hoc assumptions.

I believe that this interpretation of the problem facing the agent who makes choices over time must be resisted, *even* if one is prepared to insist, with Hume, that there is no plausible theory of the self as a continuing entity over time.[22] The argument sketched earlier for a resolute approach to sequential choice problems is designed to form part of a brief for such an alternative view. It suggests that the agent does not have to conceive of himself as having no leverage with respect to the preferences of his own future self – that he has the capacity to be other than a passive spectator to his own future behavior.

If one adopts a different view of rational intrapersonal choice – as captured by the notion of being resolute under certain conditions – the analogy between the intrapersonal and the interpersonal models is still there to be exploited: The two-person sequential game remains an analogue to the situation in which a single person must make a sequence of choices. But now the direction of argument can be reversed. If one is prepared to break away from the traditional analysis for the intrapersonal case, one can also consider an alternative analysis of rational choice for the interpersonal case. Might not separate players who have to play in turn, no less than separate time slices of the same self, manage to coordinate their choices in some fashion when it would be to their mutual advantage to do so? Once this question is seriously entertained, a similar question can be raised in the more general setting of game theory as a theory of simultaneous but interdependent choice.

In the modern theory of games, the Archimedean point has always been the concept of an equilibrium of respective strategy choices, one for each player – based on the notion that each player who knows the other players to be fully rational can in principle take the choice behavior of all the other players as a given, as something to be anticipated by him, and against which he must reactively choose so as to maximize his own expected utility. It is well known, however, that such equilibrium solutions are typically suboptimal. If, then, the theory of resolute choice offers a solution to the problem of intrapersonal suboptimality (or inefficiency), one may hope to find in it a model of a solution to the problem of interpersonal suboptimality (or inefficiency). More generally, all of this suggests that the modern theory of rational choice, with its commitment to the separability principle, may formalize – both for the case of individual, independent sequential choice and for the case of interdependent choice – not only an overly restrictive theory of rationality, but one that must be judged, on pragmatic grounds, to be inadequate.

1.11 The organization of the book

In order to develop this whole argument and to mark clearly the respects in which it differs from other arguments that have recently been put forward, I have found it necessary to deal head on with a number of rather complex topics. One concerns the relation between choice and preference. Here a natural starting point is the recent work of economists on revealed preference theory.[23] I find, however, that there are a number of conditions on orderings that those who work in the revealed preference tradition have not always distinguished from one another with sufficient clarity. The result is that quite plausible conditions on rational preference may appear to be sufficient for the intended constructions, whereas a much more problematic condition, which is necessary for those constructions, can easily be ignored. Chapter 2, then, is devoted to sorting out a variety of conditions of rational choice and preference. Again, those who have claimed that the independence principle is normative for choice have often contented themselves with appealing to a rather limited and intuitively plausible version of the principle, without making clear that the expected utility and subject probability theorems require a considerably stronger principle. Chapter 3 is devoted to identifying and marking the relationship between different versions of the independence principle.

In Chapter 4, I take up for the first time the justificatory issue. I argue that while a number of defenses of the ordering and independence principles have been offered, many of them are considerably less than compelling. Chapter 5 is devoted to outlining several versions of what I take to be the most powerful argument that can be offered for either principle – a pragmatic or consequentialist argument. It turns out, however, that the strongest versions of these arguments all presuppose a dynamic choice framework in which the agent is understood to confront the problem of making a sequence of choices over time. Chapters 6 and 7 sketch a somewhat general, but, I hope, useful account of dynamic choice problems and formulate some possible conditions on rational dynamic choice. Here I employ, but also modify, the framework assumptions and conditions to be found in several recent discussions of dynamic programming and decision trees.[24] The principal modifications I make are those necessitated by my interest in explicitly formulating rationality conditions that are typically only implicitly invoked or presupposed by those who have previously written on the subject of dynamic choice.

In Chapters 8 through 10 I return, in a more formal way, to the analysis and critique of various pragmatic arguments. Chapter 8 deals specifically with, and rejects, what I take to be the most ambitious and formal of these arguments – the one to be found in the work of Hammond. Chapter 9 suggests that Hammond's dynamic choice framework, even if it cannot be used to recover the ordering and independence principles as theorems, can be used to offer a powerful diagnosis of the problem facing the agent who wants to relax either the ordering or the independence principle. There I formulate three distinct ways to deal with potential changes in preferences and the pragmatic difficulties to which they expose the agent: the myopic, the sophisticated, and the resolute approaches. In Chapter 10 I then argue that these models can be used to reveal a variety of weaknesses in a wide range of pragmatic arguments.

Chapter 11 brings the whole analysis of the pragmatic arguments to a controversial conclusion, namely, that although a sophisticated or a resolute approach will allow the agent to escape the difficulties inevitably faced by a myopic agent, the resolute approach is, from the very pragmatic perspective that has now become central, clearly superior. Chapter 12 seeks to show that the notion of resolute choice is considerably less quixotic than it might, at first, appear to be. Although I do not expect to lay to rest all of the doubts that many will have about such an approach to dynamic choice, I hope that the discussion contained there will encourage others to reconsider the whole issue of how one should conceptualize the relation between an agent and his own future self and thereby the question of what plans are really feasible. Chapter 13 briefly surveys other recent discussions of the problem of dynamic inconsistency and concludes that the solution invariably recommended is some form or other of sophisticated, as distinct from resolute, choice.

In Chapter 14 I explore the implications of the analysis of the preceding chapters for the justificatory issue concerning the ordering and independence principles. Finally, in Chapter 15 I briefly consider the implications of a theory of resolute choice for two closely related matters: the account of interdependent choice to be found in the modern theory of games and the proverbial question of the relation between rational and moral choice.

To conclude these introductory remarks, let me say that in what follows I have sought to focus on conceptual, as opposed to formal, issues, hoping thereby to make the argument accessible to a larger intellectual community. This has incurred an inevitable cost in terms of a less rigorous presentation than would otherwise have been possible. I have, in fact, chosen to avoid certain complex questions that must eventually be raised concerning appropriate structural conditions and other controlling background assumptions. In particular, I have simply presupposed a setting in which the probabilities of conditioning events are independent of choice of actions and of other conditioning events, with respect to both the static choice situations examined and the dynamic counterparts into which these static choice problems can be embedded. I have also chosen to develop the dynamic choice argument in terms of relatively simple versions of ordering and independence conditions. The framework set out here, then, is clearly not adequate to a full treatment of dynamic choice problems; moreover, the results obtained are not to be construed as dispositive of all the important issues that can be raised. I have contented myself wherever possible with setting out only as much of a general framework as is necessary to deal effectively with the kind of dynamic choice argument offered by Hammond and others in defense of the modern theory of rational choice. For those with a passion for the more technical issues, I offer a discussion of more formal matters in the notes and provide an appropriate set of references.

I have presupposed that the reader is familiar at least with the outlines of the modern theory of preference and utility and with some version of the argument that employs the weak ordering and independence principles to characterize rational choice in terms of the maximization of expected utility. For those who are uncertain of this background but who are (admirably) resolved to work through the following text, I would suggest that they start by reviewing one of the standard axiomatic treatments of expected utility theory.[25]

2

The ordering principle

2.1 Weak preference orderings

It is a cornerstone of the modern theory of utility and subjective probability that a rational decision maker must have coherent preferences with regard to the set of options that he faces in any decision problem. On the usual account, "coherent" is taken to mean that the agent's preference ordering over any set of options must be both connected and fully transitive. In what follows I adopt the usual convention of using P to denote the (strict) preference, I to denote the indifference, and R to denote the preference-or-indifference (weak preference), relation. Correspondingly, I take X to be the set of (mutually exclusive and exhaustive) options that define a decision problem for an agent. In terms of these conventions, connectedness and transitivity are defined in the following manner:

> An agent's ordering of X is *connected* just in case for any x and y in X, either $x R y$ or $y R x$ (possibly both).

> An agent's ordering of x is *fully transitive* just in case for any x, y, and z in X, if $x R y$ and $y R z$, then $x R z$.[1]

When the agent's preferences over any set of options satisfy both the connectedness and full-transitivity conditions, the convention is to speak of his preferences as constituting a *weak ordering* of X. The qualifier "weak" derives from the consideration that the ordering in question leaves open the possibility that two distinct elements may be ranked indifferently to one another.[2] As I shall argue in Section 2.6, the requirement that preferences define a weak ordering, as it has figured in standard results pertaining to preference and choice, and in particular the expected utility and subjective probability theorems, presupposes something more than connectedness and transitivity; but it is clear enough that these two conditions are necessary for those results. From a conceptual point of view, of course, it is not a *defining* feature of an ordering that it be connected. Unconnected orderings, or partial orderings, as they are sometimes called, have been studied extensively.[3] What one has when the agent's preference ordering over

X is both connected and transitive is a *connected* ordering of X. It could be said, then, that what is central to the generic notion of an ordering is the satisfaction of the transitivity condition.

2.2 Preference and choice

It is also customary, particularly among economists, to treat the concept of preference as being closely related to that of choice – to think of the agent's preference as "revealed" (in some sense of that term) in the choices he makes. As a number of writers have noted, however, there are two very different ways in which a preference ordering and choice can be related – both of which have played a role in classic discussions of revealed preference theory.[4] The first involves treating the notion of a preference ordering as the primitive concept and taking the agent's choice of an option as something that is determined by his preference ordering over the set of options.

Suppose, in particular, that the agent can weakly order the set X of available options and that he prefers one of the options to all the others. One expects that he will choose that option. Of course, it may well happen that there is no uniquely preferred option; but still one expects that he will choose from among those that are weakly preferred to all the others. Stated somewhat more formally, on the supposition that there exists some antecedently specified weak ordering of the set X of options, one can utilize this underlying ordering to define the notion of a preference-based choice set:[5]

Let x in X be *a best option* with respect to an underlying relation R iff for all y in X, $x R y$; and let $C(X, R)$, the *preference-based choice set* for X, be the set of best options in X.

On this interpretation, preference is antecedent to choice. That is, it is presumed that the agent has some sort of preference ordering R over the set of options and that he will choose an option x in X such that $x R y$ for every y in X. Alternatively put, he will maximize with respect to his preference ordering over the set of options. Moreover, since there may be a number of options in X, all of which are weakly preferred to every other element in X, there is no guarantee that the preference-based choice set is a unit set. Since, however, observed choice is always of a singleton, the concept of a preference-based choice *set* is once removed from anything that is directly observable.[6]

A second, "choice-based" approach to preference takes the concept of an abstract choice set as the primitive and simply defines preference in terms of it. Such an (abstract) choice set is obviously related, but conceptually distinct from $C(X, R)$, the preference-based choice set just introduced. Since in this instance, choice is to be taken as the primitive, the reference to some underlying preference ordering R must be dropped. In somewhat more formal terms:

> Let the *choice set* $C(X)$ of X be that subset of X consisting of all the options in X that the agent regards as acceptable or choice-worthy (by whatever criteria are being employed).

By appeal to such an "abstract" choice set, a variety of choice-based preference constructs are possible.[7] The most useful of these for present purposes is one based on choice from pair sets, that is, *pair-set-"revealed" weak preference* (the subscript "c" signals a choice-based notion of preference):

> $x R_c y$ just in case x is in $C(\{x, y\})$,
> $x P_c y$ just in case x is in $C(\{x, y\})$ and y is not in $C(\{x, y\})$
> $x I_c y$ just in case both x and y are in $C(\{x, y\})$.

Since $X = \{x, y\}$ is presumed to be a set of mutually exclusive options, the agent can choose only one option from X. As the definition of I_c makes clear, however, $C(X)$ may not be a unit set. If both x and y are choice-worthy, then $C(X) = \{x, y\}$.[8]

2.3 Choice functions and coherence

Consider some set X of options, with a corresponding choice set $C(X)$. What are the implications for the choice set if X is limited to some subset S thereof? Formally speaking, if S is a subset of X, then $C(S)$ is the set of options the agent would regard as "choice-worthy" were he to find himself limited to selecting from this subset of X. Limitation of choice to options in S rather than X may, of course, mean that the agent is now forced to choose between what were judged – in the context of X itself – to be inferior options; that is, S and $C(X)$ may be altogether disjoint, but the notion is that when subject to such a constraint on the available set, the agent will still be able to form a judgment as to the *relative* acceptability of what is left. Since this can be said to hold for any arbitrarily selected subset S of X, it can be presumed to hold for all such subsets S of X. This, in turn, suggests the useful notion of a choice function:

A *choice function* $C(\cdot)$, defined on some underlying domain of possible alternatives X, is a functional relation such that the choice set $C(S)$ is nonempty for every nonempty subset S of X.

The bulk of the literature on abstract choice functions is devoted to formulating and exploring the relation between, and the implications of, various "coherence" or "consistency" conditions that any given choice function may or may not satisfy. Alternative factorings of such conditions have been proposed, but in each instance the conditions require, in effect, that certain inclusion relations obtain between the choice set for X and other related choice sets. On the factoring most often employed, the relevant conditions are formulated in the following manner:[9]

> *Alpha:* A choice function $C(\cdot)$ defined on X satisfies Alpha just in case for all x in S, and all $S*$ such that $S*$ is a superset of S, if x is not in $C(S)$, then x is not in $C(S*)$.

Alternatively put, Alpha requires that if x is rejected (not chosen) from any set S, then it must be rejected from any superset $S*$ of S.

> *Beta:* A choice function $C(\cdot)$ defined on X satisfies Beta just in case for all x and y in S, and all $S*$ such that $S*$ is a superset of S, if both x and y are in $C(S)$, then either x and y are both in $C(S*)$ or neither is in $C(S*)$.

Alternatively put, if both x and y are in some choice set, then they must be choice inseparable in any larger set containing both of them – either both are in the choice set or neither is.

Since terms like "coherence" and "consistency" are evaluatively charged, I shall use somewhat more neutral terminology and speak of these as "context-free" conditions on choice functions. This terminology is apt, since what Alpha and Beta require is that the choice-worthiness of various alternatives not be influenced in certain specific ways by the presence or absence of other alternatives. More specifically, what they require is that if an alternative is not choice-worthy, adding new options should not result in that option being transformed into one that is choice-worthy; and if two options are both choice-worthy, adding new options should not result in one being choice-worthy and one not. In what follows I shall designate the conjunction of the pair of these conditions as the context-free choice condition:

> An abstract choice function $C(\cdot)$ satisfies the *context-free choice condition* (CF) just in case $C(\cdot)$ satisfies both Alpha and Beta.

As will become evident shortly, a major preoccupation of this work will be with the question whether CF constitutes a rationality condition on choice, where "rationality" is understood to have normative force. In particular, my concern will be with whether it can be shown, by some argument or other, that an agent should (in some nonmoral sense of this term) so evaluate options that the corresponding choice functions satisfy this condition. For the present, however, it will prove useful to continue to focus on conceptual connections and, in particular, to explore somewhat more fully the important set of relationships that obtain between weak orderings and choice functions and, more specifically, choice functions that satisfy condition CF.

2.4 Weak orderings and choice functions

On the standard account, weak orderings and choice functions that satisfy CF are connected in a number of important respects. Consider a case in which there is an antecedently specifiable weak preference ordering defined over X. By appeal to the notion of preference-based choice sets one can specify the choice set not only for X itself, but for any subset S of X. Formally speaking, for the set X itself, $C(X, R)$ is defined as before; that is, it consists of all those elements x in X such that $x R y$ for every y in X. But since R defines a weak ordering over X, the *restriction* of R to S, where S is a subset of X, trivially constitutes a weak ordering over S. One can then consider an arbitrary subset S of X and specify a choice set $C(S, R)$ by reference to the restriction of R to S. In the event that the choice sets so constructed are nonempty for every subset S of X, one can speak of a preference-based choice function defined on X:

> A *preference-based choice function* $C(\cdot, R)$, defined on X, is a functional relation such that the choice set $C(S, R)$ is nonempty for every nonempty subset S of X.

Here $C(S, R)$ is the preference-based choice set for subset S of X and is determined by taking the restriction of the weak ordering R to the subset S.

The most important connections between the existence of such an underlying weak ordering R and the existence of a choice function $C(\cdot, R)$ having various properties can now be captured by the following propositions:

Proposition 2.1. If R is a weak ordering defined over a finite set X, then there exists a choice function $C(\cdot, R)$ defined on X.[10]

Proposition 2.2. If there exists an underlying weak ordering R defined on X, then the choice function $C(\cdot, R)$ that can be constructed from R will satisfy condition CF.[11]

Moreover, if there exists an abstract choice function $C(\cdot)$ defined over X that satisfies CF, one can "derive" (i.e., construct from it) a weak ordering R defined on X:

Proposition 2.3. If there is a choice function $C(\cdot)$ defined on X that satisfies CF, then the pair-set choice-constructed ordering R_c on X is a weak ordering.[12]

Finally:

Proposition 2.4. If there exists a weak ordering R defined on X, and if one employs the choice function that can be derived from it to define a pair-set choice-based preference ordering R_c, then R_c will coincide with R.[13]

In the light of these results, it is natural to treat the presupposition that there exists a weak ordering R defined on X as essentially equivalent to the assumption that there exists a choice function $C(\cdot, R)$, defined for all finite subsets S of X, that satisfies CF. That is, it would seem that one can, in effect, move smoothly back and forth between a choice function satisfying the context-free conditions Alpha and Beta and a preference ordering R having the property of being connected and fully transitive.

2.5 The minimax risk rule

On a careful formulation, however, the connections that can be established are somewhat more complicated. This can best be shown by exploring a particular decision principle, the minimax risk rule for the evaluation of uncertain prospects.[14] The minimax risk rule is designed to apply to cases in which the outcome of the decision is partially a function of which of a number of mutually exclusive and exhaustive events occurs and in which the agent is completely uncertain as to the likelihood of these conditioning events. The rule calls upon the agent to fix on a particular event, determine what would be the best option to choose if he could correctly anticipate that event, and then determine the difference between the value of the outcome in that case and the value of the outcome for each available option paired with that fixed event. The difference can be said to measure the risk to which he is exposed if he chooses the option in question and that event takes place. This "risk" evaluation is then to be repeated for each option paired with each of the other possible conditioning events. Once this is done, the rule calls upon the agent to ascertain the maximum risk to which each option exposes him and to choose an option that minimizes this measure of maximum risk.

As an illustration of the rule and its implications, suppose the agent is faced with choosing among the following three gambles:

	E_1	E_2	E_3
g_1	$10	$ 5	$ 1
g_2	0	10	4
g_3	5	2	10

where the E_i's are mutually exclusive and exhaustive events whose likelihoods are completely unknown by the agent. If E_1 does in fact occur, then one's best choice is g_1, for a payoff of $10.[15] Suppose, however, that one chooses g_2 instead (playing, say, on a hunch that E_2 will take place). If it turns out that E_1 rather than E_2 takes place, one wins $0 instead of the $10 one would have won had one selected g_1 (the best alternative given that E_1 will occur). Thus, the pair (g_2, E_1) has associated with it a "risk" factor of $10. This is the difference between what one in fact receives ($0) and what one would have received ($10) if one had anticipated that E_1 would occur and had chosen the best option available on that hypothesis. Similar calculations can be made for the other option – event pairs, yielding the following "risk" matrix:

	E_1	E_2	E_3	Maximum risk
g_1	0	5	9	9
g_2	10	0	6	10
g_3	5	8	0	8

As applied to this problem, then, the minimax risk rule ranks g_3 over g_1 and the latter over g_2. Alternatively put, one can think of the rule as determining a choice set $C(\{g_1, g_2, g_3\}) = \{g_3\}$.

Suppose now that one were to discover that g_1 is in fact not available, so that the problem is reduced to choosing between g_2 and g_3:

	E_1	E_2	E_3
g_2	$0	$10	$ 4
g_3	5	2	10

The corresponding regret matrix can now be calculated for this problem:

	E_1	E_2	E_3	Maximum risk
g_2	5	0	6	6
g_3	0	8	0	8

The option g_2 ranks above g_3 in virtue of exposing the agent to less risk, and so the required choice is now g_2. In choice-set terms, $C(\{g_2, g_3\}) = \{g_2\}$.

The minimax risk rule, then, generates an ordering over the feasible set that is not context free. When the feasible set contains all three alternatives, g_3 ranks over g_2, whereas for the case in which just g_2 and g_3 are available, g_2 ranks over g_3. In particular, this means that if one takes the ordering generated by the rule over all three options and considers the restriction of that ordering to just g_2 and g_3, that restricted ordering does not coincide with the ordering generated by the rule over g_2 *and* g_3, when just those two options are available.

This in turn poses a problem for the characterization of preference-based choice sets. One alternative is to have the choice sets reflect the manner in which the minimax risk rule operates when it is applied anew to each feasible set. In particular, letting R_m designate the ordering derived from application of the minimax risk rule for the set $\{g_1, g_2, g_3\}$, $C(\{g_1, g_2, g_3\}, R_m) = \{g_3\}$, since the minimax risk rule ranks g_3 over g_2 over g_1. But for the set $\{g_2, g_3\}$, $C(\{g_2, g_3\}, R_m) = \{g_2\}$, since the rule ranks g_2 over g_3. Thus, on this way of specifying the choice sets, $C(\cdot, R_m)$ violates condition Alpha. Notice, however, that the minimax risk rule still generates a connected and fully transitive ordering over each set of feasible alternatives. This suffices to ensure that there is a nonempty preference-based choice set that can be associated with each set of feasible alternatives. In short, the contextually defined orderings are "locally" well behaved, and preference-maximizing choice is possible.

Alternatively, one can take $C(\cdot, R_m)$ to be specified by considering the ordering generated over the largest "relevant" set of alternatives (e.g., in the problem given earlier, the set consisting of all three alternatives) and then taking the restriction of *that* ordering to S as the basis for determining $C(S, R_m)$. On that interpretation, $C(\cdot, R_m)$ will not only exist but also satisfy condition CF.

There are two serious drawbacks to this way of specifying $C(\cdot, R_m)$. In the first place, suppose that after some set of options has been identified, the rule applied, and the corresponding choice set determined, it becomes clear that some one of the options is in fact not feasible. Why should the agent persist in viewing the decision problem in terms of results obtained on the basis of information that is now outdated? The very point of the minimax risk rule is to evaluate each option by means of a test that appeals to what one could have achieved had one chosen a different option; but that presupposes one could have chosen the other option, just what is now being denied. The very logic of the rule seems to demand that in the light of new information about the members of the feasible set, the situation be reevaluated, that is, $C(S, R_m)$ not be determined by taking the restriction of R_m to the subset S.

There is another, more practical objection. Any such decision rule must be able to deal not only with situations in which what were thought to be feasible options are suddenly discovered to be not feasible (contractions in the feasible set), but also with situations in which new options suddenly become available (expansions in the feasible set). In any practical application (with choice behavior spread out over time), if the minimax risk rule responds to expanding possibilities, the implied choice function can fail to satisfy the context-free conditions – even if the second of the two ways of specifying choice sets is employed. One can avoid such violations only by proceeding in the following fashion: At the earliest relevant time, one would have to determine the set of all possibly feasible options (most likely an infinite set), apply the minimax risk rule to this "largest" set of possible options, compute the maximum risk values, and then select from among the set of really feasible options one whose associated maximum risk value was minimum for that feasible set. Since it will be hard, if not impossible, to meet these requirements, dynamic violations of CF will continue to occur, and thus little will be gained by utilizing this alternative method for constructing the choice function.

2.6 Reinterpreting the standard results

I propose to proceed on the assumption that preference-based choice sets are to be determined by reference not to the preference ordering over the "largest" set of (logically) possible alternatives but, rather, to the ordering of whatever happens to be the feasible set of alternatives. Given this interpretation, what implications does the employment of the minimax risk rule have for the constructions we have been considering? Consider, first, Proposition 2.2. If the minimax risk rule is taken to generate an ordering of a set X of feasible options in some decision situation, and also an ordering of each subset S of X, as the example in Section 2.5 illustrates, the choice function constructable from these orderings will, as noted, fail to satisfy CF. But then Proposition 2.2 implies that these underlying orderings cannot be taken collectively to constitute a weak ordering. This is true enough, but note that it is still the case that each of the orderings that the minimax rule generates – one over X and one over each distinct subset of X – is connected and fully transitive. In short, the problem is not that the orderings, which form the basis for choice *sets* (and thereby the choice function), fail to have connectedness and transitivity properties; rather, it is that the orderings are relativized to feasible sets and cannot be "pieced together" to form an ordering that coincides with the ordering that the rule generates over the union of all these feasible sets.

This suggests, in fact, an important *disconnection* between a decision rule generating a connected, transitive ordering and its generating a choice function satisfying condition CF. More specifically, as the example of the minimax risk rule makes clear:

Proposition 2.5. That for each feasible subset S of X, the underlying ordering of S (which is possibly relativized to S) happens to be connected and fully transitive is not a sufficient condition for generating a preference-based choice function (over all such subsets S) that satisfies CF.

Alternatively put, a given decision rule can fail to generate a preference-based choice function satisfying condition CF and yet still generate a connected and fully transitive ordering over any specific set of alternatives to which it is applied.

This proposition might seem to conflict with Proposition 2.2, which makes satisfaction of condition CF by a preference-based choice function defined on X a necessary condition for the underlying ordering being a weak ordering R on X. But the conflict is only apparent. What Proposition 2.5 forces us to recognize is that the properties of a weak ordering that ensure that Proposition 2.2 is true are not exhausted by connectedness and full transitivity. More specifically, what is only implicit in the usual formulation of the weak ordering requirement, but essential to it, is a condition that is quite distinct from either of these – and that forms a natural analogue to the context-free condition on choice functions:

Context-free ordering (CFO). The ordering R defined over any set of alternatives X is not changed by adding new alternatives, that is, by expanding X to some superset Y.

To frame this in terms of the preference relation that obtains between any two elements x and y in the set of available options, CFO requires that whatever preference relation obtains between x and y must hold regardless of whatever other options are available. That is, if x and y are in S, and $x\,R\,y$, then for any set S^* such that x and y are in S^*, it must be the case that $x\,R\,y$. I shall characterize this as a "context-free" condition for reasons analogous to those introduced in connection with the discussion of condition CF. The requirement is that the ordering over any set of elements be independent of the context of other alternatives that also happen, on some particular occasion, to be available.

Now if a method of evaluation generates an ordering over some set X that satisfies CFO, then the restriction of that ordering to some subset S of X will clearly coincide with the ordering generated by that same method over S itself when that subset is considered in isolation from any other alternatives, that is, in isolation from the other elements in X. From a practical point of view this also means that the ordering over any feasible set S can be built up piecewise, by ascertaining what ordering relation obtains between pairs of options considered in complete isolation from any other options and then combining these results. That is, when this condition is satisfied, one need not be concerned that the ordering between any pair of alternatives will vary, depending on whether those two options constitute the feasible set or are simply elements of some larger set of feasible alternatives.

The earliest explicit formulation of this condition is that of Milnor, who distinguishes an "ordering" requirement involving connectedness and full transitivity from just such a context-free condition. Working within a framework in which the alternatives available to the agent can be represented as rows in a matrix, Milnor characterizes this as a "row adjunction" condition: The ordering of old rows is not changed by the addition of a new row.[16] For the most part, however, the condition is merely implicitly presupposed. Whether tacitly presupposed or explicitly introduced, CFO turns out to be an essential feature of the concept of a weak ordering, as the latter has figured in the literature on revealed preference theory. Stated more formally:

> *Weak ordering (WO).* An agent's preference ordering R of X constitutes a weak ordering R of X just in case R is connected, is fully transitive, and satisfies CFO.

At issue here is not just a terminological point. What Proposition 2.5 establishes is that Propositions 2.2 and 2.4 will fail to hold unless CFO is taken as a defining feature of a weak ordering. Proposition 2.2 must be understood to assert that if there exists an underlying connected, fully transitive, *and context-free* ordering R over some set X, then the choice function $C(\cdot, R)$ that can be constructed from R will satisfy condition CF. Similarly, the antecedent to Proposition 2.4 must be understood to make reference not simply to a connected and fully transitive but, in addition, to a *context-free* ordering R of X.

In the light of this reinterpretation of Propositions 2.2 and 2.4, the tendency to treat the concept of an underlying weak ordering casually in terms of just the connectedness and transitivity conditions has one unfortunate consequence. Although a full discussion of this matter will be deferred until Chapter 4, the transitivity conditions are arguably bedrock. An "ordering" that fails to satisfy these conditions seems hardly intelligible. Perhaps even more to the point, cycles in the "ordering" threaten to defeat choice altogether: If when confronted with the set of options $\{x, y, z\}$ the agent ranks x over y and y over z, but also ranks z over x, what is the agent to choose? What counts in this context as choosing so as to maximize one's preference ordering over the set of options? As Arrow has succinctly put the matter, "In the absence of transitivity, choice may whirl about in circles."[17] The context-free condition CFO, however, requires for its defense a considerably more elaborate argument. As the minimax risk rule suggests, so long as the method of evaluation generates a connected and fully transitive ordering over any set to which it is applied, the agent is not precluded from choosing so as to maximize his preference ordering over any given set of feasible alternatives. Within a preference-based framework, then, the casual identification of a weak ordering with just the transitivity and connectedness properties obscures a substantial issue – whether CFO is really an essential part of a normative theory of choice.

What reinterpretations are required within a framework that takes choice as the primitive concept? Interestingly, Proposition 2.3 still holds even if a weak ordering is defined as an ordering that is connected and fully transitive, but not necessarily context independent. That is, if there is a choice function $C(\cdot)$ defined on X that satisfies CF, the derived ordering R_c will be both connected and fully transitive. Connectedness of R_c is ensured by the presupposition that $C(\cdot)$ is defined on X. Transitivity of R_c is ensured by the presupposition that $C(\cdot)$ satisfies CF.

However, the full import of Proposition 2.3 is that if there exists a choice function defined on X that satisfies CF, then one can show that not only is the choice-constructed preference relation R_c on X connected and fully transitive, but it also satisfies CFO. What ensures this? Surprisingly, this result can be secured in a rather trivial manner by employing as one's choice-based construct pair-set-revealed preference (as defined at the end of Section 2.2). In that case satisfaction of CFO is a simple artifact of the manner in which the ordering was obtained. That is, if the underlying choice function $C(\cdot)$ exists, then one can proceed to define an ordering over any set X by simply looking at the choice sets for pair sets of feasible options. Since it is not assumed that $C(\cdot)$ satisfies CF, the derived ordering R_c may well fail one or more of the transitivity conditions, but the ordering will still be – given the way in which it was constructed – context free. But this way of securing CFO does not prove to be very interesting. If $C(\cdot)$ fails to satisfy CF, then R_c, constructable though it is, will not connect in any way with choice from sets larger than pair sets.

What is at issue here can be captured by considering a choice-based analogue to Proposition 2.4:

> **Proposition 2.6.** If $C(\cdot)$ is defined over X and satisfies CF, and if one derives a pair-set-revealed preference relation R_c from it and uses this in turn to define a new choice function $C(\cdot, R_c)$, then $C(\cdot, R_c)$ will coincide with $C(\cdot)$.[18]

Even if the underlying choice function $C(\cdot)$ fails to satisfy CF, one can still define R_c, but one may not be able to use R_c in turn to get a choice function $C(\cdot, R_c)$. Moreover, even if $C(\cdot, R_c)$ does exist, it may not coincide with $C(\cdot)$.[19]

Even when CFO is explicitly introduced into the definition of a weak order, there is one final qualification to be imposed on the notion that choice-based and preference-based approaches can be used more or less interchangeably. To be sure, it is still the case that within a choice-based preference framework, CFO as well as connectedness and full transitivity can be secured easily enough by supposing that there exists an underlying choice function $C(\cdot)$ that satisfies CF. This is just what Proposition 2.3 establishes: If one takes choice as primitive and assumes the existence of a choice function satisfying CF, the derivable preference relation will satisfy all the conditions of a weak order. And if one takes some preference relation R as the primitive, then imposition of CFO, connectedness, and full transitivity on R will ensure that the derivable choice function $C(\cdot, R)$ satisfies CF. But there remains another important *disconnection* between the property of a rule's generating a weak ordering and the property of its generating a choice function satisfying condition CF – a disconnection that becomes clear within a framework in which preference is taken as the primitive concept:

> **Proposition 2.7.** That a rule generates a connected, fully transitive, and context-free ordering on X is a sufficient but not a necessary condition for its generating a choice function defined on X satisfying CF.

The reason for this is simple. It is always possible that the respects in which the orderings over isolated subsets of X are context dependent pertain only to "losing" or unacceptable elements in each subset.

Thus, it could happen that R as defined on X fails to satisfy CFO and yet the derivable choice function defined on X does satisfy CF.

2.7 General preference-based choice functions

Suppose that the method of evaluation employed generates a connected and fully transitive ordering R of any feasible set, albeit an ordering that is contextually bound to the set over which it is defined; that is, the ordering defined on each set S is relativized to S. In such a case, let $R(S)$ be the ordering of the elements in S, when S is the feasible set. Then in place of R there will be a set of orderings $\{R(S)$, for all subsets S of $X\}$, each member of which is explicitly relativized to the set of elements over which it is defined.

Correspondingly, one can introduce, as a generalization of $C(S, R)$, the notion of an $R(S)$-based choice set:

The $R(S)$-*based choice set* $C(S, R(S))$ is the set of elements x in S such that for every element y in S, $x\, R(S)\, y$.

Now it is obvious from the preceding explorations that if, for each S, $R(S)$ is connected and fully transitive, then corresponding to each S there will exist a nonempty choice *set* $C(S, R(S))$, and for each finite set X together with all its subsets S, there will exist a family of choice sets $\{C(S, R(S))$, for each subset S in $X\}$, each member of which is nonempty. Recall, however, that the defining characteristic of an abstract choice *function* defined over a finite X is simply that for each subset S in X the choice function picks out a nonempty subset of S, namely, the R-best elements in S. Thus, even though there is not a single underlying ordering R, but only a family of orderings $\{R(S)$, for all subsets S of $X\}$, it is still the case that a choice function exists. More specifically:

Let $C(\cdot, R(\cdot))$ be a *preference-based choice function* defined on X, relative to an underlying set of orderings $\{R(S)$, for all subsets S of $X\}$.

Then by a straightforward and uncontroversial extension of proposition 2.1, we have directly the following:

Proposition 2.8. If $R(S)$, for each and every subset S of X, is connected and fully transitive, then there exists a choice function $C(\cdot, R(\cdot))$ defined on X.

2.8 Necessary conditions on choice functions

One direct implication of the generalization given in the preceding section is that the nonemptiness of the preference-based choice set, and hence the existence of a choice function, does *not* presuppose an underlying context-free ordering. Notice, moreover, that Proposition 2.1 formulates only a sufficient, rather than a necessary, condition for the existence of a choice function. What, then, qualifies as a necessary condition?

Consider first the standard framework, in which it is presupposed that the underlying ordering R is context free. Within that framework the following is a well-known result:

Proposition 2.9. Connectedness of R on X is a necessary condition for the existence of the choice function $C(\cdot, R)$ on X.

To see this, suppose there exists a context-free ordering R that fails to be connected over X, so that for some x and y in X it is neither the case that $x R y$, nor the case that $y Rx$. In this instance, it is not true that the set $C(S, R)$ is nonempty for every finite S. In particular, $C(\{x, y\})$ is empty.

What role does transitivity play in all of this? It turns out that transitivity is not a necessary condition for the existence of a preference-based choice function (of the traditional sort). A set of weaker conditions, namely, reflexivity, connectedness, and transitivity of just strict preference, suffice to ensure the existence of a choice function:

Proposition 2.10. If R is reflexive, connected, and transitive with respect to strict preference over a finite X, then a choice function $C(\cdot, R)$ is defined over X.[20]

And this can be weakened even further:

Proposition 2.11. If R is reflexive, connected, and acyclical over X, then a choice function $C(\cdot, R)$ is defined on X,[21]

where

R is *acyclical* over X iff for all $x_1, \ldots, x_j$ in X, if $x_1 P x_2$ & $x_2 P x_3$ & $\ldots$ & $x_{j-1} P x_j$, then $x_1 R x_j$.

But here, finally, one does reach another necessary condition:

Proposition 2.12. A choice function $C(\cdot, R)$ is defined on X only if R is acyclical on X.[22]

Cycles in a context-free relation pose a fatal problem for the existence of a choice function: One has only to identify the chain of options that form the cycle and consider the set S_c consisting of just those options. For S_c, the corresponding choice set will be empty: There will be no member x of S_c such that $x \, R \, y$ for every y in S_c.

What happens to Propositions 2.9 through 2.12 in the more liberal framework of $R(S)$ instead of R, in which orderings may be context dependent? Proposition 2.10 can be generalized in a straightforward manner to cover the case in which, instead of R, there is an underlying set of (context-dependent) orderings $\{R(S)\}$. Proposition 2.11 also continues to hold. Proposition 2.12, however, does not. The reason is that if the ordering is not context free and some set X contains a cycle, it may still be the case that (a) the cycle does not involve "top-ranked" elements, that is, the cycle occurs among losers, and (b) when just the elements involved in the cycle are isolated as a distinct feasible set, the cycle disappears.[23] For similar reasons, Proposition 2.9 no longer holds. If the choice sets are based on context-dependent orderings $R \, (S)$, rather than a single underlying ordering R, failure of connectedness of $R(S)$ between "unacceptable" options in a given feasible set S need not jeopardize the nonemptiness of the choice set $C(S, R(S))$ and, hence, the existence of the choice function $C(\cdot, R(\cdot))$ defined on X, that is, on all subsets S of X.

2.9 Another generalization

Are there other frameworks that are permissive in some respect other than that of allowing the underlying orderings to be context dependent, and yet in which constructable choice functions will still exist? Sen (1970) provides an important case in his exploration of a setting in which R is presumed to be context free but not necessarily connected, an exploration that reveals that even the requirement of connectedness is dispensable. As already noted, failure of connectedness of R jeopardizes the existence of a choice function. But all that one need do in this case, as Sen himself makes clear, is to generalize the notion of a choice set to that of a "maximal" set:[24]

Let x be a *maximal element* of X with respect to the underlying relation R iff it is not the case that there exists a y in X such that y is strictly preferred to x; and let the set of all such elements be the *maximal set* $M(X, R)$.

This, of course, neatly obviates the need to assume that R is connected. If it is not the case that $x\,R\,y$ nor that $y\,R\,x$, then, as noted before, $C(\{x, y\})$ is empty. But still, neither element is strictly preferred to the other, and thus $M(\{x, y\}) = \{x, y\}$.[25] It can also be noted, although Sen does not explore this point, that the definition of a maximal set leads naturally to that of a maximal set function:

> A *maximal set function* $M(\cdot, R)$ defined over X is a functional relation such that the maximal set $M(S, R)$ is nonempty for every nonempty subset S of X.[26]

Within a framework in which choice is characterized in terms of maximal sets, Propositions 2.9 through 2.12 undergo substantial modification. For the case in which there is a single context-free underlying ordering R, Proposition 2.9 no longer holds; Propositions 2.10 and 2.11 hold in the weakened form that results by dropping the connectedness condition, and in Proposition 2.12 the acyclicity condition can be weakened to P-acyclicity, where R is *P-acyclical* over X iff for all $x_1, \ldots, x_j$ in X, if $x_1\,P\,x_2$ & $x_2\,P\,x_3$ & $\ldots$ & $x_{j-1}\,P\,x_j$, then it is not the case that $x_j\,P\,x_1$.

2.10 A maximally permissive framework

Moving beyond the concept of a maximal set function, is there a choice framework that presupposes even less structure? Clearly there is. The maximal set framework still presupposes that R is a context-free relation, and as I have already observed satisfaction of this condition is not required for the existence of a choice function.

The most general framework of all is one in which it is possible that the method of evaluation employed by the agent issues in nothing more than a simple division of options into those that are acceptable and those that are not. In the generic sense in which I have been employing the term, this can still be thought of as involving an ordering: Certain options are ranked as superior to others. As a specific example, consider the proposal recently put forward by Levi for decision making under conditions of radical uncertainty, where probabilities are indeterminate.[27] As an illustration of his proposal, consider the following decision problem, in which p and $1 - p$ specify the probabilities with which the associated monetary payoffs will be received:

$$g_1 = [\$7, p; \$2, 1 - p],$$
$$g_2 = [\$2, p; \$7, 1 - p],$$
$$g_3 = [\$4, p; \$4, 1 - p], \quad \text{i.e., } \$4 \text{ with certainty.}$$

For the purposes of this example, assume that when probabilities are well defined, the agent is prepared to order gambles of this type solely in terms of expected monetary return. Given that assumption, for any specific value of p, the agent will be able to order completely the set $\{g_1, g_2, g_3\}$. Now suppose that the agent suddenly confronts this problem with no information at all, or only partial information, about the value of p. For dealing with this kind of case, Levi invokes what he terms the principle of *E-admissibility*. In the present context, a given option is E-admissible just in case for some permissible determinate probability value, that option bears maximum expected monetary return as compared with the other available options. In the above example, if p is taken to be completely indeterminate, then any value $0 < p < 1$ is permissible. If p is only partially indeterminate – for example, it is known to lie on some more restricted interval, say, on the closed interval between ¼ and ⅜, then any value of p that lies on that closed interval will be permissible.

Levi allows for the possibility that an agent might take E-admissibility in such cases as a sufficient criterion of choice. The orderings generated by application of the principle of E-admissibility are clearly contextually dependent. Suppose that the agent is limited to choosing just between g_1 and g_3; that is, let $G = \{g_1, g_3\}$ and let p be completely indeterminate. In this case, both are E-admissible, since there are permissible values of p for which g_1 will have a greater expected monetary return, for example, $p = .75$, and those for which g_3 will have a greater expected monetary return, for example, $p = .25$. But for $G^* = \{g_1, g_2, g_3\}$, there is no value of p such that g_3 has as great or greater expected monetary return than both g_1 and g_2: Whatever the value of p, either g_1 or g_2 will have greater expected value than g_3. Thus, when g_2 as well as g_1 is available, g_3 turns out to be E-*in*admissible. That is, g_3 fails to be E-admissible when taken in comparison with both g_1 and g_2. The implied orderings here, then, are not context free. Recast explicitly in terms of choice, the choice function to which such evaluative rankings give rise will fail to satisfy Beta.

In a setting such as this, one may also consider the possibility that evaluation takes place in stages. That is, it is possible that the feasible options are evaluated by reference to one criterion, and then options passing that test are subjected to another test. Levi, for example, suggests that one might supplement his principle of E-admissibility with a security or S-admissibility rule. To illustrate one version of such a security rule, if two uncertain prospects are both E-admissible and one of them guarantees a higher minimum payoff than the other, then it is acceptable (although not required), on Levi's account, to use a maximin criterion. Consider again the problem introduced to illustrate E-admissibility. In a pairwise comparison between g_1 and g_3, both are E-admissible; but g_3 ensures a payoff of at least \$4, whereas g_1 does not. Thus, if the criterion of S-admissibility is used to supplement the E-admissibility principle, g_3 will be chosen over g_1, for the feasible set $G = \{g_1, g_3\}$. When, however, the feasible set is $G^* = \{g_1, g_2, g_3\}$, g_3 is ruled out by E-admissibility alone, and by application of S-admissibility to the remaining options, the acceptable set consists of both g_1 and g_2. When E- and S-admissibility are employed in this way, the resulting ordering is once again not context free. In pairwise comparison, g_3 ranks over g_1, whereas in three-way comparison g_1 and g_2 rank over g_3. Recast in terms of choice, the choice function to which these orderings can be said to give rise will violate both Alpha and Beta.

Again, within such a framework, there is no reason to suppose that once the options have been evaluated, all those found acceptable must be regarded as equally good. Since the method of evaluation employed may not yield a connected ordering of the options, there is no reason to assume that any particular comparisons have been made among those options that remain, that is, that have not been rejected. Levi again provides a case in point. He would argue that it would be a mistake to think of the principle of E-admissibility as requiring that for $G^* = \{g_1, g_2, g_3\}$, g_1 and g_2 must be regarded as equally good in the sense of being preferentially indifferent to each other. E-admissibility is a criterion by appeal to which certain options can be rejected, not a criterion for judging two options to be equally good. Alternatively expressed, one can think of the approach Levi advocates as not necessarily generating a connected ordering of the members of any feasible set. So construed, Levi's proposal involves a method of evaluation that supports the existence of a maximal set function rather than a choice function. But as I suggested at the outset of this section, Levi's whole approach fits even more naturally within a maximally permissive framework in which orderings consist of nothing more than a separation of feasible options into those that are acceptable and those that are not – a framework within which the question of connectedness, as it is usually conceived, does not even arise. If, on completion of the evaluation, there are a number of options, all of which are judged acceptable by whatever criteria have been employed, then the agent's final task will be to *pick* one from among those that are acceptable.

Levi's admissibility rules suggest that one should begin with a conception of choosing that is applicable in the widest possible range of settings. Choosing, on this view, can be understood as expressive of whatever evaluative criteria are being employed and of whatever (perhaps only partial, perhaps even context-dependent) ordering of the available options has been effected by the use of those criteria. Choosing, then, amounts to the act of identifying in the feasible set a subset of elements all of which are acceptable, in the sense of passing the various tests to which they have been subjected. Of course, at this level of abstraction, this is simply the notion of a choice set $C(\cdot)$, as introduced in Section 2.2. However, the "choice" set, in this sense, may be determined by reference to an underlying relation, which may or may not be context free and may or may not be connected. To signal that these matters are being left open for now, I propose to use a more general notation:

> Let the *acceptable set* $D(X)$ of any set X be that subset of X consisting of just those alternatives in X that are judged acceptable by whatever criteria are being employed.

If the acceptable set is determined by reference to a context-free, connected ordering, this can be indicated by relativizing the "choice" set to that ordering and using a subscript "c" to indicate that the set consists of best options (as defined in Section 2.2). In this case, the appropriate notation will be $D_c(X, R)$. If the underlying preference ordering is context dependent, but still connected, the appropriate notation will be $D_c(S, R(S))$. If, however, the context-free, or context-dependent, underlying ordering is not connected, this can be indicated by subscripting D with "m" to indicate that these sets consist of options that are not bettered by any other options in the set (per the definition of a maximal set given in Section 2.9); that is, the appropriate notations will be, respectively, $D_m(X, R)$ and $D_m(S, R(S))$.

Whichever of the above is the case, if the evaluative method proceeds by the generation of an ordering (or orderings) as a basis for choice, it is reasonable to suppose that the ordering (or orderings) is such that the corresponding acceptable-set function $-D_c(\cdot, R)$ or $D_m(\cdot, R)$ or $D_c(\cdot, R(\cdot))$ or $D_m(\cdot, R(\cdot))$, as the case may be $-$ is defined on X; that is, the acceptable set is nonempty for every subset S of X.

But as the definition of $D(X)$ makes clear, one need not think just in terms of "ordering-based" acceptable sets. One can start, more generally, from the notion of an abstract "acceptable set" and assume simply that the method of evaluation employed, however it works, at the very least gives rise to nonempty acceptable sets. That is, stated somewhat more formally, one can propose the following:

> *Minimal intelligible choice (MIC).* The evaluative method must be such that it generates a nonempty acceptable set for each

subset of X, that is, such that there exists an acceptable-set function $D(\cdot)$ defined over X.

In effect, this is what is left if one starts with the requirement that a preference-based choice function proper exists and strips away all that is not necessary to ensure that intelligible choice is possible. But notice how little constraint this places on any method of evaluation. The issue here, just as in the case of choice functions, concerns the possibility of intelligible choice. To be sure, this is not something that can be guaranteed simply by assuming that the feasible set consists of a set of mutually exclusive and exhaustive options. That ensures that the agent will do something, not that he will intelligibly choose (in any recognizable sense of that term). Nor is it something guaranteed by the notion of an evaluative method as such. This is one very important respect in which *choosing* as I have explicated the notion here in terms of the concept of an acceptable set is more specialized than the evaluation on which I have supposed it is predicated. Evaluation is not necessarily confined to a set at least one element of which must eventually be chosen. One can proceed to evaluate or grade a barrel of apples and come to the conclusion that the whole barrel contains nothing but rotten, and thus unacceptable, apples. As it turns out, nothing measures up, passes the grade. But when evaluation or grading is directed toward choosing, matters are somewhat different. If every available apple is rotten, and no finer discriminations are made but some apple must still be selected, then rather than its being the case that the acceptable set is empty, one can meet the requirement of intelligible choice by supposing that every apple is in the acceptable set.

2.11 A more structured framework

What substantive requirements in addition to MIC must be imposed on any abstract acceptable-set function $D(\cdot)$ if one is to recover the more traditional setting of a context-free, connected weak ordering? It turns out that all that must be assumed in addition is the context-free condition CF. That is:

> **Proposition 2.13.** If $D(\cdot)$ is well defined over X and satisfies CF, then there exists a pair-set choice-constructed preference relation R_c defined on X that constitutes a weak ordering of X (i.e., R_c is context free, connected, and fully transitive).

Proposition 2.3 establishes that if a *choice* function $C(\cdot)$ satisfies CF, then one can define a weak ordering R_c on X. Proposition 2.13 will be established if it can be shown that this result transfers to the case in which one starts out with an acceptable-set function rather than a choice function. But this is trivially true. An acceptable-set function is just a choice function that has been freed of any trace of connection to an underlying context-free or connected ordering relation. That is, an acceptable-set function is just an abstractly conceived choice function.

If then, in addition, $D(\cdot)$ satisfies CF, then by Proposition 2.3, one can employ a choice-constructed preference concept such as R_c to get from there to a reflexive, connected, transitive, and context-free preference ordering. It is true, of course, that this does not imply that the constructed ordering R_c coincides with the ranking that is directly produced by the method of evaluation being employed and that is taken as a basis for the definition of acceptable sets. One can recall in this connection that Proposition 2.4 establishes that if R is a context-free, fully transitive, and connected ordering and $C(\cdot, R)$ is the corresponding preference-based choice function, then $C(\cdot, R)$ can be employed in turn to define *an* ordering R_c that does coincide with R. The trouble is that this result presupposes that R is context-free. It would appear that there is nothing like a corresponding result for general (as distinct from context-free) orderings.[28]

It is possible to argue, however, that this is a "don't care" matter. Recall that the notion of an acceptable set was introduced to capture the implications *for choice* of whatever method of evaluation is being employed. If it turns out that $D(\cdot, R(\cdot))$ really does satisfy CF, then the agent's acceptable sets – and hence his choice behavior – will be just like those of a person who is maximizing a context-free connected ordering. That is, at the level of the implications of any evaluative method for *choice*, the agent behaves as if he were basing his choice on maximizing with respect to a weak ordering. As will become evident shortly, the pragmatic arguments with which I shall be concerned turn on a comparison of the consequences of different approaches to sequential choice. That is, the focus will be on the pragmatic implications of methods of evaluation as methods of choosing – not as methods of ranking as such. For my purposes, then, the results just outlined should suffice. That is, MIC and the context-free condition CF together suffice to capture for present purposes what is contained in the traditional requirement that the agent have a weak preference ordering over X.

2.12 Summary

I have proposed in the foregoing a particular factoring of the traditional weak ordering requirement. The account I have offered makes the context-free condition CF pivotal. Given that evaluation proceeds in such a way as to ensure, for any given feasible set, that at least one element is not ranked below others, MIC is satisfied, and thus $D(\cdot)$ is well defined. Beyond this it suffices for the purposes of securing the weak ordering principle to suppose that the acceptable-set function satisfies condition CF. That is, if the method of evaluation employed generates acceptable sets that satisfy both MIC and CF, then one can interpret the agent as choosing as if he were maximizing with respect to a weak ordering R defined on X. In subsequent chapters, I shall proceed on the assumption that the task for the foundations of decision and utility theory with respect to the weak ordering requirement is to formulate an argument in defense of CF.

In this respect, my analysis coincides at least in part with that which has been put forward by advocates of the so-called theory of revealed preference. In particular, like them, I suppose that the weak ordering requirement can be reconstructed in terms of conditions on choice functions. My analysis does differ, however, in two important respects from traditional revealed preference theory.

First, I have argued that although satisfaction of MIC and CF together suffices (by appeal to choice-based preference constructs) to establish the existence of orderings that are fully transitive and connected over the relevant set of options X, CF is hardly a necessary condition for the existence of an ordering with such properties. In particular, it is possible that the method of evaluation generates context-dependent orderings whose corresponding preference-based choice sets fail to satisfy condition CF, yet the ordering over any given feasible set will still be both connected and fully transitive. This point, it seems to me, has not been made with the clarity it deserves. Where this is not clearly marked, it is easy to miss the fact that the conjunction of CF and one or another choice-based preference construct is considerably more powerful than the transitivity conditions on orderings: CF and the definition of R_c together guarantee, in addition, that R_c is relevant to choice and satisfies the logically distinct context-free condition CFO. As I shall show in more detail in Chapter 4, failure to note that CF as a condition on choice functions is a much stronger condition than transitivity on the preference ordering can lead to real confusion when it comes to justifying CF as normative for choice. Transitivity of the ordering over any feasible set of alternatives is a relatively weak and plausible condition; CF is much more problematic.

Second, in making the context-free condition CF central, I intend no capitulation to a "behavioral" approach to preference of the sort favored by empirically oriented psychologists or economists studying microbehavior. Within the framework proposed, in which it is not assumed that choice sets are unit sets, my willingness to employ both the choice-(set!)-based concept of a preference ordering and the preference-based concept of a choice set does not imply acceptance of an excessively behavioral approach to preference. Nonunit choice sets, after all, are not much more observable than "preferences in the head."[29]

3

The independence principle

3.1 Alternative formulations of independence

The weak ordering principle discussed in the preceding chapter pertains to the ranking of any set of alternatives, regardless of the nature of the alternatives themselves. The second of the cornerstones of the modern theory of utility and subjective probability, the independence principle, is more specialized. As formulated in Chapter 1, it places the following restriction on the ordering of options that involve risk or uncertainty (in suitably defined senses of each of these terms):

> *Independence (IND).* Let g_1, g_2, and g_3, be any three alternative gambles. Then $g_1 R g_2$ iff $g_{13} = [g_1, p; g_3, 1 - p] R g_{23} = [g_2, p; g_3, 1 - p]$,

where $g_{ij} = [g_i, p; g_j, 1 - p]$ is a complex gamble in which there is p probability of being exposed to the gamble g_i, and $1 - p$ probability of being exposed to g_j, and $0 < p \leq 1$.[1]

IND invites further extension and/or specialization in a variety of ways. By way of illustration, note first of all that since an outcome involving no risk (a "sure" outcome) can be viewed as a "gamble" in which one gets that outcome with probability 1, IND yields a constraint on preference in the special case of gambles whose component outcomes themselves involve no risk:

> *Independence for sure outcomes (ISO).* Let o_1, o_2, and o_3 be any three outcomes (monetary prizes, etc.). Then $o_1 R o_2$ iff for $0 < p \leq 1$, $[o_1, p; o_3, 1 - p] R [o_2, p; o_3, 1 - p]$.

IND is formulated above in terms of weak preference. It can also be particularized by reformulation in terms of the strict preference relation or, alternatively, in terms of the indifference relation.[2] Again, as formulated above, IND deals with simple gambles over two prospects, but the principle can be easily extended to more complex forms of gambles, and once again in a variety of ways. For example, some introduce an independence assumption in the form of a substitution principle, in which replacement of some component of a gamble with something indifferent to that component results in a gamble that is indifferent to the original one. Stated somewhat more formally, this yields the following:

Substitution (SUB). Let $g_{1x} = [\ldots g_1 \ldots]$ and $g_{2x} = [\ldots g_2 \ldots]$ be two complex gambles that are alike in every respect except that in one or more places where g_{1x} has g_1 as a component outcome, g_{2x} substitutes g_2, then $g_1 \, I \, g_2$ iff $g_{1x} \, I \, g_{2x}$.[3]

It can also be shown that IND immediately implies the following principle:

Independence for constant outcome (ICO). For any $0 < p \leq 1$ and any four gambles g_1, g_2, g_3, and g_4, $g_{13} = [g_1, p; g_3, 1 - p] \, R \, g_{23}$ $= [g_2, p; g_3, 1 - p]$ iff $g_{14} = [g_1, p; g_4, 1 - p] \, R \, g_{24} = [g_2, p; g_4, 1 - p]$.[4]

All of the versions of independence mentioned so far are framed with respect to well-defined probabilities. But the principle has a natural extension to cases in which the agent faces prospects the likelihoods of whose outcomes may not be well defined (in any frequency or "logical" sense of probability). Savage introduces such a principle in *The Foundations of Statistics*. There the independence requirement is formulated without reference to probabilities at all, but only to the notion of mutually exclusive and exhaustive events, which condition the consequences of various acts, and to the notion of two or more acts coinciding with respect to their consequences as conditioned by some particular event. Stated somewhat less rigorously than it is in Savage but in a manner that clarifies its connection with the constant-outcomes version (ICO) of the independence principle, the relevant principle is as follows:[5]

Savage independence (SI). Let E and $-E$ be mutually exclusive and exhaustive events conditioning the various components of four gambles $g_{13}, g_{23}, g_{14}, g_{24}$, and let the schedule of consequences be as follows:

	E	$-E$
g_{13}	g_1	g_3
g_{23}	g_2	g_3
g_{14}	g_1	g_4
g_{24}	g_2	g_4

Then $g_{13} \, R \, g_{23}$ iff $g_{14} \, R \, g_{24}$.

In very general terms, the particular formulation to which appeal is made in a given axiomatic construction typically depends in part on the strength of the other axioms employed and in part on considerations of simplicity and/or formal elegance. Since the aim of any axiomatic structure is to present a set of results as the logical consequences of the simplest and weakest set of postulates possible, the concern of those who seek to provide an axiomatic reconstruction of a theory may diverge sharply from the concerns of those who seek to assess the adequacy of that theory. That is, although a rather weak version of a given axiom may well suffice for the derivation of a particular theorem, what counts in favor of a relatively weak version of the axiom may also serve to underpin a much stronger version of the same axiom. In general, and in particular from the perspective of a foundational exploration, it will serve the purposes of conceptual clarity and evidential support to focus on more general (and hence stronger) versions of various postulates. In what follows, then, I shall take IND itself as an appropriate representative of the independence requirement.

3.2 Reduction principles

Constructions that employ an independence principle invariably invoke some form or other of what has come to be known as the reduction principle. This requires, in effect, that a rational agent be indifferent between any two gambles that yield the same outcomes with the same probabilities (or uncertainties). The notion is that regardless of the "internal" structure of a given gamble – the number of stages or conditioning events it involves – it is always possible, by multiplying through and combining the specified probabilities of the various conditioning events, to associate with that gamble a "reduced" version, the structure of which consists of a simple set of outcomes, together with a (more or less determinate) probability distribution over those outcomes. Such a reduction principle requires an agent to be indifferent, for example, as to whether he gambles at the roulette table or at cards or with dice, so long as these different "games" offer him the same odds of winning the same amounts of money. Similarly, it requires him to be indifferent between a complex lottery in which the first-stage prize is a ticket in a second lottery, and so on, and a simple, single-stage lottery, so long as the amounts to be won and their respective odds are the same.

For most of the constructions to be explored, the version of reduction that Luce and Raiffa employ will suffice. They formulate the principle in the following manner:[6]

Reduction (RD). Any compound gamble is indifferent to a simple gamble with $o_1,\ldots,o_r$ as outcomes, their probabilities being computed according to the ordinary probability calculus. In particular, if

$$g^{(i)} = [o_1, p_1^{(i)}; o_2, p_2^{(i)}; \ldots; o_r, p_r^{(i)}], \qquad \text{for} \quad i = 1,\ldots, s,$$

then

$$[g^{(1)}, q_1; g^{(2)}, q_2; \ldots; g^{(s)}, \quad q_s] \, I \, [o_1, p_1; o_2, p_2; \ldots; o_r, p_r],$$

where

$$p_i = q_1 p_i^{(1)} + q_2 p_i^{(2)} + \cdots + q_s p_i^{(s)}.$$

3.3 Independence and noncomplementarity

The introduction of the term "independence" was motivated by a perceived analogy to the economic concept of independent goods, in which the value of a bundle of various quantities of different goods can be represented as an additive function of the value of the quantities of the various separate goods that make up that bundle. It is, of course, well known that independence with respect to the value of a bundle of commodities can fail. The value of the combination of x amount of one good and y amount of another good may not be equivalent to the sum of the value of x amount of the one good and the value of y amount of the other good. Failure of independence in such cases is said to be due to complementarity or interaction. That is, the value of one good may be enhanced if the good is combined with some other good, as, for example, in the proverbial case in which white wine is said to complement fish and red wine to complement beef.

It is usually argued, however, that for decision making under conditions of risk and uncertainty this sort of complementarity problem does not arise and, thus, that the appeal to an independence principle in this context is warranted. Samuelson, for example, explicitly marks the analogy and, while acknowledging that complementarities can arise in the case of (conjunctive) bundles of goods, insists that the nature of a disjunctive (or stochastic) bundle, in which one is to get just one of the disjunctions, makes it plausible to impose independence as a condition on preferences for gambles. Addressing a simple variant on IND, according to which if lottery ticket g_1 is (as good as or) better than g_2, and lottery ticket g_3 is (as good as or) better than g_4, then an even chance of getting g_1 or g_3 is (as good as or) better than an even chance of getting g_2 or g_4, he argues as follows:

Within the stochastic realm, independence has a legitimacy that it does not have in the nonstochastic realm. Why? Because either heads *or* tails must come up: if one comes up, the other cannot; so there is no reason why the choice between g_1 and g_2 should be "contaminated" by the choice between g_3 and g_4.[7]

When independence is treated in terms of the concept of noncomplementarity, the substitution version SUB invites interpretation as implying a preference version of the principle that the addition of equals to equals preserves equality: What it requires is that substitution of a component with something indifferent to it preserve indifference. Correspondingly, IND itself can be interpreted as implying a preference version of the principle that adding unequals to equals results in an inequality in the same direction: That is, it requires that substitution of a component with something weakly preferred to it result in a new gamble weakly preferred to the old.

Viewed from this perspective, the independence principle formulates for the case of preferences over gambles a condition analogous to one employed in a wide range of other axiomatizations of preferences, including preferences for commodities that can be described in terms of multiple attributes and social (or collective) preferences. In each case the role that it plays is the same: It is the postulate that secures a theorem to the effect that preferences for (or of) "wholes" can be represented in terms of some additive function of preferences for (or of) components.[8]

3.4 Independence and sure-thing reasoning

The presupposition that noncomplementarity characterizes the manner in which the values of the components of disjunctive bundles enter into the value of such wholes is only one of two basic ways in which the independence condition has been conceptualized. Starting in the fifties one can mark a very different interpretation, one that relates independence to what subsequently came to be known as the "sure-thing principle."[9] One of the earliest appeals to this principle is that of Friedman and Savage, who introduce it in the following manner:

... suppose a physician now knows that his patient has one of several diseases for each of which the physician would prescribe immediate bed rest. We assert that under this circumstance the physician should, and unless confused, will prescribe immediate bed rest whether he is now, or later, or never, able to make an exact diagnosis.

Much more abstractly, consider a person constrained to choose between a pair of alternatives, g_{13} and g_{24}, without knowing whether a particular event E does (or will) in fact obtain. Suppose that, depending on his choice and whether E does obtain, he is to receive one of four gambles, according to the following schedule.

Choice	Event	
	E	$-E$
g_{13}	g_1	g_3
g_{24}	g_2	g_4

The principle in sufficient generality for the present purpose asserts: If the person does not prefer g_1 to g_2 and does not prefer g_3 to g_4, then he will not prefer the choice g_{13} to g_{24}. Further, if the person does not prefer g_{13} to g_{24}, he will either not prefer g_1 to g_2 or not prefer g_3 to g_4 (possibly both).

We anticipate that if the reader considers this principle, in the light of the illustration that precedes and such others as he himself may invent, he will concede that the principle is not one he would deliberately violate.[10]

The *conceptual* thrust of the principle is clear enough. Consider once again the abstract problem given in the quotation from Friedman and Savage. If $g_1 P g_2$ and $g_3 R g_4$, then choice of g_{13} offers a sure thing in the following respect: One cannot do worse having selected g_{13}, regardless of the turn of events $(E, -E)$, and one may end up doing better. If $g_1 P g_2$ and $g_3 P g_4$, then choice of g_{13} offers a sure thing in an even stronger sense: It is guaranteed that one will do better having chosen g_{13}, regardless of the turn of events.

As Savage was to make clear two years later, what is being invoked here is essentially the dominance principle that had been employed by many statisticians as a basic admissibility criterion.[11] Recast in n-ary form, the principle as it applies to the case of gambles with well-defined probabilities can be formulated in the following manner:

General dominance for fixed probabilities (GDP). For $g = [g_1, p_1; \ldots; g_n, p_n]$ and $g^* = [g_1^*, p_1; \ldots; g_n^*, p_n]$, if $g_i R g_i^*$ for all i, then $g R g^*$; and if, in addition, $g_j P g_j^*$ for some j, then $g P g^*$.

One can abstract from probabilities, however, and reformulate the principle in terms of a partition of mutually exclusive and exhaustive conditioning events $(E_1, \ldots, E_n)$:

General dominance for a fixed partition of events (GDE). For $g = [g_1, E_1; \ldots; g_n, E_n]$ and $g^* = [g_1^*, E_1; \ldots; g_n^*, E_n]$, if $g_i R g_i^*$ for all i, then $g R g^*$; and if, in addition, $g_j P g_j^*$ for some j, then $g P g^*$.

With the reformulation of the sure-thing principle or dominance principle in terms of a partition of events rather than probabilities, it becomes necessary, of course, to introduce important qualifications in the scope of the principle. On the usual account, one necessary restriction can be framed in terms of a requirement that the choice of a gamble not differentially affect the probabilities of the conditioning events – that is, for each E_i that conditions both an outcome of g and an outcome of g^*, the conditional probability of E_i, given that one chooses g, must be equal to the conditional probability of E_i, given that one chooses g^*.[12] Alternatively, some have suggested that the restriction should be reframed in terms of the notion that there should be an absence of certain kinds of *causal* connection between the choice of a gamble and the occurrence of conditioning events.[13]

These formulations of the dominance principle are to be specifically understood as applying to cases in which outcomes are themselves risky prospects or gambles. In this sense, the "outcome" of an event E_i is simply what happens – what prospect the agent faces – conditional on E_i taking place. Of course, such principles, like IND, can be particularized to the case in which outcomes are not gambles but sure amounts of money or other goods. This yields the following:

> *Dominance in terms of sure (riskless) outcomes (DSO).* For $g = [o_1, E_1; \ldots; o_n, E_n]$ and $g^* = [o_1^*, E_1; \ldots; o_n^*, E_n]$, if $o_i \, R \, o_i^*$ for all i, then $g \, R \, g^*$; and if, in addition, $o_j \, P \, o_j^*$ for some j, then $g \, P \, g^*$.

3.5 Independence and dominance

Some sense of the intuitive connection between independence and sure-thing or dominance reasoning can be gained by considering how one might get from a simple version of dominance to a version of independence. Consider again dominance as formulated with respect to two components:

(A) For all $0 < p \le 1$ and all g_1, g_2, g_3, and g_4, if $g_1 \, P \, g_2$ and $g_3 \, R \, g_4$, then $g_{13} = [\, g_1, p; g_3, 1 - p] \, P \, g_{24} = [\, g_2, p; g_4, 1 - p]$.

But since indifference implies weak preference, this yields immediately the following:

(B) For all $0 < p \le 1$ and all g_1, g_2, g_3, and g_4, if $g_1 \, P \, g_2$ and $g_3 \, I \, g_4$, then $g_{13} = [\, g_1, p; g_3, 1 - p] \, P \, g_{24} = [\, g_2, p; g_4, 1 - p]$.

And on the plausible assumption that any component is indifferent to itself, this in turn implies the following:

(C) For all $0 < p \leq 1$ and all g_1, g_2, and g_3, if $g_1 P g_2$, then $g_{13} = [g_1, p; g_3, 1 - p] P g_{23} = [g_2, p; g_3, 1 - p]$.

Now principle (C) makes the ordering of the two gambles – with fixed probabilities and one component in common – a simple function of the relative ordering of the other component: This appeals to independence, since it implies that the ordering of the two gambles is to be independent of the way the agent would preferentially rank the component they have in common. Principle (A), in contrast, appeals to sure-thing reasoning, since it implies that if the components of one gamble are uniformly at least as good as the ones with which they are paired in the other gamble, and in one case better, then this determines the ordering of the two gambles.

The line of reasoning from principle (A) to principle (C) is also reversible. Principle (C) requires that g_{13} and g_{23} share a common component g_3. And by extension of this line of reasoning, one then considers the case in which there is some g_3 and some g_4, which is not identical with, but nonetheless indifferent to, g_3 – the case covered by principle (B). But given (B) it also seems plausible to accept principle (A). In the presence of various additional assumptions, in fact, one or another version of independence will typically suffice for the derivation of a dominance condition.

Friedman and Savage run a version of the first of the two arguments sketched above, reasoning from a version of dominance framed in terms of a partition of events rather than probabilities, together with the reduction principle discussed in Section 3.2, to a version of principle (C).[14] More recently, Arrow has offered a construction in which the standard dominance principle is factored into a pair of principles. The first introduces the concept of a *conditional preference* for one act a_1 over another a_2, given that a particular event is assumed to obtain, ($a_1 P a_2/ E$), and is glossed by Arrow in the following manner:

> The first assumption special to the theory of choice under uncertainty may be put this way: what might have happened under conditions that we know won't prevail should have no influence on our choice of actions. Suppose, that is, we are given the information that certain states of nature are impossible. We reform our beliefs about the remaining states of nature, and on the basis of these new beliefs we form a new ordering of the actions. The principle of conditional preference, which we will now introduce, asserts that the ordering will depend only on the consequences of the actions for those states of the world not ruled out by the information.

Following Arrow, one can refer to this as the principle of conditional preference (CP). The other postulate is a dominance principle framed in terms of the notion of conditional preferences and with respect to a partition, that is, a finite or infinite collection of events

$P = \{E_1, E_2, \ldots\}$ that are mutually exclusive and jointly exhaustive of the possibilities:

> *Arrow dominance (AD).* Given two acts a_1 and a_2, if, for every event E_i in the partition P, $a_1 \, R \, a_2/E_i$, then $a_1 \, R \, a_2$; and if, in addition, there exists a collection of P' of events in P whose union is nonnull, that is, the union defines an event not deemed to be impossible, and such that $a_1 \, P \, a_2/E_i$ for all events E_i in P', then $a_1 \, P \, a_2$.

These two postulates in turn form the basis for a proof of the expected utility theorem that relates it to the economic concept of independent goods.[15] That is, CP and AD (together with a version of the reduction principle RD) are shown, within such a framework, to imply a version of the independence principle IND.

Since it was Savage himself who originally framed the sure-thing or dominance principle and who, together with Friedman, used it to secure a version of independence, one might have expected that he would introduce it as a postulate in his subsequent book *The Foundations of Statistics.* There, however, he adopts just the reverse approach. It is the independence principle that is given the status of a postulate. The appeal to "sure-thing" considerations serves initially to motivate the independence postulate *informally,* although a specific version of dominance is then shown to be derivable as a theorem.[16]

In very general terms, a survey of various alternative axiomatizations of utility and subjective probability theory suggest, then, that in the typical framework some version of dominance and some version of independence can be employed more or less interchangeably: that one can be taken as a postulate and the other derived as a theorem. In the next chapter I shall consider in somewhat greater detail the import of this interchangeability. For the moment, however, it should be noted that although many (starting with Friedman and Savage) have viewed the dominance principle as intuitively more compelling, and have thus viewed this as an effective way to secure an independence condition, the same line of reasoning can be used to undermine the intuitive status of dominance principles. That is, if one had evidence that within some domain independence were suspect – say, due to some problem of complementarity – one could conclude that since such independence is a logical consequence of a dominance principle (together with certain other unproblematic postulates), dominance in that context must also be regarded as suspect. In effect, what counts in favor of independence, via modus ponens, can count against dominance, via modus tollens.

More important yet, whether one takes dominance or independence as basic, what is requisite for the expected utility and subjective probability constructions is some version or other of a relatively strong axiom – for example, IND, which applies to gambles defined over gambles, or a generalized dominance principle such as GDP or GDE. In particular, neither independence for sure outcomes (ISO) nor dominance with respect to sure outcomes (DSO) will suffice. This point has not always been stated with the clarity that it deserves. In many expositions, independence or dominance is illustrated with reference to a case involving "sure" outcomes (e.g., monetary payoffs), but what then is employed in the construction is the much more highly generalized version of the principle. In the case of certain other axioms or postulates, as I have already remarked, this need pose no particular problem, since the postulate in question may well be one whose plausibility is not increased by being rendered in a less general form. But this is not the case with regard to either independence or dominance. As I shall argue in subsequent chapters, the very particularized versions of independence and of dominance (namely, ISO and DSO) can be motivated in a fashion that does not carry over smoothly to the more general forms (i.e., IND and GDP or GDE). Alternatively put, there are objections to IND and GDP (or GDE) that do not undermine ISO and DSO.

3.6 Stochastic dominance

There remains one conceptually distinct approach to the imposition of an independence condition. Luce and Raiffa, for example, introduce a proof of the expected utility theorem that makes use of a very limited version of the substitution version of independence (SUB), as formulated in Section 3.1. In addition they appeal to the following axiom:[17]

> *Monotonicity (MO).* If o_1 and o_2 are two sure (nonrisky) prizes such that $o_1 P o_2$, then for any two gambles of the form $g_p = [o_1, p; o_2, 1 - p]$ and $g_q = [o_1, q; o_2, 1 - q]$, $g_p P g_q$ iff $p > q$.

This invokes a very restricted version of the concept of first-order stochastic dominance, which is defined as follows:[18]

> One probability distribution over a set of sure outcomes *first-order stochastically dominates* another probability distribution over the same set of outcomes iff one can obtain the former from the latter by shifting at least some of the probability mass from less

to more desirable payoffs and none of the mass from more to less desirable payoffs.

Consider now some finite set of sure outcomes and all well-defined gambles over subsets thereof. For agents who are concerned solely with outcomes and the probabilities with which such outcomes will be received, one can regularize the gambles in question by supposing that each such gamble constitutes a probability distribution defined over the total set of sure outcomes, with zero probability being assigned to outcomes that are not possible at all. For example, if $S = \{o_1, o_2, o_3, o_4\}$ and $g_{14} = [o_1, p; o_4, 1 - p]$, one can rewrite this as $g_{14} = [o_1, p; o_2, 0; o_3, 0; o_4, 1 - p]$. This permits one to compare any two gambles in a straightforward way to determine if one first-order stochastically dominates the other. Within this sort of framework, one can now formulate the following:

> *Principle of first-order stochastic dominance* (FSD). For any two gambles g_1 and g_2 defined over the same set of sure outcomes, if g_1 first-order stochastically dominates g_2, then $g_1 P g_2$.

There is an obvious parallel between dominance with respect to sure outcomes and first-order stochastic dominance. The outcome dominance conditions are designed to apply to cases in which probabilities are held fixed and the outcomes are varied. Now assume once again that the agent is concerned only with outcomes and the probability distribution over those outcomes, that is, that his preference behavior satisfies the simple reduction principle discussed in Section 3.2. Under that condition, the intuition is (to put the point somewhat informally) that if the probability distribution is held constant, the desirability of a gamble will increase when the value of the outcomes is increased in an unambiguous fashion – for example, if substitutions are made only in favor of more desirable outcomes. But then the principle of first-order stochastic dominance simply complements that intuition, by specifying, in parallel fashion, that for cases in which the set of outcomes is held fixed, the desirability of the gamble will increase when the probability distribution itself is shifted in a particular fashion – for example, if at least some of the probability mass is shifted to more desirable outcomes and none of the mass is shifted from more to less desirable outcomes.

As it turns out, if the reduction principle RD and transitivity of weak preference are assumed to hold, the two conditions are linked even more closely. In the first place, note that if RD holds and if g_1 first-order stochastically dominates g_2, then it will be possible to construct gambles g_1^* and g_2^* such that (1) $g_i I g_i^*$, $i = 1, 2$, and (2) g_1^*

dominates g_2^* with respect to sure outcomes. To illustrate, let $g_1 = [\$0, .7; \$100, .3]$ and $g_2 = [\$0, .8; \$100, .2]$. Then g_1 stochastically dominates g_2. Now arrange the following partition of events conditioning the payoffs of the two gambles,

	E_1	E_2	E_3
g_1^*	$\$0$	$\$100$	$\$100$
g_2^*	0	0	100

where $P(E_1) = .7, P(E_2) = .1$, and $P(E_3) = .2$. Here g_1^* weakly dominates g_2^* with respect to sure outcomes. Notice, however, that if the agent accepts RD, it will be the case that $g_1^* I g_1$ and $g_2^* I g_2$, since g_1 and g_1^* (and, correspondingly, g_2 and g_2^*) offer the very same probabilities of receiving the very same set of outcomes, the difference between the elements in each pair being simply a matter of the way in which the conditioning events are arranged. But now, on the assumption that the agent's preferences satisfy FSD and transitivity of weak preferences, it will follow that we must regard g_1^* as strictly preferred to g_2^*. This suggests, then, the following more general proposition:

Proposition 3.1. Within a framework in which both the reduction principle and transitivity of weak preference are assumed to hold, if the agent is committed to DSO, then he will also have to be committed to FSD; that is, failure to respect FSD will imply, in turn, violations of DSO.

To see this, suppose that g_1 first-order stochastically dominates g_2 but that $g_2 R g_1$. Construct now g_1^* and g_2^* in the manner described above. Since $g_1^* I g_1$ and $g_2^* I g_2$, by transitivity, $g_2^* R g_1^*$; but, by construction, the latter dominates the former with respect to outcomes. Thus, DSO is violated.

Can this argument be run in reverse? Suppose there is a partition of states $[E_1, \ldots, E_n]$ such that g_1 weakly dominates g_2 with respect to sure outcomes, so that the decision problem can be schematized in the following fashion,

	E_1	E_2 $\ldots$ E_n	
g_1	o_{11}	o_{12}	o_{1n}
g_2	o_{21}	o_{22}	o_{2n}

where each o_{ij} is a sure outcome, and for each j, $o_{1j} R o_{2j}$, and for some j, $o_{1j} P o_{2j}$. Now let $p(E_j) = p_j$, and reinterpret g_1 and g_2 as follows:

$$g_2^* = [o_{21}, p_1; \ldots; o_{2n}, p_n; o_{11}, 0; \ldots; o_{1n}, 0],$$
$$g_1^* = [o_{21}, 0; \ldots; o_{2n}, 0; o_{11}, p_1, \ldots; o_{1n}, p_n].$$

By inspection, g_1^* can be got from g_2^* by taking each probability weight p_j and shifting it from o_{2j} to o_{1j}. However, since by construction o_{1j} is always at least as good as o_{2j}, and sometimes better, this implies that none of the probability mass has been shifted from more to less preferred outcomes, and some of it has been shifted to more preferred outcomes. Thus, g_1^* first-order stochastically dominates g_2^*. But then, by reasoning in a manner strictly parallel to that used above, we may conclude the following:

> **Proposition 3.2.** Within a framework in which both the reduction principle and transitivity of weak preference hold, if the agent is committed to FSD, then he will also have to be committed to DSO. That is, failure to respect DSO will imply violations of FSD.

Thus, within a framework in which the reduction principle and transitivity of weak preference are presupposed, FSD and DSO are essentially equivalent. Commitment to either one implies a commitment to the other.[19]

Given the connection between FSD and DSO and the fact that DSO is itself a special case of the much stronger condition GDP, the question naturally arises as to whether there is a comparably stronger version of FSD and, if so, whether it is essentially equivalent to GDP. The generalization of FSD is straightforward enough: One has only to extend the principle so that it applies to any set of outcomes (as opposed to simply "sure" outcomes), that is, to treat it as a condition on distributions over distributions. Such a principle – which can be characterized as the *generalized* first-order stochastic dominance principle (GFSD) – stands to FSD just as GDP stands to DSO. In particular, GFSD is a significantly stronger principle than FSD. To see the difference, suppose that $g_2 = [\$20, .4; \$80, .6] \, P \, g_1 = [\$0, .3; \$100, .7]$. Then GFSD requires that $g = [g_1, .2; g_2, .8] \, P \, g^* = [g_1, .3; g_2, .7]$. Multiplying the probabilities through and once again appealing to the assumption that the agent is concerned with just outcomes and the probability distribution over them, $g \, I \, [\$0, .6; \$20, .32; \$80, .48; \$100, .14]$ and $g^* \, I \, [\$0, .9; \$20, .28; \$80, .42; \$100, .21]$. FSD is now applicable in principle, since both of these are simple distributions over sure outcomes, but neither first-order stochastically dominates the other. Moreover, the logical relation between GFSD and GDP is easy enough to establish. Recall the arguments in support of Propositions 3.1 and 3.2. By inspection it is clear that neither of these arguments presupposes that each o_{ij} is a sure outcome. Each argument, then, can be run once again, in terms of generalized outcomes of the form g_{ij}, in support of the conclusion that GFSD is essentially equivalent to GDP.

Now consider once again the Luce and Raiffa construction mentioned at the outset of this section. What one has, in effect, is a suggestion that one can employ a weak form of independence – such as SUB – and capture the rest of what is required for the utility and probability theorems by invoking a very simple, and highly plausible, version of stochastic dominance (or, given the interchangeability between stochastic dominance and dominance with respect to sure outcomes, a very plausible version of outcome dominance). Of course, in view of the results sketched in Section 3.5, according to which outcome dominance and independence conditions are also essentially interchangeable, this should not be surprising. The independence condition employed, SUB, is, to be sure, weaker than IND (more precisely, weaker than an n-termed, as distinct from a two-termed, version of IND), but the slack has been taken up by introducing MO, the monotonicity axiom, a simple version of the stochastic dominance condition FSD, which is itself essentially equivalent to a very plausible version of independence, namely, ISO. More to the point, the independence principle that is explicitly retained, SUB, is not really that weak at all, since it allows for substitution in the context of complex gambles whose components are themselves gambles. That is, SUB corresponds to an n-termed version of IND, not an n-termed version of ISO. What Luce and Raiffa have factored out, in effect, by introducing MO is the most plausible of all of the conditions explored so far; but what remains, SUB itself, still captures the essential (and somewhat more problematic) condition that independence hold with respect to gambles over gambles.

3.7 A choice-set version of independence

The suggestion of Chapter 2 is that a reconstruction of the weak ordering condition in terms of conditions on choice functions, rather than in terms of conditions on preferences, can prove useful. Correspondingly, the independence condition can also be treated as a constraint directly on choice (or acceptable) sets rather than on preference rankings. More specifically, then, and once again utilizing the concept of an acceptable set (as formulated in the preceding chapter), the independence principle can be formulated as follows:

Independence for choice (CIND). Let g_1, g_2, and g_3 be any three gambles, let $g_{13} = [g_1, p; g_3, 1 - p]$ be a gamble over g_1 and g_3

such that one stands to confront the gamble g_1 with probability p and the gamble g_3 with probability $1 - p$, and let $g_{23} = [\, g_2, p; g_3, 1 - p]$ be similarly defined. Then g_1 is in $D(\{g_1, g_2\})$ iff for $0 < p \le 1$, g_{13} is in $D(\{g_{13}, g_{23}\})$.[20]

Within the framework of constraints on rational choice that imply satisfaction of CF and, hence, the existence of an induced weak binary-based preference order defined over any set of feasible options, IND can be derived from the choice version CIND. That is, within a framework defined by certain more technical and structural assumptions, an agent whose choice behavior satisfies CIND and CF can be interpreted as choosing as if he were maximizing a preference ordering over options that satisfies the condition IND. In effect, if one can provide a basis for CIND, this will also, within that framework, provide an underpinning for IND.[21]

3.8 The expected utility result

The foregoing discussion suggests that an independence condition can be introduced into a formal construction in a variety of ways – by direct appeal to an independence or noncomplementarity principle, to an outcome dominance principle, or, finally, to a principle of stochastic dominance. Moreover, as the very elementary presentation found in Luce and Raiffa makes clear, it can even be secured by a conjunction of what appear to be relatively weak versions of independence and stochastic dominance – substitution and monotonicity. What even the most cursory survey of alternative constructions indicates, however, is that the expected utility and subjective probability results require appeal to more than just ISO, DSO, FSD, or some combination of those principles – that is, principles governing the ordering of "simple" gambles whose components are sure (riskless) prizes. Specifically, the constructions require some principle whose scope extends to gambles over gambles. In the Luce and Raiffa construction, this is achieved by a version of SUB, which explicitly allows for replacing simple component prizes in a lottery with lotteries and thereby creating a compound lottery.[22] In more elaborate constructions, it is typically achieved by assuming that the requisite independence condition holds not only for gambles over prizes but for gambles over gambles.[23]

My sense is that preoccupation with the logically interesting task of finding alternative ways to reconstruct the expected utility and subjective probability theorems – in terms of intuitions with regard to conditions of noncomplementarity, or dominance with respect to outcomes, or dominance with respect to probabilities – has deflected attention from a much more pressing issue, namely, whether any of these principles, when given the requisite scope, is plausible. Moreover, when various writers have sought to "motivate" or rationalize the independence principle, they have typically illustrated it with reference to the special case in which components are sure (riskless) outcomes.[24] Since such "motivation" is typically understood to be informal, there is no logical error involved here, of course. It it also true that unlike the case discussed in the preceding chapter, in which the context-free condition tends not to figure explicitly in the argument at all, the need for an extended version of independence is usually fairly obvious. Finally, as I shall show in the next chapter, those who have criticized the constructions have presented counterexamples that explicitly involve cases of gambles over gambles – and this permits the issue to be joined in the proper manner.[25]

Nonetheless, the failure of most writers to draw attention to the need for an extended version of the principle obscures matters. One wonders, indeed, whether there would be anything like a foundational issue that has to be joined here were it not that some have all too casually extrapolated from intuitively secure special cases. At any rate, as these remarks suggest, the time has come to turn to the question of the justification of these various principles.

4

The problem of justification

4.1 Introduction

What arguments can be offered for taking WO and IND (or alternatively CF and CIND) as normative for choice? The question of the validity of normative principles of choice poses a methodologically troublesome problem. Since a norm prescribes rather than describes human behavior, it cannot be treated as a hypothesis or a theory about human behavior that is subject to the usual sort of empirical test. On the more traditional way of thinking about the logic of the justification of norms, there is no alternative but to appeal to even more "fundamental" principles from which the one in question can be derived. And, of course, to avoid an infinite regress, this appeal to higher authority must at some point come to an end with principles that simply recommend themselves to intuition.[1]

For some, the end comes much sooner, with a suggestion that either WO or IND is intuitively acceptable.[2] Most theorists, however, have tried to say something by way of defending the principle in question – by relating it to other, more familiar conditions, by responding to counterarguments, or simply by telling some sort of story. Arrow, for example, defends the ordering condition by appeal to the notion of what is necessary if choice is to be possible, and Samuelson (as already noted) suggests that reflection on the logical nature of disjunctive prospects reveals that the sort of noncomplementarity that is presupposed by IND is very plausible.[3] Unfortunately, many of these "motivating" accounts are presented in a rather casual manner, so that the conviction they are designed to secure has a bothersome way of vanishing when they are examined more closely. Typically, what one finds is a gap between what can be shown to be plausible and what must be presupposed in order to generate the desired results.

Philosophers who are drawn to the more recent coherence approach to epistemology will be inclined, no doubt, to see the problem of justification of these principles somewhat differently. It might be argued, for example, that these two principles provide a logically impeccable basis for modes of evaluation on which there exists a broad consensus. On one version of this argument, a given principle can be defended on the ground that it yields results (theorems) – for example, the expected utility principle or subjective measures of belief that satisfy the standard axioms for probability – that strike one as highly plausible in their own right. On another version, the suggestion is that they codify ways of evaluating gambles that enjoy widespread acceptance.[4] On the latter sort of coherence account, the fact that they, together with various other conditions, suffice for the derivation of the expected utility theorem is simply something on the order of an elegant bonus.

The attractiveness of the coherence approach is not to be denied. It provides a neat escape from a long-standing foundational problem. On such a way of thinking there is no need to reach continually backward for even more basic principles, until some point is reached at which intuition is invoked. The testing ground of principles of choice is to be found in their own public acceptability or that of their logical implications, not in the acceptability of more general (and typically more abstract) principles from which they in turn can be derived.

Whatever approach one adopts, it would seem that argument must come to an end somewhere – in "first" premises that are alleged to be intuitively secure, in conclusions that are taken to be independently plausible, or in relatively secure "specific case" judgments that the principles in question can then be understood to codify. Granting this, if any such line of argument is to work, the resting place must command the widest assent possible. Otherwise, the argument speaks only to some special community of persons – say, those who just happen to embrace some principle or the more specific judgments that the principle in question serves to codify. But in that case, the argument has no more or less force than, say, the argument that motivates the members of a particular religious or ideological community. Ideally, then, what one seeks is something on which there is a virtual consensus among thoughtful, informed persons.

This is precisely what poses the problem, however. In point of fact, something considerably less than such a consensus obtains with respect to either WO (more particularly CFO and the connectedness condition) or IND as normative for choice. The issue of the acceptability of IND arose very shortly after the development, by von Neumann and Morgenstern and Savage, among others, of versions of the expected utility and subjective probability theorems.[5] Objections to CFO and the connectedness condition arose somewhat later, although an important foreshadowing is to be found in the protracted debate that took place over a condition analogous to CFO that Arrow employed in his work on social welfare functions.[6]

To be sure, a good deal of the criticism was directed at the theories of expected utility and subjective probability as descriptive theories. And in turn many of those who were initially inclined to defend these constructions as both normative and descriptive came to acknowledge their problematic status as descriptive of preference and choice behavior. In short, the manner in which that debate took place managed to leave relatively untouched the issue of the status of these principles as norms.[7] In more recent years, however, increasing attention has been paid to the issue of the normative validity of both WO (particularly the CFO factor) and IND. Indeed, one can mark the emergence of a number of proposals for a normative theory of risk and uncertainty, each of which involves some substantial relaxation of one or the other of these two principles.[8]

In the sections to follow I shall examine a variety of arguments that have been offered in support of either WO or IND, with a view to defending the suggestion made above that many arguments fail, either because the conclusions they can support are too limited or because the considerations to which appeal is made are not the subject of a sufficiently broad consensus. Before turning to these arguments, however, I want to consider what can be said in support of the reduction principle mentioned in Section 3.2, for its normative status seems especially problematic.

4.2 The reduction assumption

Many have treated the reduction principle RD as if it were, at least from a normative perspective, beyond question. Careful reflection suggests otherwise. Suppose that an agent finds that he has a preference regarding the form of gambles – for example, he finds that he prefers complex, multistaged to simple one-stage gambles. If his preference turned on a belief that his chances of winning any specified amount of money were better when the gamble was multistaged, and if that belief could be shown to be false – if it could be shown that the odds of winning were in fact better in the case of the simple gamble – then this implied violation of RD would be subject to an obvious criticism – and this by appeal to an uncontroversial instrumentalist criterion of rationality. That is, the agent would fail to choose so as to promote his own objective, namely, the maximization of his chances of winning. To consider another example, imagine that the agent does not believe that multistage lotteries offer him a better chance of winning, but he still finds himself drawn to such forms of gambling, despite the fact that he is in the business of, say, professionally managing portfolios of risky and uncertain prospects. If he were to sacrifice a greater expected return for the sake of satisfying his preference for certain types of gambles, his violation of RD would once again be subject to criticism and, again, by reference to an un-controversial instrumentalist criterion applied in this case from the perspective of the goals or objectives of those for whom he acts as agent.

Suppose, however, that the agent gambles only infrequently and purely for the fun of it. Since such gambling has its own rewards for him – in terms, say, of the sense of danger or risk or excitement – it might well be that he derives more enjoyment from participating in multistage as distinct from one-stage gambles. Perhaps, for example, he likes to prolong the experience of excitement as much as possible. If he does prefer a multistage gamble over a simple one that offers him the same monetary payoffs with the same probabilities (or even, perhaps, better odds), he will violate RD. In this case, however, it is not clear how RD can be defended as a norm for choice. Certainly not by reference to the sort of instrumentalist criterion invoked in the previous two cases! He deliberately chooses the more complex gamble with a (correct) view to thereby furthering an important objective – the experience of excitement (or drama, etc.).

Of all those who have written on this subject, Harsanyi has offered the clearest articulation of what is at issue here and also offered the most plausible way to defend RD in the face of the objection raised by the third case presented above. What he suggests is that the principle must be taken as normatively valid for any decision maker who acts in an essentially public capacity, that is, who makes decisions as an agent for other persons.[9] The reason for this, he argues, is that although individuals can have direct preferences for forms of gambles, these preferences must be understood as purely personal – as thus, pre-sumably, they will vary significantly from one individual to another. It is reasonable, then, to require that a person who is charged with making decisions in a public capacity abstract from his own likes and dislikes with respect to features of gambles that do not pertain to outcomes and probabilities. And this means, unless there is some clear consensus among those for whom he acts as an agent (which due to the idiosyncratic nature of these preferences will be very unlikely) that he must make decisions as if such features were irrelevant. Alterna-tively put, RD can be taken to be satisfied by the preferences of a certain class of decision makers, and the remaining principles of ra-tionality (e.g., WO and IND) are then to be understood as setting further constraints on those whose basic preferences happen to satisfy this prior condition.

Von Neumann and Morgenstern were aware of the problematic nature of RD – that it precludes somewhat arbitrarily any preferences for gambling as such, or for one form of gambling over another. They simply acknowledge that within the construction they propose (which includes a version of RD), "a 'specific utility for gambling' cannot be formulated free of contradiction."[10] My sense is that the problematic nature of the principle as a normative principle has remained somewhat submerged because most of those who have worked in this area have been interested in applying expected utility concepts to agents who act in a public as distinct from a private capacity.[11] I still think, however, that the most interesting issue concerns what it is plausible to take as normative for choice and preference within a framework in which RD is presupposed. Thus, for the balance of this work I shall take the RD as setting a valid constraint on rational choice. In particular, I shall focus on the issue of whether agents who are self-consciously concerned only with outcomes and probabilities must (at least insofar as they are rational) also satisfy WO and IND.

4.3 The weak ordering condition

In an ambitious and comprehensive exposition of the theory of choice under uncertainty, Arrow offers the following laconic defense of the weak ordering condition: "An ordering is usually taken to be a hallmark of rationality; in the absence of connectedness, no choice at all may be possible; in the absence of transitivity choice may whirl about in circles."[12] How compelling are these considerations? Consider the connectedness condition first. The analysis of Chapter 2 suggested that connectedness of the underlying ordering is not indispensable to maximizing choice. In its absence, one can compensate by characterizing rational choice in terms of *maximal* set functions rather than *choice* functions. Arrow's argument for connectedness succeeds, then, only on the questionable presupposition that rational choice must be characterized in terms of choice as distinct from maximal sets.

What about transitivity? If the underlying ordering is presumed to satisfy CFO, the results of Section 2.8 can be invoked, but these do not even establish that transitivity of strict preference is a necessary condition for rational choice, that is, for the existence of a choice function. To be sure, according to Proposition 2.12 acyclicity of R is a necessary condition for the existence of a choice function, and this is surely the sort of result that prompts Arrow's remark. But as already noted, this result presupposes a choice-set framework, which in turn means that connectedness of the underlying ordering R has been presupposed. If R is not connected but satisfies CFO, the concept of a maximal set function is still available. Within that framework, as reported in Section 2.9, what emerges as necessary for "choice" is simply that R be P-acyclical. Finally, once CFO is brought into question, even P-acyclicity is not necessary. That is, if the method of evaluation employed is taken to generate only a context-dependent ordering $R(S)$ over each set S, it is not even necessary to "choice" that $R(S)$ be P-acyclical over each set S. All that is required, per MIC, is that the method of evaluation generate a ranking over each set S such that at least one element in S is acceptable.

Sen offers an alternative, but equally laconic defense of the connectedness condition: "A man with a preference relation that is complete [i.e., connected] knows his mind in choices over every pair."[13] But once again the possibility of reformulating rational choice in terms of maximal sets undercuts this argument. Faced with incomparable pairs, only the agent who demands that his choice always be generated by a connected preference-based choice set, that is, $C(\cdot, R)$, will be at loss as to what to do. A less demanding agent who is willing to settle for a maximal set approach, that is, for $M(\cdot, R)$, can reassure himself that in *picking* either x or y from $\{x, y\}$ in the face of incomparability between x and y, he still selects in such a way that what he picks is never dispreferred to something else available. Such an agent does know his own mind. In confronting x and y under the stated conditions, he does not believe x to be superior to y, does not believe y to be superior to x, and does not believe x and y to be equally good; but he does believe that neither is inferior to any other alternative and this suffices to allow him to at least pick (if only arbitrarily) between them.

What is most problematic from this perspective, however, is CFO itself. As the remarks in Section 2.10 make clear, the consideration of what is necessary for choice simply does not suffice to establish CFO itself. This is the import of the factoring proposed in Sections 2.10 and 2.11 of the "choice-set" version of the weak ordering condition into MIC and CF: MIC captures the requirement that effective choice be possible; and CF captures what is not part of *that* requirement, yet still part of the usual conception of a weak ordering. This is the lesson to be learned from the minimax risk criterion or Levi's E- and S-admissibility rules. Each serves as a reminder that effective choice is possible from a feasible set even when the method of evaluation employed does not generate an underlying ordering R that satisfies CFO, nor an acceptable-set function that satisfies CF.[14]

4.4 The transitivity condition

Broome has recently offered a quite distinct argument in favor of the transitivity condition.[15] His discussion proceeds by reference to the following example: Suppose that some individual, George, prefers visiting Rome (R) to mountaineering in the Alps (M), and prefers staying at home (H) to visiting Rome. However, if he were to have a choice between staying at home and mountaineering in the Alps, he

would prefer to go mountaineering in the Alps. Here, then, appears
to be a violation of transitivity of strict preference.

Broome suggests, however, that one need not draw that conclusion.
Alternatively, the agent can be understood to distinguish between two
different versions of H – between $H1$, that of "not rejecting a mountaineering trip and staying at home" (the option available when he is
choosing between visiting Rome and staying at home), and $H2$, that of
"rejecting a mountaineering trip and staying at home" (the option
available when he is choosing between staying at home and mountaineering). He does not, then, prefer H to R and R to M. He prefers
$H1$ to R, R to M, and M to $H2$. Indeed, as Broome sees the matter,

it is never a possibility that George might be rational and at the same time not
have transitive preferences. If it would be rational for George to choose to go
mountaineering rather than to stay home, that can only be because it is
rational for him to distinguish $H2$ from $H1$ and prefer the one to the other.
[But then] his preferences are transitive.[16]

Now what Broome characterizes as a violation of transitivity is,
more particularly, a violation of the transitivity of the pair-set choice-
determined preference relation R_c. That is, Broome never considers
a case in which the agent has all three options available, and then
ranks H over R, R over M, and M over H. His story concerns how the
agent would choose from pair sets of feasible options. Moreover, such
pair-set choice behavior is taken by Broome as a necessary condition
of preference: that N prefers A to B implies that if N were to have a
choice between A and B only, he would choose A. Within that framework, and assuming that a choice function exists, violation of the
transitivity of the pair-set-determined preference relation implies violation of Alpha. That is, if A is preferred to B and B is preferred to
C, but C is preferred to A, then A is in $C(\{A, B\})$, B is in $C(\{B, C\})$, and
C is in $C(\{C, A\})$; and this, in turn, implies that if $C(\{A, B, C\})$ is nonempty (which it must be if the choice function exists), then Alpha is
violated. Thus, the argument that Broome presents amounts to an
argument for Alpha.

But on closer inspection, there really is no argument here for Alpha
(or the transitivity of pair-set-determined strict preference). Broome
has merely suggested how one might save the hypothesis that Alpha
is a rationality condition in the face of what appears to be a rational
person whose choices violate Alpha. The saving move is to assume
that the relevant pair sets are $\{H1, R\}$, $\{R, M\}$, and $\{M, H2\}$, in which
case there is no violation of transitivity of R_c or of Alpha, since the
choice sets are the following: $C(\{H1, R\}) = \{H1\}$, $C(\{R, M\}) = \{R\}$, and
$C(\{H2, M\}) = \{M\}$.

If there were some independent defense of Alpha or transitivity of
the pair-set choice-determined preference relation, Broome's move to

save the hypothesis would make sense; but in fact Broome never offers any such argument. Recent work in epistemology reminds us, moreover, that any hypothesis – even a hypothesis rejecting, in effect, this or that fundamental principle of logic – can be saved if one is prepared to make a sufficient number of adjustments in one's other beliefs.[17] Yet for all this, Broome clearly thinks that transitivity of the pair-set choice-determined relation is an obvious rationality condition. I conjecture that this is because he conflates that condition and the much weaker condition that simply requires transitivity of the ordering as it is defined over a given feasible set. And that, I suspect, is because he has simply taken for granted a framework in which the context-free conditions (on choice functions or on underlying orderings) are satisfied. On my reading, he has not touched the real issue at all: the status of CFO (or, alternatively, CF) as a rationality condition.

4.5 Disjunctive noncomplementarity

As I noted in the preceding chapter, some have treated the independence principle for risky prospects as ruling out complementarities among the components of disjunctive bundles of goods. Characteristically, this condition has been argued for on the ground that complementarities of the sort that arise in connection with conjunctive bundles cannot arise in the case of disjunctive bundles.[18] This line of reasoning is not very compelling. Disjunctive bundles may not be subject to the problem of commodity complementarity, but this does not rule out the possibility of forms of "complementarity" that are special to disjunctive prospects.[19] As an illustration, consider the type of decision situation presented in Figure 4.1 and first isolated by Allais.[20] A significant proportion of subjects prefer g_1 to g_2 but prefer g_4 to g_3.[21] For one who accepts both WO and the reduction principle RD, such a preference pattern leads to a violation of IND. To see this one can, following Savage, consider how the agent would choose in the related situation shown in Figure 4.2, in which the conditioning events are the numbered tickets to be drawn in a lottery, with various associated prizes (in units of $100,000) attaching to each.[22] Here the set of alternatives consisting of $\{g_1^*, g_2^*\}$ differs from the set of alter-

g_1: [$500,000 for certain]

g_2: [$2,500,000, .1; $500,000, .89; $0, .01]

g_3: [$500,000, .11; $0, .89]

g_4: [$2,500,000, .1; $0, .9]

Figure 4.1

	Lottery ticket number		
	1	2–11	12–100
g_1^*	5	5	5
g_2^*	0	25	5
g_3^*	5	5	0
g_4^*	0	25	0

Figure 4.2

natives consisting of $\{g_3^*, g_4^*\}$ only with respect to the level of the constant prize associated with ticket numbers 11–100. And with an appropriate repartitioning of conditioning states – letting E be the state in which the ticket drawn has a number between 1 and 11, and not-E be the state in which the ticket drawn has a number between 12 and 100 – one can then directly appeal to SI, Savage's version of the independence principle, to show that if g_1^* is preferred to g_2^*, then g_3^* must be preferred to g_4^*. In this setting, if the agent accepts both WO and RD and prefers g_1 to g_2 and g_4 to g_3, then he must prefer g_1^* to g_2^* and g_4^* to g_3^*, in violation of SI.

Consider, however, an agent who interprets risk in terms of the dispersion in the monetary value of the various prizes and who, other things being equal, prefers less to more dispersion. The gamble g_1 has zero dispersion, and this may, despite its lower expected return, make it attractive relative to g_2. When g_1 and g_2 are transformed, respectively, into g_3 and g_4 by a reduction in the payoff for lottery tickets 12–100 from 5 to 0, the expected value of both g_3 and g_4 is reduced by the same amount. Matters are different with respect to dispersion: The increase in dispersion from g_1 to g_3 is greater than the increase from g_2 to g_4, regardless of how dispersion is measured. If dispersion considerations are relatively important, then the fact that in the case of g_4 the alteration in payoffs results in less increase in dispersion might tip the balance in its favor.

The way in which dispersion considerations can result in preference patterns that fail to conform to IND can be illustrated in an even more striking manner by reference to an example offered by Kahneman and Tversky.[23] Suppose the agent is to make a selection from each of the two sets of paired alternatives given in Figure 4.3. Again, a significant number of persons prefer g_1 to g_2 but also prefer g_4 to g_3.

g_1 [$2400]

g_2 [$2500, $33/34$; $0, $1/34$]

g_3 [$2400, $34/100$; $0, $66/100$]

g_4 [$2500, $33/100$; $0, $67/100$]

Figure 4.3

Consider gambles $g_3^* = [g_1, {}^{34}\!/_{100}; \$0, {}^{66}\!/_{100}]$ and $g_4^* = [g_2, {}^{34}\!/_{100}; \$0,$ ${}^{66}\!/_{100}]$. By direct appeal to IND, g_1 is at least as good as g_2 iff g_3^* is at least as good as g_4^*. And by appeal to RD, g_3 is indifferent to g_3^*, and g_4 is indifferent to g_4^*. Given the stated preferences with regard to g_1 through g_4 and satisfaction of both WO and RD, then, the agent must prefer g_1 to g_2 and g_4^* to g_3^*, in violation of IND.

The preferences in question can arise, however, if the agent ranks the options by appeal to the following dispersion-sensitive rule. Suppose the agent prefers, other things being equal, a higher expected monetary return to a lower one but also prefers, other things being equal, a smaller expected shortfall, where expected shortfall is defined as the expected deviation below the mean. Assume, for the sake of simplicity, that these are the only relevant factors and that the agent's implicit trade-off rate between expected return and expected shortfall, and hence his rule for evaluating such gambles, is given by the following linear function,[24]

$$V(g) = E(g) - kS(g),$$

where $V(g)$ is the value to him of the gamble, $E(g)$ is the expected return (mean value) of the gamble, $S(g)$ is expected shortfall, and k is some constant, defined on the interval $[0, 1]$. For illustration, let $k = \frac{1}{2}$. Then one gets the values presented in Figure 4.4. If this method of evaluation – based on the specified linear function of expectation and shortfall (dispersion) – is used, then g_2 will be preferred to g_1 but g_3^* will be preferred to g_4^*, in violation of IND.

Now the natural way to interpret this violation of IND is by appeal to the notion that for agents who are concerned about dispersion there is a special kind of complementarity that can arise in the concatenation of risky prospects. To see this, consider more closely SUB, which isolates, in effect, the noncomplementarity implications of IND. SUB requires that if components are indifferent to one another, there can be no "utility-enhancing" (or "utility-disenhancing") effect that results from substituting one for the other in some more complex gamble. In the example just discussed, g_1 is presumed to be preferred to g_2. But suppose that g_1's payoff is reduced to \$2390.80, and the agent employs the rule stated above. Then one obtains the values shown in Figure 4.5. The gambles g_1^* and g_2 are now indifferent to

	E	S	$E - .5S$
g_1	2400	0	2400
g_2	2426.5	71.4	2390.8
g_3^*	816	538.56	546.72
g_4^*	825	552.75	548.625

Figure 4.4

	E	S	$E - .5S$
g_1^*	2390.8	0	2390.8
g_2	2426.5	71.4	2390.8
g_3^*	812.872	536.50	544.62
g_4^*	825	552.75	548.625

Figure 4.5

each other, but g_4^* is still preferred to g_3^*. In this instance, then, when g_2 is substituted for g_1^* in the more complex gamble, even though g_1^* and g_2 are indifferent to one another, the latter enhances the value of the resultant complex gamble more than does the former. Moreover, there is no mystery as to what accounts for this differential impact on the value of the resultant complex gamble. The rule employed makes the value of the complex gamble – the whole – a function of mean value and shortfall. The expectation factor's impact is "well behaved." The embedding of g_1^* in the more complex gamble results in a proportional decrease in expected value that is strictly equal to the proportional decrease that results from embedding g_2: $E(g_1^*)/E(g_3^*) = E(g_2)/E(g_4^*)$. The differential impact is due to the shortfall factor. That is, the proportional increases in shortfall are not equivalent. Thus, for one who is concerned with shortfall, even though g_1^* is indifferent to g_2 when the two are considered in isolation, there is a better "fit" between g_2 and [·, $^{34}/_{100}$; $0, $^{66}/_{100}$] than there is between g_1^* and [·, $^{34}/_{100}$; $0, $^{66}/_{100}$]. Combining g_2 with the balance results in a smaller proportional increase in shortfall than that which results from combining g_1^* with the balance.

There is another, much discussed counterexample to the independence principle which suggests a distinct type of complementarity that can arise in the concatenation of risky prospects. The example is due to Ellsberg and is directed not at IND but at Savage's version, SI.[25] Ellsberg considers a situation in which the agent is to choose among various gambles based on drawing a ball at random from an urn that contains red, black, and yellow balls, with monetary payoffs specified as in Figure 4.6. In addition, one is supplied with the following infor-

	(30) Red	(60) Black	(60) Yellow	Range of E
g_1	$ 100	$ 0	$ 0	33⅓
g_2	0	100	0	0–66⅔
g_3	100	0	100	33⅓ – 1
g_4	0	100	100	66⅔

Figure 4.6

mation: There are 30 red balls in the urn, and 60 that are either black or yellow; thus, the relative proportion of black and yellow is unknown. Since the probabilities of the conditioning events are only partially defined, one cannot associate with each option an unambiguous expected return E. But as the column to the far right indicates, one can still specify the possible range of such values.

Suppose one has to choose between just g_1 and g_2. Ellsberg notes that many people prefer g_1 to g_2, while preferring g_4 to g_3, and that the following rule of evaluation generates this preference ordering: Rank options in terms of increasing minimum expected return. However, preferences based on this rule violate SI. In particular, notice that the pair of options g_1 and g_2 differ from the pair of options g_3 and g_4 only with respect to the payoffs in the event that a yellow ball is drawn. But in each case the amount to be received if a yellow ball is drawn is constant. Thus, once again with an appropriate repartitioning of the states, SI applies and requires that g_1 be preferred to g_2 just in case g_3 is preferred to g_4, contrary to the described preferences.

Again, it is possible to interpret what is happening here in terms of the notion of complementarities with respect to the value of disjunctions of outcomes. The shift from a situation in which, under the condition of drawing a yellow ball one receives \$0, regardless of which act is chosen, to a situation in which, under the same chance conditions, one receives \$100, regardless of which act is chosen, results in "contamination" (to use Samuelson's term for complementarity).[26] Moreover, there is no mystery here as to how this happens. The person who adopts Ellsberg's rule can be characterized as uncertainty (or, as Ellsberg himself terms it, "ambiguity") averse: Uncertain prospects (as distinct from those whose associated expected return is well defined) are discounted to their minimum expected return.[27] Although one can think of g_3 and g_4 as resulting from a modification of g_1 and g_2, respectively – in each case the addition of \$100 to the payoff under Y – this proportional increase in payoffs has a differential impact with regard to uncertainty or ambiguity. In the case of choice between g_1 and g_2, it is g_2 that presents an uncertainty; but given the substitution, it is now the counterpart to g_1, namely, g_3 (and not the counterpart to g_2) that presents the uncertainty.

Here is another example of decision making under uncertainty in which the potential for "disjunctive complementarity" is even clearer and where IND itself is violated.[28] Suppose that the agent is asked to choose among the three gambles shown in Figure 4.7, where E is some event whose likelihood is completely unknown and (H, T) are the two possible outcomes of a toss of what the subject presumes to be a fair coin, so that he assigns a subjective probability of ½ to each of H and T. Many persons report that they prefer g_3 to both g_1 and g_2 but that

g_1 [$100, E; $0, not-$E$] g_4 [g_1, H; g_2, T]

g_2 [$0, E; $100, not-$E$] g_5 [g_1, H; g_1, T]

g_3 [$100, H; $0, T],   Figure 4.8

Figure 4.7

(predictably) they are indifferent between g_1 and g_2. Such a ranking typically expresses itself as a willingness to pay more for g_3 than for either g_1 or g_2. Alternatively put, for constant prizes or outcomes, persons typically prefer even-chance odds to ambiguous (i.e., uncertain) odds. Consider now the compound gambles shown in Figure 4.8, based on the above options (where, once again, "H" and "T" refer to the outcomes of the flip of the same fair coin). By appeal to the standard rules for combining the probabilities of independent events, an agent who accepts RD must rank g_4 as indifferent to g_3. Moreover, by analogous reasoning, g_5 must be ranked indifferent to g_1. Hence, given the preferences projected above for g_3 and g_1 and acceptance of WO, the agent must prefer g_4 to g_5. But this violates IND – and, more specifically, the substitution version SUB: g_4 and g_5 differ only in that where g_4 has an occurrence of g_2, g_5 has an occurrence of g_1, but by hypothesis, the agent is indifferent between g_1 and g_2; hence, by SUB, g_4 should be indifferent to g_5.

The agent who prefers g_3 to g_1, however, has a natural rejoinder and one that appeals once again to a special kind of complementarity for disjunctive prospects – a complementarity that occurs when the agent's method of evaluation is sensitive to ambiguity or uncertainty. Although the agent is indifferent between g_1 and g_2, the combination of the two in an even-chance lottery results in the ambiguity or uncertainty of the odds associated with each gamble taken separately canceling each other out. That is, an even-chance disjunctive combination of (ambiguous) g_1 with (ambiguous) g_2 results in a prospect that involves no ambiguity. This is not due to anything pertaining to g_1 or g_2 taken separately. The resolution of the ambiguity is a function of the way in which the two component gambles are combined.

It should be emphasized that what has been isolated here is distinct from the complementarity that arises in connection with conjunctive bundles. Here there is no question of some sort of interaction between prizes, both of which are to be received. It arises in the context of a disjunctive concatenation of prizes or goods and turns on the implication of combining both well-defined and indeterminate odds. But it bears all the marks of being a type of complementarity. The gambles g_1 and g_2 are clearly indifferent to one another when considered in isolation. When each is disjunctively combined in the manner suggested to form g_4 and g_5, however, there is a "fit" that obtains in the case of g_4 that does not obtain in the case of g_5. The fit, moreover, is perfectly explicable: The rules for combining probabilities imply that g_4 involves no ambiguity with respect to the odds of receiving \$100, whereas the same rules imply that g_5 is maximally ambiguous. For one who is uncertainty (or ambiguity) averse, then, it does make a difference as to which of the (indifferent) components are combined with which.

The implication of both the Ellsberg and the Allais examples is quite clear. One cannot infer that IND is a plausible condition to impose on the ordering of disjunctive bundles simply by appeal to the consideration that complementarities of the type that arise in connection with conjunctive bundles cannot arise in connection with disjunctive bundles. That argument is a nonstarter, for it ignores a kind of "complementarity" that is unique to disjunctive bundles and that forms an intelligible basis for discriminating among prospects, if one is (as in the case of the Allais example) concerned with dispersion or (as in the case of the Ellsberg examples) concerned with uncertainty (ambiguity).

4.6 The independence principle

Broome offers a quite distinct argument in defense of IND and SI.[29] Recall that if E and not-E are mutually exclusive and exhaustive events conditioning the various components of four gambles, g_{13}, g_{23}, g_{14}, g_{24}, and the schedule of consequences is as follows,

	E	not-E
g_{13}	g_1	g_3
g_{23}	g_2	g_3
g_{14}	g_1	g_4
g_{24}	g_2	g_4

then SI requires that g_{13} be at least as good as g_{23} iff g_{14} is at least as good as g_{24}. As Broome chooses to construe this sort of example, g_1 stands for the (possible) world that would come about – all that would be the case – if g_{13} were chosen and E were to occur, and so on for the other possibilities.

Broome thinks that the following consideration supports SI: A person may have a reason for preferring g_{13} to g_{23} (or vice versa). Whatever reasons he has, however, must derive from what would be the case if E were to occur. To be more exact, they must derive from the difference between g_1 and g_2. No reason can derive from the difference between the world that comes about if g_{13} is chosen and not-E occurs and the world that comes about if g_{23} is chosen and not-E occurs, because these worlds belong to the same possibility, g_3, and consequently do not differ in any relevant respect. Similarly any reason there is for preferring g_{14} to g_{24} (or vice versa) must derive from the difference between g_1 and g_2. Notice also that the world that comes about if g_{13} is chosen and E occurs and the world that comes about if g_{14} is chosen and E occurs belong to the same possibility g_1, so they do not differ in any relevant respect. Likewise, the world that comes about if g_{23} is chosen and E occurs and the world that comes about if g_{24} is chosen and E occurs do not differ in any relevant respect. Consequently, as far as relevant considerations are concerned, any difference between the world that comes about if g_{13} is chosen and E occurs and the world that comes about if g_{14} is chosen and E occurs is also a difference between the world that comes about if g_{23} is chosen and E occurs and the world that comes about if g_{24} is chosen and E occurs; that is, everything comes down to a difference between g_1 and g_2. So any reason there may be for preferring g_{13} to g_{23} (or vice versa) is also a reason for preferring g_{14} to g_{24} (or vice versa). If, therefore, a rational person prefers g_{13} to g_{23}, he should also prefer g_{14} to g_{24}.

Broome notes that the step in this argument most often criticized is the first, the claim that the reasons for preferring one gamble to another must derive from what would be the case – what possible world would result – if E were to occur or if not-E were to occur, that is, by comparing the outcomes of the alternative gambles, conditioning event by conditioning event. This event-by-event comparison is really the essence of SI, he claims, and once it is granted the rest of the argument simply amounts to a recital of the obvious.

Can one object to limiting evaluation to such an event-by-event comparison? Might this not ignore any possible interaction between what would be the case if one event were to occur and what would be the case if another event were to occur? Broome replies that his way of individuating the possibilities – the worlds that result from a choice of an action and an event occurring – makes sure that any interaction like this is taken into account in the step-by-step comparison. The justification of step-by-step comparison, then, he argues, is simply that it takes account of everything there is to take account of. He illustrates this point by reference to the Allais gamble. Adjusting his remarks to the version of the Allais problem given in Section 4.5, Figure 4.2, his argument proceeds as follows:

It might be argued that there is a reason for preferring g_1^* to g_2^* that is not derived either from what would be the case if ticket 1 came up, or what would be the case if one of the tickets 2–11 came up, or from what would be the case if one of the tickets 12–100 came up. It is derived from all of these together: taking them together it emerges that gamble g_1^* gives a certainty of winning $500,000. Certainty, then, has a special value, and this gives a reason for preferring g_1^* to g_2^* that is not also a reason for preferring g_3^* to g_4^*.[30]

What is the special value of certainty? Broome suggests that a variety of rationalizations have been offered. Choosing g_1^* rather than g_2^* may be a way to avoid anxiety – until the prize is announced, any of the other gambles will keep you worrying that you may get nothing. Again, picking g_1^* may be a way of avoiding the chance of suffering bitter disappointment – if you pick g_2^* instead and get nothing, perhaps your extreme bad luck will make you unhappy, whereas in the choice between g_3^* and g_4^*, whichever you choose you are unlikely to win, so you will not be particularly disappointed if you lose.

Now a common feature of all such rationalizations, according to Broome, is that they depend on feelings. Besides the money prizes there are good and bad feelings to take into account; and these feelings can be written into the table of outcomes. On this interpretation, the problem as given in Figure 4.2 will now look something like that given in Figure 4.9.

In this case, however, preference for g_1^* over g_2^* but g_4^* over g_3^* does not violate SI. Broome concludes that the very arguments that aim to show that it is rational to prefer g_1^* to g_2^* but g_3^* to g_4^* also show, if they succeed, that these preferences do not violate SI. That principle appears to be violated in this sort of case only if one individuates outcome possibilities by money prizes alone, ignoring feelings, while at the same time allowing feelings to rationalize preferences.

More generally, Broome concludes that if outcome possibilities are more finely individuated, Allais-type preferences will be revealed to be compatible with SI. Indeed, he notes, if one were to adopt the finest individuation and classify each possible world as a different possibility, SI would place no constraints at all on (practical) preferences.[31]

	Lottery ticket number		
	1	2–11	12–100
g_1^*	5	5	5
g_2^*	0, disappointment	25	5
g_3^*	5	5	0
g_4^*	0	25	0

Figure 4.9

Now it might seem that Broome's argument provides an efficient way to deal with a number of objections that have been raised to SI. But once again, as in the case of the argument he constructs for transitivity of pair-set choice-based preference, what one has here is not so much an argument for SI as a suggestion as to how one might try to save SI. Quite revealingly, Broome insists that the burden of proof lies with the person who proposes to violate SI: "Suppose someone has preferences that seem to conflict with [SI], and claims they are rational. What I am saying amounts simply to this: her claim will need justifying."[32] But why should the burden lie there? Why suppose that it is SI that must be saved? In the next chapter I will suggest some reasons for not taking one's stand there. Following a way of thinking to be found in Hume's *Treatise*, I think one must see this, at root, as an example of unwarranted legislating with regard to norms of rationality. For the moment, however, one can at least observe that since no independent argument in support of SI is given and no defense is made of the meta-claim that it is the violator of SI that must justify his position, the argument is rather incomplete.

Moreover, Broome's objections to allowing Allais-type preferences do not deal with the counterargument presented in the preceding section, concerning dispersion considerations. To see why this is the case, notice, first, that Broome does not suppose it necessary, in order to justify taking into account the probability distribution over outcomes, that one translate concern about probabilities into a "feeling" that attaches to outcomes. That is, there is no suggestion that one regard getting $500,000 when the odds of that happening were $1/100$, as a different outcome from getting $500,000 when the odds of that happening were $89/100$. So not everything that is relevant to rational evaluation is "loaded" into the description of outcomes: The probability distribution itself is not to be treated in that way.

For Broome (as for others committed to the expected utility theory), the appropriate way to incorporate concern for probabilities is to view each gamble as representable by its expected value – the sum of the discounted values of its several outcomes, with the discount being given in each case by the probability of receiving that outcome. Alternatively put, he regards the rational approach as consisting in treating any probability distribution over a set of values as if its central moment – the mean or expected value – captures all that is relevant about that distribution of values. This is clearly *one* way to think about evaluating gambles; but it is hardly the only way. In the preceding section I suggested that a rational agent may well want to take into account more than the first moment (the mean) of the probability distribution; in particular, he can choose to evaluate probability distributions over valued outcomes by reference to a two-termed function of mean value and some measure of dispersion.

Now consider once again Broome's implicit assumption that the agent's concern with the expected return (mean value) implications of the probability distribution over values is not to be interpreted in terms of special feelings attaching to outcomes. If this is correct, there is no reason to suppose that the agent who is concerned not simply with the mean of the distribution but also with the dispersion of values must be interpreted as responding to some special feeling about outcomes that alters the nature of the problem (and thereby renders SI inapplicable). But then it is not correct, as Broome would have us believe, that all arguments for the rationality of Allais-type preferences can be dismissed on the grounds that they simply presuppose a finer individuation of outcomes, in terms of, say, special feelings toward nonmonetary aspects of those outcomes – an individuation by reference to which it can be seen that SI simply does not apply.

4.7 Sure-thing reasoning and independence

I have already remarked that a different approach to IND is possible, namely, one that appeals to dominance considerations. There is no question that dominance principles are intuitively very plausible and that they offer what appears to be the most promising way to ground the independence principle. Recall, once again, the argument presented by Friedman and Savage in support of IND.[33] A version of IND follows directly from GDE, in the presence of the reduction principle RD. Now GDE mandates preference for g_1 over g_2 if, no matter what the turn of events, the outcome of choosing g_1 is at least as good as the outcome of choosing g_2 and, for *some* turn of events, the outcome of choosing g_1 is better than the outcome of choosing g_2. And that seems plausible enough. If you strictly prefer the consequences of g_1 to those of g_2, given that the event E occurs, and if you regard the consequences of g_1 to be at least as good as those of g_2, given that the event not-E occurs, then a choice of g_1 over g_2 promises a "sure thing" with respect to consequences: By choosing g_1 you cannot do worse, and may end up doing better, than if you choose g_2.

Despite the fact that many have taken this to be a decisive consideration in favor of IND, this line of reasoning is flawed.[34] GDE (alternatively, GDP) is *very* strong. It is framed with respect to the outcomes that can be associated with arbitrarily selected partitions of conditioning states. The principle requires that if there exists *any* event partition for which the outcome of g_1 is at least as good as the outcome of g_2 for each event in the partition, then g_1 is at least as good as g_2. In particular, the principle is not limited in its application to outcomes that can be characterized in nonprobabilistic terms, that is, sure outcomes.

This brings up a substantial issue. Consider, for example, the problem presented in Figure 4.3 and in the accompanying text. By hypothesis, the agent prefers g_1 to g_2, but $g_4^* = [g_2, {}^{34}\!/_{100}; \$0, {}^{66}\!/_{100}]$ to $g_3^* = [g_1, {}^{34}\!/_{100}; \$0, {}^{66}\!/_{100}]$. Here is a partition, then, for which the associated outcomes satisfy the conditions for dominance: g_1 is preferred to g_2, and (trivially) $0 is at least as good as $0. Thus, by GDP (rather than GDE, since in this case the probabilities are well defined), the agent should rank g_3^* over g_4^*. But what qualifies these outcomes as relevant to assessing the choice between g_3^* and g_4^* from a sure-thing perspective? Within the framework of a *finer* partitioning of events – and one that is an *explicit* feature of the problem – it is simply not true that one does as least as well by choosing g_3^* as by choosing g_4^*, regardless of the turn of (all relevant) events. By inspection, one possible outcome of g_4^* is \$2500, which is, by hypothesis, strictly preferred to any of the possible outcomes of g_3^*. I do not mean to suggest, of course, that one can undercut the application of GDP in such cases simply by displaying *some* other partition of events such that preferences for the outcomes under that partition fail to satisfy the antecedent condition of GDP. The issue here concerns the propriety of appealing to a partition under which the antecedent conditions are satisfied even though there exists an explicit *refinement* of that partition for which the antecedent conditions are not satisfied. If there is such an explicit refinement, then by reference to the consequences under that (refined) description, appeal to sure-thing considerations, it seems to me, is thereby undercut.

Savage himself is well aware of the full scope of GDE, for example, and explicitly raises the question of whether it might be appropriate to restrict it to cases in which the outcomes themselves are not defined in probabilistic terms. This amounts, of course, to a proposal to restrict GDE to an event-defined version of DSO – dominance with respect to *sure* outcomes. Focusing on the case of event-defined gambles over "sure" amounts of money, he rejects this suggestion on the following grounds: "A cash prize is to a large extent a lottery ticket in that the uncertainty as to what will become of a person if he has a gift of a thousand dollars [for example] is not in principle different from the uncertainty about what will become of him if he holds a lottery ticket."[35] This amounts to denying that there is anything like a bedrock level of certainty. On this account, it is risk all the way down. But granting that this undercuts the attempt to distinguish between GDE and an event-defined version of DSO, what makes this an argument for accepting GDE, and correspondingly GDP, rather than rejecting these much stronger principles?

Consider once again the Kahneman and Tversky example (Figure 4.3). Suppose that E is the chance event that is to occur with probability $34/100$, whereas not-E occurs with probability $66/100$; and F is the event whose probability is $33/34$ and that conditions the agent's getting \$2500 in the event he ends up confronting g_2. Since the agent, by hypothesis, prefers g_1 to g_2, GDP requires him to prefer $g_3^* = [g_1, E; \$0, \text{not-}E]$ to $g_4^* = [g_2, E; \$0, \text{not-}E]$. But rendering subsequent chance events more explicit, and repartitioning (at that finer level of discrimination) to collect events that yield the same monetary return, g_4^* is equivalent to the following: [\$2500, $E \& F$; \$0, not-E or $E \& \text{not-}F$], and this gamble is *not* dominated with respect to simple (i.e., monetary) outcomes by g_3^*, since it involves the possibility of getting as much as \$2500, which is greater than any of the possible monetary prizes associated with g_3^*.

The agent can acknowledge, of course, that if he chooses g_4^* over g_3^*, then he moves *through* a state in which a dominance relation obtains. More specifically, no matter what the outcome of the E-events, and before the F-events are run, the prospect the agent then faces, if he has chosen g_4^*, is dispreferred to the prospect he would then be facing if he had chosen g_3^*. He could argue, however, that this is something that he suffers only *en passant*, and since he is concerned only with outcomes and their probabilities, it is of no consequence to him.

Now Savage's reply, as reported earlier, is that, in effect, it is always a matter of what we face *en passant*, that it is risk all the way down. This means, however, either because it is an explicit feature of the problem or because (following Savage) even "sure" prizes involve an element of risk – even if it is not explicitly specified – that the agent can never be sure he will always do better choosing one way rather than another. But why not, then, simply take Savage's point, turn it upside down, and regard it as undercutting the whole idea of an appeal to dominance with respect to outcomes?

There is no need, however, to take such a drastic position. Any principle such as GDP or GDE must be interpreted as constraining preferences among alternatives, *under a given description* of those alternatives. If the agent has not refined his description of certain component gambles and treats them as simply possible outcomes over which he has a preference ranking, then it can be argued that it is appropriate to appeal to dominance considerations. Suppose, however, that he has refined his description of those outcomes – recognizing explicitly the nature of the further risks to be encountered. In such a case, since at *that* level of discrimination the principle is revealed not to apply, it is unclear what force there is to an argument that appeals to dominance as applied at the coarser level of description.

I conclude, then, that whereas sure-thing considerations provide a highly plausible basis for DSO, there is little to support the extension of this line of reasoning to either GDP or GDE. This is, moreover, very worrisome. The thrust of the counterexamples offered in Section 4.5 is that IND is too strong a condition. It might seem, however, that at least some leverage against those counterexamples could be provided by grounding IND in what have been alleged to be very plausible dominance principles such as either GDP or GDE. But the conclusion of this section is that only DSO has the requisite plausibility, and DSO does not suffice for the derivation of IND (and hence for the expected utility and subjective probability theorems).

Similar remarks, I suggest, apply to the counterpart stochastic dominance conditions, FSD and GFSD. The latter is a much stronger condition and cannot be connected easily with "maximizing" principles. As the example in Section 3.6 was intended to establish, one complex gamble can stochastically dominate another with respect to component gambles (i.e., the two can be ordered by GFSD) without its being the case that the reduced versions of each can be ordered by FSD. In appealing to stochastic dominance considerations, then, it is important to make clear which version of the principle is being invoked. Once again, what may be required for a particular argument to work is that one be able to assume the stronger (and much more problematic) condition.[36]

4.8 Summary

My concern in this chapter has been to examine a variety of standard arguments that have been offered in support of this or that presupposition of the modern theory of rational choice. For the most part, these arguments must be judged as nonstarters. In particular, with regard to those that pertain to the context-free ordering principle (CFO) and the independence principle (IND), there is a gap between these principles and supporting intuitions that enjoy a sufficiently broad consensus. To be sure, it makes sense to require that the ordering over any feasible set be transitive and that preferences respect dominance with respect to "sure" outcomes – but such a simple transitivity condition will not suffice to secure CFO, and dominance with respect to sure outcomes will not secure IND. Similarly, although everyone can agree with Samuelson that complementarities of the classical sort, namely, those that arise in connection with considering (conjunctive) bundles of commodities, cannot arise in connection with disjunctively defined prospects, still this does not preclude the possibility of complementarity-like effects that are special to disjunctive combinations of goods. Broome, for his part, though he inventively shows how both the transitivity of R_c and the independence principle might be "saved," fails to show why we should want to do this. And, finally, there has been a tendency to trade on an ambiguity between very plausible versions of dominance conditions, such as DSO and FSD, and much stronger and less plausible versions, such as, respectively, GDP and GFSD.

5

Pragmatic arguments

5.1 Introduction

If the arguments examined in the preceding chapter are essentially nonstarters, there are two other, much more substantial and very closely related lines of reasoning that have yet to be considered. The first of these can be characterized as a pragmatic argument, and the second – following a suggestion of Hammond – can be termed a "consequentialist" argument.[1] It is a distinctive feature of each that it can be put to work to support both the ordering and the independence principles. That is, from a consequentialist or pragmatic perspective on foundational issues, the two cornerstones of the modern theory of rational choice are revealed to stand on a par with each other. If either one of these arguments goes through, then the agent who is concerned to maximize with respect to consequences will have good reason to accept *both* WO and IND. This is rather striking, for historically at any rate the two principles have been regarded as grounded in quite distinct intuitions.

In very general terms, the pragmatic argument seeks to show that failure to accept the ordering and independence principles can work to the practical disadvantage of the agent – to his doing less well (in terms of the promotion of personally defined interests) than he otherwise could have done in a certain class of situations. Arguments of this general sort have surfaced repeatedly in the history of decision theory. Both Ramsey and de Finetti, for example, argue that an agent whose subjective probabilities fail to satisfy the usual axioms of probability can have "book" made against him, that is, can be placed in a situation in which he will accept a certain collection of bets, despite the fact that regardless of the turn of events, he must end up less well off than he would have been had he refused the whole set of bets.[2] Again, Davidson, McKinsey, and Suppes offer a defense of transitivity of pair-set choice-determined preference (and hence also of the Alpha factor of CF) that runs along similar lines. The suggestion is that preference cycles in this context can make the agent liable to exploitation. Someone else can offer the agent a sequence of options, which he will be disposed in each case to accept, such that he ends up poorer for having accepted the sequence of choices than he would have been had he refused them all. In short, such an agent can be "pumped" for money (and, at that, repeatedly). Others have sought to construct a similar argument in defense of the strong independence principle, by showing that those who violate this principle will end up violating DSO, the principle of dominance with respect to sure outcomes.

The consequentialist argument, which is due to Hammond, is much more complex, and its full explication will have to await the development, in the next two chapters, of a more formal account of dynamic choice. Briefly, however, Hammond argues from an "almost unquestioned hypothesis of modern normative decision theory," namely, that acts are valued by their consequences.[3] This principle of consequentialism, as he characterizes it, has only modest implications in the context of static choice: Choice of an action is to be judged acceptable if and only if the consequences of such an act (more generally its risky and uncertain consequences) lie in the choice set corresponding to the feasible set of consequences associated with all possible actions available to the agent in that setting. This means, of course, following the distinctions set forth in Chapter 2, that choice of an action is acceptable if and only if the consequences of that action are maximally preferred by the agent – if and only if the agent chooses so as to maximize with respect to his preference ordering over consequences. Hammond argues, however, that the principle of consequentialism has both a natural and a very powerful extension to dynamic choice contexts in which the agent is called upon to make a sequence of choices over time. Within such a framework, consequentialism requires two things. First, choice at each successive point in time must be oriented to whatever consequences remain open at that point. Second, the structure of the dynamic decision problem – the particular sequence of choice and chance events – is irrelevant in the following sense: If two decision problems expose the agent to the same set of (perhaps risky or uncertain) possible consequences of action, then acceptable choice in each case must expose the agent to the same set of consequences. So interpreted, consequentialism can then be shown, Hammond argues, to imply both WO and IND. As I shall argue in Chapter 7, a particularly clear version of his argument can be captured by factoring his extended consequentialist principle into three conditions on dynamic or sequential choice and then showing that this set of conditions logically entails both CF and CIND – the choice versions of the context-free ordering and the strong independence conditions. In very general terms, then, the thrust of this sort of argument is simply that the two key principles of a static theory of choice, WO and IND, are recoverable as theorems in a theory of dynamic choice.

Although this is a point that will become much clearer when each is presented in greater detail, the pragmatic and consequentialist arguments are clearly connected. A pragmatic approach is, after all, one that looks to consequences. Consequentialism, for its part, requires that the agent at each choice point select an action whose consequences are maximally preferred, while the thrust of the "pragmatic" argument is that one who fails to satisfy certain choice conditions will end up with a less preferred consequence than he could have achieved if his choice behavior always satisfied the conditions in question. The difference between the two arguments seems, in fact, to come to this: Hammond thinks his principle of consequentialism logically entails certain conditions on choice functions, whereas the pragmatic argument proceeds by showing that failure to satisfy those conditions would lead to unfortunate or undesirable consequences for the agent. One might then think of them as, at least roughly speaking, simply two different ways to make the same logical point. However, for reasons that will become clearer shortly – namely, that I think Hammond's argument turns out to be a special-case version of a much more general "consequentialist" or pragmatic argument – I shall continue to distinguish between the two.

5.2 A pragmatic/consequentialist perspective

The perspective exemplified by the two arguments discussed in Section 5.1 is expressive of a fundamentally individualistic and practical way of approaching choice. On such a view, it is the personal preferences of the individual with respect to outcomes or consequences that form the appropriate reference point for the evaluation of alternative courses of action open to him; and to be "rational" in such a setting is basically simply a matter of choosing so as to maximize with respect to those preferences or, more colloquially, choosing so as to promote one's interests.

Such a view of "rationality" is also profoundly permissive in a certain very important respect. If what best serves a given set of interests is a question of fact, and thus something to be resolved by reference to public criteria of evidence and so on, still it is essential to such a view of rationality that the agent's interests themselves – as expressed in terms of his preferences with regard to outcomes – are not subject to a critique in terms of principles of rationality. Alternatively put, rationality pertains to the choice of means to ends, not the choice of ends themselves.

This sort of *permissive* view of rationality finds expression in the quotation from Hume that I have taken as an epigraph to this volume. Two theme notes are struck there. Hume is, first of all, concerned to offer protection to those with unorthodox preferences. To this end he resists allowing much to count as irrational. From that perspective, choice is subject to criticism *only* insofar as it is insufficient to its designed end: Being inadequate with respect to its intended objective is a *necessary* condition of choice being irrational. Put somewhat more carefully, inadequacy of means to given ends is only one of two respects in which an "affection" can be criticized. It can also be unreasonable when it is founded on false supposition. One might, in the interests of parsimony, consider trying to subsume this second case under the first – that of means insufficient to chosen ends. The suggestion would be that the problem with acting on false beliefs is that one is likely to be frustrated in the pursuit of one's chosen ends. This, it could be argued, is true whether one's ends are intellectual (to realize a true account of some aspect of the world) or nonintellectual (to realize happiness, to contribute to the well-being of others, to live up to some moral ideal, to create something of value, or even just to play).

In virtue of being demanding as to what can count as irrational, this part of Hume's test is permissive with respect to what can count as rational. In very general terms, choice is never irrational per se – only irrational relative to given ends or interests of the agent. Hume does not shrink from the implications of this. He remarks that it is not necessarily unreasonable to prefer the destruction of the entire world to the suffering of a small scratch on one's own finger. If one refuses to go beyond Hume's test, much that many have insisted is irrational turns out simply to reflect some particular person's (perhaps very unusual) set of preferences.[4]

For all this, however, there is a second, less permissive theme. Inadequacy with respect to intended end is a *sufficient* condition of irrationality. Thus, the permissiveness implied in the setting of a necessary condition for irrationality is bounded by a sufficient condition: Choices that fail to serve the ends of the agent are thereby subject to criticism.

Notice also that the proposed tests are presumably to be understood as providing criteria for "objectively" rational choice. Actual agents, facing inevitable limits with respect to memory, computational ability, data processing, and the like, will end up choosing means that are in fact insufficient to their ends or that are based on false suppositions. Both criteria, then, must be recast in subjective terms. But for purposes of criticizing choice, the objective formulation remains indispensable. A cogent argument has been offered against any choice that rests on a false presupposition or is inadequate to the realization of the agent's own ends.

It will not be lost on the historian of ideas that Hume's concept of rationality fits comfortably with Adam Smith's theories concerning the economic motivation of individuals. And more generally yet, of course, this sort of "minimalist" or "thin" theory of rationality is central to the modern economist's notion that basic preferences lie beyond criticism and that the task of normative economics is essentially confined to questions of individual and group efficiency – questions of what constitutes effective ways to realize the interests of a given individual or the interests of a group of such individuals.[5]

The arguments to be explored in the next few chapters need not be interpreted as embracing the full version of Hume's test. The pragmatic and consequentialist arguments constructively proceed via appeal to the "if" portion of Hume's test of irrationality: The intention is to show that some methods of evaluation must be judged irrational because they lead to choice of means insufficient to our ends. But if, as I hope to show, these arguments are less than fully successful, then the real thrust of Hume's test lies in the "only if" part: These are the *only* grounds on which choice can be criticized.

Such a way of proceeding has the virtue not merely of addressing a consideration that all are prepared to accept as relevant to assessing the rationality of choice, but of *avoiding* an appeal to considerations on which, it would seem, there is nothing like an informed consensus. Where there is no consensus, it is important to proceed with the greatest of caution. Otherwise, one ends up legislating for all about matters best left to individual discretion. I propose to see how far one can get, then, if one proceeds in the spirit of the full version of Hume's test; that is, not only accepting constraints on choice that can be pragmatically justified, but also refusing to impose constraints that cannot be so justified.

5.3 Refining the pragmatic perspective

The pragmatically oriented person, as I have characterized him, is oriented to consequences; that is, he views the various plans open to him in terms of their associated consequences or, in cases involving risk, their associated prospects (i.e., a probability distribution over a set of outcomes). Commitment to the reduction principle RD can be taken to express such a decidedly pragmatic orientation. The agent who accepts RD does not concern himself with the manner or mode in which the risky prospect is presented to him – such as whether the gamble is single-staged or multistaged, whether the odds are determined by the toss of a coin or the play of cards, and so on. Instead, he is concerned only with the possible outcomes and their respective likelihoods. The manner in which the risky option is presented to him is viewed simply as a way of accessing an associated prospect.

As I have already indicated, however, one must proceed with caution in this regard. If commitment to RD is characteristically to be associated with being pragmatically oriented, still rejection of that principle does not necessarily imply rejection of that perspective. As Harsanyi has suggested, it remains open to the individual agent (who is acting, say, in a purely private capacity and who is not concerned with developing a policy for maximizing his return over the long run from risky investments) to have preferences with regard to forms of risk. Following this line of reasoning, I will treat cases in which persons have such preferences with regard to structural features of gambles as "special cases" to which certain of the principles of decision theory are simply not applicable. For the balance of the discussion in this and the next two chapters, I shall suppose that the considerations and arguments brought forth in support of this or that principle of choice are addressed to an agent who does not, as a matter of fact, have such "special preferences" and whose pragmatic orientation is partially expressed by his commitment to RD.[6]

A much more pressing problem, I think, concerns the implications such a pragmatic perspective has for situations in which the agent faces a dynamic or sequential decision problem. Suppose, to take the simplest case first, the agent is faced with making a series of choices over time, but it is presumed that there are no chance events that will affect the outcomes in any significant fashion – or at least no chance events that occur before the choices are to be made. I shall suppose that the mark of a pragmatically respectable approach to choice in such a context is that the agent seeks to execute a course of action or plan – a sequence of choices – the associated outcome, or consequence, of which is maximally preferred among those that could be realized by execution of any of the possible courses of action open to the agent in that decision situation. That is, just as he is committed to RD, so also he will regard the particular concatenation and order of choices to be made as having no significance or value in itself – as simply providing an access route to the consequences he wishes to realize.

This suggests, in turn, an extension to the case in which the decision problem involves an intermixing of chance and choice "moves." The notion, once again, is that a pragmatically oriented agent will execute a course of action or plan whose associated risk or uncertain consequence (as predicated on the relevant conditioning events) is maximally preferred among all the possibly risky or uncertain consequences to which the agent has access, given the decision problem in question. The agent will view any particular concatenation and order of chance events and choice possibilities strictly in terms of the prospects that it is thereby possible to access.

There is another pressing problem. Although appeal to a pragmatic perspective does presuppose that the agent can identify some (perhaps risky or uncertain) consequence in any possible set of such consequences that is not ranked below any others, the individualistic and instrumentalist features of that perspective preclude making any substantive assumption about the agent's preferences with respect to consequences. But how, then, can such a pragmatic perspective be employed to criticize an agent's failure to conform in his preference (or choice) behavior to WO and IND (or, alternatively, CF and CIND)? Doesn't an Allais-type or Ellsberg-type pattern of preferences, for example, bring up a substantive point – that is, what in fact the agent prefers and hence what, from Hume's perspective, lies beyond criticism?

The answer (which is to be elaborated in the next few sections) turns on three distinct points. First, it should be recalled that on any account WO and IND rule out only certain *patterns* of preferences. To take the Allais example, as given in Figure 4.1, nothing constrains the agent as to his preference with regard to g_1 and g_2: He may prefer g_1 to g_2, prefer g_2 to g_1, or be indifferent between the two; all that is required is that whatever his preferences in this regard, his preferences with regard to g_3 and g_4 conform (in the stated respect) to those other preferences. Similarly, CF imposes no constraint on choice from a pair set; it simply expresses the idea that what is judged acceptable in the pair set $\{x, y\}$ has implications for the acceptable subset of any superset of $\{x, y\}$. Second, what is characteristic of the pragmatic arguments is the presupposition that these constraints on patterns of preference can ultimately be rooted in considerations of *pragmatic* consistency – of choice of means adequate to desired ends. The claim is that the agent who violates one of these constraints on preference can be "caught out" in a pragmatic inconsistency. Third, the pragmatic arguments do involve one modest presupposition, namely, that there is some good or commodity (say, money) that the agent does prefer more of to less and quantities of which are capable of division into arbitrarily small units. They do not presuppose, however, that there is some one commodity such that all agents prefer more of it to less; all that is presupposed is that for each such agent there is some commodity having the properties in question.

Using these very general (and admittedly still somewhat tentative) remarks about a pragmatic orientation as a background, I want to consider now in somewhat greater detail the sort of pragmatic argument that might be constructed in favor of both CF and CIND. The arguments to be discussed in the following two sections are to be taken as merely illustrative. They are offered here simply to prime the more formal discussion to follow in subsequent chapters, by establishing the potential value of a dynamic choice framework when it comes to arguing for various rationality conditions.

5.4 Money-pump arguments

I argued in Chapter 2 that the failure of an evaluative method to determine an acceptable-set function satisfying CF need not pose a cycling problem for choice from a fixed set of options, that is, "static" choice: Context-dependent orderings may yet be fully transitive and connected over any given feasible set. It would appear, however, that failure of the acceptable-set function to satisfy CF will give rise to a troublesome cycling phenomenon with respect to choice in a dynamic setting, where one successively confronts a series of feasible sets. Imagine, for example, the following situation: x is chosen from $\{x, y\}$, y is chosen from $\{y, z\}$, and z is chosen from $\{z, x\}$. This amounts to a violation of Alpha, since if a choice function exists, it must also make a selection from $\{x, y, z\}$, and by Alpha and the information just given, none of x or y or z can be chosen from this larger set. Now suppose the agent begins with y; then it seems that he should be willing to exchange y for x and also willing to exchange x in turn for z and z in turn for y. In this case, then, there is a cycle over time; the agent ends up back where he started.

It would appear, moreover, that this sort of cycle can make the agent liable to a serious pragmatic difficulty. The agent whose choices cycle in the fashion just described can be placed in a situation in which he will end up failing to maximize with respect to his own preferences. The so-called money-pump argument, as originally formulated by Davidson, McKinsey, and Suppes, offers a particularly striking version of this line of reasoning. Here is how they introduce the problem:

Mr. S. is offered his choice of three jobs by a cynical department head. . . . He can be a full professor with a salary of $5,000 (alternative x), an associate professor at $5,500 (alternative y) or an assistant professor at $6,000 (alternative z). Mr. S. reasons as follows: $x P y$ since the advantage in kudos outweighs the small difference in salary; $y P z$ for the same reason; $z P x$ since the difference in salary is now enough to outweigh a matter of rank. What arguments can be given to show that this is an irrational set of preferences?[7]

Their response to this question takes the form of the following scenario:

The department head, advised of Mr. S's preferences, says, "I see you prefer y to z, so I will let you have the associate professorship – for a small consideration. The difference must be worth something to you." Mr. S. agrees to slip the department head $25. to get the preferred alternative. Now the department head says, "Since you prefer x to y, I'm prepared – if you pay me a little for my trouble – to let you have the full professorship." Mr. S. hands over another $25. and starts to walk away, well satisfied, we may suppose. "Hold on," says the department head, "I just realized you'd rather have z than x. And I can arrange that – provided . . ."[8]

Notice, first of all, that nothing in this story precludes Mr. S from effectively choosing in each of a number of possible situations. The story explicitly indicates what his choice is from each pair set; and those choices (as well as any underlying preference ordering on which they might be based) do not preclude choice from the triplet $\{x, y, z\}$. To be sure, if he is also prepared to evaluate the options in the triplet and if the acceptable set $D(\{x, y, z\})$ is nonempty, then Alpha will be violated. That is to say, he will be revealed to have an ordering over feasible sets that is not context free. But choice will still be possible. As the story makes clear, Mr. S's problem is quite different. He can choose, but his choices are subject to criticism from a pragmatic perspective.

This story can, moreover, be generalized to any situation in which there is a cycle in pair-set-revealed strict preference P_c over a triple of options $\{x, y, z\}$, that is, where in terms of acceptable sets, only y is in $D(\{y, z\})$, only x is in $D(\{x, y\})$, and only z is in $D(\{x, z\})$. Suppose the agent holds rights to z. Since he strictly prefers y to z, he should be willing (so the argument goes) to exchange z, together with a small amount of cash, say, $\$a$, for y when an entrepreneur offers him just those two options. Once that trade is effected, the entrepreneur proceeds to offer to take back y, together with some small amount of cash, say $\$b$, in exchange for x. Since, by hypothesis, x is preferred to y, when just these two options are available, the agent should be willing to make this exchange also. But now the entrepreneur proposes to work one more trade, offering back what he originally took for y, namely z, in exchange for x and a small amount of money, $\$c$. Once again the agent should be prepared to trade. The net effect, then, is that he ends up where he started, with z, except that he has paid out the sum of $\$a + \$b + \$c$. In principle, if the agent continues to have this preference pattern, it should be possible for the entrepreneur to continue to work the series of exchanges over and over, to the ever increasing disadvantage of the agent.

The story just told concerns the case in which the agent has a pair-set strict preference cycle: $x\,P_c\,y$, $y\,P_c\,z$, but $z\,P_c\,x$. What about the case in which the agent's preferences with respect to pair sets can be characterized, for example, as $x\,P_c\,y$, $y\,P_c\,z$, but $z\,I_c\,x$? Translating this once more into choice-set terms, the case concerns one in which $D(\{x, y\}) = \{x\}$, $D(\{y, z\}) = \{y\}$, and $D(\{x, z\}) = \{x, z\}$. There need be no violation of Alpha implied here, but if Alpha is satisfied, then Beta will be violated.[9] That is, by appeal to Alpha, it must be that $D(\{x, y, z\}) = \{x\}$, but this conflicts with the requirement of Beta according to which since $D(\{x, z\}) = \{x, z\}$, either both x and z are or neither is in $D(\{x, y, z\})$. Can an agent committed to this sort of choice behavior also be turned into a money pump?

Suppose, once again, the agent holds rights to z. Since he is committed to choosing y in preference to z in pairwise choice, he should be willing to exchange z together with a small amount of cash, say, $\$a$, for y. Once this trade is effected, the entrepreneur proceeds to offer to take back y, together with some small amount of cash, say $\$b$, in exchange for x. Since, by hypothesis, the agent is committed to choosing x in preference to y in pairwise choice, the agent should be willing to make this exchange also. But now the entrepreneur proposes to work one more trade, offering back what he originally took in exchange for y, namely, z plus a small amount of money, $\$c$, in exchange for x. By hypothesis, the agent is indifferent between z and x; presumably, then, he will prefer the option of having z and a small amount of money, $\$c$, to retaining x. Moreover, if he is really indifferent between x and z, the entrepreneur need not offer all of the amount $\$a + \$b$ that he has already collected from the agent in order to effect the trade back to z. That is, we may suppose that he need only offer some amount $\$c < \$a + \$b$. Once this trade has been made, the agent is back where he started, in the sense that he has z again, except he is poorer by $\$a + \$b - \$c > 0$. In principle, if the agent continues to violate Beta, it should be possible for the entrepreneur to continue to work the series of exchanges over and over, to the ever increasing disadvantage of the agent.[10]

5.5 Violations of IND and DSO

Objections to allowing violations of IND have usually been cast not in terms of money-pump considerations, but in terms of the closely related notion that such violations make the agent liable to violations of DSO – the principle of dominance with respect to sure outcomes. One of the first, and best known, of these arguments is due to Raiffa.[11] The argument turns on a variation on the original Allais problem (Figure 5.1), involving two pairs of gambles whose sure monetary outcomes (in millions of dollars) are conditioned by the draw of a colored ball from an urn, with balls of each color in the stated proportions. Raiffa casts his argument in terms of a series of direct questions to the reader. Suppose you are prepared to rank g_1 over g_2, and g_3 over g_4, in violation of the independence axiom. If you have this preference

		Green (10)	White (1)	Orange (89)
Problem 1	g_1	$1M	$1M	$1M
	g_2	5M	0	1M
Problem 2	g_3	5M	0	0
	g_4	1M	1M	0

Figure 5.1

		Green (10)	White (1)	Orange (89)
Problem 1*	g_1	$1M	$1M	$1M
	g_2^*	5M + 10	0 + 10	1M + 10
Problem 2*	g_3	5M	0	0
	g_4^*	1M + 10	1M + 10	0 + $10

Figure 5.2

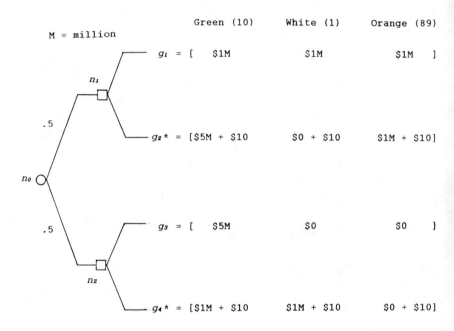

Figure 5.3

ordering, he suggests, you will likely also, when presented with the problems shown in Figure 5.2, rank g_1 over g_2^*, and g_3 over g_4^*. That is, augmenting each of the possible payoffs in g_2 and g_4 by $10 is not likely to make any difference.

Suppose now, Raiffa continues, the experimenter tosses a fair coin to determine which of the two problems, 1* or 2*, he is going to let you play. In tree-diagram form, your problem can be represented as in Figure 5.3. The suggestion is that since you prefer g_1 to g_2^*, and prefer g_3 to g_4^*, you will, upon arriving at n_1, choose g_1 over at g_2^*; and you will, upon arriving at n_2, choose g_3 over g_4^*. Raiffa now continues: "If the experimenter asks you to announce your intention before the toss of the coin, would you assert that you would take g_1 if heads, and g_3 if tails?"[12]

	Green (10)	White (1)	Orange (89)
s	[$1M, .5; $5M, .5]	[$1M, .5; $0, .5]	[$1M, .5; $0, .5]
r	[$5M + $10, .5 $1M + $10, .5]	[$0 + $10, . 5; $1M + $10, .5]	[$1M + $10, .5; $0 + $10, .5]

Figure 5.4

The language in which this question is couched is somewhat unclear, involving as it does talk of both choice and prediction. But the use
of the term "intention" suggests that Raiffa is asking you, the reader as
hypothetical decision maker, to consider what plan you would be prepared to adopt at the outset, it being understood that the plan must be
implemented by choices to be made after the toss of the coin.[13] That
is, the question concerns how you would be prepared to evaluate com-
paratively the following two plans, at the outset, before the coin is
tossed: plans s, which calls for you to choose g_1 if the coin comes up
heads, and g_3 if the coin comes up tails; and plan r, which calls for you
to choose g_2^* if the coin comes up heads, and g_4^* if the coin comes up tails.
Moreover, as Raiffa sees the matter, the answer to this question is clear:
You should regard s as the best plan and r as the worst.

Raiffa now proceeds to offer an analysis of the options from a
somewhat different perspective.[14] Let us, he suggests, examine the
payoffs for the preferred plan s and the dispreferred plan r on the
supposition that the experimenter will toss a coin to determine which
problem (problem 1* or 2*) he will assign to you. More particularly,
"suppose the experimenter draws a ball without disclosing the result
to you, and holds it in his left hand; he then tosses a coin, also without
disclosing the results to you, and holds it in his right hand." If you
adopt plan s and he has a green ball in his left hand, Raiffa continues,
then what confronts you is simply a $1M or $5M return, depending on
whether he has "heads" or "tails" in his right hand, and so on for the
other possibilities. In table form, the payoffs are as shown in Figure 5.4.
Now suppose that the ordering of plans replicates the ordering of associated prospects. Then since you prefer plan s to plan r, you must
prefer the prospect associated with plan s, namely, $g_s =$
[($1M, .5; $5M, .5), .10; ($1M, .5; $0, .5), .01; ($1M, .5; $0,.5), .89] to
the prospect associated with plan r, namely, $g_r =$ [($5M + $10, .5; $1M
+ $10, .5), .10; ($0 + $10, .5; $1M + $10, .5), .01;($1M + $10, .5;
$0 + $10, .5), .89]. It is easy to ascertain, however, that RD and WO
in turn imply that given this ordering of g_s and g_r, one must also order
the first of the following two gambles over the second:

$$g_s^* = [\$1M, .5; \$5M, .05; \$0, .45],$$
$$g_r^* = [\$1M + \$10, .5; \$5M + \$10, .05; \$10, .45].$$

But it can also be seen, by inspection, that the second, g_r^*, dominates the first, g_s^*, with respect to sure outcomes.

To recapitulate briefly the steps in his argument, Raiffa has reasoned that if you have a preference for g_1 over g_2 and g_3 over g_4, you must have a preference for g_1 over g_2^* and g_3 over g_4^* and also (combining the two more preferred gambles and the two less preferred gambles) a preference for g_s over g_r. But by appeal to RD and WO, this means that you must prefer g_s^* to g_r^*, and this violates DSO. Thus, the original preferences in question lead to a violation of DSO.

Raiffa's argument, to be sure, is rather complicated: Not only must he presuppose various other principles of rationality as fixed, but, what is somewhat more worrisome, he simply presumes, without any discussion, that the choice problem given in Figure 5.4 is the same as the one specified in Figure 5.3. But a much simpler version of the same type of argument was presented in connection with the decision problem in Figure 1.1. There, it will be recalled, it was suggested that the agent whose ordering of certain gambles fails to conform to IND will end up violating DSO.[15]

As a last example of this type of argument, consider a case, somewhat similar to the one presented by Ellsberg (and discussed in Section 4.5), in which the agent prefers some outcome g_1 to g_2 and some other outcome g_3 to g_4, but prefers the lottery $g = [g_2, H; g_4, T]$ to the lottery $g^* = [g_1, H; g_3, T]$, where both are based on the outcome of the toss of a fair coin. By appeal to RD and WO it can be shown that this sort of preference pattern violates IND. Now suppose that the agent possesses rights to g^*. One can imagine an entrepreneur who now offers to trade him g in exchange for g^* and a small amount of money, $\$a$. Since the agent definitely prefers g to g^*, we may presume that for small enough a, he will be willing to trade. Once the trade is effected, the experiment is run and either H or T occurs. If H, the agent is now in possession of rights to g_2, and the entrepreneur proceeds to offer to exchange g_2 together with a small amount of money $\$b$ for g_1. Since by hypothesis the agent prefers g_1 to g_2, it would seem that he should be willing to accept this trade, at least if $\$b$ is small enough. If T, the agent is now in possession of g_4, and the entrepreneur proceeds to offer to exchange it together with a small amount of money $\$c$ for g_3. Again, since by hypothesis the agent prefers g_3 to g_4, the agent should be willing to make the trade, at least if $\$c$ is small enough. But now, regardless of the lie of the coin, the agent ends up just where he would have been had he engaged in no trades – he now has either g_1 or g_3 – except that he is either poorer by $\$(a + b)$ or poorer by $\$(a + c)$. That is, looking at the prospect associated with the full sequence of these contingent choices – the prospect of ending up with g_1 and a capital loss of $\$(a + b)$ in the event that H, and g_3 and a capital loss of $\$(a + c)$ in the event that T – one immediately sees that this prospect is dominated with respect to sure outcomes by the prospect of refusing any of the trades at all (regardless of the internal composition of g_1 and g_3) – for that prospect is simply g_1 if H, and g_3 if T. Thus, once again, it would seem, the agent who violates this version of IND can be trapped into a violation of DSO.

5.6 Dutch books

One can also identify a type of argument involving an appeal to DSO in support of various principles governing belief (subjective probability) rather than preference, versions of which can be traced back as far as Ramsey and, independently, de Finetti. In Ramsey's case, the argument amounts to no more than a suggestion: After sketching an axiom system for degrees of belief satisfying the usual laws of probability, he remarks that if anyone violated these laws, "he could have book made against him by a cunning bettor and would then stand to lose [money] in any event."[16] This suggestion and the much more explicit argument to be found in de Finetti were subsequently explored very thoroughly in a series of articles by Lehmann, Kemeny, and Shimony.[17] In each case, the argument is that one who fails to accept the laws of probability will be disposed to accept various bets, even though by doing so he ends up facing a *monetary* loss, regardless of how events transpire, and even though he could have chosen alternatively to accept none of the bets (and hence, though not gaining anything, avoid any loss). Once again, this amounts to a pragmatic argument for making "coherent" probability assignments to various sets of related events.

As a very simple example of how this argument works, consider two mutually exclusive events, E and F. On the usual account, the probability to be assigned to the disjunction of E and F should be equivalent to the sum of the probabilities assigned to E and to F, that is, $P(E \text{ or } F) = P(E) + P(F)$.[18] Suppose, contrary to this rule, that the probabilities assigned by the agent are as follows: $P(E) = .3, P(F) = .4, P(E \text{ or } F) = .5$. Now on the assumption that the agent's willingness to take bets on these various events is strictly a function of expected return, it follows that he should be willing to (1) pay up to $.3(\$S)$ for a bet that yields him $\$S$ if E occurs and $\$0$ if not, (2) pay up to $0.4(\$S)$ for a bet that yields him $\$S$ if F occurs and $\$0$ if not; and (3) demand a payment of $.5(\$S)$ to be exposed to a bet that will cost him $\$S$ if either E or F occurs and $\$0$ if not. Suppose, further, there is someone willing to offer him all of these bets, at the stated limits of acceptable odds. Then, so the argument goes, he will take all of them. There are, now, three contingencies to consider. Either E

occurs or F occurs or neither does (since E and F are mutually exclusive). Suppose E occurs. Then the agent wins $\$S - .3(\$S) = .7(\$S)$ on bet (1), loses $0.4(\$S)$ on bet (2), and loses $\$S - 0.5(\$S) = .5(\$S)$ on bet (3) and thus incurs a net loss of $.2(\$S)$. Suppose F occurs. Then he loses $.3(\$S)$ on bet (1), wins $.6(\$S)$ on bet (2), and loses $.5(\$S)$ on bet (3) and thus incurs a net loss of $.2(\$S)$ again. Finally, suppose that neither E nor F occurs. Then the agent loses $.3(\$S)$ on bet (1), loses $.4(\$S)$ on bet (2), and wins $.5(\$S)$ on bet (3) and thus incurs a net loss of $.2(\$S)$. In short, regardless of which of a series of mutually exclusive and exhaustive events occurs, he loses money. But since he would break even, regardless of which of those events occurred, were he to accept none of the bets in question, his choice behavior violates DSO. By systematic extension of this sort of reasoning, it can be shown that he can avoid such violations of DSO only by assigning probabilities to E and to F and to $(E$ or $F)$ that satisfy the constraint $P(E) + P(F) = P(E$ or $F)$.

Both Kyburg and Schick have argued convincingly that arguments of this sort – including the versions found in Kemeny, Lehmann, and Shimony – are badly flawed. They have shown that the argument goes through only on the assumption that if the agent is willing to accept bet A, and also willing to accept bet B, then he must be willing to accept *both* A and B.[19] This presupposes, however, that the problem of complementarity does not arise in connection with *conjunctive* combinations of bets. Whatever one wants to say about the possibility of complementarity in connection with *disjunctive* combinations (as discussed in Section 3.3), it is implausible to assume that noncomplementarity holds for conjunctive combinations. Indeed, the most natural conclusion to draw from the examples presented by those who have advocated the dutch-book argument is precisely that noncomplementarity frequently fails to obtain in such cases. Since I find Kyburg's and Schick's arguments dispositive, I shall ignore the dutch-book line of reasoning and focus instead on pragmatic arguments that do not presuppose conjunctive noncomplementarity.

5.7 Summary

I have suggested in this chapter that there is a family of arguments in support of either the ordering or independence principle that turn on the notion that a rational agent is one who chooses a course of action so as to maximize his preferences with respect to the consequences associated with such actions. The more accessible versions of this type of argument involve the notion of turning a violator of the principle in question into a money pump or trapping him in a situation in which he violates DSO. Now one thing that marks these arguments is that the liabilities in question arise within a context in which the agent is called on to make a sequence of choices over time. That is, in each case the argument turns on showing that a certain pattern of preference over some set of consequences gets the agent in trouble once these consequences are embedded in a dynamic or combinatorial choice situation. And again, it is a common feature of these arguments that the notion of rationality to which appeal is implicitly made here is that the agent avoid choice or preference patterns that can result in his being placed in a "no-win" situation, that is, in a situation in which despite his efforts to maximize his preferences with regard to out-comes, at each choice point, the net effect of just that effort is that he ends up with a less preferred outcome. Thus, these arguments have a distinctively pragmatic thrust. They address the interests or prefer-ences of the agent himself and purport to show that he stands to lose (on terms that make reference to his own ends or goals) if his pref-erence rankings or choices fail to satisfy the principle in question.

In this respect, moreover, the money-pump argument and the ar-gument that appeals to DSO are really very closely connected. The dominance argument suggests that regardless of which of two or more mutually exclusive and exhaustive events occurs, the violator of independence ends up, as a result of his own choices, in a financial state that he disprefers to the one that he would have been in had he not traded at all. But the money-pump argument introduces what is essentially a variation on the same theme. It suggests that the agent who fails to satisfy CF can be placed in a situation in which he ends up, as a result of his own choices, in a financial state that he disprefers to the one that he would have been in had he not traded at all. What links the two arguments, of course, is simply the intuitive sense that failure to respect DSO is an instance of failing to maximize with respect to preferences for outcomes or consequences.

All of this suggests a potentially powerful line of reasoning in sup-port of essential factors of WO and the independence principle IND. This sort of argument, then, promises to provide a solid underpin-ning for the two main cornerstones of the modern theory of utility. The above stories, however, run their course a bit too smoothly and quickly. The agent in each case has been described as if he had blind-ers on – as if he never considered anything but the immediate choice problem presented to him at each point in time. Alternatively put, the agent is presumed to choose at each stage myopically and incrementally – without consideration of what he did at previous choice points and without consideration of what he can anticipate doing at subsequent choice points. In this respect, if the dynamic framework provides a natural setting in which to explore what happens when choice fails to satisfy certain conditions, still more groundwork has to be laid before it can be concluded that an agent whose method of evaluation of static choices fails to satisfy these conditions *must* choose in the manner described when the set of choices is spread out over time. What is needed in particular is a much more systematic account of dynamic as distinct from static choice and a careful exploration of the ways in which these two types of decision framework can be linked. Moreover, such an exploration is just what is needed for a proper understanding of Hammond's considerably more formal and complex consequentialist argument.

6

Dynamic choice problems

6.1 Dynamic choice and decision trees

In very general terms, a dynamic choice problem can be characterized as one in which the agent is called upon to make a sequence of choices over time, in response to situations that are a function of his own earlier choices and (perhaps also) certain randomly determined events. The classic representation of such a problem is that of a "decision tree," with branch points defining either choices to be made by the agent or possible outcomes of chance events determined by nature (Figure 6.1). By convention, choice branches (n_0, n_2) are designated by squares; chance branches (n_1) by circles. A particular sequence of choice and/or chance events takes the agent from the initial node or branch point (n_0) in the tree to some terminal node or outcome of the tree $(o_1, o_2,$ etc.). For example, if the agent elects to take the upper branch at n_0, then chance events (to which determinate probabilities may or may not be assignable) determine whether he ends up at n_2 with another choice to be made, between $s(n_2)$ – the branch leading to outcome o_1 – and $r(n_2)$ – the branch leading to outcome o_2 – or whether he ends up simply confronting the outcome o_3.

Such a representation, of course, involves what some will regard as an arbitrary conceptual cut. The suggestion will be that each decision a real-life agent makes occurs at a point that is the continuation of a decision tree sequence that began only with the first deliberate decision he made and that will terminate only (if then?) with his death. A decision tree, on this view, is always an arbitrarily defined segment of a larger sequence of choices. Against this, however, it can be argued that the representation of a decision problem as bounded is perfectly appropriate. As for starting points, agents *do* initiate projects. From the perspective of the deliberation over alternative plans, not every point calling for decision is to be understood as a continuation of an earlier project. As for terminal points, one can appeal to the familiar notion of a time horizon. That is, there is a limit as to how far into the future the agent is able (or willing!) to project what choices he will make, what "natural" events will condition various logical possibilities, and thus what the consequences of his choices will be.

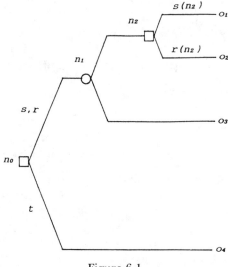

Figure 6.1

Granting the intelligibility of the concept of a *bounded* sequential decision problem, it will prove useful to develop a set of basic notation conventions for talking about such problems.

6.2 Trees and terminal outcomes

Let T be a bounded sequential decision problem. Such a problem can be schematized in terms of some initial chance or choice node, a set of subsequent choice and/or chance nodes, any one of which the agent may or may not end up encountering, depending on circumstances, and a set of terminal nodes or outcomes. Each terminal node or outcome o_i can be thought of as the consequence of a particular concatenation of choices made by the agent and randomly determined events (choices made by "nature"). For any T, let $O(T) = \{o_1, \ldots, o_n\}$ be the set of outcomes or consequences associated with T. In keeping with the notion of a bounded sequential decision problem, I shall suppose that with regard to whatever description of o_1, o_2, and so on, is relevant for purposes of evaluating the choices faced by the agent, there is no explicit reference to chance events and probabilities. That is, insofar as chance events and probabilities *explicitly* enter into the description of some outcome, I shall suppose that the outcome in question does not constitute a *terminal* node.[1]

6.3 Plans

The temporal thickness that characterizes a dynamic choice problem necessitates consideration of something that does not figure at all in static choice, namely, the notion of a plan – the specification of what is to be chosen, at one or more future points in time, subject to various contingent events taking place. A plan for a decision problem T, as I shall use the term here, consists of a complete specification of what choice is to be made at each choice node in T reachable as a result of the implementation of earlier portions of the plan. If T consists of just choice nodes, a plan will typically pick out a unique path through the tree, from an initial choice node n_0 to a particular terminal node o_i. If T also contains chance nodes, a plan specifies a unique path through the tree for each possible concatenation of randomly determined events. That is, in this case it constitutes a contingency plan that specifies what is to be chosen at each possible choice node, where the particular choice nodes at which the agent actually finds himself is partially a function of certain randomly determined events.[2] For any T, let $S(T)$, or S, where there is no ambiguity, be the set of plans available to the agent in T, and let s, r, and so on be elements of $S(T)$.

6.4 Truncated trees and plans

For any decision tree T, let $T(n_i)$ be the truncated part of the tree from node n_i to whatever terminal nodes can be reached from n_i. What the agent confronts at n_i can be thought of simply as a set of truncated plans, each of which calls for some sequence of choices to be made, the first member of the sequence being the choice to be made at n_i (if n_i is a choice node) or at some point reachable from n_i (if n_i is a chance node). Let $s(n_i)$ be a truncated plan available to the agent at point n_i. Correspondingly, let $S(n_i)$ be the set of plan truncations available at node n_i.

Given the notion of a truncated tree and that of a truncated plan, a plan itself can be specified in terms of what truncated plan it calls upon the agent to choose at each and every choice node in T reachable as a result of the implementation of some earlier portion of the plan. As an illustration, consider again Figure 6.1. The agent in this case has available a total of three plans. Plan s consists in choosing to head toward n_1 and then, if chance takes him to n_2, selecting $s(n_2)$, the path leading to the outcome o_1. Plan r consists in choosing to head toward n_1 and then, if chance takes him to n_2, selecting $r(n_2)$, the path leading to the outcome o_2. Plan t consists in choosing directly at n_0 the path leading to o_4.

6.5 The evaluation of plans

I shall suppose that even if the agent does not have an actual choice to be made at the outset of the decision tree – it being the case that nature has one or more moves to make before the agent does – still he can contemplate the plans available to him and, by application of what he takes to be relevant criteria of evaluation, rank them. All of this becomes not just possible but pressing, of course, once he reaches the first choice node. In keeping with the suggestions made in Chapter 2, I shall suppose that such evaluation is for the sake of deciding which plan is to be adopted, but I will not suppose that the criteria the agent employs to rank the alternatives must provide the basis for a uniquely acceptable choice.

Following the suggestion made in Section 2.10, the (partial) ranking on any given set of plans S can be taken to determine a set of acceptable plans $D(S)$. That is, for a given S, $D(S)$ is the subset of S consisting of those plans judged by the agent to be acceptable, by whatever evaluative criteria he employs. Since I do not assume that the evaluative approach adopted necessarily generates a connected ordering of the feasible set S, I do not assume that for any s and r in S, if s and r are in $D(S)$, then s and r are equally good. It might be that neither is ranked inferior to any other options, yet the method of evaluation leaves them unranked vis-à-vis each other. Similarly, the evaluative perspective may be such that within the context of some feasible set S, a plan s is judged acceptable while another plan r is not, but this is specifically *not* to be interpreted as implying that r would be judged inferior to s in pairwise comparison. This means that insofar as acceptable sets of plans can be thought of as determined by reference to some underlying ordering, that ordering is not necessarily either connected or context free. Correspondingly, there is no implication here that the acceptable sets so defined satisfy the context-free condition CF. However, since a decision tree is supposed to describe a forced-option situation in which the agent must choose some course of action, I shall suppose that insofar as the method of evaluation of plans he employs gives rise to any sort of ranking at all, that ranking is at least minimally coherent in the following sense: For any decision tree for which there is defined a finite set of plans, there is at least one plan that he does not rank below others. More generally, whether or not acceptable sets are determined by reference to some underlying ranking, I shall assume that $D(S)$ is nonempty for any $S(T)$. But, once again, since I want to adopt the most permissive framework possible, I will not assume that these nonempty acceptable sets can give rise, via some choice-based concept of preference, to a preference relation that is either connected or context free.

There is another limitation, one imposed by the very nature of decision trees and corresponding plans. Within the framework of sequential decision problems, sets of feasible plans are defined by the corresponding decision tree. On the usual account, given some S and corresponding $D(S)$, one can, in principle, go on to consider the family of sets $\{D(A): A$ is a subset of $S\}$. But the acceptable-set concept can

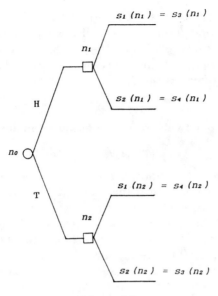

Figure 6.2

be adapted to plans only with a substantial modification. If S is the set of plans available to the agent given decision tree T, it does not follow that corresponding to every subset A of S there is a well-defined decision tree offering just the set of plans A. If s and t and r are plans in S, it may be that if the tree is altered so that r is no longer available, then t will no longer be available either. Consider, for example, the tree shown in Figure 6.2. In this instance, the agent has available four plans:

s_1 Take $s_1(n_1)$ if H; take $s_1(n_2)$ if T,
s_2 Take $s_2(n_1)$ if H; take $s_2(n_2)$ if T,
s_3 Take $s_3(n_1)$ if H; take $s_3(n_2)$ if T,
s_4 Take $s_4(n_1)$ if H; take $s_4(n_2)$ if T.

But there is no tree corresponding to the subset $A = \{s_1, s_3, s_4\}$. If s_2 is not available, then neither is s_4.

Thus, although I shall assume that the method of evaluation employed gives rise to a nonempty subset D for the set of plans S associated with each decision tree, one cannot suppose that D is defined for every subset A of S. Technically speaking, this means that one cannot assume that an acceptable-set function $D(\cdot)$ exists. The problem here, however, has nothing to do with potential "incoherences" in the underlying ordering; it is the result of the fact that in a decision tree framework, not every subset A of S is well defined; that is, the nature of decision trees is such that plans may not be structurally separable from one another. It is still possible to assume, however, that $D(A)$ is nonempty for every well-defined, that is, structurally separable, subset A of S, and this will suffice to ensure that MIC is, for all intents and purposes, satisfied.

6.6 Evaluation at subsequent nodes

Evaluating truncated plans

Suppose that the agent finds himself at a chance or a choice node n_i – how this happened is for the moment of no concern. What the agent now faces is a truncated tree $T(n_i)$, corresponding to which there is defined a set $S(n_i)$ of truncated plans, each of which describes a contingency plan for the sequence of choices that he can make from the point n_i on. Just as I have assumed that the agent is capable at the outset of evaluating the various alternative plans available to him, so I assume that at point n_i he is capable of evaluating the alternatives in $S(n_i)$ – the set of truncated plans that remain open to him at n_i. Correspondingly, let $D(S(n_i))$ be the set of truncated plans that the agent judges to be acceptable from the new vantage point of n_i.

Plan continuations and their evaluation

There is another perspective from which the agent can view the truncated plans available to him at any point n_i. The set S being the set of all plans available to the agent at the outset, which of those original plans can the agent continue to implement – either by making some choice at n_i, if n_i is a choice node, or by making some choice at a point reachable from n_i, if n_i is a chance node – if and when he arrives at n_i? Typically, upon arriving at n_i the agent will no longer be in a position to implement certain plans. That is, earlier choices will have resulted in a loss of certain opportunities. But by the same token, at n_i there must be plans in S that the agent is in a position to continue to implement. More specifically, for each truncated plan $s(n_i)$ that is available at n_i, there must exist some s in S such that $s(n_i)$ is the continuation of plan s from the point n_i forward. Alternatively put, each truncated plan $s(n_i)$ also specifies the balance of what *some* plan s requires to be done from node n_i on. This must be true of each truncated plan $s(n_i)$, since if n_i is reachable within the tree T and $s(n_i)$ is available at n_i, then it is possible to frame at the outset a contingency plan that calls upon one to implement $s(n_i)$, either by choosing $s(n_i)$ at n_i or by making some appropriate choice at a choice point reachable from n_i, if and when one arrives at n_i. Notice, however, that the relationship between truncated plans $s(n_i)$ and continuations of plans in S is not one – one: $s(n_i)$ may be the continuation of two distinct plans in S (which differ only with respect to what they require the agent to do at some other choice point in the decision tree).[3]

Thus, at n_i the agent can also think of himself as being faced not with a set of truncated plans, but with a set of plan continuations. When the agent conceptualizes the options at n_i in this manner, he is bound also to consider which of the plan continuations now available to him are among those he initially judged to be acceptable, that is which are continuations of members of $D(S)$. It can happen, of course, that for some arbitrarily selected node n_i, this node is not one that can be reached from any s in $D(S)$. In this case I shall say that $D(S)$ is not defined from node n_i on. But if the agent initially settled on a plan and proceeded to implement it, then (barring inadvertent moves on his part or other special conditioning circumstances) any point n_i at which the agent finds himself is one such that $D(S)$ will be defined. That is, if he has *intentionally* reached n_i, there will be some plan s in $D(S)$ that he can implement, either at n_i itself or at some choice point that can be reached from n_i.

More generally, and more formally, for any chance or choice node n_i, let $D(S)(n_i)$ be the set of all plans in $D(S)$ that the agent can still implement from the vantage point of n_i. Alternatively put, for any node n_i such that $D(S)$ is defined, $D(S)(n_i)$ is the restriction of $D(S)$ to just the continuations from n_i onward of plans in $D(S)$.

The distinction between acceptable truncated plans and acceptable plan continuations

$D(S(n_i))$ must be carefully distinguished from $D(S)(n_i)$. The latter encapsulates the implications for choice at n_i of the agent's evaluation of all the logically possible plans available to him, before any move in the tree by himself or by nature. In contrast, $D(S(n_i))$ encapsulates the implications for choice of the agent's evaluation of the options available at n_i from the vantage point of n_i itself.

Technically, this distinction between $D(S)(n_i)$ and $D(S(n_i))$ can be said to hold even in the special case in which $n_i = n_0$, the first node in the decision tree. It is reasonable to suppose, however, that whether n_0 is a choice or a chance node, $D(S) = D(S)(n_0) = D(S(n_0))$. The left-hand equation is immediate: At n_0, nothing has yet been closed out; thus, we must have $D(S) = D(S)(n_0)$. The right-hand equation follows from one (albeit not the only) way to settle a boundary matter. If the agent were to mark out the set of acceptable plans at some point before n_0 and then, upon arriving at n_0 itself, found himself evaluating the options differently, it would be just as intelligible to think of the agent as having reconsidered – as having made a tentative evaluation at some point before n_0, but then having firmed this up somewhat differently at n_0 itself. Since no move by the agent or by nature has yet taken place, it would seem that nothing hinges on how one chooses to describe this situation.

Evaluating truncated plans as de novo trees

The two perspectives that give rise to the distinction between $D(S)(n_i)$ and $D(S(n_i))$ do not exhaust those from which the truncated plans at n_i can be evaluated. To characterize the agent at n_i as being faced with choosing from the feasible set $S(n_i)$ is still to think of him as facing a choice against the background of past choices made and past events; of collateral but now counterfactual paths – that is, paths he could have taken but did not and of outcomes that might have been realized but will not be – all of which, taken together, define T. To think of the choice problem then confronting him in this manner is certainly natural, since the question is how the agent should choose at a certain point *within* a particular decision tree. But history and collateral (and now counterfactual) paths may be of no particular concern to him. This brings me, then, to a second fundamental evaluative distinction. It is possible that what the agent now conceives himself to be facing (from the vantage point of n_i) is a completely new decision tree, and one that presents him with a new set of options. From such a vantage point, once again, his concern is with the plans that are available to him, their respective outcomes, and the likelihoods of these various outcomes.

Formally, this can be expressed in the following manner. For any decision tree T and truncated tree $T(n_i)$ define another tree, $T(n_i)^d$, which is just like $T(n_i)$ except for having no history or collateral paths. That is, $T(n_i)$ is the tree truncation $T(n_i)$ conceived as a tree that begins de novo at choice point n_i. $T(n_i)^d$, unlike the truncated tree $T(n_i)$, is to be understood as a "full" tree in its own right. Correspondingly, define $S(n_i)^d$ as the set of plans available to the agent in $T(n_i)^d$, and $D(S(n_i)^d)$ as the set of plans for $T(n_i)^d$ that the agent judges to be acceptable. In contrast to $T(n_i)^d$, $T(n_i)$ denotes a decision tree situation with a past. The point is not simply that any agent who confronts $T(n_i)$ has some history that brought him to this juncture point but, rather, that for any choice point in T other than the initial choice point, $T(n_i)$ is, by definition, the continuation of some decision tree situation, which continuation poses for the agent options at n_i that he presumably anticipated, evaluated, and made plans about at some earlier point.

Summary of the three perspectives

For a given agent who finds himself at some point n_i in a decision tree T, there are three perspectives from which he can judge the plans available to him at that point – the plans associated with the truncated tree $T(n_i)$. First, he may consider which of the (truncated) plans now available at n_i are continuations of plans judged by him to be acceptable at the outset of T itself. This is given by the set $D(S)(n_i)$. Second, he may simply ask himself what he is now disposed to do at this point n_i, taking it as the appropriate vantage point from which to evaluate the options remaining. This defines the set $D(S(n_i))$. Third, he may ask himself what he would be disposed to do if he were presented with a choice problem just like the one he now faces, only it would be understood to be a de novo decision problem, that is, if he abstracted completely from the consideration that what brought him to this point was in part the partial execution of plans previously decided upon, and so on. To view his present problem in this way is to focus on the set $D(S(n_i)^{\mathrm{d}})$. I shall shortly consider what relationship, if any, should obtain among these three sets, that is, what the concept of rationality suggests about how they should be related; for the present it suffices to remark that the three sets are conceptually distinct.

6.7 Prospects

If a decision tree T consists just of choice nodes, then each plan s will typically have associated with it a unique consequence or outcome. The association is determined in the following manner: Let s be the plan in question. On the assumption that it calls for the agent to make a series of determinate choices, one at each of the choice nodes encountered, s can be said to pick out a unique path through the decision tree to a specific terminal outcome o_i. Alternatively put, o_i can be said to be the outcome that the agent can expect – on the assumption that he adopts and correctly executes s, that is, chooses, at each relevant choice point n_i, with probability 1 (or something approximating thereto), the plan continuation $s(n_i)$.

It is possible to imagine an even more complex sort of plan than those that meet the definition of "plan" given earlier. Up to this point I have assumed that the set of all plans is determined in a relatively simple manner by the structure of the decision tree and, thus, for example, that for any choice point n_i at which there are m distinct branches, $s_1(n_i), \ldots, s_m(n_i)$, there must be, correspondingly, at least m plans in S – one for each distinct choice available at n_i. But it is possible, of course, to extend the concept of a plan. It is open to the agent, upon arriving at n_i, to choose probabilistically between the m truncated plans available there. For example, he might, upon arriving at n_i, select an option there by the device of tossing a coin or rolling a die. Correspondingly, it is open to the agent to plan to choose probabilistically if and when he reaches n_i. In this case, even if the tree as initially defined consists just of choice points, some plans will have associated with them not a unique outcome, but a probability distribution over a set of such outcomes. As it turns out, plans that call for the agent to choose probabilistically at some choice node n_i play a key role in settling some issues about just what plans are feasible for a given agent in a given tree, and so this is a matter to which I shall have to return.[4]

For the present, however, it will suffice to note that if recognizing such special plans will complicate the mapping of plans into outcomes, just this sort of complication is unavoidable if the decision tree involves chance as well as choice nodes. Suppose, to take the simplest case first, the decision tree has chance nodes, but that there is a well-defined probability distribution over the set of alternative branches at each chance node and that these probability distributions are independent of one another and of the choices the agent makes. In such a case, it will be possible to associate with each plan s a risky prospect g_s, which consists of a well-defined probability distribution over some set of terminal outcomes. The relevant set of terminal outcomes is simply the set of all those terminal outcomes any one of which might possibly eventuate, given the implementation of plan s. The distribution can be computed by appeal to the usual addition and multiplication rules for independent events, taken in conjunction with the specified distributions over the relevant chance events and the assumption, once again, that if plan s calls for the agent to select a particular plan continuation $s(n_i)$ at n_i, and the agent has adopted that plan, then the agent will, with probability 1 (or something approximating thereto), select that continuation.

As an illustration, consider again the decision tree in Figure 6.1 and, in particular, plan s. Plan s calls for the agent to take $s(n_2)$, the path to o_1, in the event that chance determines that he gets to n_2. If the probability of ending up at n_2 is p and if, contingent upon his acting on plan s, the probability of his selecting $s(n_2)$ can be presumed to be (or closely approximate to) 1, then plan s has associated with it the prospect of getting o_1 with probability $(p)(1) = p$ and o_3 with probability $1 - p$.

In the case of more complicated trees, with chance events occurring serially, the prospect associated with any plan can be computed by first characterizing it in multistage form (involving gambles defined on gambles, as determined by all the possible serial orders of chance events) and then, by appeal to the reduction principles RD, reducing it to a simple gamble on some set of terminal outcomes. Thus, the notion of a prospect, as it will be employed here, appeals to what I have presupposed from the outset, that the agent's preference ordering over gambles satisfies condition RD. That is, regardless of the other features of his ordering of gambles, he is indifferent to all gambles that can be reduced to the same probability distribution over the same set of outcomes.[5]

In the event that probabilistic dependency of one sort or another obtains, matters are more complicated. Presumably, however, it will still be possible, for example, by appeal to principles governing conditional probabilities, to specify a prospect of the sort mentioned above. That is, so long as the relevant probability distributions are well defined, it will be possible to project some probability distribution over the set of relevant terminal outcomes.

Suppose, finally, that the decision tree involves chance nodes, but the probability distributions are not well defined. In this case, obviously, it would prove very useful if there were a theory of indeterminate probabilities to which appeal could be made, a theory that proposed a way of conceptualizing uncertainties and that specified principles (if any) governing the combining of indeterminate probabilities under conjunctive and/or disjunctive concatenations of events. At the same time, in view of the consideration that the dynamic choice setting may prove useful for providing an underpinning for the theory not only of expected utility but also of subjective probability, it is desirable to leave the dynamic framework relatively open in this regard. In particular, what is needed is a general characterization that leaves open the possibility that the best one can do – at least initially – is to associate with each plan s some more or less determinate prospect – some set of possible terminal outcomes plus some (perhaps only partial) specification of the likelihoods of reaching each such terminal outcome.

It should be noted here, however, that just as in the static setting of simple choices among gambles, the way in which certain particular events concatenate can lead to some plausible inferences concerning the determinateness of associated probability distributions. For example, suppose the agent confronts the following sequential version of the second of the Ellsberg counterexamples discussed in Section 4.5 (see Figure 6.3). That is, a fair coin is to be tossed and if it comes up heads (H) the agent has a choice between rights to the uncertain prospect $g = [\$0, E; \$100, \text{not-}E]$ or \$25 outright, whereas if it comes up tails (T) he has a choice between the uncertain prospect $g^* = [\$100, E; \$0, \text{not-}E]$ or \$25 outright. Let s be the plan that calls

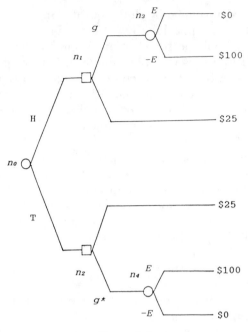

Figure 6.3

upon him to select g if H and g^* if T. This plan has terminal outcomes of $0 and $100. Once again, following the reasoning developed in Section 4.5, it makes no difference, from the perspective of n_0, if the probability distribution over $\{E, \text{not-}E\}$ is completely or partially unknown. On the assumption that the toss of the coin and the turn of events $\{E, \text{not -}E\}$ are independent of one another and that the agent expects that if he acts on plan s he will with probability (approximating to) 1 choose g in the event that E, and will with probability (approximating to) 1 choose g^* in the event that not-E, plan s has associated with it the well-defined even-chance prospect of getting either $0 or $100.

In very general terms, then, for any tree T and associated plan s in S, let g_s be the prospect that can be associated with s and let G_S be the set of prospects that can be associated in this manner with T. Notice, moreover, that the distinctions made above carry over smoothly to the case in which what are contemplated are the prospects to be associated with a truncated plan $s(n_i)$. Correspondingly, then, for any tree T and associated truncated plan $s(n_i)$ defined at n_i, let $g_{s(n_i)}$ be the prospect that can be associated, from the perspective of n_i itself, with $s(n_i)$; and let $G_{S(n_i)}$ be the set of prospects that can be associated with the truncated tree defined by $S(n_i)$.

6.8 An important qualification

The framework just described, it should be noted, is minimal. It certainly would not suffice for a comprehensive and constructive treatment of actual dynamic choice problems.[6] Nor is it particularly elegant from a formal point of view. The reader will find a more sophisticated, and much more formal, characterization of decision trees in, for example, Hammond.[7] My concern here, however, is exclusively with sorting out certain foundational issues. To this end, I have sought to get out just enough of a formal framework to capture the essence of the consequentialist version of pragmatic reasoning employed by Hammond, to explore what I think are its significant limitations, and finally to establish a basis for a more careful formulation of certain other pragmatic arguments.

7

Rationality conditions on dynamic choice

7.1 Introduction

The preceding chapter focused exclusively on distinctions and notation conventions that should prove useful for characterizing the logic of dynamic choice. In this chapter I shall explore a set of conditions that some have thought might plausibly be imposed on any pattern of dynamic choice that is to qualify as rational.

By way of anticipating the substance of the next chapter, the conditions in question can be read as providing one way in which one can factor Hammond's consequentialist principle for dynamic choice, although one must proceed with caution in this regard, since (as indicated at the close of the preceding chapter) Hammond's own construction is considerably more elaborate, and (as I shall indicate more carefully as I proceed) he views the notion of "dynamic consistency" somewhat differently than I do. Roughly speaking, however, the conditions to be explored do capture what Hammond regards as a consequentialist approach, and collectively they can be seen to suffice for the derivation of CF and CIND, the choice-set versions, respectively, of CFO and IND. As such, they manage to provide a simplified and thus, one would hope, perspicuous model of the sort of consequentialist argument that he and others have thought could be constructed in favor of these two basic presuppositions of the modern theory of rationality.

In the presentation to follow, however, I shall develop these conditions in isolation from Hammond's own arguments. That is, I shall approach them as conditions each one of which has at least some (if only minimal) claim to qualify as a rationality condition and which can be motivated without reference to Hammond's rather ambitious and elaborate project. In part, this is because I think each of these conditions does have a certain prima facie plausibility. But even more to the point, the particular set of conditions to be isolated has, I believe, significant implications for a more general pragmatic approach. In this sense, the present chapter (together with the preceding chapter) provides a framework not only for understanding Hammond's consequentialist argument but for fully appreciating what turns out to be a much more general class of pragmatic arguments – the class of arguments that are the focus of Chapters 9 through 12.

7.2 Simple reduction

The first, and perhaps least controversial, of the conditions I want to consider amounts to a modest extension to the dynamic choice framework of the simple reduction condition RD, which I mentioned in Section 3.2 and discussed again in Section 4.2. The suggestion made there was that (at the very least) rational agents who act in some sort of public or professional capacity and who are faced with evaluating gambles will be concerned only with outcomes and probability distributions over outcomes.

Now consider the very special and limiting case of a decision tree in which each plan available to the agent requires for its implementation a single initial choice by the agent; that is, n_0 is a choice node and all subsequent nodes are chance nodes. Under these conditions, the agent faces a decision tree problem that is essentially equivalent to a simple nonsequential choice among various gambles. And if we are prepared to presuppose that the agent's static choice among gambles is constrained by the consideration that only outcomes and probabilities count, that is, by RD, then it is plausible to impose an analogous condition here and require that the ranking of plans in this limiting case of a dynamic choice problem be a function of the ranking of the prospects that can be associated with each of those plans. Reformulating this as a condition on acceptable sets, this yields the following:

Simple reduction (SR). Let T be any decision tree with associated set of plans S such that each plan s in S requires for its implementation a single choice "up front" by the agent, and let G_S be the set of prospects associated with such plans. Then for any plan s in S and associated prospect g_s in G_S, s is in $D(S)$ iff g_s is in $D(G_S)$.

7.3 Plan reduction conditions

The reduction condition SR itself has an extension that is more controversial. The extension is achieved by simply dropping the qualifier "such that each plan s in S requires for its implementation a single choice 'up front' by the agent." The motivation for this condition involves, once again, an extension of the reasoning in support of SR. That is, it is natural to think of choice as being undertaken for the sake of what one expects to realize thereby and, hence, to think of the value of a given plan as essentially a function of the value one is prepared to assign to its associated prospect. The notion here is that what counts is not the plan itself but what can result from pursuing that plan, together, in the case of trees involving chance events, with the likelihoods of these possible outcomes.

Specifically, one can consider postulating that if at the outset there are two plans whose associated prospects are judged by the agent to be equivalent in value, the two plans should be assigned the same value, regardless of how the plans may themselves differ – with respect to order of events and choices, and so on. Since the thrust of such a principle is to say that for purposes of evaluation any plan can be reduced to its associated prospect, that is, a schedule of possible outcomes and more or less determinate information about likelihoods, this amounts to a *reduction* principle. And, once again, it will prove sufficient to utilize a version of this principle that is formulated in terms of acceptable sets. What is required is that there be a coincidence between the acceptable sets defined over prospects and the acceptable sets defined over the plans that map into these prospects:

> *Plan reduction (PR).* Let T be any decision tree with associated set of plans S, and let G_S be the set of prospects associated with such plans. Then for any plan s in S and associated prospect g_s in G_S, s is in $D(S)$ iff g_s is in $D(G_S)$.

So formulated, PR is a strong condition. The prospect to be associated with a plan is the prospect defined by supposing that the agent flawlessly executes that plan regardless of the turn of events. Thus, PR makes no concession to inadvertent error or, even more important, to the proverbial problem of weakness of will or, more generally, to any qualifying belief the agent might come to entertain concerning the likelihood that he will carry through on the plan. I shall subsequently consider how this condition might be weakened.[1] For the moment, however, it should be noted that appreciation of the strength of the condition does not automatically undercut its plausibility. Insofar as the agent conceives himself as a deliberative being, his projection of his own future behavior may well be a function (at least in certain settings) of what he judges to be the relative attractiveness of the prospects associated with the different plans. That is, although one may want to insist that there are conditions under which the agent will come to entertain doubts concerning whether he will in fact carry through on some plan, it would also seem clear that one natural basis on which a person might come to expect that he will execute some plan is precisely his concluding that the plan in question has associated with it a prospect that is more attractive than that associated with any other plan open to him.

The more limited reduction condition SR is a special case of, and hence immediately implied by, PR. It will prove useful, however, to factor PR. What PR adds to SR is that there is no evaluative distinction to be made between plans in *normal* and *extensive* form, to borrow a bit of terminology from the theory of games.[2] By way of explaining this distinction, consider any plan s in $S(T)$, and suppose that T is altered so that at the very outset the agent can implement any plan in T simply by means of a single choice. More concretely, suppose that for any plan s, there is some mechanism such that if it is actuated at the very outset it will automatically and flawlessly execute all the subsequent choices called for by s, subject to the relevant contingencies. Let s^n be the *normal-form* version of s, T^n be the normal-form version of T, and S^n be the set of plans in T^n. The requisite condition, then, can be formulated as follows:

Normal-form/extensive-form coincidence (NEC). Let T be any decision tree with associated set of plans S, and let T^n be the decision problem that results by converting each s in S into its normal form, so that each s in S is mapped into s^n in S^n. Then for any plan s in S, s is in $D(S)$ iff s^n is in $D(S^n)$.

The relation between SR, NEC, and PR can be formally captured in the following propositions:

Proposition 7.1. NEC and SR together imply PR.

Proof. Since NEC ensures that the acceptable set of plans $D(S)$ associated with any tree coincides with the acceptable set of normal-form plans $D(S^n)$ that can be associated with that same tree, and SR ensures that the acceptable set of normal-form plans $D(S^n)$ coincides with the acceptable set $D(G_{S^n})$ for the corresponding prospects, SR and NEC together yield that s is in $D(S)$ iff g_{s^n} is in $D(G_{S^n})$. But recall that by the construction device described above, normal- and extensive-form versions of plans map into the same prospects, that is, $G_{S^n} = G_S$; hence, s is in $D(S)$ iff g_s is in $D(G_S)$.

Proposition 7.2. PR implies both NEC and SR.

Proof. The more restricted condition SR is simply a special case of PR; hence, PR implies SR. But also, by construction, both s and s^n map into the same prospect. Hence, by PR, if s is in $D(S)$, then $g_s = g_{s^n}$ is in $D(G_s) = D(G_{S^n})$, and by PR again, if g_{s^n} is in $D(G_{S^n})$, then s^n is in $D(S^n)$. Thus, if s is in $D(S)$, s^n is in $D(S^n)$.

Since the argument is reversible, one has the desired conclusion.

This immediately yields the following:

Proposition 7.3. PR is logically equivalent to the conjunction of NEC and SR.

7.4 Dynamic consistency

Consider any finite decision tree that an agent confronts. Whatever method he uses to evaluate the plans available to him, that evaluation will form the basis for deciding what plan to pursue. But even if he decides on a plan s, it does not follow that he will end up implementing plan s. In fact, there are clearly circumstances under which he will depart from that plan. For example, he may acquire new information concerning the outcomes of this or that plan, in which case he will have to redescribe the terminal nodes. Alternatively, he may learn that the order of events has been altered or that the likelihood of the conditioning events is other than he originally thought them to be, in which case he will have to redescribe the structure of the tree itself. In either case, the new information may (although it need not) require a reevaluation of available plans and a revision of his commitment to the plan on which he originally settled. Of course, deviation from adopted plans is also possible in cases in which the agent comes into possession of no new information of the kind just mentioned. Given inherent limitations in computational ability and other related skills, one cannot rule out the possibility of inadvertent error. As a result, even the most rational agent may simply fail to execute the plan on which he originally settled. Thus, there could be nothing like a blanket assumption that a rational agent will always adhere to the plan he originally adopted.

Abstracting from cases involving new information or the problem of unintentional error, it does seem reasonable to require, however, that there be consistency between planned choice and actual choice. Ceteris paribus, one expects that a rational agent will proceed to implement the plan he initially adopts, particularly when the choice of a plan is based on some systematic evaluation of alternative plans. To adapt a term that has acquired some currency in the literature, one can refer to this as a requirement that choice be *dynamically consistent.*[3]

As an illustration of the requirement of dynamic consistency, consider the tree in Figure 6.1. Suppose that the agent *correctly* anticipates the structure of choices, chance events, payoff possibilities, and so on that are about to unfold, looks ahead to the possible outcomes of the choices available at n_2 and the likelihood of being in a position to make such a choice, and then either judges both t and r to be unacceptable, and so chooses s, or judges both t and s, but not r, to be acceptable, and then picks s. In the former case, since s is the only acceptable alternative and since it can be realized only by a move toward n_1, and then, in the event that he arrives at n_2 choosing $s(n_2)$ rather than $r(n_2)$, the agent moves toward n_1, planning to choose $s(n_2)$ if and when the opportunity presents itself. In the latter case, finding both s and t acceptable, he ends up adopting plan s and, hence, moving toward n_1, planning to choose $s(n_2)$ if and when the opportunity presents itself. Given either account of how he comes to head toward n_1, it remains possible that if and when he gets to n_2, he may find (even though he is in possession of no new information) that he now regards $r(n_2)$ as the only acceptable choice, despite his earlier intentions, and accordingly ends up choosing $r(n_2)$ instead of $s(n_2)$.

Under the conditions specified, the agent acquires between n_0 and n_2 no new information – there is no unanticipated change in his prospects – but there is still a disparity between what from the vantage point of n_0 he intended to choose at n_2 and what he ends up choosing at n_2 upon arriving at that point in the decision tree. To be sure, upon arriving at n_2, the agent knows, after the fact, the outcome of the random event at n_1; but the presumption is that at n_0 he was fully aware that he would come to know the outcome of the chance event at n_1, in the event that he chose to head toward n_1 and that he took this into account in his original deliberations.

Notice, moreover, that the type of inconsistency here under consideration cannot be explicated in terms of the notion that the two choices in question cannot implement one and the same plan. Each available choice at any given choice point is always consistent with *some* plan that it is then open to the agent to execute. For every truncated plan at a choice point there is a corresponding plan; that is, each truncated plan is the continuation of a plan the implementation of which has not yet been ruled out by the agent's previous choice behavior. In moving through the tree, he continually reduces the number of plans he can still implement. But each one whose implementation has yet to be ruled out is a plan whose next stage could be implemented at the next node, and the decision to do this is, then, consistent with all choices made previously. Thus, any two (or more) actual, successive choices will always be consistent with one another in the sense that both can be understood as implementing steps in the execution of some particular plan. In short, if dynamic consistency means consistency in this sense, then however the agent chooses as he goes through the tree, he chooses in a dynamically consistent manner.[4]

I have suggested diagnosing dynamic inconsistency in terms of a disparity between the plan originally adopted and subsequent choice. I have also assumed that the plan adopted by the agent is one that he judges to be acceptable at n_0 and that the particular choice that he makes at some subsequent choice point will be from among those truncated plans he finds acceptable from that vantage point. This suggests formulating the condition of dynamic consistency in terms of some sort of inclusion relation between $D(S)$, the acceptable set of plans, and in particular what $D(S)$ implies with regard to each subsequent choice node, that is, $D(S)(n_i)$, and $D(S(n_i))$, the set of acceptable truncated plans available to the agent at n_i. That is, the requirement of dynamic consistency can be formulated in terms of a condition on the relation between what the agent judges from the standpoint of the initial node of the tree to be an acceptable choice to make at n_i (if and when he gets to that choice point) and what he judges from the standpoint of n_i itself to be an acceptable choice to make at n_i.

Construed in this way, dynamic consistency requires at the very least that at any given choice point n_i in the decision tree for which $D(S)(n_i)$ is nonempty, the intersection of $D(S)(n_i)$ and $D(S(n_i))$ be nonempty. Since evaluation is for the sake of choice, one may suppose that the plan adopted is a member of $D(S)$ and, correspondingly, what is chosen (or picked) at choice point n_i is a member of $D(S(n_i))$. If the intersection is empty, then upon finding himself at n_i, the agent will have to choose in a manner that is not consistent with the plan adopted. In more formal terms:

Intersect. For any choice point n_i in a decision tree T, if $D(S)(n_i)$ is nonempty, then $D(S)(n_i)$ intersect $D(S(n_i))$ is nonempty.

Intersect has a natural extension. Suppose that $D(S)(n_i)$ is nonempty and, hence, that n_i is a choice point at which the agent can arrive by implementing an acceptable plan. Specifically, let s be a plan in $D(S)$ for which $s(n_i)$ is defined and let $s(n_i)$ be in $D(S(n_i))$, thereby ensuring that the above condition is satisfied. Now let $r(n_i)$ be a plan continuation from choice point n_i onward of some plan r, and suppose that $r(n_i)$ is also in $D(S(n_i))$, but that there is no plan r in $D(S)$ for which $r(n_i)$ is the continuation. In this case, it will be possible that upon arriving at n_i the agent will pick $r(n_i)$ rather than $s(n_i)$, thereby choosing at n_i in a fashion that is not consistent with the adopted plan. To avoid this, one can require that there must be *some* acceptable plan in $D(S)$ whose continuation at n_i is $r(n_i)$.[5] Stated more formally:

Inclusion (DC-INC). For any choice point n_i in a decision tree T, if $D(S)(n_i)$ is nonempty and $s(n_i)$ is in $D(S(n_i))$, then there is some plan $s*$ in $D(S)$ such that $s(n_i) = s*(n_i)$ is the plan continuation of $s*$ at n_i, and hence such that $s(n_i) = s*(n_i)$ is in $D(S)(n_i)$.

Clearly, this is much stronger than the previously formulated intersect condition and implies it.

The question now arises whether the converse must also hold. If s is in $D(S)$ and s calls for choice of $s(n_i)$ at n_i, must $s(n_i)$ be in $D(S(n_i))$? One can notice, first of all, that if $D(S)$ is a unit set, then clearly the agent will end up choosing in a manner inconsistent with his plan unless $s(n_i)$ is in $D(S(n_i))$. But suppose that both s and r are in $D(S)$, both are defined for n_i, and $s(n_i)$ is, while $r(n_i)$ is *not*, in $D(S(n_i))$. If and when the agent arrives at n_i, the intersection of $D(S)(n_i)$ and $D(S(n_i))$ is nonempty – $s(n_i)$ is by hypothesis in both – and every plan continuation in $D(S(n_i))$ is in $D(S)(n_i)$ – namely, $s(n_i)$ – so both of the aforementioned conditions are satisfied. By hypothesis, since only $s(n_i)$ is in $D(S(n_i))$, the agent will never choose other than $s(n_i)$ at n_i. Thus, $r(n_i)$ will never be chosen. By hypothesis, however, r is in $D(S)$, and it is therefore possible that the agent adopts r at the outset. On such occasions the agent will, then, adopt a given plan s only to choose subsequently in a manner inconsistent with s. One can rule this possibility out by requiring the following:

Exclusion (DC-EXC). For any choice point n_i in a decision tree T, if $s(n_i)$ is defined and $s(n_i)$ is not in $D(S(n_i))$, then s is not in $D(S)$.

Note the parallel here to the way in which DC-INC was explicated. There it was argued that if n_i is reachable by partial execution of an acceptable plan and $s(n_i)$ is in $D(S(n_i))$, then $s(n_i)$ may well be chosen at n_i; thus, if there is no corresponding plan s in $D(S)$, whose plan continuation at n_i is in $D(S)(n_i)$, the agent may well end up choosing at n_i in a manner inconsistent with his plans. In the present case, the requirement is that plan s *not* be in $D(S)$ if there are conditions under which it will never be executed. If s is an acceptable plan, the agent may well adopt s as his plan. But if there exists a choice node n_i at which $s(n_i)$ is defined but never chosen, then there will be occasions on which the agent will end up choosing in a manner inconsistent with his plan. That is, in the one case, s is to be included in $D(S)$ because it is projected that under certain conditions $s(n_i)$ will be selected; in the other case, s is to be excluded from $D(S)$ on the grounds that in the event that the agent arrives at n_i, the continuation $s(n_i)$ will never be chosen.

The combination of the inclusionary and the exclusionary conditions yields the following:

Dynamic consistency (DC). For any choice point n_i in a decision tree T, if $D(S)(n_i)$ is not empty and $s(n_i)$ is in $D(S(n_i))$, then $s(n_i)$ is in $D(S)(n_i)$; and if $s(n_i)$ is in $D(S)(n_i)$, then $s(n_i)$ is in $D(S(n_i))$.

I have proceeded as if consistency of plans with future choices is consistency between what is adopted at some initial planning session and what is done at some future occasion for choice. But the agent continues to plan (i.e., intend) as he moves through the tree. At any given node prior to some last choice to be made by the agent (in a bounded decision tree), one can mark the agent's plans with respect to whatever choices remain to be made and then observe whether he subsequently chooses in a manner consistent with those plans. In terms of the use to be made of the dynamic framework, however, this more general characterization of dynamic inconsistency is unnecessary. It will suffice to consider a simple decision tree, with plans being settled on at the first choice point and full implementation not effected until a selection is made at a subsequent choice point.

7.5 Separability

One additional condition remains to be considered. Recall that when an agent has settled on a plan and arrives at some intermediate point n_i, what he then confronts is a truncated tree $T(n_i)$. In turn, $T(n_i)$ has associated with it a set of truncated plans $S(n_i)$, and each $s(n_i)$ in $S(n_i)$ has associated with it a prospect $g_{s(n_i)}$ in $G_{S(n_i)}$, where the latter consists of the set of prospects that correspond one to one with the truncated plans in $S(n_i)$. Moreover, this set of prospects would seem to provide a natural reference point for the evaluation of the corresponding truncated plans, and hence for the determination of $D(S(n_i))$.

Indeed, the intuition of many has been that $G_{S(n_i)}$ provides not just *a* natural reference point, but *the* appropriate reference point, for the evaluation of the options at n_i. The details of the case for this will vary, depending on what kind of decision problem is being modeled. For the type of decision problem with which I shall shortly be very much concerned – involving just two stages of choice and where, in virtue of a commitment to SR, the agent is disposed to view plans simply as access routes to prospects – this intuition is captured in a principle to the effect that the prospects the agent confronts at the subsequent point in the tree are *controlling* for choice at that point.

Such a principle constitutes an extension of the plan reduction condition PR. It will be recalled that PR makes the ordering of prospects controlling for the ordering of plans. However, PR is limited to whole plans. This suggests, in turn, the following extended requirement:

> *Truncated plan reduction (TR).* Let n_i be any node in a decision tree T, and let $S(n_i)$ be the set of truncated plans that can be associated with $T(n_i)$. Then $s(n_i)$ is in $D(S(n_i))$ iff $g_{s(n_i)}$ is in $D(G_{S(n_i)})$.

TR requires that the ordering of the set of plan truncations be a function of the ordering of the set of associated prospects that are still open to the agent at that point in the decision tree – considered in isolation from any other possibilities. That is, if TR holds, one can look at the ordering of prospects associated with any truncated tree and be assured as to the ordering of plan truncations, regardless of the larger tree in which those truncations are embedded. This means in particular that the ordering of the truncated plans at point n_1 is independent of what prospects might have been available to the agent at previous points in the decision tree. What are from the perspective of point n_i counterfactual possibilities – prospects that the agent might have realized had he chosen differently at some earlier point in the tree and/or had nature made a different move – can have no influence on the ordering of prospects, and hence truncated plans, at n_i.

As an illustration, consider once again the simple tree in Figure 6.1. There is a choice node n_0, at which one can either choose t or proceed forward, deferring choice between s and r until node n_2. If TR holds, we can be sure that the ranking between $s(n_2)$ and $r(n_2)$ is invariant in the following sense: For any other tree T^* and choice node n_i^*, at which there are only two plan truncations $s(n_i^*)$ and $r(n_i^*)$ whose associated prospects $g_{s(n_i^*)}$ and $g_{r(n_i^*)}$ are such that $g_{s(n_i^*)} = g_{s(n_2)} = o_1$ and $g_{r(n_i^*)} = g_{r(n_2)} = o_2$, the ordering between $s(n_i^*)$ and $r(n_i^*)$ will be the same as that between $s(n_2)$ and $r(n_2)$, regardless of what other choices are available in T^*.

Since PR is simply TR restricted to the case where $n_i = n_0$, TR immediately implies PR. But once again, it will prove useful to factor TR. This can be accomplished by distinguishing between $T(n_i)$ and $T(n_i)^d$, between the truncated tree that results from considering T just from node n_i onward and a tree that is like $T(n_i)$ in every respect except that it begins de novo at that node n_i.

Now suppose that PR holds. Then it holds for T^d, since it is a whole tree. By PR, then, $s(n_i)^d$ is in $D(S(n_i)^d)$ iff $g_{s(n_i)^d}$ is in $D(G_{S(n_i)^d})$. Note, however, that by construction, $G_{S(n_i)^d} = G_{S(n_i)}$. That is, the set of prospects associated with the truncated tree $T(n_i)$ is equivalent to the set of prospects associated with the de novo version of $T(n_i)$. Thus, we have that $s(n_i)^d$ is in $D(S(n_i)^d)$ iff $g_{s(n_i)}$ is in $D(G_{S(n_i)})$. Thus, if we can assume, in addition, that $s(n_i)$ is in $D(S(n_i))$ iff $s(n_i)^d$ is in $D(S(n_i)^d)$, TR will then be secured; that is, it will then follow that $s(n_i)$ is in $D(S(n_i))$ iff $g_{s(n_i)}$ is in $D(G_{S(n_i)})$.

What is needed, then, in addition to PR, is the following condition, linking $D(S(n_i))$ and $D(S(n_i)^d)$:

> *Separability (SEP).* For any tree T and any node n_i within T, let $T(n_i)^d$ be a separate tree that begins at a node that corresponds to n_i but otherwise coincides with $T(n_i)$, and let $S(n_i)^d$ be the set of plans available in $T(n_i)^d$ that correspond one to one with the set of truncated plans $S(n_i)$ available in $T(n_i)$. Then $s(n_i)$ is in $D(S(n_i))$ iff $s(n_i)^d$ is in $D(S(n_i)^d)$.

That is, SEP requires that the agent choose in $T(n_i)$ as if he were choosing from the separate tree $T(n_i)^d$ that corresponds to $T(n_i)$.[6]

From this, moreover, Proposition 7.4 immediately follows:

Proposition 7.4. The conjunction of PR and SEP implies TR.

Thus, TR is best understood as a derivative condition – one that can be secured by adding SEP to the conditions already delineated.

As an explication of SEP itself, notice that it requires that choice at n_i not be based on what might have happened, or what alternatives would have been available, under conditions that do not in fact obtain at choice point n_i. The suggestion is that at any point in the tree the agent is faced with a particular feasible set, determined by what the state of the world is, where that state is itself to be understood as a function of which immediately preceding chance branch was selected by nature or, alternatively, which choice the agent made at an immediately prior choice point. It can be argued, then, that the acceptable options in the feasible set he now confronts should be independent of what might have been had nature, or he himself, chosen differently at some prior node. That is, choice from the present feasible set should be independent of those other sets that are associated with alternative but counterfactual choices or moves by nature. What such a requirement precludes, then, is treating counterfactual aspects of one's position at n_i as part of the discriminatory basis for choice at n_i.[7]

7.6 Summary of dynamic choice conditions

I have been concerned here with three basic conditions special to a theory of dynamic choice. DC requires that choice in a decision tree be dynamically consistent: The (series of) choice(s) that an agent makes should be consistent with the plan that the agent adopts at the outset (subject, of course, to a caveat permitting a change in plans in the light of new information). NEC requires that choice be invariant with respect to normalization: it should make no difference to choice whether one is presented with the normal- or the extensive-form version of any plan. SEP requires that dynamic choice satisfy a separability condition: How one is prepared to evaluate the options still available at some point within the context of the tree – in the context of choices and chance events already executed – should be independent of that context. More specifically, how one would choose if one were to confront those options de novo should determine how one would choose among them at any given point within the decision tree.

In addition to these three conditions, I have also introduced a condition that represents a very modest extension of the reduction assumption RD that is central to the theory of static choice. This is SR, according to which the ordering of simple, nonsequential plans should be a function of the ordering of the prospects associated with those plans. That is, how one would choose among abstractly presented sets of prospects should determine how one chooses among simple plans that directly access those prospects.

7.7 The relation between SR, NEC, DC, and SEP

What logical relation, if any, obtains between each of these four conditions and the others? As it turns out, no one of the conditions is logically entailed by any one, or any pair, or even the conjunction of all three, of the other conditions. More specifically, consider the following:

Proposition 7.5. If choice in decision trees satisfies SR, NEC, and DC, it does not follow that it satisfies SEP.

Proof. This is immediate. SR and DC set restrictions on acceptable sets internal to a given decision tree and its related prospects, whereas NEC and SEP require a link between the acceptable set for plans in one tree and the acceptable set for plans in a logically distinct tree. Moreover, the linkage required by NEC, pertaining to the relation between $D(S)$ and $D(S^n)$, is entirely distinct from that required by SEP, which pertains to the relation between $D(S(n_i))$ and $D(S(n_i)^d)$.

Proposition 7.6. If choice in decision trees satisfies SEP, NEC, and DC, it does not follow that it satisfies SR.

Proof. Let T, T^n, and $T(n_2)^d$ be the decision trees shown in Figure 7.1. Plan s calls for selecting $s(n_2)$, and plan r calls for

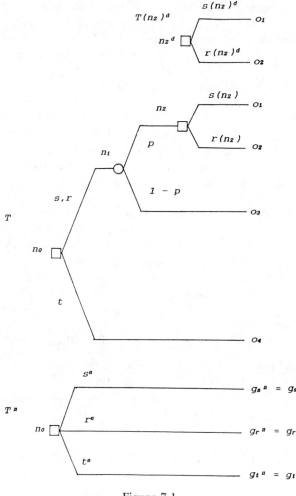

Figure 7.1

selecting $r(n_2)$ in the event one arrives at n_2. The truncated plan $s(n_2)$ has as outcome o_1 and the truncated plan $r(n_2)$ has as outcome o_2. There is a probability of $1 - p$ of ending up with outcome o_3 if one selects either s or r, and n_0 is the choice node at which one must choose to pursue either s or r, on the one hand, or some other plan t, on the other. At n_0, plan s accesses the prospect $g_s = [o_1, p; o_3, 1 - p]$ and r accesses $g_r = [o_2, p; o_3, 1 - p]$. Decision tree T^n is the normal-form version of T, with normal-form plans $s^n r^n$ corresponding to s, r, and $t^n = t$. $T(n_2)^d$ is the de novo version of $T(n_2)$, with plan $s(n_2)^d$ leading to o_1 and $r(n_2)^d$ leading to o_2.

Now suppose that both $s(n_2)^d$ and $r(n_2)^d$ are in $D(S(n_2))^d$, and both $s(n_2)$ and $r(n_2)$ are in $D(S(n_2))$. Then SEP will be satisfied. Suppose also that both s and r are in $D(S)$; then DC is satisfied for T. Finally suppose both s^n and r^n are in $D(S^n)$. Then NEC is satisfied. But nothing so far constrains the ranking over o_1 and o_2 and over g_s^n and g_r^n. Suppose, for example, that o_1 is, and o_2 is not, in $D(\{o_1, o_2\})$. Then SR is violated in $T(n_2)^d$. And if g_s^n is, and g_r^n is not, in $D(G_{S^n})$, then SR is violated in T^n.

Proposition 7.7. If choice in decision trees satisfies SEP, SR, and DC, it does not follow that it satisfies NEC.

Proof: Consider again the trees in Figure 7.1. Suppose $s(n_2)^d$ is, and $r(n_2)^d$ is not, in $D(S(n_2)^d)$, and $s(n_2)$ is, and $r(n_2)$ is not, in $D(S(n_2))$. Then SEP is satisfied. If s is in $D(S)$ but r is not, then DC is satisfied for T. If o_1 is, and o_2 is not, in $D(\{o_1, o_2\})$, then SR is satisfied for $T(n_2)^d$, and if both s^n and r^n are in $D(S^n)$ and both g_{s^n} and g_{r^n} are in $D(G_{S^n})$, then SR is satisfied for T^n. But in this case, NEC fails to be satisfied, since r is not in $D(S)$, whereas r^n is in $D(S^n)$.

Proposition 7.8. If choice behavior in decision trees satisfies SR, NEC, and SEP, it does not follow that it satisfies DC.

Proof. Consider again the trees in Figure 7.1. Suppose that all of the following are true:

(1) o_1 is, and o_2 is not, in $D(\{o_1, o_2\})$,
(2) $s(n_2)$ is, and $r(n_2)$ is not, in $D(S(n_2))$,
(3) $s(n_2)^d$ is, and $r(n_2)^d$ is not, in $D(S(n_2)^d)$,
(4) only r is in $D(S)$,
(5) only g_r is in $D(\{g_s, g_r, g_t\})$,
(6) only r^n is in $D(S^n)$.

From (1) and (3), it follows that SR is satisfied for acceptable plans in $T(n_2)^d$; (5) and (6) imply that SR is satisfied for acceptable plans in T^n; (4) and (6) imply that NEC is satisfied; and (2) and (3) imply that SEP is satisfied. But (4) together with (2) implies a violation of DC, since (4) and DC imply that $r(n_2)$ is in $D(S(n_2))$, which contradicts (2). In this instance, then, DC fails to be satisfied while all of SR, NEC, and SEP are satisfied.[8]

Combining Propositions 7.5 through 7.8, one obtains the following:

Proposition 7.9. No one of the four conditions SR, NEC, SEP, and DC is logically implied by the conjunction of the other three, nor is it, then, implied by any subset of the other conditions.

It is also possible to show that all of the conditions in question can be jointly satisfied in any (finite) decision tree:

Proposition 7.10. There exist preference orderings defined over a given set of outcomes (or prospects), as well as orderings defined on the subsets thereof, such that regardless of the tree structure into which such outcomes and prospects are embedded, the implied acceptable sets for all of the relevant sets (and subsets) of plans will satisfy all of SR, NEC, SEP, and DC.

Proof. Anticipating material to be discussed in Chapter 8, Hammond has shown that if a preference ordering defined over outcomes (and prospects) satisfies WO and certain independence requirements, then his consequentialist principle will be satisfied for all finite decision trees. But on my reading, his consequentialist principle implies all of SR, NEC, SEP, and DC.[9] Thus, if preferences for outcomes and prospects satisfy WO and various independence conditions, all of SR, NEC, SEP, and DC will be satisfied in any finite decision tree.

This is not to say, of course, that all of SR, NEC, SEP, and DC can be satisfied regardless of the preference orderings defined on prospects (or consequences). As I shall show in the next chapter, if the agent's choice behavior in decision trees satisfies all of these four conditions, this implies some significant constraints on his preference ordering of prospects. In particular, the ordering must satisfy CFO and IND. The point here is simply that it is possible for an agent to have preferences with respect to prospects that permit satisfaction of all four conditions.

8

Consequentialist constructions

8.1 Introduction

Hammond has recently developed an approach to dynamic choice problems that closely parallels the one taken in Chapter 7.[1] He does not explicitly appeal to the four conditions, SR, NEC, DC, and SEP. Instead, he appeals to a "consequentialist principle," according to which acts are to be valued by their consequences. But the manner in which he glosses and applies this principle indicates that he has adopted a framework that is closely related to one defined by these four conditions.

His commitment to SR is clearly revealed in his remarks concerning the implications of his consequentialist principle for normal-form decision problems (i.e., problems requiring a single choice "up front"): "In a normal form decision problem, consequentialism means that behavior [i.e., choice of a normal-form plan] is judged to be acceptable if its consequences (or, more generally, its risky and uncertain consequences) lie in the choice set corresponding to the feasible set of consequences resulting from all possible decisions."[2]

Treated as a constraint on choice at the initial choice point in the tree, Hammond's consequentialist principle also implies NEC. This is clearly indicated when he remarks that "whenever two decision trees T and T' are consequentially equivalent . . . then behavior in the two trees must also be consequentially equivalent. . . . [and] thus the structure of the decision tree must be irrelevant to the consequences of acceptable or recommended behavior."[3] Since T^n, the normalized form of T, does not (by construction) differ with respect to consequential possibilities from T – it differs only with regard to structural features – it follows that for the set S of all logically possible plans in T, $D(S) = D(S^n)$, which is just NEC. This, together with SR, of course, yields PR.

With regard to choice at a subsequent point in the decision tree, which he describes as a "continuation" tree, he holds that "consequentialism applies to . . . continuation strategies in the continuation decision trees no less than to complete strategies in complete decision trees."[4] As his subsequent remarks make clear, the "continuation tree" defined at a point n_i in some tree T is what I have characterized as $T(n_i)^d$ – the de novo version of $T(n_i)$.[5] Thus, Hammond's claim that consequentialism applies to continuation strategies as well as complete strategies means simply (as must be the case) that NEC (and hence PR) apply to these segments of the original tree when they are treated as separate trees in their own right. What, then, ensures "consistency" between what is chosen within the context of T at n_i and what is chosen at the initial choice point of $T(n_i)^d$? That is, what secures SEP? Hammond treats this as a "consistency" condition that is logically distinct from the consequentialist principle but nonetheless one that, he insists, is very weak and highly plausible:

> Consistency is a natural requirement given that the [consequentialist] norm should apply to continuation trees as well as complete trees. Essentially, the norm must prescribe behavior in any continuation tree which is a restriction of the behavior prescribed in the original tree. That is, the behavior in the original tree and in the continuation tree must specify the same subset of [successors to n] at any decision node of the continuation tree.[6]

This is just SEP, and with the addition of PR, as identified above, this means that Hammond is committed to TR. This leaves only DC to be accounted for. It turns out that DC plays no explicit role in Hammond's construction. The reason for this is that it presupposes a notion of choice that transcends that of selection at a given choice point n_i in the tree of an immediate successor to n_i. In particular, it presupposes the "adoption" of a plan, which the agent may then proceed to implement or fail to implement as he confronts the more specific choice points in the tree. Hammond tends to favor limiting discussion to behaviorally ascertainable choices – choices of an immediate successor. But, of course, within that sort of framework one can speak of the plan that an agent has adopted: It is the plan that is "revealed" in the series of choices that he subsequently makes. Moreover, with regard to the plan that is adopted in this sense, it turns out (as noted in Section 7.4) that the agent cannot fail to act on this plan, since every subsequent choice that he makes is consistent with the plan that is thereby revealed. Thus, in effect, condition DC is implicit in Hammond's framework; it is simply that Hammond interprets plans adopted and plans executed in such a way that the agent cannot fail to satisfy this condition.[7]

One can readily see why Hammond introduces the term "consequentialism" in connection with his principle. Each of the reduction conditions that it implies – SR, PR, and TR – has "consequentialist" import. Each makes the ordering of plans or truncated plans dependent on the ordering of associated consequences or, in cases involving risk and uncertainty, disjunctive sets of consequences – prospects. Of course, TR is the strongest of these conditions, and it captures at least one way to interpret the full import of "consequentialism" in a dynamic framework.[8] It implies that at *every* choice point the agent's choice among the options then available is determined by his evaluation of the corresponding prospects to which he can still expose himself from that vantage point. One who accepts TR, then, can be said to be thoroughly oriented to prospects – that is, risky or uncertain consequences. As I have already noted, however, TR is directly implied by three of the four conditions in question: SR, SEP, and NEC. Constructions that employ all of SR, SEP, and NEC can then be said to be consequentialist in their approach.

The significance of Hammond's dynamically interpreted consequentialist principle lies in its potential implications for expected utility and subjective probability theory. What he claims is that the principle suffices for the derivation of both the ordering and independence principles.[9] I will not replicate his proofs here, but content myself with showing that, correspondingly, the four conditions on dynamic choice presented in the preceding chapter collectively achieve the same results. More specifically, it is possible to show that CF and CIND, the acceptable-set versions of the ordering and independence principles, follow logically from the conjunction of SR, NEC, DC, and SEP.

8.2 Derivation of the context-free principle

As discussed in Chapter 2, CF can be factored into Alpha and Beta. Applying the characterization given in that chapter to an arbitrary set of prospects G, let $D(G)$ be the set of all prospects in G that are judged acceptable. Alpha then requires that if g_1 is in $D(G)$ and g_1 is in any subset G^* of G, then g_1 is in $D(G^*)$. Beta requires that if both g_1 and g_2 are in $D(G^*)$ and G is a superset of G^*, then either g_1 and g_2 are in $D(G)$ or neither g_1 nor g_2 is in $D(G)$.

> **Theorem 8.1.** If choice in decision trees satisfies SR, NEC, SEP, and DC, then acceptable-set functions defined on prospect sets will satisfy both Alpha and Beta.
>
> *Comment.* The strategy used to establish this result turns on the consideration that if the agent is disposed to rank the elements in a given set of prospects in some manner or other, one can always construct a very simple dynamic choice problem in which subsets of the full set of prospects can be reached only by passing through some particular choice node. One can then show that if the sequence of choices that the agent makes satisfies conditions SR, NEC, SEP, and DC, then acceptable-set

$G = \{g_1, g_2, g_3, \text{etc.}\}$

$G^* = \{g_1, g_2, \text{etc.}\}$, i.e., g_3 not in G^*

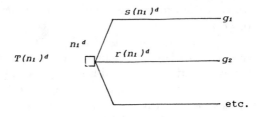

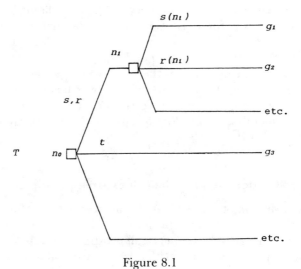

Figure 8.1

functions defined on prospect sets must satisfy both Alpha and Beta. Alternatively put, if acceptable-set functions defined on prospect sets fail to satisfy either Alpha or Beta, then it will be possible to construct a very simple dynamic choice problem in which he must end up violating one or another of the four conditions on dynamic choice. In the formal demonstration that follows, repeated use is made of Proposition 7.1, namely, that the conjunction of SR and NEC implies PR.

Proof. Consider first Alpha. Suppose g_1 is in $D(G)$. Construct a decision tree T consisting just of choice nodes, in which s has as outcome g_1, r has as outcome g_2, and so on, that is, with a plan corresponding to each outcome in G and with n_1 providing access to some subset G^* of G, which contains g_1; and construct also the de novo version of $T(n_1)^{\text{d}}$ of $T(n_1)$ (Figure 8.1). Now suppose that g_1 is in $D(G) = D(G(T))$. It follows by PR that s is in $D(S)$. Since $s(n_1)$ is defined, it follows by DC that $s(n_1)$ is in $D(S(n_1))$. But then, by SEP, $s(n_1)^d$ is in $D(S(n_1)^d)$, and from this together with PR applied to $T(n_1)^d$ it follows that g_1 is in $D(G_{S(n_1)^d})$. But the latter set is, by construction, equivalent to $D(G^*)$. This establishes Alpha.

Consider now Beta. Construct trees T and $T(n_1)^d$ as in Figure 8.1. Now suppose that both g_1 and g_2 are in $D(G^*) = D(G_{S(n_1)^d})$. By PR applied to $T(n_1)^d$, it follows that both $s(n_1)^d$ and $r(n_1)^d$ are in $D(S(n_1)^d)$. But then, by SEP, both $s(n_1)$ and $r(n_1)$ are in $D(S(n_1))$; and by DC, either $D(S)(n_1)$ is empty or both $s(n_1)$ and $r(n_1)$ are in $D(S)(n_1)$. If $D(S)(n_1)$ is empty, then by definition of $D(S)(n_1)$, neither s nor r is in $D(S)$. But then, by PR, neither g_1 nor g_2 is in $D(G)$. If both $s(n_1)$ and $r(n_1)$ are in $D(S)(n_1)$, then there are at least two plans in $D(S)$ whose continuations are, respectively, $s(n_1)$ and $r(n_1)$. In this case, however, by construction, these are s and r. Thus, s and r are in $D(S)$, and by PR, both g_1 and g_2 are in $D(G)$. Thus, either g_1 and g_2 is in $D(G)$, or neither is. This establishes Beta.

8.3 Derivation of the independence principle

Consider the independence principle IND, and in particular its acceptable-set version, CIND. The relation between the conditions on dynamic choice and CIND is given by the following:

Theorem 8.2. If behavior in decision trees satisfies SR, NEC, SEP, and DC, then acceptable-set functions defined on prospect sets will satisfy CIND.

Proof. Construct a decision tree T and the corresponding de novo version of $T(n_1)$, $T(n_1)^d$, with plans s and r, each yielding g_3 with probability $1 - p$, and choice point n_1 with probability p, $s(n_1)$ accessing g_1 and $r(n_1)$ accessing g_2 (Figure 8.2). Suppose g_1 is in $D(\{g_1, g_2\})$. Then by PR, $s(n_1)^d$ is in $D(S(n_1)^d)$, and by SEP, $s(n_1)$ must be in $D(S(n_1))$. Now in this very simple model, any plan defined at the outset is also defined at n_1. Thus, if $D(S)$ is nonempty, it must be that $D(S)(n_1)$ is nonempty, and given this and the fact that $s(n_1)$ is in $D(S(n_1))$ it follows by DC that $s(n_1)$ must be in $D(S)(n_1)$ and that s must be in $D(S)$, since by construction s is the unique plan in T that involves choosing $s(n_1)$ in the event that one arrives at n_1. But s accesses the prospect g_{13}; hence, by PR, g_{13} is in $D(\{g_{13}, g_{23}\})$. The argument is reversible. Let g_{13} be in $D(\{g_{13}, g_{23}\})$; then s is in $D(S)$, and by DC, $s(n_1)$ is in $D(S(n_1))$; and by SEP, in turn, $s(n_1)^d$ is in

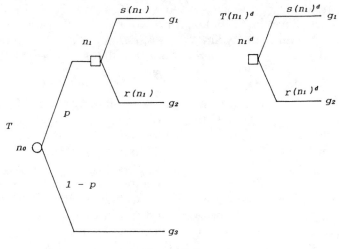

Figure 8.2

$D(S(n_1)^{\mathrm{d}})$. But then by PR applied to $T(n_1)^{\mathrm{d}}$, g_1 is in $D(\{g_1, g_2\})$.
Thus, g_1 is in $D(\{g_1, g_2\})$ iff g_{13} is in $D(\{g_{13}, g_{23}\})$, which is the
desired conclusion.

8.4 Plausibility of the construction

Theorems 8.1 and 8.2 establish that if the agent's choice behavior
satisfies SR, NEC, DC, and SEP in all decision trees, then his choice
behavior with respect to sets of prospects must satisfy both CF and
CIND.[10] Moreover, taken by itself, each of the conditions explored
seems to be a plausible enough consistency condition. SR requires
consistency between $D(S)$ and $D(G)$, for the limit case of trees containing only a single choice point n_0. SEP requires consistency between
$D(S(n_i))$ and $D(S(n_i)^{\mathrm{d}})$, where $T(n_i)^{\mathrm{d}}$ is the de novo tree that coincides
with T from n_i on. NEC requires consistency between $D(S)$ and $D(S^n)$,
where T^n is the normalized counterpart to T. And, finally, DC requires consistency between $D(S)(n_i)$, insofar as it is nonempty, and
$D(S(n_i))$. In this sense, no one of these conditions nor, for that matter,
any combination of them determines what plans (or prospects) qualify
as acceptable: Each requires only that if a given plan or prospect is
acceptable, then so also must some related plan or prospect be acceptable. What provides content here, then, is simply the acceptable-
set functions defined over prospects.

That content is provided, however, not only by the agent's judgments concerning the acceptability of the various prospects he faces
at n_0, but also the prospects he faces at each and every subsequent choice point n_i, for $i \neq 0$. And this, it could be argued, poses

a problem for the construction in question. Notice, in particular, that what prospects the agent finds acceptable among those to which he is exposed at n_i, together with SEP and SR, determines what truncated plans he will judge acceptable at the tree-continuation point n_i, and thus fixes the composition of $D(S(n_i))$. But what prospects the agent finds acceptable among those to which he is exposed at n_0, together with NEC and SR, determines what must be judged acceptable at the outset, and thus fixes the composition of $D(S)$ and more particularly $D(S)(n_i)$. Now the last of the consistency conditions, namely DC, requires that $D(S)(n_i)$, insofar as it is nonempty, coincide with $D(S(n_i))$. But given that dynamic choice satisfies all of SR, NEC, and SEP, and given acceptable sets of prospects, there is no guarantee that DC can be satisfied. That is to say, given no further constraints on acceptable sets of prospects – in particular, if they fail to satisfy either CF or CIND – there will be no assurance that some particular plan that the agent finds acceptable at n_0, and may then intend to implement, will still be regarded by him as acceptable and thus something he is prepared to continue to implement at n_i. Alternatively, if the agent is committed to DC and if acceptable sets of prospects fail to satisfy either CF or CIND, then something else will have to give.

One possibility would be to reconsider NEC. As formulated, NEC requires coincidence between the acceptable set of all logically possible plans in a given tree and the acceptable set for the counterpart set of normal-form plans. This, it might be argued, presupposes that the set of plans feasible for the agent in any extensive-form tree is simply the set of all logically possible plans; and this presupposition, it might be argued, is not beyond question.

Consider the plans in T^n – the tree in normal form. Since execution of any plan in T^n requires only a single, initial choice by the agent, it seems plausible to suppose that every s^n in S^n is feasible, that is, a plan that the agent can execute, if at that moment he desires to do so, since it requires only that initial act of choice on his part to ensure that the plan is implemented. In contrast, extensive plans pose a distinctive problem of implementation, since implementation comes only by co-ordination of choices over time. Although the agent may well be disposed at n_0 to choose to begin implementation of the desired plan, it may also happen that at some subsequent choice point n_i he will no longer be disposed to make the choice required if that plan is to continue to be implemented. This in turn means that even though an agent would (ideally) choose to implement some particular (extensive) plan, he may come to regard that plan as not feasible on the grounds that he expects that were he to adopt and begin implementation of that plan, he would fail to do what was required at some subsequent choice point. Moreover, if the agent judges a plan s to be not feasible in this sense, then he will not regard the plan as acceptable. That is, plan s will fail to be in $D(S)$. This, of course, would constitute a violation of NEC – but one that might seem altogether intelligible. Indeed, abstracting for the moment from NEC, the triplet of conditions SR, SEP, and DC could be said to model just this type of situation. They, together with acceptable sets of prospects to which he is exposed at n_i, determine what truncated plans are acceptable at n_i, and this implies that, in at least certain cases (e.g., when the agent employs methods of evaluation that fail to satisfy either CF or CIND), the agent will be disposed at n_i to choose differently than he had intended when evaluating plans from the perspective of n_0. Here, then, it could be argued, is a situation in which not all logically possible plans are feasible and, hence, a situation in which NEC must be rejected.[11]

8.5 Formalizing restricted feasibility

To pursue the notion of a more restrictive criterion of feasibility in a more formal manner, one could argue that at the very least NEC (as previously characterized) must be factored into two conditions. The first, which I shall here designate full feasibility (FF), specifies what is to count as the set of feasible plans in any given decision tree, namely, all logically possible contingency plans. The second, NEC proper, requires that if one constructs a decision problem T^{nf} consisting of normalized versions of all the *feasible* plans in T, then $D(S(T))$ must coincide with $D(S(T^{\mathrm{nf}}))$.

Once FF is distinguished from NEC proper and the latter is taken to hold with respect to feasible plans, it is possible to imagine a much more restricted scope for NEC, that is, where one does not simply presuppose that for any tree T, all logically possible contingency plans are feasible. As a first approximation to such a more restrictive criterion of feasibility consider the following:

> *Restricted feasibility* (RF). A plan s is feasible iff $s(n_i)$ is in $D(S(n_i))$ for every *choice* point n_i, $i \neq 0$, for which s is defined.[12]

The great advantage of RF is its generality. It involves a condition reminiscent of DC-EXC (see Section 7.4), but reformulated as a requirement for s being feasible, rather than as a requirement for s being in $D(S)$, and as a necessary and sufficient condition instead of only a necessary condition.

Now within a framework in which SEP holds, RF immediately implies the following:

> *Separable feasibility* (SF). A plan s is feasible iff $s(n_i)^{\mathrm{d}}$ is in $D(S(n_i)^{\mathrm{d}})$ for every *choice* point n_i, $i \neq 0$, for which s is defined.

This serves as a reminder that it is really SEP (or some very similar condition) that in accordance with the line of reasoning pursued in Section 8.4, requires a more restricted conception of feasibility. More precisely, other conditions determine what plans in the separable tree are acceptable, but it is SEP that provides for an independent determination of the acceptability of the truncated plans at any point n_i in T – that is, one not determined by what the agent finds acceptable at n_0.

In the presence of SF, NEC can now be understood to apply only to sets of plans that qualify as separably feasible. Corresponding to this restrictive conception of feasibility, one can also introduce the following restricted version of PR:

> *Restricted plan reduction (RPR).* For any plan s, such that s satisfies SF, s is in $D(S)$ iff g_s is in $D(G_s)$.

Predictably, what RPR requires is simply that the mapping of acceptable plans in T into acceptable plans in T^n – the normalized version of T – pertains not to all logically possible plans in T, but only to those that are separably feasible.

RPR serves very effectively to capture at least part of the implications for feasibility of supposing that SEP constrains $D(S(n_i))$ independently of the constraints implied by the combination of PR applied at n_0 and DC. It can be argued, however, that RPR does not capture all the relevant implications. The above discussion focuses exclusively on the problem of tracing out the implications for feasibility of the supposition that SEP together with other assumptions rules out certain truncated plans at n_i. But any general characterization of feasibility, it could be argued, must also be responsive to what is implied in situations in which at some subsequent choice node more than one plan continuation is acceptable, that is, where $D(S(n_i))$ is not a unit set.

Suppose that $D(S(n_i)) = \{s(n_i)\}$; that is, it is a unit set. Then the agent will expect that if and when n_i is reached, $s(n_i)$ will be chosen with certainty (probability of 1). If, however, $D(S(n_i))$ is not a unit set, if, for example, $D(S(n_i)) = \{s(n_i), r(n_i)\}$, what expectation is the agent to form with respect to what he will do if and when he reaches n_i? It would appear that there can be no *a priori* answer to this question. Perhaps the agent is in the habit of using a randomizing device when he is confronted with a number of equally acceptable courses of action. But perhaps, to the contrary, he uses some other much more casual approach. He himself may have a fairly good sense of what he is likely to do; but then again he may not. He may, plainly and simply, be completely uncertain, from the perspective of n_0, as to what he would in fact do were he to arrive at some successor node. At best, then, he can project only that he is just as likely to select any one of the plan continuations at n_i as any other; in this case, what he expects to do is select what can be characterized as a well-defined mixed plan. And in the event that he is not inclined to use some well-defined random device to determine which of a number of equally acceptable plans he will select, what he now confronts is an indeterminate mixed plan. In either case, however, if $s(n_i)$, $r(n_i)$, and so on are all equally acceptable, then what he now confronts is a plan that involves, if and when he arrives at n_i, choosing (equiprobably or indeterminately) between $s(n_i)$ and $r(n_i)$, and so on.

This forces a much more radical reinterpretation of what can be taken to be a feasible plan. If the agent projects that $s(n_i)$ and $r(n_i)$ are equally acceptable, any plan that calls on him to select $s(n_i)$, if and when he reaches n_i, is not feasible. Under the stated conditions, he simply cannot expect ex ante that he will definitely choose $s(n_i)$ if and when he reaches n_i. Thus, the set of feasible plans available to him at the outset (and, by extension, the set of feasible truncated plans at any subsequent point) is not equivalent to the set defined by SF. What is needed here is not simply the exclusion of plans that call for selection of what will be an unacceptable plan continuation at some choice point; in addition, in cases where a number of plan continuations are equally acceptable, one must exclude all but plans that leave open the disjunction of acceptable plan continuations. More formally:

> *Very separable feasibility (VSF).* If s and r are such that both satisfy the "only if" part of SF but there exists some n_i, $i \neq 0$, such that both s and r are defined at n_i, then neither s nor r itself is a feasible plan; what is feasible is (1) a modified version of s, which is just like s except that at n_i it calls for choosing either $s(n_i)$ or $r(n_i)$, and (2) a modified version of r, which is just like r except that at n_i it calls for choosing either $s(n_i)$ or $r(n_i)$.[13]

VSF places even more stringent restrictions on the mapping of acceptable plans in the normal-form version T^n of any decision tree T back into the acceptable plans in T itself: Normal-form versions that are acceptable in T^n have counterparts that are acceptable in T, so long as the latter meet the conditions of feasibility set forth in VSF. Correspondingly, the necessary restriction on PR will now have to be formulated in the following manner:

> *Very restricted plan reduction (VRPR).* For any plan s in any tree T, such that s satisfies VSF, s is in $D(S)$ iff g_s is in $D(G_S)$.

Working in the framework of VSF (as distinct from SF), it should be noted, requires a somewhat more careful interpretation of DC. Recall,

first of all, that DC was assembled from what were termed its exclusionary and inclusionary factors (see Section 7.4). The problem arises
with respect to DC-INC. Heretofore, it sufficed to assume that when
the antecedent conditions are satisfied, there is some plan s in $D(S)$ for
which $s(n_i)$ is the unique plan continuation – such that choice of $s(n_i)$ is
required if the plan is to be implemented. But now the condition must
be "liberalized" to read as follows: There has to be some plan s in $D(S)$
such that choice of $s(n_i)$ is consistent with – a possible way of – executing that plan.

8.6 Theorems for separable feasibility

What happens to Theorems 8.1 and 8.2, which provide a grounding
for CF and CIND, when SF is adopted as the framework assumption
governing feasibility and PR is correspondingly weakened to RPR? As
it turns out, certain important results can still be secured. Recall here
that one key version of the independence axiom governs substitution
of a component gamble with some other gamble indifferent to it, that
is, SUB (as defined in Section 3.1). Formulated as a condition on
acceptable sets this becomes the following:

> *Equivalent choice independence (CIND-E).* For any g_1, g_2, and g_3,
> and $0 < p \le 1$, if both g_1 and g_2 are in $D(\{g_1, g_2\})$, then both g_{13}
> and g_{23} are in $D(\{g_{13}, g_{23}\})$, where $g_{13} = [g_1, p; g_3, 1 - p]$ and
> $g_{23} = [g_2, p; g_3, 1 - p]$.

Can CIND-E be derived within a framework in which feasibility is
characterized in terms of SF? First of all, one can establish the following:

Theorem 8.3. If choice in decision trees satisfies SF, RPR, SEP,
and DC-INC, then acceptable-set functions defined on prospect sets will satisfy CIND-E.

Proof. Consider once again the decision trees in Figure 8.2. For
definiteness, but without loss of generality, suppose contrary to
the hypothesis to be established that (1) both g_1 and g_2 are in
$D(\{g_1, g_2\})$, while (2) $g_{13} = [g_1, p; g_3, 1 - p]$ is, and $g_{23} = [g_2, p;
g_3, 1 - p]$ is not, in $D(\{g_{13}, g_{23}\})$. By (1) and RPR (indeed, the
even weaker condition SR), it follows that both $s(n_1)^{\mathrm{d}}$ and $r(n_1)^{\mathrm{d}}$
are in $D(S(n_1)^{\mathrm{d}})$, and by SEP, both $s(n_1)$ and $r(n_1)$ are in $D(S(n_1))$.
But both s and r, then, are feasible, since by the sufficiency part
of SF, $s(n_i)^{\mathrm{d}}$ is in $D(S(n_i)^{\mathrm{d}}$ for every choice point n_i, $i \ne 0$,
for which s is defined, and $r(n_i)^{\mathrm{d}}$ is in $D(S(n_i)^{\mathrm{d}})$ for every choice

point n_i, $i \neq 0$, for which r is defined. This, together with RPR applied at n_0 and (2), implies that s is in $D(S)$; thus, $D(S)(n_1)$ is defined. But then, since $r(n_1)$ is also in $D(S(n_1))$, DC-INC implies that there must be a plan in $D(S)$ that has $r(n_1)$ for its continuation at n_1. By construction, however, this is r. Thus, r is in $D(S)$. This together with RPR applied at n_0 implies that g_{23} is in $D(\{g_{13}, g_{23}\})$, which contradicts (2).

But one can also establish the following:

Theorem 8.4. If choice in decision trees satisfies SF, RPR, SEP, and DC-INC, then acceptable-set functions defined on prospects will satisfy Beta.

Proof. Consider once again the decision trees in Figure 8.1, with $G = \{g_1, g_2, g_3, \text{etc.}\}$ and G^* a subset of G that does not contain g_3 but does contain g_1 and g_2. For definiteness but without loss of generality, suppose contrary to the hypothesis to be established that (1) both g_1 and g_2 are in $D(G^*)$, whereas (2) g_1 is, and g_2 is not, in $D(G)$. By (1) and RPR (or SR), both $s(n_1)^d$ and $r(n_1)^d$ are in $D(S(n_1)^d)$, and by SEP, both $s(n_1)$ and $r(n_1)$ are in $D(S(n_1))$. But both s and r, then, are feasible, by appeal to the sufficiency part of SF. That s is feasible, together with RPR applied at n_0 and (2), implies that s is in $D(S)$; thus, $D(S)(n_1)$ is defined. But then, since $r(n_1)$ is also in $D(S(n_1))$, DC-INC implies that there must be a plan in $D(S)$ that has $r(n_1)$ for its continuation at n_1. By construction, however, this is r. Thus, r is in $D(S)$. This together with RPR applied at n_0 implies that g_2 is in $D(G)$, which contradicts (2).

It turns out, however, that within the framework of SF, with PR weakened to RPR, the balance of the results contained in Theorems 8.1 and 8.2 cannot be secured:

Proposition 8.1. Violations of Alpha by acceptable-set functions defined on prospects are compatible with choice in decision trees that satisfies SF, DC, SEP, and RPR.

Proof. Consider once again the decision tree in Figure 8.1. Let $G = \{g_1, g_2, g_3, \text{etc.}\}$ and let G^* be a subset of G that does not contain g_3 but does contain g_1 and g_2. For definiteness, but without loss of generality, consider the following violation of Alpha: just g_1 and g_2 are in $D(G)$, but only g_2 is in $D(G^*)$. Let just $r(n_1)^d$ be in $D(S(n_1)^d)$; then RPR is satisfied for $T(n_1)^d$. Now let only $r(n_1)$ be in $D(S(n_1))$; then SEP is satisfied. And if we let only r be in $D(S)$, then RPR is satisfied at n_0 and DC is satisfied. Of course, if FF and PR held, s would also have to be in $D(S)$, but s involves sequential choice, and $s(n_1)$ is not in $D(S(n_1))$. Hence, s not being in $D(S)$ is compatible with RPR, even though g_1 is in $D(G)$. Here, then, is a model in which all of SF, RPR, DC, and SEP hold but Alpha is violated.

Notice that for T^n, the normal-form version of T, with s^n, etc., corresponding to s, etc., RPR together with the assumption that $D(G) = \{g_1, g_2\}$ implies that $D(S^n) = \{s^n, r^n\}$. Thus, as one should expect, although the above pattern of acceptable sets for prospects is compatible with SF, RPR, DC, and SEP, it leads to a violation of unrestricted NEC.

Theorem 8.1 focuses on CIND-E, which can be described as the "indifference" factor of CIND. What remains of CIND, once CIND-E is factored out, is the following requirement:

Strict choice independence (CIND-S). For any g_1, g_2, and g_3, and $0 < p \leq 1$, if g_2 is not in $D(\{g_1, g_2\})$ then g_{23} is not in $D(\{g_{13}, g_{23}\})$, where $g_{23} = [g_2, p; g_3, 1 - p]$ and $g_{13} = [g_1, p; g_3, 1 - p]$.

This constraint, which stands to CIND-E as Alpha stands to Beta, also cannot be derived within the weakened framework:

Proposition 8.2. Violations of CIND-S by acceptable-set functions defined on prospects are compatible with choice in decision trees that satisfies SF, RPR, DC, and SEP.

Proof. Consider once again the decision trees in Figure 8.2. For definiteness, consider the following violation of CIND-S: g_1 is, but g_2 is not, in $D(\{g_1, g_2\})$, whereas both g_{13} and g_{23} are in $D(\{g_{13}, g_{23}\})$. If $s(n_1)^d$ is, but $r(n_1)^d$ is not, in $D(S(n_1)^d)$, then RPR as applied to $T(n_1)^d$ is satisfied. If $s(n_1)$ is, but $r(n_1)$ is not, in $D(S(n_1))$, then SEP is satisfied. Finally, if s is, but r is not, in $D(S)$, then RPR is satisfied at n_0, and DC is also satisfied. Of course, if FF and PR held, then r, being feasible, would also have to be in $D(S)$, since by hypothesis g_{23} is in $D(\{g_{13}, g_{23}\})$. But implementation of r involves sequential choice, and by hypothesis, $r(n_1)$ is not in $D(S(n_1))$. Hence r's not being in $D(S)$ is compatible with RPR, even though g_{23} is in $D(\{g_{13}, g_{23}\})$. Here, then, is a model in which all of SF, RPR, DC, and SEP are satisfied but CIND-S is not.

Notice once again that RPR applied to normal-form versions s^n and r^n of s and r, of course, requires that r^n be in, and s^n not be in, $D(S^n)$. Thus, the above pattern leads to a violation of unrestricted NEC.

8.7 Results for very separable feasibility

The results presented in Theorems 8.3 and 8.4 might seem promising enough if it were possible to hold the line on a more restrictive principle of feasibility and argue for RPR but not VRPR. The problem is that the reasoning that drives one to RPR naturally leads one to endorse VRPR. If future behavior pertaining to the discrimination between acceptable and unacceptable options must be taken into account, then surely also must future behavior in the face of more than one acceptable option. Translating into the language of preference rather than choice, one is enjoined by RPR to take into account the implications of future strict preference relations, while VRPR plausibly extends this injunction to include taking into account future indifferent relations. It is hard to see why future strict preference behavior should be relevant to the issue of feasibility whereas indifference behavior is not.[14]

Once VSF is in place, however, even the more modest results captured in Theorems 8.3 and 8.4 can no longer be secured:

Proposition 8.3. Violations of Beta by acceptable-set functions defined on prospects are compatible with choice in decision trees that satisfies VSF, VRPR, DC, and SEP.

Proof. Consult the decision tree in Figure 8.1 and, for definiteness, consider the following violation of Beta: Let $D(G) = \{g_1, g_3\}$, while $D(G^*) = \{g_1, g_2\}$. If just $s(n_1)^d$ and $r(n_1)^d$ are in $D(S(n_1)^d)$, then VRPR is satisfied; and if just $s(n_1)$ and $r(n_1)$ are in $D(S(n_1))$, then SEP is satisfied. Suppose further that only t is in $D(S)$; then, since no plan distinct from t is in $D(S)$, $D(S)(n_1)$ is empty, and thus DC-INC is trivially satisfied for T. Since nothing excluded from $D(S(n_1))$ is included in $D(S)$, DC-EXC is also trivially satisfied for T. PR applied to T itself would require, of course, that s be in $D(S)$, as would RPR, but the weaker condition VRPR does not require s to be in $D(S)$, since with both $s(n_1)$ and $r(n_1)$ in $D(S(n_1))$, s itself is not feasible at n_0. This is a model, then, in which all of VRPR, SEP, and DC are satisfied but Beta is violated.

If RPR is applied to the normal-form T^n version of T, with normal-form plans s^n and r^n corresponding to s and r (t, recall, is already in normal form), then s^n as well as t must be in $D(S^n)$. Thus, the above pattern of acceptable sets satisfies the other conditions on dynamic choice but at the expense of violating unrestricted NEC.

Proposition 8.4. Violations of CIND-E by acceptable-set functions defined on prospects are compatible with choice in decision trees that satisfies VSF, VRPR, DC, and SEP.

Proof. Consult Figure 8.2 once again and, for definiteness, consider the following violation of CIND-E: g_1 and g_2 are both in $D(\{g_1, g_2\})$, whereas g_{13} is, and g_{23} is not, in $D(\{g_{13}, g_{23}\})$. If both $s(n_1)^d$ and $r(n_1)^d$ are in $D(S(n_1)^d)$, then RPR applied to $T(n_1)^d$ is satisfied. If both $s(n_1)$ and $r(n_1)$ are in $D(S(n_1))$, then SEP is satisfied. Now by appeal to VRPR, neither s nor r is feasible; what is feasible is the plan mix(s, r), which calls for selection of either $s(n_1)$ or $r(n_1)$, if and when choice point n_1 is reached. On the other hand, DC-INC is satisfied, since both $s(n_1)$ and $r(n_1)$ specify possible ways in which mix(s, r), the uniquely feasible plan in $D(S)$, can be continued at n_1. This is a model, then, in which all of VSF, VRPR, DC, and SEP are satisfied but CIND-E is violated.

RPR applied to normal-form versions s^n and r^n of s and r, of course, requires that r^n be in, and s^n not be in, $D(S^n)$. Thus, the above pattern of acceptable sets satisfies the other conditions on dynamic choice but at the expense of violating unrestricted NEC.

All of this is very disturbing. If one is prepared to reformulate the criterion of feasibility along lines that seem to be required by the introduction of SEP or, for that matter, any other condition that provides an independent basis for the evaluation of tree-continuation choices, the constructive results presented in Sections 8.2 and 8.3 are in deep trouble. Not only will they have to be weakened considerably, as detailed in the intermediary results reported in Section 8.6, but abandoned altogether, as detailed in the results reported in this section. And with this, it would appear, goes the whole dynamic choice argument for both CF and CIND.

8.8 Modifying the separability assumption

Given the paucity of results for a framework constrained by VSF, is there some way to salvage FF and, hence, a strong version of NEC? Recall that the problem here concerns a possible tension, given DC, between the presupposition that all logically possible plans are feasible, on the one hand, and SEP, SR, and specified acceptable sets of prospects, on the other. The results of Sections 8.6 and 8.7 presuppose that SEP, SR, and the specified acceptable sets of prospects are not subject to criticism and that, therefore, adjustments must be made with respect to the presupposition regarding what is feasible. But it remains possible to consider making adjustments in the reverse direction.

There is, in fact, a natural fit among NEC, DC, SR, and the conception that all logically possible plans are feasible. The fit here turns on the notion that NEC and SR provide a model in which future choice cannot be predicted without reference to present plans and, thus, in which ex post choice is constrained by ex ante adoption of a plan – so that ex ante evaluation of prospects turns out to be controlling not only for the adoption of a plan but for its implementation. In that model it is SEP that is problematic. If ex ante evaluation of full plans can be regulative for ex post choice, then an agent can be disposed to choose at some ex post choice point n_i (against the background of having adopted some plan) differently than he would have chosen had he confronted n_i de novo. In such a case, the agent would violate SEP.[15]

I shall return in the next three chapters to the question of the relative merits of restricting SEP in this manner rather than retaining SEP and introducing a more restrictive criterion of feasibility. For the moment, however, note that if SEP is weakened, then the intended consequentialist construction – the derivation of both CF and CIND – is once again jeopardized.

Proposition 8.5. Violations of CF and CIND by acceptable-set functions defined on prospects are compatible with choice in decision trees that satisfies SR, unrestricted NEC, and DC.

Proof. This can be established by appeal once again to the trees in Figures 8.1 and 8.2. Suppose, for example, with reference to the decision trees in Figure 8.1., that (1) only g_1 is in $D(G)$, while only g_2 is in $D(G^*)$, in violation of Alpha, and let all of the following be true: (2) $r(n_1)^d$ is, and $s(n_1)^d$ is not, in $D(S(n_1)^d)$; (3) $s(n_1)$ is, and $r(n_1)$ is not, in $D(S(n_1))$; and (4) s is, and r is not, in $D(S)$. From (1) and (2) it follows that PR is satisfied in $T(n_1)^d$; from (1) and (4) it follows that PR is satisfied in T; from (3) and (4) it follows that DC is satisfied; but from (2) and (3) it follows that SEP is violated. Here, then, is a model in which a violation of CF can be reconciled with SR, and NEC and DC at the expense of SEP. Analogous arguments can be made with respect to Beta and also with respect to the S- and E-factors of CIND.

8.9 Implications for Hammond's construction

Looking back over the results of Sections 8.4 through 8.8, it would seem that if one is convinced that there is a conflict between accepting both SEP and FF, one can resolve this matter in at least two different ways. More specifically, if one is prepared to retain SEP, one can reinterpret the scope of NEC, that is, think through more carefully what is to count as the set of feasible plans to which NEC is applicable. On that way of thinking, NEC as originally formulated is too strong a constraint on rational choice – precisely because it presupposes that every logically possible plan is feasible. Alternatively, as suggested in Section 8.8, if one wants to retain FF and PR, but finds the argument of Section 8.4 convincing, then one can weaken SEP in some fashion or other. The punch line here, of course, is simply that whichever adjustment is made – the introduction of a more restrictive criterion of ex ante feasibility, which thereby limits the scope of NEC, or the placing of restrictions on SEP – Hammond's consequentialist construction will have to be reassessed. In particular, neither modification leaves conditions strong enough to secure both CIND and CF.

It remains to consider, however, whether anything forces one to the conclusion that either FF must be replaced by the much more restrictive condition VSF or SEP weakened. What precludes Hammond from arguing simultaneously for the strong version of NEC (applied to all logically possible plans as defined by the decision tree structure) and all of DC, SR, and SEP? The suggestion that motivated the formal explorations of Sections 8.6 through 8.8, as expressed in Section 8.4, was that the four conditions SR, NEC, DC, and SEP do not form a *plausible* set of conditions to impose on rational choice and preference with respect to plans. But these four conditions do, after all, constitute a consistent set of conditions. As established by Proposition 7.10, there are preference orderings over sets of prospects that will satisfy all of SR, NEC, DC, and SEP.

Thus, although it is certainly true that if one is determined to defend methods of evaluation that violate CF or some version of independence, one will have to argue against accepting all of SR, NEC, DC, and SEP, still Hammond is entitled to turn that point around and insist that in the light of the reasonableness of all of SR, NEC, DC, and SEP, such "nonconforming" methods must be judged unacceptable. In short, Hammond is entitled to counter the modus tollens argument against his position by appeal to the modus ponens form of the very same argument.

All of this, it seems to me, is simply a reminder that if one is determined to take certain assumptions as fixed points, that is, beyond question, one thereby arms oneself with a powerful lever to use against certain other assumptions. Such a way of proceeding, however, is not likely to engender any consensus. All that happens is that different theorists line up on opposing sides.

8.10 An additional problem

There is, however, one other aspect of Hammond's construction that should be explored. If the combination of SR, NEC, DC, and SEP is taken as definitive of a consequentialist perspective, this combination of conditions appears to impose a severe constraint on what can count as a consequence. On a first reading, at any rate, consequentialism so defined would seem to rule out allowing choice at any point within the tree to be influenced by commitment to plans previously adopted, lost opportunities, sunk costs, regrets, and so on. One natural response here is to insist that this undercuts the plausibility of this brand of consequentialism – that it excludes too much. Hammond is well aware of this problem. In the opening remarks of his most recent publication he writes:

> It would be false if missed opportunities, regrets, sunk costs, etc. affected behaviour and yet were excluded from the domain of consequences. As a normative principle, however, consequentialism requires everything which should be allowed to affect decisions to count as a relevant consequence – behaviour is evaluated by consequences, and nothing else. If regrets, sunk costs, even the structure of the decision tree itself, are relevant to normative behaviour, they are already in the consequence domain.[16]

If this serves to defuse the objection of a too narrow conception of consequentialism, it seems to do so at the cost of the theory having much content. Hammond, it would seem, is willing to pay the price:

> . . . the content of a normative theory of behaviour is then largely a matter of what counts in practice as a relevant consequence, rather than whether consequentialism and other abstract axioms are satisfied. For example, the standard economists' injunction to ignore sunk costs is a *practical* normative principle. Whereas expected utility maximization is a principle which has no practical content (beyond continuity of behaviour with respect to changes in probabilities) until the consequences which are the arguments of the utility function have been specified. . . . my subject is the implications of consequentialism for the structure of normative behaviour – in particular, the extent to which consequentialism implies that behaviour must maximize expected utility. Consequentialism *per se* is not about practical normative theories.[17]

If the domain of consequences can be enlarged in this way, it is still open to us to consider what implications this has for the status of SEP. Hammond himself takes the position that SEP formulates a principle distinct from consequentialism.[18] It might seem, then, that enlarging the domain of consequences to include "even the structure of the decision tree itself" leaves SEP intact. But is this correct?

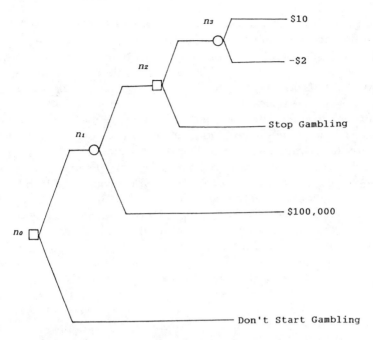

Figure 8.3

To appeal once again to the sort of example that Broome discusses, suppose, say, that one is contemplating participating in a sequential lottery situation having the structure shown in Figure 8.3. Following Hammond's and Broome's suggestion, one might suppose that the outcome of receiving the prize of $10 in this lottery can be rede-scribed as "getting $10 when one could have had as much as $10,000," and so on. But what sense is to be made of SEP in this context? SEP requires that choice at point n_2 in the decision tree T not differ from what it would be were the tree to start de novo at n_2. But there cannot be a truncated, and separable, tree $T(n_2)^d$ that involves no background (now counterfactual) possibility of getting $10,000 and yet that still includes as part of the description of one of the terminal consequences leading out from n_2 precisely that same counterfactual possibility.

There are similar implications for conditions like SR and NEC. If the path taken as well as the "outcome" (in the ordinary sense of that term) can figure in the description of the consequences of a certain plan, then two different paths yielding the same probability distribu-tion over what would otherwise be the same set of "outcomes" may in fact differ with respect to consequences. In such a setting, neither SR nor NEC will have the same prescriptive force.

It may be argued, of course, that what happens in this sort of situation is not that one or more of these conditions is violated, but simply that their scope becomes more restricted. That is, the trees in question, then, cannot be separated in the fashion that would make SEP applicable, and trees that NEC or SR ordinarily requires be treated in the same fashion will be treated differently. This would "save" SEP, NEC, and SR, but at the price of restricting the domain over which they operate.[19]

I conclude, then, that the project of grounding the three conditions on dynamic choice in an intuitively secure consequentialist "pre-axiom" (as Hammond describes it) faces a dilemma. If the concept of a consequence is given a narrow interpretation, the scope of application of conditions such as SR, NEC, and SEP is considerable; but then it is no longer clear that "consequentialism" is an intuitively acceptable principle. Alternatively, the concept of a consequence can be formulated in a much more inclusive sense. In this case, although the principle of consequentialism gains intuitive plausibility, it no longer has the same normative force. In particular, conditions like SEP, SR, and NEC will have a considerably narrower scope of application.

A more general question can also be raised here. It is not clear what is gained in terms of a more *secure* grounding for the modern theory of expected utility and subjective probability by an appeal to "intuitively plausible" conditions for dynamic choice. The decision tree framework hardly presents itself as one whose basic axioms are somehow significantly more intuitively acceptable than those governing, say, static choice among gambles. With respect to intuitive standing, it might be argued, one cannot improve on something like the set of axioms for static choice employed by Luce and Raiffa or by Herstein and Milnor.[20] Against this, it might be urged that the sequential choice problem is more general – that the choice problems forming the object of the standard expected utility theory can be construed as special cases of dynamic choice problems. On this account, the recasting of the theory in the dynamic framework represents a deepening of results in the sense that expected utility theory as governing static choice can now be seen to connect systematically with other types of choice problems. But once again it is not clear that a decision tree or dynamic choice framework must be taken as the more general framework. Viewed from another perspective, it would seem, nothing could be more general than the more traditional approach, with its notion of an abstractly defined feasible set of options.

8.11 A return to a more pragmatic perspective

The problems raised in Sections 8.9 and 8.10 are not likely to be resolved, I suggest, in a framework that seeks to deduce the traditional principles of choice from "intuitively secure" conditions on dynamic choice. In particular, if the impasse identified in Section 8.9 is to be resolved, one must develop some independent standpoint from which these rival ways of thinking about Theorems 8.1 and 8.2 can be assessed. As the reader may well have anticipated by now, I hope to find just such an independent standpoint in the kind of pragmatic approach first surveyed in Chapter 5. Moreover, as I anticipated in Section 5.1, it is possible to view Hammond's own consequentialist construction in this somewhat different manner, that is, as presenting a frankly pragmatic argument in support of the certain principles of choice. Viewed in this way, the central question becomes whether a thoroughly pragmatic perspective really forces one to accept all of SR, NEC, DC, and SEP, or whether working with some weakened set of conditions can be shown to be fully compatible with such a pragmatic perspective. This is the matter to which I now turn.

9

Reinterpreting dynamic consistency

9.1 Introduction

Chapter 8 began with two constructive theorems (8.1 and 8.2) concerning CF and CIND. The conclusion finally reached, however, was that these two theorems do not suffice to establish CF and CIND as principles of rationality. In particular, certain feasibility issues remain to be resolved, and, moreover, the conceptual connection between all of the dynamic choice conditions employed in these constructions and an intuitively secure notion of consequentialism was found to be questionable.

In this chapter I shall consider Theorems 8.1 and 8.2 from a somewhat different perspective. Even if one grants that these two theorems do not settle the question whether CF and CIND are principles of rationality, still they are diagnostically useful. In particular, they serve as a reminder that if the agent employs certain methods of evaluation, he can be placed in a situation in which he is liable to choose in a manner that is dynamically inconsistent, that is, in violation of DC. Theorems 8.1 and 8.2 provide a formal model for this. They imply that if the agent's method of evaluation fails to satisfy either CF or CIND, then it will be possible to construct a decision tree in which, if the agent chooses in a manner that satisfies all of SR, NEC, and SEP, he will end up violating DC.

9.2 Strotz on dynamic inconsistency

There is within economic theory a large body of literature that is concerned with this sort of dynamic inconsistency and that takes as its touchstone an important article by Strotz (1956). For Strotz, the problem of dynamic consistency is posed not by an agent who employs evaluative methods that fail to satisfy either CF or CIND, but by one who is faced with choosing among consumption schedules and who finds that his preferences for (or dispositions to choose from) such schedules change over time. Here is Strotz's introduction to the problem:

An individual is imagined to choose a plan of consumption for a future period of time so as to maximize the utility of the plan as evaluated at the present moment. His choice is, of course, subject to a budget constraint. Our problem arises when we ask: If he is free to reconsider his plan at later dates, will he abide by it or disobey it – *even though his original expectations of future desires and means of consumption are verified?* Our answer is that the optimal plan of the present moment is generally one which will *not* be obeyed, or that the individual's future behavior will be inconsistent with his optimal plan. If this inconsistency is not recognized, our subject will typically be a "spend-thrift". . . . If the inconsistency is recognized, the rational agent will do one of two things. He may "precommit" his future behavior by precluding future options so that it will conform to his present desire as to what it should be. Or, alternatively, he may modify his chosen plan to take account of future disobedience, realizing that the possibility of disobedience imposes a further constraint – beyond the budget constraint – on the set of plans that are attainable. It is in this way that the individual becomes "thrifty."[1]

This problem, of course, is not special to choice of consumption schedules. Strotz takes the story of Ulysses and the Sirens as an epigraph for his article and as illustrating another situation in which there is a potential for such a temporal shift or change: Ulysses prefers now (before he hears the Sirens' song) that he not subsequently choose to follow the Sirens, but he projects nonetheless that if he does hear them, he will choose to follow them. The potentiality for shifts of this sort is, Strotz thinks, a common feature of dynamic choice situations.

Strotz also argues that shifts of this sort, when they do in fact occur, are subject to criticism. The agent who adopts a plan and then fails to abide by it – despite the fact that there has been no intervening change in relevant information – chooses in a dynamically inconsistent manner. Moreover, since he assumes that the potentiality for such shifts is a common feature of dynamic choice situations, Strotz concludes that a rational agent will anticipate the problem and adopt appropriate measures. Accordingly, he characterizes one who fails to do so as myopic or shortsighted.

The distinctions set forth in Chapters 6 and 7 provide a concise way to characterize such myopia. For Strotz's dynamically inconsistent agent there is some plan s such that s is in $D(S)$, but there also exists a subsequent choice node n_i such that $s(n_i)$ is not in $D(S(n_i))$. That is to say, Strotz's myopic agent exhibits choice behavior that violates DC.

Strotz's article prompted a series of papers, two of which (Hammond, 1976, 1977) are of particular relevance to the foundations of utility theory. Like Strotz, Hammond presupposes that changes in plans that are not predicated on the receipt of new and relevant information involve the agent in a form of "inconsistency" and as such constitute a departure from rationality. He, like Strotz, confines himself to situations in which risk or uncertainty plays no role. But Hammond explicitly generalizes beyond the case of consumption patterns, by characterizing the general class of situations in which there is a potentiality for such a shift in plans as those where the agent's

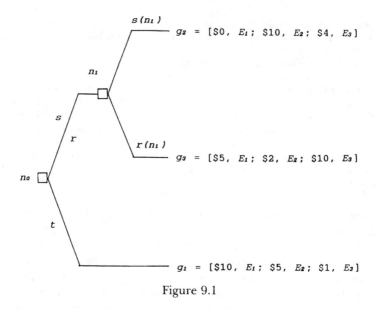

$s(n_1)$

$g_2 = [\$0, \ E_1; \ \$10, \ E_2; \ \$4, \ E_3]$

n_1

s

r

$r(n_1)$

$g_3 = [\$5, \ E_1; \ \$2, \ E_2; \ \$10, \ E_3]$

n_0

t

$g_1 = [\$10, \ E_1; \ \$5, \ E_2; \ \$1, \ E_3]$

Figure 9.1

preference ordering over outcomes gives rise to acceptable-set functions that fail to satisfy CF. Since he abstracts from considerations of risk and uncertainty, the analysis in these early articles can proceed by reference to decision trees that involve only choice nodes. It is only in the subsequent articles (Hammond, 1988a, b), as discussed in Chapter 8, that the analysis is extended to decision trees involving chance nodes as well.[2] There it is shown that the same potential for change in plans arises with respect to those whose preference ordering of (risky) prospects give rise to acceptable-set functions that fail to satisfy CIND.

Strotz's diagnosis of this type of problem as involving a violation of DC can be applied to the kinds of cases with which Hammond is concerned.[3] Consider, as a first example, an agent who is committed to Savage's minimax risk rule and who faces the following sequential version of the problem presented in Section 2.2, where $g_1 = [\$10, E_1; \$5, E_2; \$1, E_3]$, $g_2 = [\$0, E_1; \$10, E_2; \$4, E_3]$, and $g_3 = [\$5, E_1; \$2, E_2; \$10, E_3]$ (Figure 9.1). A minimax risk approach ranks the prospect associated with plan r as superior to the prospect associated with either plan s or plan t, when all three are available. Thus, one who judges plans and truncated plans in terms of their associated prospects could be expected to regard plan r as the only acceptable plan. If the agent chooses accordingly, he will head for n_1. However, from the perspective of n_1, where t (and its associated prospect g_1) is no longer available, the maximin risk criterion implies that the prospect associated with $s(n_1)$ is ranked over the prospect associated with $r(n_1)$. This suggests that only $s(n_1)$ will be acceptable at n_1. Thus, the agent is

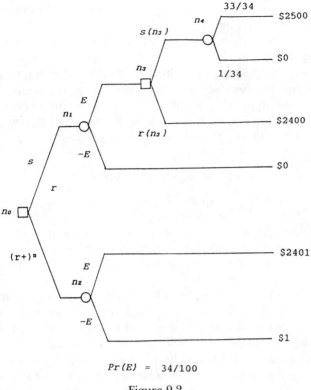

Pr (E) = 34/100

Figure 9.2

caught in a potential situation of dynamic inconsistency. At n_0, he will
be inclined to adopt r rather than s; but at n_1, he will be inclined to
choose $s(n_1)$ rather than $r(n_1)$. The formal conditions delineated in
Chapter 7, moreover, provide a model of just such behavior. Adoption of r at n_0 is mandated by PR (i.e., SR and NEC); choice of $s(n_1)$
rather than $r(n_1)$ is mandated by the combination of SR and SEP. If
the agent is faithful to all of SR, NEC, and SEP, then he will in fact
end up violating DC.

Similar remarks apply to the Kahneman and Tversky example first
discussed in Section 1.6, Figure 1.1, where it is assumed that the agent
prefers g_1 to g_2, but also prefers g_4 to g_3+ and g_3+ to g_3. Adopting
the notational conventions for plans and plan continuations adopted
in Chapter 6, we can incorporate these prospects into the decision tree
shown in Figure 9.2. SR and NEC mandate that s is in $D(S)$ while r is
not; SR and SEP mandate that $r(n_3)$ is, and $s(n_3)$ is not, in $D(S(n_2))$. The
agent who ranks g_1 over g_2 and g_4 over g_3+ and g_3+ over g_3, and accepts
SR, NEC, and SEP, will adopt plan s at n_0 and, if and when he arrives

at n_3, choose $r(n_3)$ rather than $s(n_3)$. In so choosing, however, he will in fact end up violating DC.

Notice that in each of the two cases just discussed an agent who is prepared to employ the methods of evaluation in question is in a position to anticipate fully that he will, in effect, abandon ex post the plan that he adopts ex ante. If, then, such an agent persists, that is, continues to employ that method of evaluation and chooses in the manner described, one can, following Strotz, characterize such an agent as behaving in a myopic or shortsighted fashion.

9.3 An interpretive problem

One can mark in Strotz's original article and in various articles written in response to it (including the early articles by Hammond) an important interpretive problem. Strotz focuses on situations in which such temporal changes in plans are due to such factors as weakness of will, habituation, addiction, or (as in the case of Ulysses) some external force that is "psychologically" overpowering. Yet Strotz's intention is to mark out a much more general – or perhaps even quite distinct – class of cases. As the title itself suggests, and later parts of the article make clear, Strotz is concerned with the more general problem of what counts as effective utility maximization within a dynamic context.

Similarly, Hammond takes the behavior of the myopic (or naive) drug user as a paradigm of "inconsistent" behavior. The myopic drug user prefers moderate use to abstention, and both of these to addiction. But as a result of acting on this preference, he starts to use the drug and ends up being addicted. The preoccupation of these articles, however, is really quite different. Hammond's objective is to utilize the analysis of dynamic choice situations to establish that the rational agent must accept CF.

Both Strotz and Hammond, then, tend to treat cases of potential changes in plans as involving something like weakness of will or addiction. This is unfortunate. In the two examples discussed in Section 9.2 what creates the problem of dynamic inconsistency is that the agent is committed to maximizing with respect to his preferences at each choice point in the decision tree. This suggests not so much a situation in which the self as executive will is simply weak or overcome by forces external to itself, as a situation in which the self is in control and is vigorously acting in its executive capacity to further what it at least takes to be its interests. In subsequent chapters I shall have much more to say in defense of sharpening this distinction between the addict and Ulysses, on the one hand, and the rational maximizer, on the other. In a sense, it is an objective of this work to make the case for *not* assimilating the problem faced by the dynamic utility maximizer to that of the drug addict or Ulysses. For the present, however, I simply want to note that the drug addict and Ulysses are potentially misleading paradigms for the type of problem I am exploring.

9.4 Sophisticated choice

On Strotz's view, the problem of dynamic inconsistency can be resolved. Resolution is achieved by means of a recognition of the problem and consequent adjustment of one's evaluation of plans – by the adoption of what Hammond subsequently characterizes as a *sophisticated* approach to choice. A sophisticated chooser has, in fact, two strategies available to him. The first, which Strotz describes as the strategy of "consistent planning," involves the agent anticipating his own future evaluations (and choices) and tailoring his present assessment of what counts as a feasible plan to these projections. Translated into the language of Chapters 6 and 7, such an agent regards a plan s as not feasible, and hence as not even a potential member of $D(S)$, if he projects that at some point n for which $s(n_i)$ is defined, $s(n_i)$ is not in $D(S(n_i))$. What this means, of course, is that unlike the myopic chooser the sophisticated chooser does not violate DC. By restricting the set of feasible (and hence acceptable) plans in this way, he ensures that he does not subsequently choose in a manner that is inconsistent with the plan he adopts at the outset.[4] Such a strategy can be illustrated by reference to the two examples discussed in the preceding section. For the problem given in Figure 9.1, an agent who accepts the minimax risk rule and adopts the strategy suggested above will project that if he were to move to n_1, he would then choose $s(n_1)$ over $r(n_1)$. From this he concludes, however, that r is not feasible and thus, that the feasible set of plans consists of just s and t. Moreover, by appeal to the minimax risk rule as applied to the prospects associated with these two remaining plans, he will conclude that t is the only acceptable plan and choose accordingly. Once again, moreover, the various dynamic choice conditions presented in Chapter 7 provide us with a precise way to model this behavior. Given his preferences for the prospects associated with these various plans and truncated plans, SR applied to $T(n_1)^d$ and SEP applied to $T(n_1)$ mandates that just $s(n_1)$ is in $D(S(n_1))$, and RPR or VRPR applied at n_0 mandates that just t is in $D(S)$. Thus, an agent who accepts the combination of conditions SR, SEP, and RPR or VRPR provides a model for what Strotz characterizes as "consistent planning" and Hammond characterizes as sophisticated choice.

Similar remarks can be made about the problem in Figure 9.2. The agent whose preferences conform to the Kahneman and Tversky pattern and who engages in "consistent planning" projects that were he to move to n_1, and were chance to take him to n_3, he would then choose $r(n_3)$ over $s(n_3)$. He thus realizes that s is not a feasible plan, and since, by hypothesis, the prospect associated with t is preferred to the prospect associated with r, he chooses t. Again, commitment to SR and SEP mandates the choice of $r(n_3)$ over $s(n_3)$, and RPR or VRPR, together with the judgment as to what is feasible at n_0, mandates a choice of t.

Strotz notes that sometimes the sophisticated chooser has available an alternative strategy, which he characterizes as "precommitment." That is, he may be able to take steps to ensure that at some subsequent point he prefers to choose (or perhaps has no alternative but to choose) in the manner he now prefers that he (then) choose. Strotz also argues that typically precommitment (where it is possible) will be rational. That is, it will be

rational for the man to-day to try and ensure that he will do tomorrow that which is best from the standpoint of to-day's desires. Unpleasant things which to-day we want to do sometime in the future are continually put off until tomorrow . . . unless we can find some way of precommitting ourselves to actually doing the task tomorrow. Consequently, we are often willing even to pay a price to precommit future actions (and to avoid temptation). Evidence of this in economic and other social behaviour is not difficult to find. It varies from the gratuitous promise, from the familiar phrase "Give me a good kick if I don't do such and such" to savings plans such as insurance policies and Christmas Clubs which may be hard to justify in view of the low rate of return.[5]

One can easily modify the decision problem given in Figure 9.2 to illustrate such precommitment. Let plan $(r+)^n$ be replaced by plan s^n, which is just like s, except that it involves a single choice to be made at n_0. A precommitment approach will then call for adoption of plan s^n rather than plan s. And with one additional modification of the problem, one can also illustrate Strotz's point that a rational agent will be willing to pay for the option of precommitment. One has only to replace s^n with plan s^n-, which calls for the sophisticated chooser to hire an agent who will undertake to execute plan s fully under all circumstances, for a modest fee of, say, \$1.[6]

9.5 Sophisticated choice and plan reduction

In very general terms, then, a sophisticated chooser is one who retains a commitment to all of SR, DC, and SEP but who is prepared, when confronted with a potential violation of DC, to deal with this by reconsidering which of the logically possible plans at n_0 are actually feasible for him. That is to say, he accepts PR only in the modified form indicated by RPR or VRPR.

It is clear, moreover, that what characterizes the sophisticated

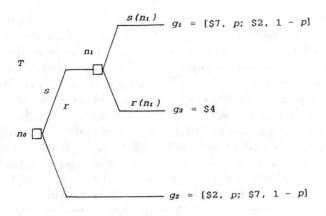

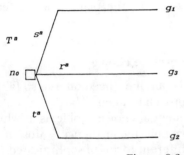

Figure 9.3

chooser's modified commitment to PR is a rejection of NEC as applicable to all logically possible plans at n_0. The sophisticated chooser resolves the potential problem of dynamic inconsistency by allowing a disparity to emerge between his evaluation of the plans before him and the evaluation he would make of those plans were he in a position to make a once-and-for-all choice. Consider, for example, a sequential choice version of the problem of decision making under uncertainty discussed in Section 2.10, where the agent is committed to Levi's principles of E-admissibility and S-admissibility (Figure 9.3). The agent who is committed to both E- and S-admissibility and who evaluates plan continuations in a manner consistent with SR and SEP will reject $s(n_1)$ in favor of $r(n_1)$ at point n_1 in T. Each of the prospects associated with these two plan contentions is E-admissible, but only the prospect associated with $r(n_1)$ is S-admissible. From the perspective of n_0, then, the decision to move on toward n_1 is tantamount to adoption and implementation of r: Plan s is simply not feasible. But, then, only r and t are feasible at n_0, and once again by application of

E- and S-admissibility to their associated prospects, the sophisticated chooser will adopt r rather than t. In the case of T^n, however, where s is available in a nonsequential form at n_0, and hence all three plans are available, the sophisticated chooser who is committed to both E- and S-admissibility will reject r and pick either t or s. Thus, whether plans are presented in normal or extensive form makes a difference.[7]

If it is clear that a sophisticated approach involves rejection of NEC, as it was originally formulated, it is also clear that it implicitly invokes something stronger than simply SR. In the example involving E- and S-admissibility rules, the sophisticated agent is prepared to rank r over t by appeal to their associated prospects. Since r can be implemented only by means of sequential choice, SR alone provides no basis for comparison between r and t. As suggested by the discussion above, then, the sophisticated chooser is quite prepared to apply a restricted version of PR such as RPR or VRPR. That is, PR is taken to hold with respect to the evaluation of t and r – the plans that are feasible by appeal to SF (and VSF).[8]

9.6 Resolute choice

On virtually all of the accounts that have been offered so far by other authors, the sophisticated approach is taken to be the only alternative to a myopic approach for sequential choice problems in which there is a potential problem of dynamic inconsistency.[9] Most have been content, in effect, to explore different forms of sophisticated choice, as Strotz does, for example, by distinguishing between "consistent planning" and "precommitment." But the factoring of conditions presented in Chapter 7 and the role that these conditions play in the constructions presented in Chapter 8 clearly suggest, in principle, one additional degree of freedom. That is, a sophisticated approach is not the only way to resolve the problem of dynamic consistency.

Note, first of all, that DC requires that future choice be consistent with present plans – that the restriction of $D(S)$ to n_i, $D(S)(n_i)$, insofar as it is nonempty, coincide with $D(S(n_i))$. But this in itself says nothing about what determines such future choice. That is, DC does not specify the basis for determining which of the alternatives at a given choice point is to be judged best: It simply requires consistency between present plans and future choices. Granting, then, that it is rational to think in terms of making plans today that are consistent with what one expects to do tomorrow, what shapes the evaluation that one expects to make tomorrow?

Sophisticated choice provides one answer. For the sophisticated chooser, the plan adopted at n_0 is conditioned by an independently based estimate of what one expects to choose at each subsequent point

n_i. And such expectations, in turn, are to be shaped by an appeal to SR, SEP, and one's preferences with respect to the prospects available at each of the de novo trees that corresponds to each subsequent point n_i. Alternatively put, projected ex post choice behavior is to constrain ex ante choice with respect to a plan; that is, $D(S)(n_i)$ is to be regimented to $D(S(n_i))$ for every n_i at which $D(S)(n_i)$ is nonempty, and $D(S(n_i))$, in turn, is to be regimented to $D(S(n_i)^d)$.

Conceptually, however, it is also possible to think of the constraint as running the other way – to think of an agent who is constrained ex post by what he judges ex ante to be the best plan available to him. That is, DC can be satisfied also if the agent applies PR at n_0 to determine $D(S)$ and then intentionally regiments $D(S(n_i))$ to $D(S)(n_i)$ for every n_i at which the latter set is nonempty.

Consider the examples previously discussed. In the case of an agent who employs the minimax risk rule in the problem in Figure 9.1, a sophisticated approach calls for selecting plan t with associated prospect g_1. By way of contrast, imagine an agent who, having judged plan r to be the best plan by appeal to SR and NEC, adopts and then proceeds to execute r by intentionally choosing $r(n_1)$ over $s(n_1)$, and thus ends up with g_3 rather than g_1. Similarly, in the version of the Kahneman and Tversky example given in Figure 9.2, sophisticated choice calls for adopting and implementing plan t, even though, by hypothesis, were s feasible the agent would prefer to have it implemented. Imagine, then, an agent who adopts plan s and then implements it by intentionally choosing $s(n_3)$ rather than $r(n_3)$ if and when he reaches n_3. Finally, in the sequential version of the problem involving Levi's E- and S-admissibility rules, as given in Figure 9.3, sophisticated choice calls for selecting and implementing plan r, the associated payoff of which is $4, even though, from the perspective of n_0, the prospect associated with that plan is not E-admissible when taken in comparison with both the prospect associated with s and that associated with t. Imagine, then, an agent who rejects plan r at n_0 (by appeal to E-admissibility considerations applied to the prospects associated with all three plans) and then, finding both plan t and plan s to be E-admissible, picks s, arrives at n_1, and then intentionally chooses $s(n_1)$ rather than $r(n_1)$.

In each of these cases, I propose to characterize the agent in question as having acted in a *resolute* manner. That is, in each case the agent can be interpreted as resolving to act in accordance with a particular plan and then subsequently intentionally choosing to act on that resolve, that is, subsequently choosing with a view to implementing the plan originally adopted. In each such case, the plan that is judged most attractive from an ex ante perspective calls for an ex post choice that the agent would otherwise not be disposed to make, but the agent consciously makes that choice nonetheless. In doing this, the agent can be said to act on his previous decision – and in so doing to choose resolutely.

Being resolute, it should be noted, is not the same as making a precommitment. The agent who precommits "ties the hands" of his future self; that is, he "deposits his will" in some external structure, so that when he arrives at the subsequent choice point, certain options are no longer available. Being resolute involves no such act of alienation. Insofar as the agent is capable of resolute choice, the ex post self is constrained not by some external structure that was created by an act of *pre*commitment on the part of the ex ante self, but by its own sense of *commitment* to a plan initiated by the ex ante self.[10]

9.7 Resolute choice and separability

The resolute chooser avoids violating DC, but he does so at the expense of SEP. There is a disparity between his ex post evaluation of plans and the evaluation he would make of those very same ex post possibilities were he to face them de novo. Consider, once again, an agent whose evaluation of risky prospects conforms to Levi's E- and S-admissibility rules and also one who is committed to the pattern identified by Kahneman and Tversky. For a resolute chooser who is committed to E- and S-admissibility rules and who faces the decision tree given in Figure 9.3, $r(n_1)$ would be ranked over $s(n_1)$ were these to be presented to the agent de novo, as $r(n_1)^d$ and $s(n_1)^d$. But plan s, which calls for a choice of $s(n_1)$ over $r(n_1)$ if and when choice node n_1 is reached, is just as acceptable as plan t, and hence a resolute agent will sometimes adopt plan s and proceed to execute it. Similar remarks apply to the case of the Kahneman and Tversky pattern of preferences, as illustrated in Figure 9.2. By hypothesis, the agent ranks the prospect associated with plan s, which calls for the choice of $s(n_3)$ over the prospect associated with plan r, which calls for the choice of $r(n_3)$. The resolute agent, then, will adopt plan s and in the event that the ex post choice point n_3 is reached will select $s(n_3)$ over $r(n_3)$. However, such an agent would also select $r(n_3)^d$ over $s(n_3)^d$.

There is, then, a disparity between how the resolute agent does in fact evaluate various options at the ex post choice point and how he would evaluate the same options were he to confront them de novo. This means, in particular, that the resolute agent's choice at a given point within the decision tree cannot be understood solely by reference to the prospects he then confronts at that choice point. Choice *within* the decision tree is shaped by a plan that is responsive to the totality of prospects that he confronted at the outset. For such an agent, choice points within the decision tree are *continuation* points:

He sees his task (at each such point) as that of continuing to implement the plan he initially settled upon, so as to ensure that the sequence of choices thus made serves to access the prospect he initially
judged to be most acceptable (or, at the very least, took to be one of
those that were acceptable). Thus, choice within the decision tree is
shaped by what can be characterized as counterfactual aspects of the
situation he then confronts. In short, the resolute agent violates SEP.[11]

Alternatively put, the resolute agent does not treat each subsequent
choice point as a new occasion for evaluation and deliberation –
unless, of course, he has received new information that requires him
to reassess his original decision. One could say that, objectively, it is
still possible for him to change his mind but, subjectively, his mind is
made up. In this sense, the resolute chooser could be said to be one
who is capable of making one grand choice at the outset and treating
every subsequent choice point as simply an occasion for the implementation of the plan previously adopted. But this means, among
other things, that the resolute chooser does not distinguish between
the extensive and normal forms of plans. That is, such an agent is
committed to PR and, in particular, to NEC.

9.8 Resolute choice and feasibility

For dynamic choice situations in which both SR and DC are taken to
be regulative, the following parallel could be said to exist between
sophisticated and resolute choice. The sophisticated chooser is prepared to discipline ex ante judgment of feasibility (and hence ex ante
choice) to what from an ex ante perspective he projects to be his own
ex post choice behavior, as independently determined, by reference
to SR and SEP. If the ex ante self projects that its ex post self would
from its own independent standpoint choose the continuation of plan
s over that of plan r, then the ex ante self regards plan r as not feasible.
The resolute chooser, in contrast, brings ex post judgment of feasibility and, correspondingly, choice into line with what, from the ex
ante perspective, he judged to be an acceptable plan. If he adopted a
plan that calls for the ex post self to select the continuation of s over
the continuation of r, then he would proceed, in effect, as if the
continuation of r were not a feasible plan. On this account, then, the
sophisticated chooser can be said to regard certain plans as simply not
feasible, given his projection of how he will on independent grounds
evaluate certain future options; and in a parallel fashion, the resolute
chooser can be said to regard certain ex post choices as simply not
feasible, given the plan that he adopted.

Despite this parallel, one can mark the following significant contrast. The sophisticated chooser's ex ante rejection of certain plans as

not feasible is a rejection based on a belief as to how the ex post self will in fact choose. The logic of the argument is straightforward: Even if he wants very much to execute a given plan, he cannot hope to realize the consequences associated with that plan unless he can count on the ex post self doing its part. Where he does not believe his ex post self will act in the required fashion, he must judge the corresponding plan to be not feasible.

The resolute chooser's ex post rejection of certain truncated plans, however, is not based on a belief that given the projected behavior of some other self, the truncated plan cannot be executed. Whereas the ex ante sophisticated agent is oriented to the idea that the ex post self is an independent self, the ex post resolute self is oriented to the idea of the ex ante self as a controlling self and, hence, to the idea of his ex post self not being completely independent. One can say, then, that whereas the sophisticated self acts under a constraint on choice imposed by the logic of *belief*, the resolute self acts under a constraint of a different sort altogether, namely, a constraint of *commitment*.[12]

9.9 Summary and anticipations

I have suggested here that contrary to the viewpoint implicit in both Strotz and Hammond, as well as most other writers in the field of decision theory, the problem of dynamic consistency can be resolved in more than one way. As an alternative to adopting a sophisticated approach to future choice, the agent can, in principle, adopt a resolute approach. I have also suggested a number of parallels and contrasts among myopic, sophisticated, and resolute choice. Myopia stands in the sharpest contrast to both the sophisticated and the resolute approaches. It involves a disparity between ex ante evaluation of ex post options and ex post evaluation of, and choice among, those options. The ex ante myopic evaluation, as characterized in the various examples I have discussed, is fully compatible with both SR and NEC, and ex post evaluation satisfies SEP. Thus, myopic choice is consistent with the strong condition TR. But the myopic approach, unlike the other two, offers no solution to the problem of dynamic inconsistency: The myopic agent fails to satisfy DC.

Unlike myopic choice, neither sophisticated nor resolute choice involves any violation of DC. In each case, ex ante and ex post evaluations coincide with one another. The sophisticated chooser achieves dynamic consistency by regimenting ex ante evaluation to projected ex post independently determined choice. By achieving dynamic consistency in this way, the chooser satisfies SEP. Satisfaction of DC in this way, however, is purchased at the price of a disparity between how the agent would evaluate the ex ante options if choice could be effected all at once and how he would evaluate them if implementation would have to take place in stages. That is, the sophisticated chooser will end up violating NEC. The resolute chooser, in contrast, achieves dynamic consistency by regimenting ex post choice to his ex ante evaluation of plans. By achieving dynamic consistency in this way, NEC is satisfied. However, satisfaction of DC in this way is purchased at the price of a disparity between how the agent would evaluate the ex post options were he faced with making the ex post choice de novo and how he would evaluate them as continuations of plans already evaluated. That is, he violates SEP.

If one abstracts from SR, then, the three approaches to the problem of dynamic consistency – myopic, sophisticated, and resolute choice – neatly triangulate the possibilities with respect to the conditions specific to a theory of dynamic choice. Myopic choice characterizes commitment to NEC and SEP at the expense of DC; sophisticated choice characterizes commitment to DC and SEP at the expense of NEC; and resolute choice characterizes a commitment to DC and NEC at the expense of SEP.[13]

The formal results of Chapter 8 establish that those who accept the simple reduction requirement SR but who employ methods of evaluation that violate either CF or CIND unavoidably face a problem. Such an agent cannot remain faithful to all of the three conditions on dynamic choice – NEC, DC, and SEP. What I have sought to do in this chapter is give a formal account or model of what amounts, then, to three possible ways to deal with this problem. The agent has, in principle, *three* degrees of freedom when confronted with various dynamic choice problems. He can take a myopic, a sophisticated, or a resolute approach.

To be sure, granting the conceptual intelligibility – the bare logical possibility – of resolute choice, it remains to be determined whether the commitment that it presupposes is realistically available to the rational agent. I propose to defer discussion of this matter, however, until Chapter 12. This is an issue that cannot be resolved until I have fully explored what an uncompromisingly pragmatic theory of rationality has to say about the problem of dynamic inconsistency discussed above. But with the setting out of the logical distinction among these three approaches, I have now completed the development of a dynamic choice framework in terms of which the pragmatic arguments first discussed in Chapter 5 can be carefully formulated and assessed. I am thus finally in a position to pick up once again the thread of argument that I temporarily put to one side at the end of Chapter 5.

10

A critique of the pragmatic arguments

10.1 Introduction

What I propose to do, in this and the following chapter, is to turn back to the explicitly pragmatic arguments that were surveyed in Chapter 4 and consider how compelling they really are when recast in terms of the framework of distinctions and conditions developed in Chapters 6 through 9. Since each of these arguments purports to show that the agent who violates either CF or CIND can be caught in a pragmatic difficulty, what I am particularly interested in determining is whether this sort of difficulty is one that arises for the agent regardless of whether he adopts a myopic, sophisticated, or resolute approach or whether, instead, the alleged pragmatic difficulty can be seen to be the consequence of adopting one, rather than another, of these approaches. In particular, what I want to determine is whether any one or another of these approaches can be shown to pass the test of not making the agent liable to be placed in a pragmatically untenable position.

My remarks at the very end of Chapter 5 hinted at what I am now in a position – thanks to the formal developments of Chapters 6 through 9 – to establish more firmly, that the pragmatic arguments presented there effectively beg the question of alternative approaches and assume that the agent behaves in a myopic fashion. That is, they tacitly presuppose an agent who is fully committed to both NEC and SEP and who, thus, unavoidably ends up choosing in a dynamically inconsistent fashion, that is, violating DC.

Once this point is established, the central question becomes that of whether any comparable pragmatic difficulty awaits either the sophisticated or the resolute chooser. If neither of these approaches can be shown to extricate the agent who is prepared to violate CF or CIND from the pragmatic difficulties that he potentially faces, then despite the objections raised in Chapter 8 to Hammond's project, there would be a consequentialist or pragmatic argument in defense of CF and CIND. The reexamination of the pragmatic arguments discussed in Chapter 5 also suggests, however, that both the sophisticated chooser and the resolute chooser escape such difficulties.

The conclusions to be arrived at in this chapter, however, are only suggestive. What is needed is a much more systematic analysis of the problem. This will be the focus of Chapter 11. There I shall defend a controversial conclusion, namely, that only the resolute approach can be judged fully acceptable from a pragmatic perspective. From this it follows, in turn, that neither CF nor CIND can be rationalized by reference to a dynamic theory of choice. Both of those principles, together with the expected utility theory that can be grounded in them, turn out to be expressive of a perfectly coherent way to think about choice, but not a way that is mandated by a pragmatic conception of rationality. If this conclusion is correct, there is a need to reconsider systematically our whole conception of rational choice.

10.2 Context-free conditions and money pumps

Consider once again the issue of the ordering requirements that might be imposed. In Section 2.9, I argued that it is reasonable to require of a rational method of evaluation that it generate a nonempty acceptable set over any set of options. That argument, of course, does *not* require appeal to money-pump considerations. It turns on the simple notion that a method of evaluation must leave the agent with something to choose, something judged acceptable. But recall also that requiring an acceptable-set function to exist does not ensure that it satisfies the various context-free conditions. Suppose, then, an agent who is disposed to choose y over z when just these two options are feasible; to choose x over y when just these two options are feasible; and, finally, to choose z over x when just these two options are feasible. If there exists an acceptable-set function, in particular, if $D(\{x, y, z\})$ is nonempty, then it will not satisfy Alpha.[1] Now according to the story told in Section 5.4, a money-pump argument can be constructed against such a violation of Alpha. That is, if the agent is presumed to hold rights to one of these, say, z, then an entrepreneur could offer him a series of trades the net effect of which would be that the agent would end up where he started, with z once again, except that he would have paid out a sum of $\$a + \$b + \$c$.

Since this story involves a series of choices made by the agent spread out over time, the decision problem in question can be represented in terms of a decision tree. For purposes of illustration, consider a decision tree in which the agent projects that the entrepreneur will continue to propose trades all the way back to z and then one more round, that is, for a total of four rounds (Figure 10.1). For the tree in question, since refusal to trade brings the chain to a close, the agent has available just the following plans and associated outcomes:

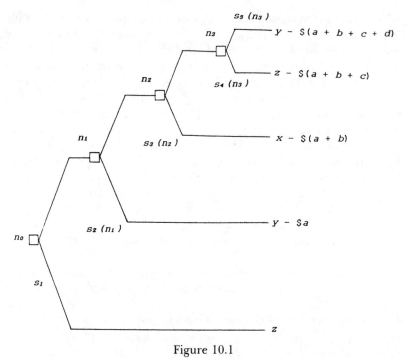

$$S_5\ (n_3)$$
$$n_3 \qquad y - \$(a + b + c + d)$$
$$z - \$(a + b + c)$$
$$S_4\ (n_3)$$
$$n_2$$
$$n_1$$
$$S_3\ (n_2) \qquad x - \$(a + b)$$
$$S_2\ (n_1)$$
$$y - \$a$$
$$n_0$$
$$S_1$$
$$z$$

Figure 10.1

(s_1) Refuse all trades, with the result that the agent retains z and pays out no money.

(s_2) Accept only the trade at n_0, with the result that the agent ends up with y and pays out the sum of $\$a$.

(s_3) Accept only the trades at n_0 and n_1, with the result that the agent ends up with x and pays out the sum of $\$a + \$b$.

(s_4) Accept only the trades at n_0, n_1, and n_2, with the result that the agent ends up with z again and is out the sum of $\$a + \$b + \$c$.

(s_5) Accept all the trades, with the result that the agent ends up with y and is out the sum of $\$a + \$b + \$c + \$d$.

Given the agent's preferences with respect to money and the three goods x, y, z, the following conclusions can be drawn concerning his preferences for the outcomes of these five plans. The outcome of plan s_5 must be dispreferred to that of plan s_2, since the latter dominates the former with respect to sure outcomes. The agent ends up in either case with y, but in the former case he is poorer by the sum of $\$a + \$b + \$c + \$d$ instead of just $\$a$. The outcome of plan s_4 must be dispreferred to that of s_1, since the latter dominates the former with respect to sure outcomes. The agent ends up in either case with z, but in the former case he is poorer by $\$a + \$b + \$c$.

The relationship between the remaining outcomes is more complicated. By hypothesis, the acceptable set of outcomes is nonempty, and
since all outcomes other than those associated with s_1, s_2, and s_3 are
clearly unacceptable, we can confine our attention to these. Given that
three prospects are still potentially acceptable, this yields a total of
seven possible specifications of the acceptable set of those outcomes
that are logically possible at n_0. Each in turn generates a sequential
decision problem that is slightly different. In order to keep the analysis as simple as possible, I shall focus on what is perhaps the most
likely case, in which the agent judges the outcome associated with s_3 to
be uniquely acceptable.[2]

Suppose, then, that the outcome associated with s_3 is uniquely acceptable. If the agent accepts PR and the ranking of the plans follows
that of the ranking of outcomes, then plan s_3 is uniquely acceptable.
This calls for the agent to move to n_1, and on to n_2, and then select
$s_3(n_2)$. At n_2, however, the agent runs into a problem. By appeal to
SEP, what is now relevant are the (truncated) plans and associated
prospects that still remain to the agent:

$s_3(n_2)$ The outcome is that the agent ends up with x and has expended
$\$a + \$b$.
$s_4(n_2)$ The outcome is that the agent ends up with z again and has
expended $\$a + \$b + \$c$.
$s_5(n_2)$ The outcome is that the agent ends up with y again and has
expended $\$a + \$b + \$c + \$d$.

From the standpoint of n_2, however, the sum $\$a + \$b$ amounts to a
sunk cost – it cannot be recovered – and thus it would seem to be
irrelevant to choice. It seems plausible to suppose, then, that the agent
will find the prospect associated with $s_4(n_2)$ more attractive than the
prospect associated with $s_3(n_2)$, and the prospect associated with $s_5(n_2)$
even more attractive. Abstracting from the sunk costs, by hypothesis
the agent was prepared to exchange x and $\$b$ for z and willing also to
exchange z and $\$d$ for y. These preferences, coupled with PR applied
to the separable situation the agent confronts at n_2, recommend adoption of plan $s_5(n_2)$. In this case, however, the agent ends up violating
DC. At n_0, s_5 is rejected in favor of s_3; but at n_2, the continuation of s_3
is rejected in favor of the continuation of s_5.

What the story describes, of course, is the situation of the myopic
chooser. Such a chooser will enter into this series of exchanges, planning, in accordance with s_2, to stop after two trades. But once the
point at which he planned to stop is reached, by reference to the
separable prospects that he then confronts, he will again prefer to
exchange for two more rounds. Thus, he trades at each point, with

the consequence that he ends up with y and is "pumped" for $\$a + \$b + \$c + \$d$. That is to say, his dynamically inconsistent behavior results, in this case, in his implementing plan s_5, the associated prospect of which, y discounted by $\$a + \$b + \$c + \$d$, is dominated with respect to sure outcomes by the prospect of y discounted by $\$a$, the prospect associated with plan s_2.

What happens to the sophisticated chooser? If no precommitment option is available, the sophisticated chooser will make just one trade; that is, he will adopt s_2. He arrives at this decision by reasoning backward from n_3. Specifically, he projects, by appeal to SEP and PR, that if he arrives at n_3, the uniquely acceptable choice there will be to trade one last time. But then, from the vantage point of n_2 and again by appeal to SEP and RPR (i.e., PR applied to what from that vantage point are judged to be feasible plans, given what he expects he will do at n_3), it is rational to trade, that is, head toward n_3, since he still prefers, we may suppose, any two trades to none. From the vantage point of n_1, however, the two feasible (truncated) plans are $s_2(n_1)$ and $s_5(n_1)$, the associated outcomes of which are, respectively, getting y at an expenditure of $\$a$ and getting y at an expenditure of $\$a + \$b + \$c + \$d$, and clearly the former of these is preferred to the latter, since it dominates the latter with respect to sure outcomes. Thus, the agent projects that at n_1 he will choose $s_2(n_1)$. At n_0, then, by RPR (or VRPR), the only feasible plans are s_1 and s_2, and s_2 is presumably the preferred one. This approach satisfies SEP and DC. But it violates PR, since from the vantage point of n_0, PR requires choice of s_3, not s_2. Yet the sophisticated chooser manages to avoid being pumped.

What about the resolute chooser? From the perspective of n_0 and PR, plan s_3 is the most attractive of the available plans. But, then, since the chooser is capable of bringing his preference ranking at the subsequent choice points into line with his ex ante evaluation of the alternative plans, he proceeds to make two trades and then stops. That is, the resolute agent will adopt plan s_3 and, then, upon arriving at n_2, execute s_3, refusing to make any further trades. The resolute agent satisfies DC and PR. But his choice behavior does not satisfy SEP. His preference ranking over the options at n_1, n_2, and so on is a function of what he judges at n_0 to be the best plan, and not a function of the prospect he faces at that choice point. In particular, we may suppose that were the resolute agent faced with a de novo choice at n_2, he would not stop but, rather, would continue on toward n_3. Yet the resolute chooser, no less than the sophisticated chooser, avoids being pumped.

It would appear, then, that both the sophisticated and the resolute chooser are protected from something to which the myopic chooser is exposed. For the problem at hand, it is only the myopic chooser who is liable to be pumped. This suggests that what is pragmatically disadvantageous is not a failure to abide by the context-free condition Alpha but rather (given that one is disposed to violate that condition) a failure to adopt an appropriate strategy at the level of dynamic choice.[3]

10.3 Independence violations

Consider the relatively simple pragmatic argument introduced in Section 1.6 against those whose preferences for well-defined risk situations conform to the pattern identified by Kahneman and Tversky. Figure 9.2 shows the decision tree representation of the problem. By hypothesis, the agent ranks $g_1 = [\$2400]$ over $g_2 = [\$2500, ^{33}/_{34}; \$0, ^{1}/_{34}]$, but ranks $g_r = [g_1, ^{34}/_{100}; \$0, ^{66}/_{100}]$ inferior to $g_s = [g_2, ^{34}/_{100}; \$0, ^{66}/_{100}]$. On the story told, the agent chooses plan s and moves to n_1, intending to choose $s(n_3)$ if and when he arrives at n_3. However, if the agent does arrive at n_3, he allegedly chooses $r(n_3)$ instead. This is, of course, the story of a myopic agent, who is neither capable of disciplining future choice to the plan adopted nor capable of anticipating his own inability in this respect. Since he is committed to both PR and SEP, he chooses s over r at n_0, but chooses $r(n_3)$ over $s(n_3)$ at n_3 and thus violates DC. Moreover, in choosing to head to n_2, the agent exposes himself to the prospect g_r, whereas if he had chosen plan $(r+)^n$ at n_0, his prospect would have been $g_{(r+)^n}$, which dominates g_r with respect to sure outcomes.

In contrast, the sophisticated chooser will anticipate that $r(n_3)$ will be chosen if and when n_3 is reached and, thus, regards r and $(r+)^n$ as the only feasible plans. Since $g_{(r+)^n}$ dominates g_r with respect to sure outcomes, he chooses plan $(r+)^n$ and, thus, avoids any violation of DSO. Correspondingly, the resolute chooser settles on plan s and chooses $s(n_3)$ if and when n_3 is reached. Thus, he also avoids any violation of DSO.[4]

A similar analysis is possible with regard to the pragmatic argument outlined in Section 5.5, which was addressed to an agent of the type identified by Ellsberg. On the assumption that the agent is fully aware of the situation, the problem he faces can be expressed in terms of the decision tree shown in Figure 10.2. Plan s has associated with it the prospect g_s, which is equivalent to $[g_2, .5; g_4, .5]$ discounted by an entry fee of $\$a$. Plan r has associated with it the prospect g_r, which is equivalent to $[g_1, .5; g_3, .5]$, discounted by entry fees amounting to $\$(a + b)$. Plan t has associated with it the undiscounted prospect of $g_t = [g_1, .5; g_3, .5]$. Now the behavior of the agent, as described in Section 5.5, is that of a myopic chooser, who accepts SR, NEC, and SEP and so violates DC. At n_0, the agent by appeal to SR and NEC chooses to

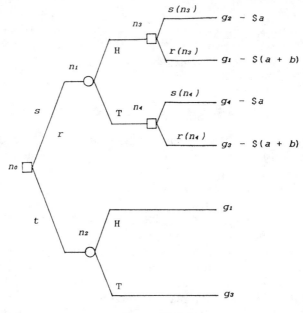

Figure 10.2

adopt plan s and, thus, trades away his right to g_t. Yet regardless of whether the coin comes up heads or tails, he is disposed, in view of his commitment to SR and SEP, to execute the continuation of plan r rather than s (in violation of DC), and thus trades again, paying out another small amount of money, $\$b$, to get either g_1 or g_3. And the price of his violation of DC in this case is that he ends up executing plan r, the associated prospect of which, g_r, is dominated with respect to sure outcomes by g_t.

The sophisticated agent, in contrast, will anticipate how he is disposed to choose in the future and hence, by appeal to SF (or VSF), will regard plan s as not feasible. Of the remaining two plans, since g_r is dominated with respect to sure outcomes by g_t, he will choose by appeal to SR and RPR (or VRPR) plan t rather than r. Finally, a resolute chooser will by appeal to PR adopt plan s and then proceed to implement it, by choosing either $s(n_3)$ or $s(n_4)$, depending on the outcome of the coin flip. Thus, once again, both the sophisticated and the resolute approaches avoid the problem of dynamic inconsistency, with its attendant violation of DSO.

10.4 Raiffa's argument

Raiffa's more complicated argument turns out to be subject to a parallel analysis. Consider an explicit tree representation of the decision problem you face when informed that the experimenter will toss a

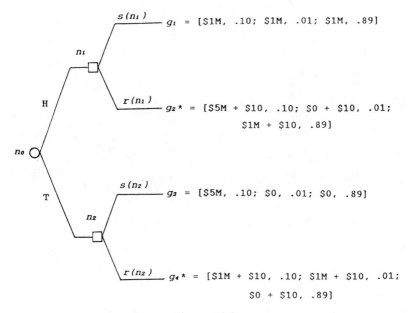

$s(n_1)$ — g_1 = [$1M, .10; $1M, .01; $1M, .89]

n_1

H

$r(n_1)$ — g_2* = [$5M + $10, .10; $0 + $10, .01;
$1M + $10, .89]

n_0

$s(n_2)$ — g_3 = [$5M, .10; $0, .01; $0, .89]

T

n_2

$r(n_2)$ — g_4* = [$1M + $10, .10; $1M + $10, .01;
$0 + $10, .89]

Figure 10.3

coin to determine whether you will play problem 1* or problem 2*
(Figure 10.3). Raiffa tacitly assumes, in effect, that preference for g_1
over g_2^* and for g_3 over g_4^* settles the question of choice at n_1 and n_2.
Translated into acceptable-set terms, his suggestion is that $D(S(n_1)) =$
$\{s(n_1)\}$ and $D(S(n_2)) = \{s(n_2)\}$. What warrant this assumption, of course,
are SEP and SR. Against that background assumption, one can now
explain his answer to the question concerning which plan you would
choose at n_0.[5] His answer is that you will choose plan s, the plan that
calls for choice of $s(n_1)$ with prospect g_1 if at n_1, and choice of $s(n_2)$
with prospect g_3 if at n_2. Translated into acceptable-set terms, $D(S) =$
$\{s\}$. Given the above determination of $D(S(n_1))$ and $D(S(n_2))$, this is
mandated by DC (indeed, by just DC-EXC), together with the assumption that $D(S)$ is nonempty. Thus, the analysis up to this point
presupposes, in effect, not the stance of a myopic, but rather that of
a sophisticated, chooser who is committed to DC, SEP, and SR. Notice,
in particular, that so far no appeal at all has been made, implicitly or
otherwise, to NEC.

Recall, however, that Raiffa then proceeds to offer a revised account
of the decision problem – as specified by Figure 5.4. Recast in decision
tree terms, this problem has the structure shown in Figure 10.4. In
this situation all plans are in normal form; the only choice to be made
is at n_0. This contrasts sharply with the problem given in Figure 10.3,
where, first, a chance experiment is conducted and then you must
make a choice.

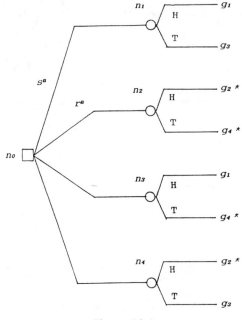

Figure 10.4

For the problem given in Figure 10.4, then, all logically possible plans are feasible. Now s and s^n have associated with them the same prospect, and similarly for r and r^n. But by appeal to Figure 5.4, g_{s^n} = g_s is dominated with respect to sure outcomes by g_{r^n} = g_r. This, taken in conjunction with SR, implies that plan s^n must be rejected in favor of plan r^n. Note, moreover, that still no appeal has been made to NEC.

Raiffa, however, assumes that his entire analysis pertains to one and the same decision problem. That is, he supposes that the problems given in Figures 10.3 and 10.4 are essentially equivalent. Specifically, he assumes that since you previously accepted his suggestion that you will choose s over r in the problem presented in Figure 10.3, then you must choose s^n over r^n in the problem in Figure 10.4. Given *that* assumption, your original favoring of g_1 over g_2^* and of g_3 over g_4^* now proves an embarrassment. You must embrace a plan whose associated prospect, g_{s^n} = g_s, is dominated with respect to terminal outcomes by g_{r^n} = g_r, the prospect associated with another plan available to you. Now what requires that if you choose s in the problem in Figure 10.3, you must choose s^n in the problem in Figure 10.4? The answer is NEC, since the decision tree in Figure 10.4 is the normal-form version of the decision tree in Figure 10.3.

Putting all of this together, it is certainly true that if you are committed to all of SR, NEC, DC, and SEP, you will face a problem here. DC, SR, and SEP require choice of s over r in the problem given in Figure 10.3; and commitment to NEC requires, then, choice of s^n over r^n in the problem given in Figure 10.4. But this choice implies, in the context of commitment to SR, that g_{s^n} be preferred to g_{r^n}, and *that* violates DSO. But this is not surprising. Such an agent is bound to get into trouble because he is implicitly described as accepting all of SR, NEC, DC, and SEP, while rejecting a logical implication of those four conditions, namely, CIND. Raiffa is right, of course, that something must give, and one possibility is that the agent abandon his preference for g_1 over g_2 and g_3 over g_4 in the original problem.

Matters turn out to be quite different, however, if we assume that the agent is committed to only two of the three conditions, SEP, DC, and NEC. First of all, if the agent is a sophisticated chooser, and thus not committed to NEC, then the embarrassment disappears. Such an agent will select s for the problem given in Figure 10.3, but r^n for the one given in Figure 10.4. If it is pointed out that r has a prospect that dominates the prospect associated with s, the sophisticated chooser's reply is simply that the "superior" plan r is not feasible.

Raiffa's argument also fails to work against a resolute agent, who will choose both r and r^n. Such an agent also avoids the charge of selecting a plan whose associated prospect is dominated with respect to terminal outcomes by another plan. The resolute agent will acknowledge, of course, that given de novo choices at n_1 and n_2 in the problem presented in Figure 10.3, he would select $s(n_1)$ if at n_1, and $s(n_2)$ if at n_2. But he will insist that n_1 and n_2 in Figure 10.3 do not present de novo options – that what he faces at each of these points are continuations of plans that were evaluated from the vantage point of n_0.

What about the myopic chooser? When presented with the problem in Figure 10.3, he will *plan* at n_0 to implement r, but in fact he will end up implementing plan s; that is, he will end up choosing $s(n_1)$ if the coin comes up heads and $s(n_2)$ if the coin comes up tails. For the problem in Figure 10.4, however, SR requires choice of r^n. Since he adopts plan r in the former and plan r^n in the latter problem, his choice behavior satisfies NEC. It would seem, then, that in this problem even the myopic chooser avoids any violation of DSO.

The myopic chooser can, however, be trapped into a violation of DSO by a simple modification of the problem. Consider the decision tree shown in Figure 10.5. Here the problem in Figure 10.3 is modified to include a prior option, namely, a version of plan r^n, with monetary payoffs discounted by some small amount $\$e$ – call this plan $(r-)^n$. Typically, it will be possible to set $\$e$ so that a myopic chooser

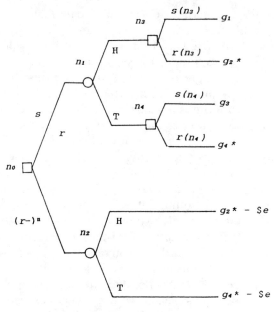

Figure 10.5

who accepts NEC (and hence PR) will not only rank r over $(r-)^n$ but also rank $(r-)^n$ over s (e.g., set $e = 5$). Note in particular that in this case the prospect associated with $(r-)^n$ still dominates the prospect associated with s in terms of sure outcomes. At n_0, the myopic chooser will head toward n_1, intending to implement plan r; but no matter what the outcome of the coin toss, he will end up abandoning that plan. If he arrives at n_3, he will choose g_1; and if he arrives at n_4, he will choose g_3. But comparing that with the alternative plan $(r-)^n$, which was available to him at n_0, the plan he ends up implementing, s, is dominated with respect to sure outcomes by $(r-)^n$. To be sure, given his myopia, the agent does not believe that he is adopting a plan that is dominated by some other plan. The agent *intends* at n_0 to implement plan r, which he does prefer to $(r-)^n$ and whose associated prospect, g_r, is not dominated by the prospect associated with plan $(r-)^n$. Indeed, g_r dominates $g_{(r-)^n}$.

In conclusion, Raiffa's counterargument turns out to be less than compelling. Once again, what generates a pragmatic difficulty for the agent is not simply his use of a method of evaluation that violates CIND; rather it is a matter of how he is prepared to deal with certain dynamic choice situations to which he can then be exposed. If he approaches these situations myopically, he does face a pragmatic problem. But if he approaches them in a sophisticated or a resolute manner, he avoids the problem.

10.5 Seidenfeld's argument

Seidenfeld has offered a somewhat related argument, which he believes poses a problem for an agent who is prepared to give up IND
(or CIND) but who accepts the weak ordering principle WO (or CF).
The argument appeals to a very explicitly formulated dynamic choice
framework, which is why I have deferred discussion of it until now.
Of the cases Seidenfeld discusses, the one on which I shall focus
concerns violations of a special version of independence, which, following him, can be designated as the mixture-dominance principle:

> *Mixture dominance (MD).* If each of two lotteries g_1 and g_2 is
> preferred (or dispreferred) to a third gamble g_3, then so too is
> any convex combination of g_1 and g_2.[6]

Here is the specific example Seidenfeld uses to diagnose the problem that arises for one who violates MD. Let lotteries g_1 and g_2 be
indifferent to each other with a sure-dollar equivalent of $5.00, and
suppose, contrary to MD, that an equal convex combination of these
two lotteries $g_3 = [g_1, .5; g_2, .5]$ is strictly preferred to either alone
and has a sure-dollar equivalent of $6.00. By continuity of preference
for monetary payoffs, one can infer that there is some fee, $\$e$, which
can be attached to each of the final payoffs in g_3, resulting in a lottery
$g_4 = g_3 - \$e = [(g_1 - \$e), .5; (g_2 - \$e), .5]$, such that g_4 is indifferent
to $5.75. It can also be assumed that there is some dollar prize, for
example, $4, which is strictly dispreferred to both $(g_1 - \$e)$ and $(g_2 - \$e)$. Putting all these specifications together yields the following
ordering:[7]

$$\$4 < (g_1 - \$e), (g_2 - \$e) < g_1 \sim g_2 \sim \$5 < g_4 \sim \$5.75 < g_3 \sim \$6.00$$

Seidenfeld now proceeds to embed these lotteries in the decision tree
shown in Figure 10.6. In contemplating the various plans open to him
in this decision tree, Seidenfeld argues, the agent must face what he
knows his preferences are at the choices he faces after the coin is
flipped. More specifically, appealing to the preferences specified
above for the lotteries in question, the agent must expect that he will
choose $5.50 if at n_3, $5.50 if at n_4, lottery $g_1 - \$e$ if at n_5, and lottery
$g_2 - \$e$ if at n_6. This means, for example, that plan r_1, which calls for
choosing g_1 if at n_3 and choosing g_2 if at n_4, is simply not available. It
is not available because it calls for the agent to make choices at n_3 and
n_4 that he knows at n_0 he will not make. Thus, the agent has available
to him only two plans, a plan s_1, whose associated prospect is a sure
payoff of $5.50, and a plan s_2, whose associated prospect is the convex
combination of $g_1 - \$e$ and $g_2 - \$e$, that is, g_4, which is valued at

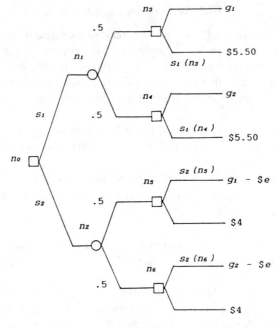

Figure 10.6

$5.75. Seidenfeld concludes, then, that the agent will choose plan s_2 over plan s_1.

Such a line of reasoning, Seidenfeld suggests, can be made more precise by appeal to the following principle:

> *Dynamic feasibility (DF).* To assess plan p at a choice node n_i, anticipate how you will choose at its (potential) "future" choice nodes n_j and declare infeasible all future alternatives under p that are inadmissible at n_j.[8]

This principle and the analysis to which it gives rise can be interpreted in terms of the set of conditions explored in Chapters 6 through 8. Seidenfeld insists that the agent must expect that he will choose $5.50 if at n_3, and so on, thereby supposing that the agent must, upon arriving at n_3, evaluate his options just in terms of the related prospects that remain open to him at that point, that is, $5.50 and g_1, and so on. This can be interpreted as an implicit appeal to SR and SEP. Moreover, DF corresponds to either condition SF or condition VSF. I shall return to the question of which is the more appropriate interpretation, but for the moment, let me continue with his argument.

Seidenfeld now suggests that the preference for s_2 over s_1 must prove an embarrassment to the agent. This part of his argument proceeds by appeal to what he terms a *coherence principle*, governing both static and dynamic choice. As it pertains to dynamic choice, the sense of coherence is this: A decision rule is *coherent* if respect for stochastic dominance is preserved under substitution of indifferent alternatives at choice points.[9] Seidenfeld claims that the agent with preferences that violate MD ends up violating this coherence principle. And while Seidenfeld does not offer a gloss on this principle, one can reconstruct from his discussion of the example just introduced what he takes its import to be. Here is his analysis:

Under the indifferences of the "ordering" postulate and the preferences induced by stochastic dominance at nodes n_3 through n_6, the upshot is a contradiction in the assessment of the sequential decision problem. The contradiction obtains as follows.

By postulate (1) [the ordering principle WO], the agent has a weak ordering of options at choice nodes n_3 through n_6. There is some sure-dollar equivalent for $g_1 - \$e$ and $g_2 - \$e$. By simple dominance, the sure-dollar equivalent for $g_1 - \$e$ (or for $g_2 - \$e$) is less than that for g_1. That is, each of $g_1 - \$e$ and $g_2 - \$e$ is worth less than \$5.00 and more than \$4.00. Since admissibility at choice nodes (such as nodes n_3 through n_6) respects indifference, anticipation and knowledge (at n_0) of one's choices at n_3 through n_6 is only up to the level of indifferents. That is, the "ordering" postulate fixes choices only up to the equivalences of indifference, $\sim$. Thus, substitution of $\sim$-indifferents at choice nodes n_3 through n_6 leaves unchanged choices at those nodes. But plan s_2 is dominated by plan s_1 when, as dictated by postulate (1), the choices at nodes n_5 and n_6 are switched for their (indifferent) sure-dollar equivalents.

. . . Hence, . . . applications of postulate (1) – "ordering" – at nodes n_5 and n_6 lead to contradictory conclusions with decisions made at node n_0.

Let us call this contradictory assessment an episode of *sequential incoherence*. That is, . . . respect for stochastic dominance is not preserved under substitution of indifferent alternatives at choice nodes.[10]

According to this line of reasoning, the problem that arises concerns a difference between the assessment of the plans when, as given in Figure 10.6, plan s_2 terminates in the lotteries $g_1 - \$e$ and $g_2 - \$e$, and the assessment of the plans when plan s_2 is *modified* into plan s_2^*, by having it terminate in the sure-dollar equivalences of $g_1 - \$e$ and $g_2 - \$e$, designated by $\$(g_1 - \$e)$ and $\$(g_2 - \$e)$. In the problem as presented in Figure 10.6, plan s_2 is preferred to plan s_1. In the altered problem, involving the replacement of plan s_2 with plan s_2^*, plan s_1 is the preferred plan. This, we are informed, means that respect for stochastic dominance is not preserved under substitution of indifferent alternatives at choice points.

Now the prospect the agent faces if he chooses s_1 is simply that of getting \$5.50, while the prospect he faces if he chooses s_2^* in the modified problem is that of getting a smaller amount of money. Thus, the former stochastically dominates the latter, and, correspondingly,

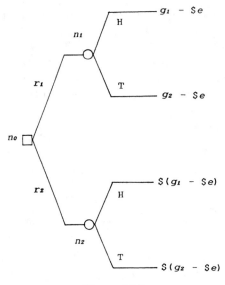

Figure 10.7

s_1 must be preferred to s_2^*. Moreover, it is clear that one can transform s_2 into s_2^* by replacing $g_1 - \$e$ and $g_2 - \$e$ with their sure-dollar equivalences. But what is required to make invoking FSD (or DSO) in this context relevant is that s_2^* be indifferent to s_2. Presumably, then, what Seidenfeld's "coherence principle" involves, in addition to FSD (or DSO) itself, is the following principle:

> *Dynamic substitution (D-SUB).* If plans s and r differ solely by a substitution of indifferents at some choice point, then s and r are indifferent.

Such a principle, as its name suggests, constitutes a dynamic choice version of the standard substitution principle SUB. To see this, consider the variation on Seidenfeld's example shown in Figure 10.7. In this instance, the agent has only a single choice up front – all subsequent moves are made by nature, and as before $\$(g_1 - \$e)$ and $\$(g_2 - \$e)$ designate the dollar equivalences for the gambles $g_1 - \$e$ and $g_2 - \$e$, respectively. D-SUB does not apply to this problem, but SUB does. That is, if the agent who confronts this problem is committed to SUB and SR, he must rank plan r_1 and plan r_2 indifferently, since each can be derived from the other by substitution of indifferent components. However, with a simple modification of this problem, one can capture the import of D-SUB. Suppose, for example, that after nature makes its move, the agent then has a second choice to make, as shown

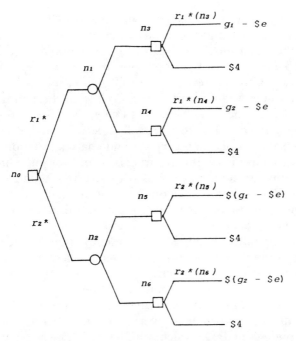

Figure 10.8

in Figure 10.8. Again, I assume that $4 is dispreferred to any of the other prospects. D-SUB now applies, and what it requires is that the agent rank plan r_1^* indifferently to plan r_2^*.

It is clear, from the very example that Seidenfeld has constructed, that the agent who is prepared to violate MD can be confronted with a situation in which he will end up violating D-SUB. Thus, holding everything else constant, the agent cannot accept D-SUB *and* order the corresponding plans in the manner discussed above, that is, rank plan s_2 over plan s_1 in the original problem (Figure 10.6), but rank plan s_1 over plan s_2^* in the modified version of that problem, obtained by replacing s_2 with s_2^*.

Granting all of this, the question is simply whether D-SUB provides any independent leverage to be used against the agent who is disposed to violate MD. One can begin by recalling that both MD and SUB are versions of an independence principle and that those who are disposed to relax MD will typically also be disposed to relax SUB. This, of course, does not require a negative response to the question posed, since D-SUB is logically distinct from SUB. SUB applies only to replacements at *chance* nodes in a decision tree, whereas D-SUB applies to replacements at choice nodes. However, within the framework in which Seidenfeld works, the extension of substitution reasoning to choice as well as chance nodes seems plausible enough – if indeed it need be thought of as any extension at all. On Seidenfeld's account, the agent must face up to what he knows his future choice will be. That is, he must figure out how he will choose in the future, by reference to the preferences he will then have for the prospects that remain open to him, and reason back from there to his present situation. I presume that Seidenfeld's agent, when confronted with the problem given in Figure 10.8, will expect that if and when node n_3 is reached, he will choose $r_1^*(n_3)$ and that expectation naturally expresses itself by his assigning a probability of 1 (or something closely approximating it) to the proposition (if I reach n_3, then I will choose $r_1^*(n_3)$). Similar assignments, moreover, can be made with respect to the various propositions regarding what he will do, conditional on reaching the other possible choice nodes.

In effect, then, the evaluation of present options proceeds by anticipating future (independently motivated) choices, using that information to reinterpret subsequent choice nodes as chance nodes, and evaluating the prospects that can be defined by reference to that reinterpretation. This implies, in turn, that the agent will reinterpret choice nodes in the problem given in Figure 10.8 as if they were "chance" nodes – nodes at which, with (virtually) probability 1, he will be exposed to certain prospects. But then he will treat the problem in Figure 10.8 *as if* it were the problem given in Figure 10.7. For such an agent, commitment to SUB in nonsequential choice situations will imply choosing in sequential choice situations *as if* he were committed to D-SUB. And turning this point around, a disposition to violate SUB will imply a disposition to choose *as if* he were violating D-SUB. This being the case, however, I do not see how an appeal to D-SUB can provide any independent leverage against violations of SUB (or MD, IND, etc.). Indeed, to argue against violations of SUB (and MD and IND) by appeal to D-SUB is to proceed in a fashion that comes uncomfortably close to begging the issue.

These are concerns that I have already expressed,[11] yet Seidenfeld continues to be convinced that D-SUB is a valid principle governing dynamic choice, at least for those committed to the ordering principle. In reply to my objections, he offers the following argument for D-SUB:

Let g_1 and g_2 be indifferent consequences. (Stability of values insures this relation is well defined over choice nodes.) Consider two sequential plans s_1 and s_2 which differ solely in that, at one designated choice node, s_1 selects g_1 and s_2 selects g_2. The two plans are identical otherwise. . . . We establish that s_1 and s_2 are indifferent as follows.

Imagine a simple sequential decision that has an initial choice between the s_1/s_2 plans and another option r, which is dispreferred to each of s_1 and s_2. Since g_1 and g_2 are indifferent, both are admissible at the designated node

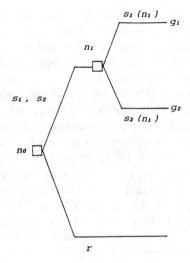

Figure 10.9

where there is a choice between them. Since s_1 and s_2 are identical otherwise, by Dynamic Feasibility, both plans s_1 and s_2 are admissible at the initial choice node, and r is inadmissible there. By ordering, then, s_1 and s_2 are indifferent.[12]

For the purposes of interpreting this argument, it will prove useful to give the decision problem an explicit dynamic representation, as in Figure 10.9. Seidenfeld here takes the indifference relation that is assumed to obtain between g_1 and g_2 as implying something about which plan continuations are admissible at node n_1. ("Since g_1 and g_2 are indifferent, both are admissible at the designated node where there is a choice between them.") In so doing, he reveals an implicit commitment to something like the combination of SR and SEP. That is, when his argument is reinterpreted explicitly in terms of those conditions, we can secure his conclusion. SR and the assumption that g_1 and g_2 are indifferent to one another yield that $s_1(n_1)^d$ is indifferent to $s_2(n_1)^d$ in the de novo tree that coincides with the tree continuation $T(n_1)$. And since this indifference also implies that both are in the acceptable set $D(S(n_1)^d)$, SEP in turn yields that both $s_1(n_1)$ and $s_2(n_1)$ are in $D(S(n_1))$.

The residual issue is how his appeal to DF is to be understood. From his gloss of DF in Section 1 of the paper from which the above quotation is taken, it seems clear that Seidenfeld is committed to something much closer to VSF (i.e., something stronger than what I have formulated as SF) for those cases in which two or more plan continuations are admissible at some choice point n_i, yet not indifferent to each other. In particular, he must invoke something like VSF if he is to respond effectively to an objection raised by Hammond, to the effect that violations of Alpha and Beta (no less than MD) will lead to a form of incoherence in dynamic choice contexts.[13] But as the quotation above also makes clear, for the case in question, where it is assumed that $s_1(n_1)$ and $s_2(n_1)$ are not simply admissible but indifferent to each other, he must take DF as having something more like the import of SF. That is, if the condition invoked were VSF (rather than SF), he could not conclude that both plans s_1 and s_2 are admissible at the initial choice node. Thus, maintaining a distinction between the criterion of feasibility that is appropriate in the case of merely admissible options and the one that is appropriate in the case where options are not only admissible but also indifferent appears to be essential to his argument as a whole. If he must make do throughout with something like SF, he may be able to justify D-SUB, but it looks as though he will have to accept Hammond's objection that violations of Beta also involve a violation in the form of dynamic incoherence. If he must invoke VSF throughout, he may have an effective rejoinder to Hammond, but it looks as though he will have to give up his defense of D-SUB.

The issue here closely parallels one explored in Chapter 8. Theorem 8.3 establishes that the conjunction of DC-INC, SEP, SR, and SF suffices for the derivation of CIND-E, the choice version of SUB, which is precisely one of the axioms of utility theory that Seidenfeld wants to retain. The problem is that according to Theorem 8.4, this set of dynamic choice conditions also yields Beta, which Seidenfeld wants to reject. Propositions 8.3 and 8.4, however, show that when SF is replaced by VSF, the resultant set of conditions does not suffice to yield either Beta or CIND-E. If, then, he could invoke something approximating VSF in the case of merely admissible options and something approximating SF in the case of admissible and indifferent options, Seidenfeld would be able to avoid the unwanted condition Beta and still secure the desired condition CIND-E. My problem here is simply that I am not persuaded that for the two cases in question – the case of options that are merely admissible versus the case of options that are admissible and indifferent to one another – different feasibility conditions are appropriate. At the very least, I believe, Seidenfeld needs to provide an explicit account of why these two cases are to be treated so differently.[14]

Regardless of how this issue is resolved, however, the reader should recall that I have no great affection for *either* SF or VSF. The point of Chapter 9 is that there is another degree of freedom possible here: One can reject SEP and think in terms of resolute choice. With regard to Seidenfeld's original discussion of MD, resolute choosers will be unimpressed by his insistence that in the problem in Figure 10.6, the agent must expect that he will choose \$5.50 if at n_3 and \$5.50 if at n_4,

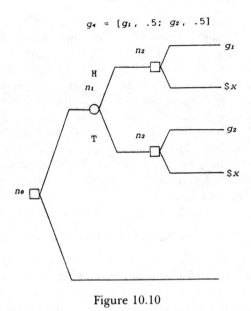

$$g_4 = [g_1, .5; g_2, .5]$$

Figure 10.10

and that he must then accept that the only feasible plan associated with heading toward n_1 is plan s_1, with its sure payoff of $5.50. To the contrary, such an agent will suppose that there is another feasible plan, r_1, which calls for him to move to n_1 and then select g_1 if chance takes him to n_3, and g_2 if chance takes him to n_4. Moreover, given the hypothesis concerning the agent's preferences (preferences that violate MD), the agent will regard r_1 as clearly superior to plan s_2 (this by appeal to FSD again) – indeed, it is the best plan of all and, hence, the one he will adopt and resolutely implement. Thus, even if Seidenfeld's argument went through, it would present no problem as such for the resolute chooser, but only for one committed to a sophisticated approach.

This difference in the logical implications of resolute and sophisticated choice becomes particularly clear when one considers in Figure 10.10 a dynamic choice version of the Ellsberg problem discussed in Section 4.5 (Figure 4.7). The hypothesis is that when the probability of E is completely unknown, the agent may well prefer g_4, which consists of an even-chance mixture of the two symmetric uncertain prospects g_1 and g_2, to getting $x outright, and prefer getting $x outright to some other inferior option available at n_0. Faced, however, with a de novo choice between g_1 and $x, he would choose $x; and, similarly, faced with a de novo choice between g_2 and $x, he would choose $x. Correspondingly, in de novo choice between $x and the dollar equivalent for g_1, $\$(g_1)$, he would choose $x. Given these preferences, a resolute chooser will plan to choose g_1 if chance takes him to n_2, and g_2 if chance takes him to n_3, and act accordingly. Now suppose that g_1 is replaced by $\$(g_1)$ and g_2 is replaced by $\$(g_2)$. In this modified version of the problem, the agent, resolute though he may be, surely now has no motive to choose $\$(g_1)$ rather than $\$x$ if chance takes him to n_2, and $\$(g_2)$ rather than $\$x$ if chance takes him to n_3. He has no such motive, because the substitution in question renders that plan decidedly inferior. Clearly, in this modified problem, his best plan is to choose $\$x$ if chance takes him to n_2, and $\$x$ if chance takes him to n_3. Thus, contrary to Seidenfeld's approach to such problems, substitution of indifferents at a given choice node may result in a radically different choice at that node.[15]

10.6 Some tentative conclusions

Looking back at the arguments discussed in this chapter, what would seem to emerge is that it is not violations per se of CF and CIND (or preference versions thereof) that lead the agent into pragmatic difficulty. Rather, given an agent who is committed to modes of evaluation that do not satisfy one or the other of these principles, it appears to be a matter of how he is prepared to approach the evaluation of plans in certain dynamic choice problems that determines whether he faces a difficulty with respect to DSO. Specifically, it appears that it is the myopic chooser who faces such difficulties. As for those who are prepared to choose in either a sophisticated or a resolute manner, the examples suggest that they face little (if any) difficulty in this regard. But this in turn suggests (if only very tentatively) that there may be nothing like a secure "consequentialist" argument in favor of either CF or CIND: Those who are disposed to violate one or the other of these two conditions may be able to avoid getting into trouble by adopting a sophisticated or a resolute approach to sequential choices.

To establish this, however, what is needed is not simply a series of illustrative or suggestive examples but rather a much more systematic argument. This is the task to which I turn in the next chapter.

11

Formalizing a pragmatic perspective

11.1 Introduction

The examples discussed in Chapter 10 suggest that agents who use methods of evaluation that violate either the CFO factor of WO (or CF) or IND (or CIND), and who thus cannot satisfy all of DC, NEC, and SEP in certain dynamic choice situations, do not necessarily fall into pragmatic difficulties – that such difficulties are reserved for those who approach these choice situations in a myopic manner. Three questions naturally arise here. First, does taking a myopic approach invariably make one subject to such difficulties? Second, does taking either a sophisticated or a resolute approach enable one to avoid whatever pragmatic difficulties arise for those who adopt a myopic approach? Third, does one of these alternative approaches turn out to be superior to the other from a pragmatic perspective?

I shall argue in response to the first two questions that it is in fact *not* true that agents who employ methods of evaluation that violate either CFO or IND can always be caught up in pragmatic difficulties. Violations of these two principles need not result in choice of a plan whose associated prospect is dominated with respect to sure outcomes by the prospect associated with some other feasible plan. To be sure, an agent who does employ such methods of evaluation and who deals with the ensuing problem of dynamic consistency in a myopic manner typically (perhaps even invariably) can be caught up in such a pragmatic difficulty. But an agent who adopts either a sophisticated or a resolute approach can avoid the specific problem to which the myopic chooser is thereby exposed.

I shall also argue that sophisticated choosers typically (perhaps even invariably) face their own version of a pragmatic difficulty – and that this difficulty is one the resolute chooser avoids. I shall argue in response to the third question that the resolute approach is pragmatically superior to the sophisticated approach. This last thesis is clearly the most controversial one. It is important to note that even if the pragmatic superiority of the resolute approach cannot be sustained (specifically on the grounds that it calls upon the agent to adopt plans that are not feasible), a sophisticated approach will then constitute a pragmatically impeccable way of dealing with situations in which not all of NEC, DC, and SEP can be satisfied. I hope to establish a strong thesis; but if this does not succeed, I have a fallback position according to which sophisticated choice can be understood to provide a pragmatically respectable way to deal with such situations.

This means that regardless of how the issue of the relative merits of resolute and sophisticated choice is settled, Hammond's consequentialist theory and the standard theory of rationality that can be derived from it remain unsupported from a pragmatic perspective. This implies that insofar as the expected utility theory is taken as a norm for rational choice, it condemns as irrational or unreasonable choice behavior that has yet to be shown to involve the choice of means insufficient for given ends. In short, from the perspective of Hume's demanding pragmatic test, the presumption is against taking the expected utility theory as setting *necessary* conditions for rational choice.

The arguments that follow are formulated in terms of acceptable-set versions of both the weak ordering and the strong independence principles, that is, in terms of CF and CIND, rather than CFO and IND. This will, I hope, allow me finally to resolve an issue posed at the end of Chapter 2, namely, whether there is any basis in pragmatic considerations for distinguishing between preference and acceptable-set versions of the relevant principles. If there are pragmatic difficulties to be encountered in connection with violations of CF and CIND, as well as CFO and IND, then whatever the merits of distinguishing between ordering and acceptable-set versions of these conditions, the basis for this distinction must lie in something other than pragmatic considerations.[1]

11.2 The problem with myopic choice

Under conditions in which not all of DC, SEP, and NEC can be satisfied, the model of the myopic chooser is that of one who holds fast to SEP and NEC and thus ends up violating DC. The myopic chooser plans to implement some plan s if and when he arrives at some choice node n_i by choosing $s(n_i)$, but in fact, when at n_i, he may choose some other plan continuation $r(n_i)$ instead. Thus he violates DC. The analysis of Chapter 10 suggested, moreover, that in each case in which the method of evaluation failed to satisfy either CF or CIND, it would be possible to embed the relevant prospects in a decision tree in such a way that a myopic agent would end up executing a plan whose associated prospect was dominated with respect to sure outcomes by the prospect associated with another plan.

With a view to formulating a generalized version of this argument, it will prove useful to explore one additional example. Consider an agent who accepts Levi's E- and S-admissibility rules and who con-

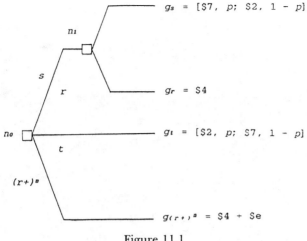

$$g_s = [\$7, \ p; \ \$2, \ 1 - p]$$

$$g_r = \$4$$

$$g_t = [\$2, \ p; \ \$7, \ 1 - p]$$

$$g_{(r+)^n} = \$4 + \$e$$

Figure 11.1

fronts the decision tree shown in Figure 11.1 (where p is completely indeterminate). Here $(r+)^n$ is to be understood as a nonsequential and enhanced version of r, in which the payoff of \$4 is increased by some small positive amount \$$e$. Once again, it should be possible to set e small enough so that by the E-admissibility criterion the prospect \$4 + \$$e$ will be rejected in the presence of the prospects associated with s and t. In particular, when p is completely indeterminate, this will be true for any \$$e < \$0.50$. Since the myopic agent accepts NEC, s and t are in $D(S)$, but neither $(r+)^n$ nor r is. The myopic agent, then, may settle upon (pick) plan s and move to n_1 with a view to selecting $s(n_1)$. If he does this, it follows from his commitment to E- and S-admissibility and the conditions PR (i.e., SR and NEC) and SEP that $r(n_1)$ is, and $s(n_1)$ is not, in $D(S(n_1))$. Thus, he will choose $r(n_1)$, thereby implementing not plan s but rather plan r. But r's prospect is clearly dominated with respect to sure outcomes by the prospect associated with $(r+)^n$, since the sure outcome associated with r, namely, \$4, is strictly dispreferred to the one associated with $(r+)^n$, namely, \$4 + \$$e$.

Notice, moreover, that the alternative plan, $(r+)^n$, is the plan that the sophisticated chooser will adopt. He will judge that plan s is not feasible and thus that the feasible set consists just of r, $(r+)^n$, and t. But since the prospect associated with $(r+)^n$ dominates the prospect associated with r, r will not be in $D(S)$. This leaves just t and $(r+)^n$, both of which are E-admissible; but only the latter is S-admissible. Thus, $D(S) = \{(r+)^n\}$. The sophisticated chooser, then, adopts $(r+)^n$ and avoids the specific pragmatic difficulty faced by the myopic chooser.

The resolute chooser also avoids this difficulty. He judges all four plans to be feasible, regards r as unacceptable in the presence of

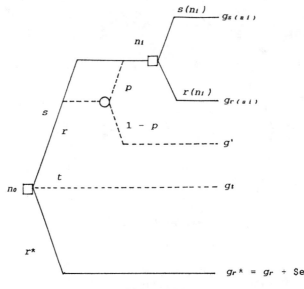

Figure 11.2

$(r+)^n$, and, by appeal to E-admissibility, regards the latter unaccept-able in the presence of s and t. Thus, only s and t are acceptable, and in the event that he decides to implement s, he will move to n_1 and then proceed to select $s(n_1)$. But whatever plan he implements – s or t – its associated prospect is not dominated with respect to sure out-comes by the prospect associated with any other feasible plan. Thus, he avoids the pragmatic difficulty faced by the myopic chooser.

Constructions of this sort are subject to the following generaliza-tion: Consider any situation in which an agent employs a method of evaluation of static choices that violates either CF or CIND. Take that choice problem and embed it in a sequential problem – involving no intervening chance event if CF is violated, or an intervening chance event if CIND is violated (and perhaps, as may prove necessary, cer-tain other intervening choice nodes or certain other options available at n_0). In diagram form, this yields the generic situation shown in Figure 11.2. If the agent's method of evaluation violates either Alpha or CIND-S, strict choice independence, it will be possible to construct a tree of this sort in which either (1) g_s is, and g_r is not in $D(G_S)$, while $g_{r(n_i)}$ is, and $g_{s\ (n_i)}$ is not, in $D(G_{S(n_i)})$ or (2) both g_s and g_r are in $D(G_S)$, while $g_{r(n_i)}$ is, and $g_{s(n_i)}$ is not, in $D(G_{S(n_i)})$.[2] If the method of evaluation violates either Beta or CIND-E, equivalent choice independence, then it will be possible to construct a tree of this sort in which (3) g_s is, and g_r is not, in $D(G_S)$, while both $g_{s(n_i)}$ and $g_{r(n_i)}$ are in $D(G_{S(n_i)})$. There are, then, three cases to consider.

Consider first case (1), in which g_s is, and g_r is not, in $D(G_S)$, while $g_{r(n_i)}$ is, and $g_{s(n_i)}$ is not, in $D(G_{S(n_i)})$. For this case, let plan $r^* = (r+)^n$ be a nonsequential enhanced version of r, whose associated prospect is $g_r + \$e$. I assume that the premium attaching to $g_{(r+)^n}$ can be made sufficiently small to ensure that $g_{(r+)^n}$ is not in $D(G_S)$, that is, that while g_r is not chosen in the presence of $g_{(r+)^n}$, the latter is not chosen in the presence of g_s.[3]

Now for a myopic agent who is committed to NEC, s is, and r is not, in $D(S)$. But at n_i, by appeal to SEP and PR (NEC and SR), $r(n_i)$ is, and $s(n_i)$ is not, in $D(S(n_i))$. Such an agent, then, violates DC. Of course, as the example of E- and S-admissibility rules makes clear, the myopic agent will not invariably move toward n_i: Some other plan t may be available at n_0, a plan that is also in $D(S)$.[4] Since s is in $D(S)$, however, the myopic chooser *may* move toward n_i, planning to select $s(n_i)$. And in such a case, if and when n_i is reached, the myopic agent will choose $r(n_i)$ instead of $s(n_i)$. Thus, he will end up implementing plan r rather than plan s. But r's prospect is dominated with respect to sure outcomes by the prospect associated with plan $r^* = (r+)^n$, and this regardless of whether there has been some intervening chance event.

By contrast, the sophisticated chooser will anticipate his own choice dispositions at n_i and judge plan s to be not feasible. Both plans r and $r^* = (r+)^n$ are feasible, however; and since the prospect associated with the latter dominates the prospect associated with the former with respect to sure outcomes, r will never be in $D(S)$. Plan t, however, may or may not be in $D(S)$. Thus, the sophisticated chooser will end up implementing either $(r+)^n$ or some other plan t, neither of which is such that its prospect is dominated by the prospect associated with any other feasible plan. The resolute chooser also avoids the difficulty. He will end up implementing either s or some other plan t, since by construction s is, t may be, and $(r+)^n$ is not in $D(S)$. But the prospects associated with both s and t are not dominated by the prospects associated with any other feasible plan.

Can this line of argument be extended to criticize the behavior of the myopic agent in case (2) violations of Alpha or CIND-S, where both g_s and g_r are in $D(G_S)$, while $g_{r(n_i)}$ is, and $g_{s(n_i)}$ is not, in $D(G_{S(n_i)})$? Once again, let $r^* = (r+)^n$, a nonsequential enhanced version of r whose associated prospect is $g_r + \$e$. In this instance, however, since, by hypothesis, both g_s and g_r are in $D(G_S)$, an enhanced version of g_r will usually end up being chosen over g_s.[5] Typically, however, it should be possible to modify g_s in a parallel fashion, to convert g_s into $g_{s+} = g_s + \$f$, such that $g_{(r+)^n}$ will not be chosen in the presence of g_{s+}, that is, so that g_{s+} is, and $g_{(r+)^n}$ is not, in $D(G_{S*})$, where $S*$ is the set of plans available in the modified version of the tree, with $s+$ substituted for s.[6] This amounts, of course, to modifying case (2)

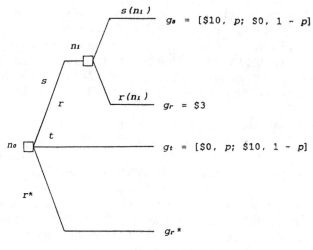

Figure 11.3

violations of Alpha or CIND-S so that they conform to type (1) violations. Where this can be done, the argument for case (1) violations will apply.

What about the behavior of the myopic agent in case (3) situations, involving a violation of either Beta or CIND-E? Here, g_s is, and g_r is not, in $D(G_S)$, while both $g_{s(n_i)}$ and $g_{r(n_i)}$ are in $D(G_{S(n_i)})$. Once again, since, by hypothesis, g_r will not be chosen in the presence of g_s, it will typically be possible to replace $g_{r(n_i)}$ with $g_{r(n_i)}+ = g_{r(n_i)} + \$e$ and devise $g_{r*} = g_{(r++)^n} = g_{r+} + \$f$, so that (1) $g_{r(n_i)}$ is chosen over $g_{s(n_i)}$, but g_s is still chosen in the presence of both g_{r+} and $g_{(r++)^n}$. Where this can be done, case (3) situations will be converted into case (1) situations, and the argument presented above will once again apply.

It would appear, however, that it will not always be possible to convert case (2) and (3) situations into case (1) situations. To see what the problem is, consider the agent who adopts just Levi's E-admissibility rule (but not S-admissibility) and who is confronted with the decision problem in Figure 11.3 (where p is once again completely indeterminate). By appeal to E-admissibility, g_r will be rejected in the presence of both g_s and g_t, but will be acceptable in the presence of just g_s. The myopic agent, then, will reject r at n_0 in favor of either s or t, but in the event that he adopts s and moves to n_1, he will then regard $s(n_1)$ and $r(n_1)$ as equally acceptable; thus, he may end up selecting $r(n_1)$. Notice, however, that the only incremental improvement in $g_r = g_{r(n_i)}$ that would *ensure* choice of $r(n_1)$ over $s(n_1)$, would be to raise \$3 to \$10. Any smaller increase will leave $g_{s(n_i)}$ E-admissible. But, of course, if g_r is raised to \$10, then r will now be chosen over both s and

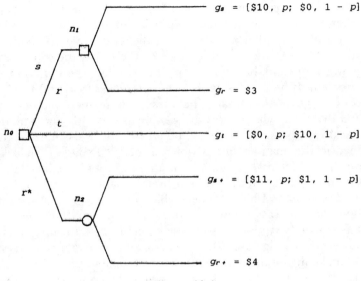

Figure 11.4

t at n_0. And, correspondingly, there could be no additional improvement, no $g_{(r+)^n}$ defining another option at n_0 such that g_s will still be chosen over it.[7]

Does this mean that a myopic chooser in this instance cannot be caught out in a violation of DSO? For the case in question, the following alternative argument can be constructed. Consider once again the problem in Figure 11.3, and define $r^* = \text{mix}(s+, r+)^n$ as a nonsequential plan whose associated prospect is a probabilistic mixture of augmented versions g_{s+} and g_{r+} of g_s and g_r, respectively, where the probabilities in question (definite or indefinite) correspond as closely as possible to what the agent himself would estimate, from the perspective of n_0, to be the odds of his choosing $r(n_1)$ rather than $s(n_1)$ at n_1. For definiteness, let $g_{s+} = [\$11, p; \$1, 1 - p]$ (instead of $[\$10, p; \$0, 1 - p]$), and let $g_{r+} = \$4$ (instead of $\$3$), as given in Figure 11.4. Here, g_s is still E-admissible in the presence of all of g_t, g_r, and $g_{\text{mix}(s+, r+)^n}$.[8] Thus, the agent may adopt plan s and move toward n_1. But then even though he plans to implement plan s, what he in fact implements is something quite different, namely, plan $\text{mix}(s, r)$, whose associated prospect $g_{\text{mix}(s, r)}$ is, by construction, dominated with respect to sure outcomes by $g_{\text{mix}(s+, r+)^n}$, the prospect associated with another plan available to the agent in question.

Once again, by contrast, the sophisticated agent who accepts VSF and VRPR avoids this problem. Even though he regards the prospect associated with plan s as E-admissible, he anticipates that, were he to head toward n_1, he would not necessarily implement plan s; thus, he regards neither plan s nor plan r as feasible. What is feasible is plan $\text{mix}(s, r)$, but since, by construction, it is dominated with respect to sure outcomes by plan $\text{mix}(s+, r+)^n$, the acceptable set reduces to just $\text{mix}(s+, r+)^n$ and t, and it is one of these that the sophisticated agent will adopt and then implement. The resolute chooser also avoids the problem. If he decides upon s, he then moves to n_1 and resolutely chooses $s(n_1)$ over $r(n_1)$; that is, he does not implement plan $\text{mix}(s, r)$.

That the agent who accepts the E-admissibility rule and who deals myopically with the problem of potential violations of DC can be trapped in this manner into a violation of DSO suggests that other instances in which case (2) and (3) situations cannot be reduced to case (1) situations can be dealt with in a similar manner. But here I must conjecture. That is, I have not been able to devise a general argument to show that any case (2) or (3) violation of CF or CIND will always lend itself to a dynamic choice construction in which the myopic agent will end up violating DSO.[9] If such an argument could be devised, it would make my thesis somewhat neater: Myopia would turn out to be invariably objectionable. But my principal concern here is to show that whatever problem besets the myopic agent, it is one that can be avoided by the agent who is prepared to adopt a sophisticated or a resolute approach. If it turns out that under certain special circumstances the myopic agent avoids being subject to violations of DSO, all that does is to underline the thesis that agents whose methods of evaluation fail to satisfy either CF or CIND are not automatically liable to make choices that are irrational by the standard of DSO.

11.3 The problem with sophisticated choice

In Section 10.6 I considered the claim put forward by Seidenfeld that those who violate independence and who approach choice in a sophisticated manner (i.e., are committed to all of SEP, DC, and RPR) end up violating DSO (or FSD). I argued in reply that his claim cannot be sustained in terms of the example that he constructs. Nonetheless, Seidenfeld's own example is illuminating.

Recall in connection with Figure 10.6 that by implicit appeal to SEP and VRPR Seidenfeld supposes that plan s_1 has associated with it the prospect of getting \$5.50. For the decision tree in question, however, one can identify an alternative plan that consists in choosing g_1 if at n_3 and g_2 if at n_4. Call this plan r. Plan r has associated with it a prospect, namely, $g_3 = [g_1, .5; g_2, .5]$, that dominates the prospect associated with plan s_2, namely, $g_4 = [(g_1 - \$e), .5; (g_2 - \$e), .5]$, with respect to sure outcomes. Moreover, plan s_2 is just the plan that Seidenfeld correctly argues will be selected by a sophisticated chooser. This suggests that whereas the myopic agent can be typically trapped into failing to execute a plan whose associated prospect is judged

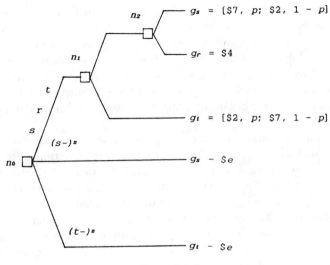

Figure 11.5

acceptable, the sophisticated agent is liable to fail to adopt and execute some plan whose associated prospect is judged more acceptable than the prospect associated with the plan he does adopt (and implement).

More generally, it can be shown that an agent whose method of evaluation involves a violation of either CF or CIND and who is disposed to employ a sophisticated approach can typically be placed in a very simple dynamic choice situation in which he will be liable to choose a plan whose associated prospect is dominated with respect to sure outcomes by the prospect associated with some other plan defined by the decision tree. Moreover, the latter plan is precisely the one that a resolute chooser will select. It should be noted, however, that the arguments to be considered now turn critically on an assumption about what plans are feasible for the agent in any given tree. Specifically, the arguments to be considered take the set of feasible plans associated with any tree to be simply all those plans that are logically possible, given the order of chance and choice nodes in that tree. Recall that the argument of Section 8.5 does not establish that VSF and VRPR are invariably appropriate; at best it establishes only that they have some plausibility when some condition such as SEP, which provides for independent determination of $D(S(n))$, is presupposed. The resolute chooser, however, is precisely one who is prepared to reject SEP.

Consider, as an illustration, the case of a sophisticated agent who accepts Levi's E- and S-admissibility rules and who faces the decision presented in Figure 11.5 (with p completely indeterminate). Here, $(s-)^n$ and $(t-)^n$ are to be interpreted as normalized but *dis*enhanced versions, respectively, of s and t. By SR, SEP, and E- and S-admissibility, $r(n_2)$ is, and $s(n_2)$ is not, in $D(S(n_2))$; thus, by VSF, the truncated plan $s(n_1)$ is not feasible, and by application of VRPR and the admissibility rules to the truncations that are feasible at n_1, only $r(n_1)$ is admissible. This in turn implies that only r, $(s-)^n$, and $(t-)^n$ are feasible at n_0; and by application of the admissibility rules and VRPR to that set, r is not admissible. Thus, the sophisticated agent will adopt either $(s-)^n$ or $(t-)^n$.

The sophisticated chooser must acknowledge, however, that whether he picks $(s-)^n$ or $(t-)^n$, he would do even better, in terms of associated prospects, if he went on to n_1. If he picks $(s-)^n$, plan s has associated with it a prospect that dominates the prospect associated with $(s-)^n$. If he picks $(t-)^n$, plan t has associated with it a prospect that dominates the one associated with $(t-)^n$. But either the agent selects $(s-)^n$ or he selects $(t-)^n$. Thus, either way, he selects a plan whose prospect is dominated with respect to sure outcomes by the prospect associated with another plan. The resolute chooser, however, is one who will select just one of these superior plans. For the resolute chooser, with his commitment to unrestricted NEC and DC, there are five feasible plans – s, r, t, $(s-)^n$, and $(t-)^n$. E-admissibility applied to the set of associated prospects, together with NEC, implies that just s and t are in $D(S)$. The resolute chooser will pick one of these and proceed to implement it. Thus, the resolute approach respects DSO in this case.

This argument can be generalized. Consider any situation in which an agent employs a method of evaluation of static choices that violates either CF or CIND. Take that choice problem and embed it in a sequential problem – involving no intervening chance event if CF is violated, or with an intervening chance event if CIND is violated (together with various other intervening choice nodes or other options available at n_0, as may be required), as shown in Figure 11.6.

Once again, there are three cases to consider. If the agent's method of evaluation violates either Alpha or strict choice independence (CIND-S), it will be possible to construct a tree of this sort in which either (1) g_s is, and g_r is not, while $g_{r(n_i)}$ is, and $g_{s(n_i)}$ is not, in $D(G_{S(n_i)})$ or (2) both g_s and g_r are in $D(G_S)$, while $g_{r(n_i)}$ is, and $g_{s(n_i)}$ is not, in $D(G_{S(n_i)})$. If the method of evaluation violates either Beta or equivalent choice independence (CIND-E), then it will be possible to construct a tree of this sort in which (3) g_s is, and g_r is not, in $D(G_S)$, while both $g_{s(n_i)}$ and $g_{r(n_i)}$ are in $D(G_{S(n_i)})$.

Take case (1) first, where g_s is, and g_r is not, in $D(G_S)$, but $g_{r(n_i)}$ is, and $g_{s(n_i)}$ is not, in $D(G_{S(n_i)})$. Let $s^* = (s-)^n$, the normalized form of a *dis*enhanced version of s whose associated prospect $g_{(s-)^n} = g_s - \$e$. By hypothesis, g_s is, and g_r is not, in G_S. Once again, I assume that $\$e$

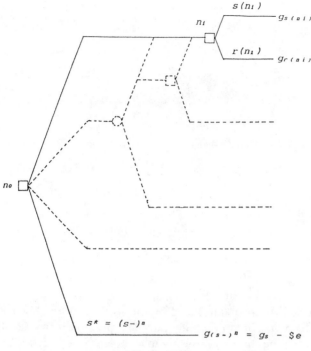

$$s^* = (s-)^n$$

$$g_{(s-)^n} = g_s - \$e$$

Figure 11.6

can be set small enough so that $g_{(s-)^n}$, which by appeal to dominance with respect to sure outcomes is clearly not in $D(G_S)$, is still sufficiently attractive that it is in $D(G_S^*)$ where $G_S^* = G_S - \{g_s\}$. More specifically, $\$e$ is to be set so that g_r is still rejected in any set containing $g_{(s-)^n}$. The sophisticated chooser anticipates that by application of VRPR and SEP at n_i, only $s(n_i)$ is in $D(S(n_i))$ and, hence, that s is not feasible. For the sophisticated chooser, then, the feasible set at n_0 consists of r and $(s-)^n$ (as well as perhaps other options available at n_0, the addition of which are needed, as indicated in the discussion above concerning E- and S-admissibility rules, to ensure the potential violation of DC). Given, then, the assumptions stated above concerning the ranking of associated prospects and VRPR, it follows that only $(s-)^n$ is in $D(S)$ (or $(s-)^n$ together with certain other constructed plans each of which is, like $(s-)^n$, inferior in the relevant respect to one of the original plans). At least sometimes, then, the sophisticated chooser will select and execute this plan. But plan s clearly dominates $(s-)^n$ with respect to associated prospects. Thus, the sophisticated chooser will select a plan whose associated prospect is dominated with respect to sure outcomes by the prospect associated with some other plan. By way of contrast, however, for the resolute chooser, who is committed to an

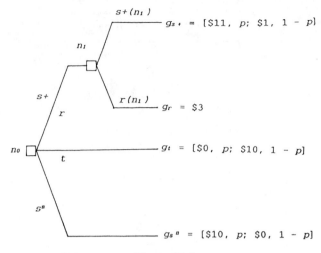

$$s+(n_1)$$
$$g_{s+} = [\$11, \; p; \; \$1, \; 1 - p]$$

$$n_1$$

$$s+$$

$$r$$

$$r(n_1)$$
$$g_r = \$3$$

$$n_0$$

$$t$$
$$g_t = [\$0, \; p; \; \$10, \; 1 - p]$$

$$s^n$$

$$g_{s^n} = [\$10, \; p; \; \$0, \; 1 - p]$$

Figure 11.7

unrestricted version of NEC, s is, and $(s-)^n$ is not, in $D(S)$, and hence he will avoid the problem faced by the sophisticated chooser.

Now this construction closely parallels the one introduced in connection with the discussion of myopic choice. The only difference, in effect, is that the constructed options are *disenhanced* as opposed to *enhanced* versions of the plans defined by the tree diagram. Typically, then, one can expect in this case, no less than in the case of myopic choice, that it will be possible to modify case (2) and (3) situations so as to convert them into case (1) situations and apply the argument just described.

To be sure, it would appear once again that there is no assurance that the requisite modifications can be made.[10]. However, the required modification can be made in the case of one who accepts just E-admissibility and who adopts a sophisticated approach. Consider in Figure 11.7 the modified version of the problem given in Figure 11.3 (with p once again completely indeterminate). Here, plan $s+$ is an enhanced version of plan s^n, and if the former were feasible, plan s^n would never be chosen. The sophisticated chooser, however, regards plan $s+$ as not feasible, since both $s(n_i)$ and $r(n_i)$ are acceptable at n_1. Thus, choice at n_0 is limited to just mix(s, r), t, and s^n. As it turns out, mix(s, r) is not E-admissible in the presence of both s^n and t, and so the sophisticated agent may well adopt s^n, a plan whose associated prospect is dominated with respect to sure outcomes by the prospect associated with s. In this instance, then, a case (3) situation can be converted into a case (1) situation.

Once again, I conjecture that if there are instances in which the requisite modifications that would convert a case (2) or (3) violation into a case (1) violation of CF or CIND, then alternative modifications can be made so as to place the sophisticated agent in a position in which he will or may choose a dominated plan. However, I do not know of any general argument by means of which this conjecture can be established. Even if this conjecture, as well as the one discussed in connection with myopic choice, cannot be sustained, it would seem very likely that for any agent who systematically employs a method of evaluation violating CF or CIND it will be possible to find specific examples of dynamic choice problems in which a myopic approach will lead to violations of DSO and also examples in which a sophisticated approach will lead to violations of DSO. And for each such case, it would appear that the resolute approach provides a way to avoid the difficulty.

11.4 Significance of the pragmatic arguments

It might be argued, of course, that the conclusions reached in the preceding section are hardly dispositive with respect to the questions of the comparative rationality of the three approaches – myopic, sophisticated, and resolute. Even if the agent gets into trouble in certain artificially modified situations, still such situations may not occur with sufficient frequency to prove worrisome. Is the problem here, then, only a problem in principle? Not if one supposes that the agent inhabits a world populated by other rational agents with typical interests and projects! Another agent will characteristically stand to make money on the dispositions of the myopic and the sophisticated chooser, and in the case of the myopic chooser, he may even have an incentive to create (at little cost to himself) the very situations in which he can make such a profit.

Exploiting the myopic chooser

Consider once again the generic decision tree for the class of situations that pose a problem for the myopic chooser, as given in Figure 11.2. One can interpret this decision tree in the following manner: Suppose that, prior to n_0, the agent possesses rights to the prospect g_{r*}. When the agent arrives at n_0, an entrepreneur announces that he is prepared to offer the agent an alternative. In exchange for rights to g_{r*}, the agent can have the opportunity, at n_i, of choosing between rights to $g_{s(n_i)}$ and rights to $g_{r(n_i)}$.

Consider first case (1) violations of CF or CIND, where the agent ranks $g_{r(n_i)}$ superior to $g_{s(n_i)}$. Since, by hypothesis, at n_0 the myopic agent ranks plan s, which calls for continuing on to n_i and selecting

$s(n_i)$ (or, if there is an intervening chance node, heading toward n_i and selecting $s(n_i)$ if and when n_i is reached) as superior to the alternative plan $r^* = (r+)^n$, to which he has rights, the myopic agent trades. Thus, the entrepreneur now possesses rights to $(r+)^n$ and is liable to have to transfer to the agent rights to $g_{s(n_i)}$ if the agent arrives at n_i. However, this liability does not worry the entrepreneur: By hypothesis, at n_i the agent ranks $r(n_i)$ over $s(n_i)$, and this is known to the entrepreneur. If and when the agent arrives at n_i, he chooses, then, $r(n_i)$ rather than $s(n_i)$, and the entrepreneur, who has purchased the rights to $(r+)^n$, for which the associated prospect is $g_r + \$e$, supplies $g_{r(n_i)}$ to the agent and retains $\$e$ for himself. In the case in which there is an intervening chance event, and matters so transpire that the agent must deliver g', this also presents no problem. The entrepreneur had rights to $(r+)^n$, and so now possesses rights to $g' + \$e$; he thus delivers g' to the agent and retains, once again, $\$e$ for himself. Thus, no matter what happens, the entrepreneur is ahead by $\$e$ and the myopic chooser has paid out that same amount. All that is required, then, for the myopic agent to be exploited in this manner, is that there be some other agent who prefers more money to less (or more of some other commodity to less, where the commodity in question is also one toward which the myopic agent has the same attitude) and who can offer various trading possibilities to the myopic agent.

To the extent that case (2) and (3) violations can be modified to produce case (1) violations, this argument will carry over. And where the requisite modifications cannot be made, there may still be alternative traps that can be laid – as the discussion of the myopic approach to the problem given in Figure 11.3 suggests. Of course, in either instance, the nature of the evaluation rule that the agent employs may require that the entrepreneur offer certain other options as well – as illustrated by the example of E-admissibility, where plan t must be present at node n_0 in order for the selection of plan r to be ruled out. And this may mean that the entrepreneur is not assured that he will always come out ahead (e.g., in the problem given in Figure 11.3, the myopic agent may choose t). In such cases, other variables will play a role, including whether the entrepreneur is risk neutral, whether he can spread his risks by repeated transactions, and what (subjective) probability he assigns to the agent choosing $r(n_i)$ over $s(n_i)$ if and when node n_i is reached, and so on. However, it seems likely that for a very wide range of cases the entrepreneur will have an incentive to set up the myopic agent in this way.

Profiting from the limitations of sophisticated choice

The possibilities open to the entrepreneur in the case of sophisticated choosers appear to be somewhat more limited. Judging from the constructions employed in the preceding section, sophisticated choosers cannot be set up, that is, exploited, in the manner in which myopic choosers can. The myopic agent is exploited by the entrepreneur taking any nonsequential choice problem the myopic agent faces and fabricating an enriched, sequential problem that is sufficiently attractive to induce the myopic agent to trade. But "exploitation" of the sophisticated agent proceeds by means of taking some already specifically defined sequential situation that the sophisticated agent faces and modifying it so as to include a nonsequential (normal-form) variation of one or more of the plans involved. It would seem, then, that entrepreneurs will be limited to offering their services in situations where the sophisticated chooser regards the most desirable prospect as one that can be accessed only by a sequence of choices that he projects he will not be disposed to make. It remains the case, however, that for every situation in which a sophisticated agent faces such a problem, there will typically be some other agent who can expect, by offering his services, to profit thereby.

Could it be argued that these are simply expenditures the sophisticated agent will be disposed to make so as to secure what he wants, just as, for example, those who are risk averse will be prepared to use resources to purchase insurance? In the insurance case it can be argued that both sides stand to benefit – the agent gets protection from certain adverse events, the insurance salesman gets money – and thus that this is an instance of productive exchange. Can the same be said about the services the entrepreneur can offer the sophisticated chooser? The two cases are not comparable. What distinguishes the expenditures for services that sophisticated choosers will be willing to pay entrepreneurs is that these, unlike insurance payments, are unnecessary. What one purchases with an insurance premium is an amelioration of the losses associated with some possible adverse event; but what the sophisticated agent purchases is a right to an outcome that he could have secured without such expenditures, simply by being resolute.[11]

In very general terms, the objection to myopic and sophisticated approaches in such situations is not simply that such approaches render the agent abstractly liable to the unnecessary expenditure of resources, but rather that either approach will provide other rational agents with an incentive to get the agent to expend resources. In the case of the myopic agent, the problem is severe. Entrepreneurs will typically have an incentive to manipulate myopic choosers by creating, and then offering to the latter, certain simple sequential choice problems. In the case of the sophisticated agent, the problem is less severe. Entrepreneurs may not be in a position to manipulate any given evaluative situation of this sort to their own advantage, that is, to create the very situations from which they can then profit. However, they can expect to profit by offering their services in a wide variety of situations.

11.5 Pragmatic impeccability of resolute choice

I argued in Sections 11.2 and 11.3 that the myopic agent is subject to violations of DSO and that the sophisticated agent is also subject to violations of DSO, at least if it can be shown that the plan selected by a resolute approach is feasible (and hence that resolute choice itself is feasible). I also argued that in each of these situations, the resolute chooser faces no such liability. That does not establish, of course, that the generic decision trees given in Figures 11.2 and 11.6 cannot be modified so that even the resolute chooser becomes subject himself to violations of DSO. However, a direct argument can be employed to show that this cannot happen. Suppose a resolute agent found himself in a situation in which some plan he contemplated choosing was dominated in this sense by some alternative plan. What would preclude the agent from adopting the latter plan instead? A resolute chooser is precisely one who is capable of shifting to a plan that is judged to be superior from the perspective of n_0 and of regimenting subsequent choice to that plan in the case of plans that require for their implementation a sequence of choices.

For the resolute chooser, then, there could be no liability of the sort faced by either the myopic or the sophisticated chooser. To identify a situation in which a resolute agent might end up choosing a dominated plan is already to provide the resolute agent with the information necessary to avoid that form of pragmatic difficulty. That is, the resolute chooser has only to shift and adopt the alternative plan. Resolute choosers, no less than sophisticated choosers, may end up choosing dominated plans as a result of misinformation or some other form of inadvertent error, but they will not deliberately choose a plan that violates DSO. It is true, of course, that the model of resolute choice presented in Chapter 9 characterizes the resolute chooser simply as one who is capable of disciplining subsequent evaluation and choice to initial evaluation: This leaves open the possibility that a resolute chooser is one whose initial self (in the temporal sequence) will dictatorially decide on a course of action. But for one who is capable of being resolute, dictatorial as its ex ante self may be, it will not knowingly choose a plan that fails to satisfy DSO.

11.6 Conclusions and anticipations

What I have argued in this chapter is that in any situation in which not all of NEC, SEP, and DC can be satisfied and the agent proceeds to adopt either a myopic or a sophisticated approach, it will be possible typically (if not invariably) to modify the situation so that whatever plan is implemented is dominated with respect to terminal outcomes by some other logically possible plan. I have also argued that entrepreneurs will characteristically have an incentive to create situations in which myopic agents can be manipulated to their own disadvantage and to the advantage of the entrepreneur, and to seek out sophisticated choosers and offer their services for a fee, services that the latter would do better to perform for themselves.

I have also argued that resolute choosers do not face any of these problems. But this means that in violating the dynamic choice condition SEP, the resolute chooser is not subject to pragmatic difficulty. This in turn suggests that from a pragmatic perspective, if some one of the dynamic choice conditions is to be relaxed, SEP seems to be a plausible candidate. That is to say, it is no longer obvious that SEP should be taken as a condition on rational dynamic choice.

It can be argued, of course, that the resolute chooser shares with the myopic chooser the liability to dynamic inconsistency. The myopic chooser does in fact end up violating DC; one who aspires to be resolute may end up violating DC if it turns out that the agent is not capable of being resolute. To argue for the possibility of resolute choice and to establish its attractiveness is not yet to show that agents *can* be resolute. This is the issue to which I must now turn.

12

The feasibility of resolute choice

12.1 An argument against resolute choice

It is central to the argument of Chapter 11 that the sophisticated chooser will in certain circumstances select a plan that is dominated with respect to sure outcomes by another plan. Specifically, situations will arise in which an entrepreneur will have a motive for offering his services for a (modest) fee, and the sophisticated agent will be disposed to accept such an offer, even though he could do better, regardless of the turn of events, by simply serving (without a fee) as his own agent. Those who are inclined to regard SEP as a plausible rationality condition on dynamic choice and, hence, who think in terms of a sophisticated rather than a resolute approach will take issue with this claim. They will do so on the grounds that the plan called for on the resolute approach – indeed, the resolute approach itself – is simply not feasible. On this view, the agent at a tree-continuation point will always choose in a manner that is consistent with de novo choice. Agents can *make* resolutions, to be sure, but they cannot carry them out. Those who set out to be resolute will end up behaving just like myopic choosers. But if resolutions cannot be effectively implemented, then the charge that the sophisticated approach is pragmatically inferior collapses. Only feasible plans can be of any relevance for determining the pragmatic respectability of sophisticated choice.

12.2 Different senses of feasibility

Many will be entirely persuaded by this argument, but I am not. As formulated, it seems to me to beg the central issue, namely, whether SEP is a rationality constraint on choice. By way of substantiating this claim, let me begin by exploring much more systematically the various senses in which a plan can be said to be feasible. Consider once again the discussion of feasibility in Section 8.4. There I suggested a possible criterion of feasibility, namely, that a plan s is feasible if it is a logically possible contingency plan, given the choice and chance structure of the decision tree in question. I propose to call any such plan an *objectively* feasible (O-feasible) plan. O-feasible plans are simply all those plans that it is in principle possible to execute, given the usual set of external constraints on the situation – as spelled out in terms of resources, the level of technical knowledge available, the laws of nature, and so on. That is, a plan is O-feasible just in case what it requires the agent to do at each choice point satisfies the following two conditions: (1) It is something the agent can do at that choice node, as determined by the natural and technological constraints on the situation, and (2) the choice node is one that the agent can reach (in the same sense of "can"), given the chance structure of the tree and given what the plan in question calls on the agent to select at choice nodes prior to the one in question. Now since the resolute approach calls for the selection of a plan that is clearly O-feasible, no argument against the feasibility of a resolute approach can be mounted from this perspective.

In Section 8.5, however, I introduced two versions (SF and VSF) of a much more restrictive concept of feasibility, and the discussion there clearly has considerable bearing on the issue of the feasibility of resolute choice. Given the various rationality conditions that do in fact (explicitly or implicitly, consciously or unconsciously) constrain the choice behavior of an agent, certain plans that are O-feasible are still clearly not feasible in an obvious sense of that term. These are plans whose implementation would presuppose that the agent is not committed to the very rationality constraints to which he is committed. Recast in subjective terms, an agent will regard a particular plan as not feasible if he believes that it calls upon him to make a choice at some future choice node that he fully expects he will not make, given the rationality conditions to which he is committed. Stated somewhat more formally, if the agent believes himself to have a continuing commitment to some rationality condition R, is at a point n_i in some decision tree, and knows that R applied to some subsequent point n_{i+} rules out selection of a truncated plan $s(n_{i+})$, then from the vantage point of n_i, he will expect that he will not select $s(n_{i+})$. This means, in turn, that he must regard any plan that calls for selecting $s(n_{i+})$ as a plan that is not R-feasible.

Plans that pass this test of feasibility can be designated as *rationally feasible* (R-feasible) plans, the "R" serving as a reminder that what determines feasibility in this sense are rationality conditions to which the agent himself is committed. For example, if rationality is to be spelled out at least in part in terms of choosing so as to maximize with respect to preferences, then insofar as the agent entertains any expectations concerning his own future preferences, these expectations will serve to delimit, at least partially, what he takes to be the set of R-feasible plans.[1]

Notice, finally, that both O- and R-feasibility have been implicitly characterized in terms of the notion of an ideally rational agent. Of course, there are likely to be substantial limits to any particular agent's capacity to make decisions in a perfectly rational manner. Even though there is some plan that is completely consistent with all the rationality constraints to which he is committed – perhaps it is even a plan that is mandated by those rationality conditions – still it does not follow that the agent will be able to execute it. Computational limitations, problems of attention or focus, various types of psychological "blocks," or other disabilities, "weakness of will," uncontrollable obsessions or drives – any of these may frustrate the agent's attempt to implement a particular plan. The agent himself, moreover, may be well aware of the limitations in this sense to which he is subject.

When the agent's capacity to implement a plan is further restricted by such considerations, one can speak of *psychologically* feasible (P-feasible) plans. It is important for the whole issue of the feasibility of resolute choice to distinguish carefully between R-feasibility and P-feasibility. The resolute agent, no less than any other agent, may confront such psychological limitations or blocks and thus come to be cautious about the extent to which he can be resolute. This point, however, belongs to a theory of imperfect rationality, that is, to a theory of what is the best course of action for the agent to take, given that he is subject to various limitations. For example, one may acknowledge that the problem of weakness of will is very real but still insist that it does not touch the theory of choice for an ideally rational agent. Similarly, Strotz's theme story of Ulysses and the Sirens and Hammond's story of the potential drug addict are more appropriately understood as models in which the self (as will) is presumed to be overcome or swamped by forces external to itself – and thus as models of imperfect, not perfect, rationality.[2] If this is correct, little is to be gained by taking these stories as paradigms for a theory of (ideally) rational behavior.[3]

Now in a foundational inquiry, where the question concerns the appropriate conditions on rational choice, it seems clear that one must *begin* with the concept of O-feasible plans. Candidates for rationality conditions are appraised against the background supposition that they apply to O-feasible plans. This, I take it, is because the only thing that could reduce the set of O-feasible plans for an *ideally* rational agent is what the theory of rationality itself implies in that setting. What is "really" feasible for an ideally rational agent is strictly a function of what conclusions can be drawn concerning the constraints on a rational agent. There is no movement from O-feasibility to "real" feasibility within a normative theory of rational choice for ideally rational agents except by establishing the appropriateness of various criteria of rational choice.

12.3 Dynamic choice and R-feasibility

I argued in the preceding question that any condition of rational choice (with any content to it at all) *may* have implications for how a rational agent will choose at tree-continuation points and, hence, implications for what is feasible at earlier choice points. Of course, any particular condition on rational dynamic choice may not have such implications. Consider the rationality conditions explored in this work. Taken by itself, PR has no such implications. It is a condition that applies to whole trees, not to segments thereof. Taken in conjunction with some assumption about the agent's ordering of prospects, PR does have, of course, definite implications for what can be chosen at n_0. But it has no implications for what is *R-feasible* at n_0 – simply because it has no direct application to any choice point except the initial one.

DC is even more vacuous. It requires consistency between what is judged acceptable at n_0 and at any point that can be reached from n_0. However, it does not specify whether, in the event of a potential disparity of this sort, ex ante judgment of acceptability is to be brought into line with ex post judgment of acceptability or vice versa. If DC is respected, one cannot shift plans in midstream. But DC does not rule any plan continuation to be unacceptable at any point n_i and, hence, implies nothing about what *plans* are R-feasible at n_0. Even the addition of some explicit assumption about how the agent orders the prospects associated with various plans and plan continuations accomplishes nothing: DC plus such an assumption still yields no conclusion about what plan continuations are acceptable and, hence, no conclusions about what plans are R-feasible.

Similar considerations apply even to SEP. Taken by itself, or in conjunction with some assumption about how the agent ranks prospects, SEP has no implications with regard to what plan continuations are acceptable at n_i and, hence, what plans are feasible at ancestors to n_i. It merely requires consistency between what one judges acceptable from a certain standpoint *within* a decision tree and what one would judge to be acceptable if one confronted what are otherwise the same prospects but from the vantage point of a de novo tree. That does constrain an agent, but, once again, not with respect to what qualifies within a given decision tree as an acceptable choice at n_i and, hence, as a component of a feasible plan at ancestors to n_i.

Matters are considerably different if one considers the conjunction of SEP and SR and some assumption about how the agent ranks prospects. As I argued in Section 8.5, this combination suffices to determine what is acceptable at some subsequent choice point n_i. This, in turn, by the argument of that section, implies something about what is feasible at each choice point that is an ancestor of n_i. It is precisely for this reason that once SR and SEP are in place it is plausible to recharacterize feasibility in terms of VSF (or at least SF).

12.4 Resolute choice and separability

One thing is quite clear: Resolute choice cannot be squared with SEP and SR. If SR and SEP are taken for granted, a resolute approach to situations in which not all of NEC, DC, and SEP can be satisfied is impossible. The strategy of the resolute chooser is to bring ex post judgments of acceptability into line with ex ante judgments. Since this involves an essential commitment to PR and DC, the agent cannot, by definition of the class of situations in question, also satisfy SEP. Turning this around, given a commitment to SEP and DC, the agent must, as a matter of logic, choose in such situations in a manner that violates NEC (and PR) and, hence, in a manner that is inconsistent with a resolute approach.

As these remarks suggest, there is a formal symmetry here. In situations where not all of DC, NEC, and SEP can be satisfied, it is true that violations of DC carry the clearest liability – namely, that one will typically be subject to exploitation by entrepreneurs. But if this serves to recommend DC, it remains an *open question* as to whether a theory of rationality that opts for SEP at the expense of NEC, or NEC at the expense of SEP, is more satisfactory. In particular, then, so long as one of the issues to be settled is precisely whether SEP is a rationality condition, one cannot appeal to SEP to argue that NEC must be qualified – and correspondingly that PR must be restricted to something like VRPR and that resolute choice is not possible, without thereby begging the issue in favor of SEP and against NEC.

Those who are determined to cling to SEP (as well as DC), and who believe, therefore, that certain plans are not R-feasible, are likely to insist that the decision tree should be revised so as to make this clear. Working with the principle of RPR, they will insist that notwithstanding the "logical" intelligibility of the standard representation of a sequential decision problem – in terms of a tree diagram with various choice nodes along the way – the only proper representation of such a decision problem for the rational agent, poised at n_0, will involve paring the "logical" tree down significantly. At every choice node n_i that is a successor to n_0, the only real choices will be among alternatives that are equally acceptable from the vantage point of n_i, that is, members of $D(S(n_i))$. If, moreover, as I have already suggested in Section 8.5, the logic of this line of reasoning pushes one not just to SF, but to VSF, then the decision tree must be pruned even more: The only "choice" at any choice point n_i that is the successor to n_0 will be a "mixture" of all the plan continuations $s(n_i)$ that are members of $D(S(n_i))$.

Notice, finally, that this line of reasoning does not easily stop at any n_i that is a successor to n_0: If n_0 is itself a choice point, it applies there as well. The point is that deliberation concerning what plan is to be adopted will typically take place before what, for purposes of representation, is taken as n_0. If n_0 is a choice point, then, at any time before that specified for n_0, the sophisticated agent will find himself faced with anticipating not simply choice points that are successors to n_0, but choice at n_0 itself. In this sense, the "sophisticated" orientation of treating one's future choices as a problem of prediction (as distinct from deliberation) leads inexorably to the conversion of all choice nodes into chance nodes, and this means pruning the decision tree down to a single contingency plan. But this, in turn, means emptying what is supposed to be a deliberative situation of anything that could count as deliberation and choice.

To be sure, those who are committed to an unrestricted version of NEC and PR have available to them an equally question-begging move. They can argue that PR does apply to the set of all O-feasible options and that it is the basis for determining what plan is to be adopted. On this way of reasoning, what remains is simply a matter of implementing the plan on which one has already settled. In effect, if the agent has made up his mind (by appeal to PR), then, for him, there are no choices left to make. Of course, in O-feasibility terms, the feasible set of choices available at each subsequent choice node has not been reduced. Moreover, the agent still has "selections" to make – steps in the master plan to be executed or implemented over time. But matters are quite different with respect to R-feasibility. If the agent has already made up his mind and, in particular, if he believes that the choice he has made is rational, it can be argued that he will subsequently regard certain options at tree-continuation points as simply not feasible.

Given this, one could now proceed to argue that SEP applies only to truncated trees from which all plan continuations that are not R-feasible have been excised. That is, the de novo tree $T(n_i)^n$, whose ordering of plans is determinative (by appeal to SEP) of the ordering of plans for $T(n_i)$ itself, must be $T(n_i)$ stripped of any truncations that do not figure in PR-acceptable plans. But then all that is left at each choice point n_i are plan continuations all of which are equally acceptable from the perspective of n_0. The argument is that SEP applies only to this reduced tree, that is, that SEP can be used to constrain choice at tree-continuation points only among options all of which are equally R-feasible, as determined by the application of PR. This would, of course, significantly restrict SEP, but in a way analogous to the way in which the imposition of VSF significantly restricts PR.[4]

More generally, then, it would seem that the claim that one must discuss proposed rationality conditions against the background of what can be established to be R-feasible and not simply O-feasible plans can mean only two things. It may amount to a more or less empty claim, as it will be if it is made before one spells out just what one takes to be an appropriate set of rationality conditions. Alternatively, if the claim has any bite, it is likely to be question begging. If the argument takes the form of a presumption by appeal to R-feasibility against resolute choice, this begs the question against PR and in favor of SEP; if the argument takes the form of a presumption, again on grounds of R-feasibility, against sophisticated choice, this begs the question against SEP and in favor of PR.

12.5 A closer look at separability

Whatever position one takes as to its plausibility or acceptability, it is clear that the separability principle SEP has played a central role in theoretical constructions pertaining to the modern theory of rational choice. Indeed, a moment's reflection suggests that many of the situations in which it seems plausible to adopt a sophisticated approach (in order to avoid violating DC) arise precisely because it is a fixed presupposition that the agent's choice behavior is governed by SEP. That is, it is the agent predisposed to approach each juncture point in the tree as if it were a new decision problem who typically faces the problem of dynamic consistency. To be sure, as the discussion of P-feasibility was intended to make clear, not all problems of dynamic consistency need be interpreted in this way. Ulysses may be genuinely concerned that his critical faculties will be overcome in the future by some force that he cannot resist. Similar considerations apply to the case of the potential drug addict, where it seems plausible to suppose that the agent's capacity for rational deliberation and choice might well be overwhelmed by forces over which he will have inadequate control. In short, P-feasible no less than R-feasible considerations can pose a problem of dynamic consistency for the agent. However, in sequential decision problems of the sort that I have been considering, it is commitment to SEP rather than something like addiction that poses the problem of dynamic consistency.

How is one to account for the hold that SEP has had on those who have been concerned with the foundations of decision theory? This entrenchment is certainly not due to unequivocal experimental evidence that agents are committed to SEP.[5] This is not surprising. There is an obvious sense in which meaning is bound up with counterfactual possibility, with the notion of what might have been. But evaluation, in turn, is clearly sensitive to – indeed quite parasitic upon – meaning in this sense, and thus one should not find it surprising that actual evaluations are conditioned by counterfactual possibilities.[6] The appeal to the empirical data of human choice can hardly be dispositive, of course. It is open to those who are committed to SEP to acknowledge that many agents do in fact violate SEP in their choice behavior but that SEP is still a valid norm for rational choice.

In very general terms, much of the support for SEP as a normative condition seems to derive from its association with the notion of a consequential approach to choice. Indeed, I am inclined to think that such a condition could be regarded as plausible *only* by one who was committed to a consequentialist perspective. Certainly evaluative rules that violate SEP are naturally described as oriented to something other than "consequences that still remain realizable," to past history, to concepts of regret, to "what might have been" rather than with what is still possible. Since orientations of this sort seem to be responsive to something other than consequences, it seems as if a rejection of SEP involves moving away from a purely consequentialist perspective.[7]

Take, for example, the version of the Kahneman–Tversky problem discussed in Section 9.2 (Figure 9.2). When the agent has the de novo option of taking $2400 outright or participating in a gamble that gives him probability $33/34$ of getting $2500 and probability $1/34$ of getting $0, the agent prefers getting $2400 outright. However, at n_0, the agent prefers that if and when he gets to n_3, he takes the option that exposes him to the gamble. Supposing for the moment that resolute choice is possible, how is one to interpret a decision at n_3 to carry through with what the agent resolved to do at the earlier choice point? To many, it will seem clear that the agent in question must be departing from a consequentialist perspective. By hypothesis, he is prepared now to choose differently than he would choose in a situation whose history is different but whose present set of alternatives and outcomes is exactly the same.

As intuitive as this line of reasoning may seem, I believe it should be resisted. In the first place, the claim that SEP is connected conceptually with a consequential perspective is problematic: One has only to recall the analysis in Section 8.10, according to which this point can be sustained only if one adopts a very narrow conception of a consequence – a conception that, in the context of the present discussion, is question begging. But this line of reasoning is even more bothersome in another respect. For those who are committed to SEP, it would appear that past preferences and plans have no force, except insofar as they are subject to independent ratification at each choice point. That is, if SEP holds, there can be no notion of a choice to be made, a path to be taken at some juncture point n_i, because the taking of that path is what one planned – made provision – to do at some point in the past or because by choosing in this manner one would finish out some project, accepted and initiated earlier, of exposing oneself to a certain prospect. Acceptance of SEP places one in a world in which there is temporal thickness to any commitment to a plan. What is decided at time t has no force at time $t + 1$, unless at $t + 1$ there is independent ratification of that plan from the consequentialist perspective of $t + 1$. That simply implies that the notion of a commitment to a plan has no meaning in the context of SEP. This implication of SEP, I want to suggest, works against its being accepted as a plausible condition on rational choice.

Consider, for example, a situation in which the agent does not even face a choice, but simply has to *pick* some option from a set of options all of which have been judged acceptable. How is he to pick? Suppose that he decides to settle it by the flip of a coin: If heads, he will pick x, and if tails, he will pick y. Let him now perform the experiment and observe its outcome. Whatever the outcome (H or T), why now should that outcome settle anything as to which one to pick? The decision to settle the matter by the toss of a coin is history. If SEP were a valid condition of "rational" picking, how could the lie of a coin tossed moments before resolve anything for a rational agent concerning whether to pick x or pick y? (To be sure, some time and energy have been expended, but those are costs incurred regardless of whether one now picks x or y.) The plain consequentialist fact is that the agent still has two options open to him: Pick x; pick y. Moreover, it is still the case that from a consequentialist perspective he has no basis for deciding which one to pick. Perhaps he should flip the coin again! Alternatively, suppose that the agent simply finds himself reaching for x rather than y and then, in the middle of the reach, the thought crosses his mind to reconsider – not to reconsider the evaluation that led to the determination that both x and y are fully acceptable, but to reconsider the settled picking of x instead of y that the reach toward x implies. From a consequentialist perspective, there is still no basis for the picking of x rather than y. Both are still open to him. Whatever impulse it was that resulted in the agent's hand reaching toward x, that impulse, given the intervening reflection, is now history.

The point is not that anyone has proposed SEP as a plausible condition on picking. Clearly it is not. But why is this? The answer, I suggest, is revealing. It is not a plausible condition on picking precisely because either it effectively blocks picking – like Buridan's ass, the agent never gets over his agony – or it makes picking costly: Time is wasted, energies expended, and so on. The person who faces the same picking problem and who resolves to let the toss of a coin decide the matter has no such problem. Once the coin has been tossed, such an agent is no longer undecided as to which of x and y to pick. The point of the experiment is precisely to provide a mechanism by which to settle this question – to enable the person to pick one of the two options. That kind of mechanism functions by orienting the agent to something other than the prospects that lie ahead. Moreover, there seems to be a clear moral to be drawn here: If SEP is so unconvincing as a condition on *picking*, one is bound to wonder about its credentials as a condition on *choice*.

12.6 Consequentialism and resolute choice

These remarks about picking point to a very different argument against SEP – a consequentialist argument for looking backward, for looking at other than what at any given point in time lies ahead. The suggestion is that those who are capable of a very simple kind of commitment and who do not always evaluate their options at each choice point simply in terms of what lies ahead can expect to do better than those who always treat each choice point as if it defined a de novo decision tree. This raises a substantial question about the plausibility of SEP from a consequentialist perspective itself – from the very perspective that has normally been taken to provide a ground for SEP. But these remarks also, of course, connect naturally with the whole argument of Chapter 11. There the objective was to show from a consequentialist perspective itself there is a case to be made for being resolute in a certain type of situation. More specifically, the resolute agent does not have to expend resources that the sophisticated agent has to expend. *That*, surely, is a consequentialist argument. What I want to do now, then, is to consider whether the argument of Chapter 11, when suitably interpreted, can be taken to make the case for the R-feasibility of resolute choice.

For such a case to be made, however, one more consideration must be put in place. The argument of Chapter 11 must be reinterpreted. There I cast the argument in terms of an appeal to the principle of dominance with respect to sure outcomes (DSO) because that principle is one on which there is something like a genuine consensus – and one that expresses something deeper than a convergence of cultural influences and/or historical accident. That is, the consensus touches something in the very logic of practical reasoning itself – the very business of effective choice of means to one's ends, regardless of what ends one happens to adopt. My hope, then, was that if the case for resolute choice could be made by appeal to DSO, this would have a certain shock value – precisely because DSO concerns something so central to our way of thinking about practical matters.

However, an appeal to nothing more than the plausibility of DSO without further remark will not suffice. The setting of Chapter 11 – in which I have argued for the superiority of resolute choice – is one in which there is in fact a potential disparity between ex ante evaluation of plan continuations (as determined by PR) and ex post evaluations of the same plan continuations (as determined by SEP and SR). In such a setting, commitment to the consequentialist perspective itself becomes problematic. One has, in effect, two consequentialist perspectives from which plans can be assessed – one via appeal to PR and the other via appeal to SEP and SR. If one distinguishes in very simple two-stage examples between these two perspectives, by speaking of the evaluations (or preferences) of the ex ante self and those of the ex post self, this means that for the cases in question, one has no assurance that the preferences of the ex ante and ex post self will coincide with regard to plans and plan continuations. If each consults just the prospects associated with the options he faces, it may happen, of course, that they concur with respect to their preferences for plans. The plan that the ex ante agent finds most attractive (in view of its associated prospect) may also be the plan the continuation of which the ex post self finds to be most attractive (once again by reference to its associated prospect). But this may not happen. It may well be that the ex ante self prefers plan s to plan r, whereas the ex post self prefers the continuation of plan r to the continuation of plan s.

Moreover, given this potential for diverging preferences with respect to plans, the structure of the decision tree that the agent confronts suddenly looms as potentially important. While the ex post self may well prefer to see plan r executed rather than plan s, it may happen that the ex ante self is in a position to choose so as to preclude the ex post self from acting on this preference. In choosing to initiate plan s he may preclude altogether the execution of plan r. In such a case, the ex post self will have to settle for the execution of some plan it judges inferior to plan s. Alternatively, however, initiation of plan s by the ex ante self may not preclude the execution of plan r. The ex post self may be in a position to choose so as to have plan r rather than plan s executed. In such a case, the ex ante self may have no choice but to settle for plan r, which he regards as an inferior plan.

Now the argument of Chapter 11 ignores this whole dimension of the problem. It is addressed to an essentially atemporal agent, who is conceived to be committed to DSO. That is, it makes no explicit attempt to address the agent as a being existing over time and whose separate, temporally defined selves can arrive at diverging evaluative judgments. In particular, it would seem that the argument of Chapter 11 is addressed to the ex ante, as distinct from the ex post, self. That is, the point of the argument is to show that if the agent thinks ahead, he will have to admit that the plan recommended by the sophisticated approach issues in a terminal outcome that is dispreferred to the terminal outcome issuing from the plan recommended by the resolute approach, regardless of the turn of intervening events. But whose preferences are these?

If the argument is addressed to the ex ante self, this provides that self with a powerful motivation to adopt a resolute approach. However, given the temporal gap between the ex ante and ex post selves, all that argument could guarantee in and of itself is a strong desire by the ex ante self to be resolute. It cannot offer any guarantee that the ex post self will be willing to respect and thus implement that resolve. Notice that the problem here is *not* solved by supposing, as I did at least implicitly, that each temporally defined self is committed to the dominance principle DSO. If preferences or judgments of acceptability change, then despite a constant commitment to DSO the ex post self may end up abandoning the plan initiated by the ex ante self.

Under what conditions might one expect that an agent would be capable of carrying through on a plan, that is, be capable of not simply wanting from the ex ante perspective to be resolute, but being able to carry through such a resolve? Alternatively put, under what conditions could one expect some effective coordination between the ex ante and the ex post selves?

Consider any case in which the ex ante self judges that the plan he would prefer to execute, plan s, is one that the ex post self is in a position to abandon in favor of plan r and, moreover, the ex post self is disposed to favor plan r over plan s. In light of this, the ex ante self may choose to initiate some other plan t instead. But it may also be the case that the ex post self prefers the prospect associated with the continuation of s to the best that self can hope to secure, given that the ex ante self chooses to initiate plan t. In this case, a cooperative arrangement, under which the ex ante self refrains from choosing some other plan and proceeds to initiate plan s and the ex post self responds by not choosing the continuation of r but rather executes the continuation of plan s instead, will have associated with it a prospect for each that is preferred to the prospect that each associates with that third plan t.

To give a somewhat more formal characterization, let a given plan s be *intrapersonally suboptimal* if there is some alternative plan r such that both the ex ante self and the ex post self rank the prospect that each associates with r over the prospect that each associates with s. Correspondingly, plan s can be said to be *intrapersonally superior* to another plan r if a shift from r to s results in both the ex ante self and the ex post self facing what each would rank to be superior prospects. If there exists no such alternative s, then a given plan r can be said to be *intrapersonally optimal*.

Of course, even if plan s is intrapersonally superior to plan r, it may still be the case that in the event that the ex ante self chooses to initiate plan s, the ex post self will find itself in a position to adopt some other plan t to complete and, ceteris paribus, will prefer to execute t rather than s (given what the ex ante self has already done). But as I have already noted, if the ex post self is disposed to act on this preference and the ex ante self is aware of this, it may well pay the ex ante self to adopt some other plan t, which it disprefers to s and which the ex post self also disprefers to s. In this case, the agent will not do as well as he could have done, both from the ex ante and the ex post perspective, if his ex ante and ex post selves had managed to coordinate on plan s. That is, he will end up executing an intrapersonally inferior plan.

What I now want to suggest is that the criterion of intrapersonal optimality can provide the basis for at least a *partial* theory of conditions under which resolute choice will be R-feasible. That is, what forms a natural condition for the self being resolute is precisely its becoming aware that there are benefits to both the present self and the future self that will have to be forgone if the self cannot act resolutely. On this way of reasoning, it does *not* turn out that resolute choice is always R-feasible. I have formally characterized resolute choice in terms of the notion of regimenting ex post evaluation (and choice) to the plan that the ex ante self has adopted. In the model of sophisticated choice, the ex ante agent takes the ex post self to have an independent set of interests that are simply given and that the ex ante self thus regards as setting limits on what it might otherwise hope to accomplish. In the model of resolute choice, the ex post self takes the plan that has been adopted by the ex ante self as setting limits on what it might otherwise prefer to accomplish. This captures a wide variety of things under the heading of being resolute, including patterns of behavior that one would not want to defend as either rational or R-feasible. To set intrapersonal optimality as a criterion of feasibility is to suggest that resolute choice will be possible only under a very constrained set of conditions – one of which is that failure to be resolute must be perceived to cost the self in terms of continuing (i.e., intertemporally defined) interests.

To argue in this fashion is to argue for a consequentialist condition on the feasibility of being resolute. The self that contemplates being resolute will have to reckon with the consideration that its feasibility is limited to a special set of cases, namely, where both the ex ante self and the ex post self can reasonably expect to benefit from such a policy. From this perspective, the issue of feasibility is not, then, whether the self can be moved solely by considerations having to do with consequences or whether it can be moved by other considerations as well. This issue is simply *from what perspective consequences are to be controlling.* The sophisticated approach presupposes an incrementalist view of how consequences enter into the calculus. The assumption is that at each choice point in a decision tree the rational agent will be disposed to maximize with respect to preferences over those consequences still open to the agent. A *feasible* resolute approach, on this account, does involve an abandonment of this incrementalist approach, but the condition of abandonment is precisely that the self come to see that the incrementalist approach is costly in terms of interests shared by the ex ante and ex post selves. On this view, the question of when to adopt an incrementalist approach and when to modify it is a matter to be settled by reference to the consequences of adopting one approach rather than the other. If one may suppose that the agent is capable of being motivated by consequentialist considerations, then it is not unreasonable to suppose that the agent is capable of being resolute under at least some circumstances.

Correspondingly, it is a consequentialist argument that tells in the end against unqualified acceptance of SEP. In the examples discussed in the preceding chapter, given an *intra*personal interest of the self in some commodity such as money, SEP's requirement that evaluation of plans be regimented to detached and independently based evaluations at every choice point in the decision tree leads to a state dispreferred or ranked inferior by both the ex ante self and the ex post self. This suggests that a rational agent will not reject SEP altogether but will be disposed to reject an unqualified version of this principle; and the basis of the recommendation in any given case that SEP should be set to one side will be that there are consequentialist advantages to so doing. SEP is to be qualified, then, not on nonconsequentialist grounds but on the grounds indigenous to the consequentialist perspective. At root, the objection is that SEP straitjackets a consequentialist perspective. It requires the agent to be disposed to an incrementalist approach to consequentialism and to be so disposed even in situations where the disposition works against the *continuing* interests of that agent.

12.7 Endogenous preference changes

What separates the theory of resolute choice from the standard view with its commitment to sophisticated choice is not rejection by the former and acceptance by the latter of some maximizing conception of rational choice. It can be argued that both theories accept such a maximizing conception. That is, rational choice calls for each of the time-defined selves to maximize preferences against what previous selves have chosen and future selves are expected to choose. Those who accept the sophisticated approach are prepared to embrace the principle that choice must maximize with respect to *exogenously* specified preferences (which is to say, in this context, preferences that satisfy SEP). The theory of resolute choice would quarrel only with the qualifier – with the presumption that at each point *within* the decision tree these preferences are to be understood as being always exogenously specified – and this by reference to some set of conditions that includes SEP.

A recent discussion in economic theory suggests itself here. In the classical model of interaction, the preferences of agents, as well as other constraints on rational self-interested choice, are taken as exogenously given, and the task is then to trace out the implications of this for interaction – where the sole principle of action for each agent is simply maximization of these *given* preferences – subject to the other constraints. But it is well known that many of these other constraints themselves can be rationalized in terms of the commitment of the agent to maximizing his given preferences. To connect the kinds of institutional constraints to which preference maximization is subjected in any organized form of social interaction to preference maximization itself is to provide what can be characterized as an *endogenous* account of such constraints. The account is endogenous in the sense that these are constraints to which preference maximizers have, on the theory in question, willingly submitted (or to which they would be willing to submit) for the sake of thereby more effectively maximizing their preferences over some projected set of interactions.[8]

In an analogous fashion, one can imagine that a rational preference maximizer who is faced with the problem of conflicts between his present and future selves might be prepared, under certain situations, to revise the preferences he would ordinarily have in the context of certain choice situations, and to do this from a sense of what would better serve the maximization of whatever antecedently specified preferences for outcomes he brings to that kind of decision situation. The notion is that a rational agent with some schedule of preferences with respect to outcomes might come to have an interest in revising the strategy with which he pursued the maximization of those preferences – specifically the procedure of giving each successive self defined over time the latitude to maximize individually from its own separable perspective – and that such an interest might be rooted precisely in his concern to maximize those preferences for outcomes. That a rational agent has such an interest might be explained, of course, in other ways. Perhaps, for example, he has been socialized into setting such restrictions on his pursuit of more specific interests. In such a case, the restrictions would not to that extent have been explained or accounted for endogenously. However, when his interest is rooted in a concern to maximize his preferences for outcomes, one can speak of the preference transformation in question as having been accounted for endogenously.

In the case of endogenous accounts of institutional constraints, to be sure, there is no suggestion that the specified preferences undergo any transformation. The institutions that rational preference maximizers might devise set external constraints on what each agent can realize. Exogenously specified preferences provide for an endogenous account of institutional arrangements. In the present case, by contrast, the suggestion is not that the rational agent might be willing to impose barriers on his pursuit of preference maximization but rather that he might be willing to undertake to transform what would have otherwise been his exogenously given preferences in certain future choice situations. Despite this difference the parallel remains. The preference transformation case is like the case of the transformation of the institutional setting in that the impetus to change in each case is to be found in the agent's belief that the original situation was one in which he could not expect to do as well as he could do if he were to effect the transformation. Since the impetus is rooted in the principle of preference maximization itself, this qualifies as an endogenous explanation of the transformation.

In summary, a full argument for the feasibility of resolute choice must make appeal to what can be termed a theory of *endogenous preference changes*. The resolute agent can be interpreted as altering his given preferences in certain situations with a view to thereby being able to improve his position – as judged both from the ex ante and the ex post perspective. The resulting preference shift can be said to be an endogenous preference shift in virtue of the fact that it is to be explained by reference to his commitment to act so as to maximize with respect to his preferences. Since the modern economic theory of motivation makes just this principle its cornerstone, those who accept this framework should be able to accommodate the claim that under certain circumstances resolute choice is R-feasible and, hence, feasible for an ideally rational agent.

12.8 Another condition of R-feasibility?

It seems likely that intrapersonal superiority cannot *suffice* as a criterion of feasibility for resolute choice. In one sense, this is obvious. What is truly feasible can be settled only by reference to considerations of the psychological limits under which any given agent acts. A theory of feasibility is incomplete without reference to P-feasibility. But I would argue that intrapersonal superiority fails to provide a sufficient criterion even when what is at issue is simply R-feasibility, feasibility for *ideally rational agents*. Within the metaphor of the divided self, there is no more reason to suppose that temporal selves will always cooperate with one another so long as mutual gains are possible than there is for supposing that distinct individuals will always cooperate so long as mutual gains are possible. A full theory of when resolute choice is R-feasible would require an exploration of the analogue to the notion of a *just* cooperative scheme among persons.[9]

Perhaps, however, with regard to the issue at hand, namely, the possibility of a resolute approach to sequential decision problems concerned with gambles over prizes, one does not have to resolve this matter. What is typically at stake for the agent concerned with choosing among such gambles are not life prospects or other substantial interests, but often no more than small amounts of money or some other valued commodity. Those who are capable of resisting the offers of others to serve for a fee and who can resolutely serve as their own agent are likely to make incremental savings in a commodity that is useful in roughly equal measure for all the relevant temporally defined selves.

12.9 Presuppositions concerning the self

I shall close this chapter with some brief remarks concerning a somewhat more philosophical issue. The parallels and contrasts between sophisticated and resolute choice that I have discussed so far suggest a marked contrast in presuppositions concerning the possible nature of intertemporal interaction between different time slices of the same self. This, in turn, is suggestive of a difference in what each theory at least tacitly conceives to be the nature of, and relation between, temporally defined aspects of the self.

One can begin by noting that resolute choice offers an interesting conceptual analogue to prudent choice – to the notion of an agent who is capable of deferring gratification. To take the example of savings, the present prudent self is imagined to be prepared to make a sacrifice now for the sake of greater gains in the future. It is not at all clear how one is to understand the motivation for, and hence the possibility of, such an act of sacrifice by the present self. For those who take seriously the Humean problem of how to establish the identity of the self over time, presumably it must be supposed that this is predicated on some sort of commitment by the ex ante self to the ex post self.[10]

The notion of a bond – or commitment – among selves, then, would seem indispensable for understanding not only the resolute but also the prudent self. The prudent self is capable of recognizing ties to its own future selves. The resolute self is capable of recognizing ties to its own former selves. Correspondingly, if it is possible for the present self to be prudentially bound to its future self, one should also be able to imagine that the present self can be resolutely bound to its former self.

Perhaps it will be argued that the manner in which such a commitment or concern can intelligibly manifest itself presupposes that one self can causally affect how well the other self does. If the ex ante self fails to attend to the interests of the ex post self, this can cause the latter to end up doing less well. Now the order of causation is presumably unidirectional – from past to future. Since the ex ante self is no more, it cannot be affected by what the ex post self does. In contrast, the ex ante self can hope to affect how the ex post self does. But while the asymmetry of causality has implications for how one self can express its commitment to another self, it does not preclude the ex post self's acting out of a sense of the concerns of the ex ante self. Such a commitment can express itself in the ex post self's executing a plan that the ex ante self initiated.

It would seem that it must be some bond of this sort that forms the basis for successful resolute choice. Moreover, the remarks of the preceding sections, concerning mutual interest and justice, can be taken as framing conditions that will have to be met if such bonds are to remain firmly in place. That is, the type of resolute choice with which I am here concerned is to be modeled in terms of a bargain struck between the ex ante and the ex post selves, in which the ex ante self must recognize the interests of the ex post self and not simply unilaterally impose a plan of its own choosing to which the ex post self must conform. Indeed, one may wonder whether some such bargain must not also be implicit in any successful form of prudential behavior. Prudence, after all, would seem conceptually distinct from mere sacrifice on the part of the ex ante self to the interests of the ex post self. If, then, following Hume's way of thinking, the problem of the ontological unity of the self over time is unresolvable, still in both the model of prudent choice and that of resolute choice one can mark the conception of the possibility of a practical unity: of cooperation made possible by a sense of a community of interest.

One can, of course, reject Hume's skepticism and seek to push the matter to a deeper level. It can be argued that the model to which it is appropriate to appeal is not that of distinct selves, but of temporal segments of some underlying continuing self – some being that conceives of itself as having a temporal thickness to its existence. Indeed, one might wonder if anything like *either* the commitment involved in resolute choice *or* the concern of the prudent self for its own future would be possible if it were not for the existence of a self that has some sense of personal identity over time. What seems essential here, in particular, is the notion of the continuity over time of the self as performing an executive function vis-à-vis the desires and interests that express themselves at any given moment. This need not be the rather authoritarian conception to be found in Plato; rather, it may come close to Butler's notion of self-love or Freud's notion of the ego.[11] Viewed from this perspective, to entertain the feasibility of resolute choice is, at the very least, to start moving in the direction of articulating the concept of a continuing self.

Consider now, by contrast, the model of pure sophisticated choice. What it assumes is that the relation of any present self to its future selves is that of strategic action predicated on a prediction of the behavior of the future self. On this view, the relation of the present self to its past is simply nonexistent unless one exogenously specifies that the present self has some (idiosyncratic) second-order interest in the interests of the former self. Moreover, since such a present self characteristically has no tie to the earlier self, the earlier self will typically seek to precommit the later self (as in the story of Ulysses and the Sirens). Indeed, under normal conditions, nothing stands in the way of the earlier self simply unilaterally imposing its will on the later self by deciding that its preference ordering will be regulative of what the later self will actually be in a position to do. This means that precommitment, and more generally sophisticated choice, presupposes that there is no bargain to be struck between such separate selves, but only strategic maneuvering.

From the perspective of sophisticated choice, the future self turns out to be something other – an alien self. That is, what is presupposed is an ontological separation of temporally defined aspects of a "self" that threatens to be as deep as that between distinct individuals. On such a view, pushed to its limits, the future self's interests are not something the fashioning of which the present self can contribute to; they are only constraints within which the present self has to work. In this sense, the model of pure sophisticated choice can be said to be caught up in a view of the self as *essentially* fragmented.

13

Connections

13.1 Other models of dynamic choice

In the preceding chapters I have been preoccupied with establishing
that resolute choice provides a pragmatically defensible solution to a
very specific problem, namely, the problem of dynamic consistency
that confronts an agent whose methods of evaluation cannot be reconciled with the standard expected utility approach. To this end, I
have refrained from saying much about the connection between this
line of reasoning and other analyses of dynamic choice, except insofar
as they have a direct bearing on the thesis I have sought to defend.
However, quite a number of significant contributions have been made
to the subject of dynamic choice. Although I will not attempt anything
like a comprehensive survey, I do want to say something in particular
about those works that have helped to shape my own thinking.[1]

13.2 Strotz's article and related literature

In Chapter 9, I discussed Strotz's seminal article in terms of the distinction it makes between myopic and sophisticated choice. His discussion of alternative ways of dealing with dynamic inconsistency is
revealing, however, in another respect. The technical portions of the
article are preoccupied in large part with a special case of dynamic
inconsistency, one that can arise when an agent overvalues consumption in the near future relative to consumption in the more distant
future. The problem of dynamic inconsistency arises in the following
way: For one who has such a discount function, today it will be rational for him to abandon the plan he judged optimal yesterday, because
today he is a different person with a new discount function – the old
one shifted forward in time.

On Strotz's account, the agent has essentially two strategies for
coping with this problem: (1) He may precommit by either irrevocably
constraining future choices or by contriving a penalty for his future
self if the latter departs from presently preferred choice; or (2) he
may make use of the technique of "consistent planning" by selecting
the present action that will be best in the light of future disobedience.

Each of these amounts to a version of what I have characterized as sophisticated choice. Strotz takes precommitment as the preferred strategy under conditions of certainty, but regards it as potentially troublesome in cases involving risk and uncertainty. In such cases, the agent who precommits may end up being disadvantaged in ways that he could not, or at least did not, anticipate.[2]

Strotz also notes that a consumption plan involving a discount for the future need not pose a problem of dynamic inconsistency. One who is called upon to reevaluate such a consumption plan may actually end up acting in a manner consistent with that plan. A sufficient condition for this is that the logarithmic rate of change in the discount function be a constant.[3] Strotz calls this the "harmony" case. His working hypothesis, however, is that we are not born disposed to a harmonious discount rate: This is something that comes about as a result of (nonrational) socialization. By contrast, "consistent planning" is characterized as something the agent is taught; that is, it is a matter of his being instructed on how to identify the best plan among those that he can really expect to execute.[4]

Strotz makes one curious remark: He suggests that the person who is instructed on how to anticipate future disobedience and plan accordingly (the person who adopts the strategy of "consistent planning") "will, from time to time, depart from the consistent pattern of behaviour, sometimes because precommitment becomes feasible . . . and sometimes because of lapses that result when the *true* weight function becomes momentarily ascendant. These lapses are the splurges, and extravagances which we all know."[5] This sounds much more like a partially successful resolute chooser. That is, if the agent chooses within each time period in terms of a "taught" discount function, even though this is not his true discount function, then he can be understood to be choosing in accordance with a plan that he previously adopted and not just by reference to what, from the perspective of that time period, he judges to be optimal. That he does not always succeed in doing this – that sometimes the true discount function becomes ascendant – does not alter the fact that he is (generally) able to be resolute, in at least one sense of that term. Thus, Strotz's discussion of this point could be taken to anticipate a version of what I have described as resolute choice – an approach that is distinct from either precommitment or the strategy of anticipating one's own future disobedience.

It remains the case, however, that the thrust of Strotz's article is to reinforce the notion that for a rational agent there is really nothing like commitment to plans. Thus, he takes having a discount function that conforms to the "harmony" case as not only a sufficient but also a necessary condition for the agent fully executing the original consumption plan. And in a revealing comment on the case where the discount function of the agent poses a problem of dynamic inconsistency, Strotz remarks that to

continue to obey a fixed consumption plan just because it was optimal when viewed at an earlier date is not rational if that plan is not the optimal one at the present date. The best plan will generally change with a change in t [the time period], and there is nothing patently irrational about the individual who finds that he is in an intertemporal tussle with himself – except that rational behaviour requires that he take the prospect of such a tussle into account.[6]

The implication is that this sort of planning (as distinct from "consistent planning") is impossible: Our commitment to such plans does not extend beyond the present time period. A rational agent, having decided on a plan with respect to consumption for periods 1 through n can be expected, upon arriving at period 2, to set a new plan for periods 2 through, say, $n + 1$. There is, it would seem, no issue here about weakness of will. It is merely that if one discounts the future according to a certain formula, then one will be disposed, at the start of each successive time period, to recalculate, according to the same formula. Compliance – doing what one originally planned to do – is to be explained in one of two ways. Either it just happens that the agent prefers at each choice point to execute the original plan (e.g., his discount function is harmonious) or he has no choice in the matter (as a result, e.g., of having precommitted).[7]

Subsequent articles by Pollack and by Blackorby, Nissen, Primont, and Russell are concerned primarily with working out certain technical problems regarding the existence of sophisticated solutions.[8] Blackorby et al. do note, however, that a sophisticated approach can generate a plan that is intrapersonally suboptimal. This last point is reiterated by Peleg and Yaari, who offer an alternative characterization of sophisticated choice in terms of the notion of a Nash equilibrium consumption plan. This is a plan that has the following "consistency" property: The agent has no motivation to change his action in any period t, nor does he have any reason to regret his action in any period, given that he acts according to the plan in all other periods. As they go on to note explicitly, the plan that uniquely satisfies this equilibrium condition may not be intrapersonally optimal. They insist, however, that while some may regard this as a serious drawback, a plan that does not satisfy the equilibrium condition "cannot be advocated seriously as a reasonable course of action for an agent with changing tastes."[9]

Now it is well known to game theorists that the analogous equilibrium condition for games derives from conceptualizing interaction in terms of a noncooperative model, while the analogue to the principle of intrapersonal optimality, namely, the Pareto-optimality principle, is central to a cooperative model of interaction. With this remark, Peleg and Yaari could be said to articulate explicitly what was only implicit in Strotz's account: A rational agent can interact strategically with his future selves, but he cannot cooperate with them. Yaari himself elaborates on this point in a later article.[10] The discussion there turns on what he takes to be a paradigmatic case of change in preference: the historical case of Indians who were sold cheap whiskey by traders and who increasingly developed such a liking for the whiskey that they were willing, over time, to offer increasing amounts of their own goods in exchange for it. The solution that Yaari offers involves appeal to a generalized version of the sort of conceptual framework set down by Strotz and Pollack in which rationality is achieved by anticipating one's own future behavior. More specifically, the rational agent selects a plan by reasoning backward from the last stage, taking it as a given that at each stage he will select a best feasible plan according to the preferences that prevail at that stage. Yaari finds this type of reasoning compelling.[11] Once again he notes that the best plan in this sense may not be Pareto optimal. Nonetheless, he argues, it would be irrational to follow the Pareto-optimal plan. The agent who has endogenously changing tastes must recognize that he can be maneuvered into

a position where rationality conflicts with Pareto-efficiency, i.e., into a position where to be efficient is irrational and to be rational is inefficient. . . . So, the disadvantage, for an economic unit, of having endogenously changing tastes is that, even with perfect information and perfect foresight, the unit may find itself forced to follow a course of action which, by the unit's own standards, is Pareto-dominated. Any other course of action would be inconsistent with itself.[12]

What is the criterion of inconsistency being invoked here? The problem with a nonequilibrium Pareto-efficient plan is simply that it cannot be squared with the requirement that the agent maximize in each period the preferences that he has in that period with regard to (then) future consumption. What is operative here, of course, is a presupposition, nowhere examined, that the agent facing this sequential choice problem has no capacity to shape his own future choices autonomously, in the sense of making them responsive to plans adopted. That is, the appeal to backward reasoning or equilibrium plans presupposes that the preferences in any particular period are determined by something exogenous to the results of *deliberation* in previous periods and that these preferences in turn determine choice.

To be sure, in the model that Yaari presents, the agent has the capacity to shape, at least partially, his own future choices, for it is assumed that future preferences are *causally* related to prior consumption patterns. That is, what the agent consumes in a given period causally affects his future preferences. Thus, even if the agent is not able to choose in a resolute manner, it would seem that he can still choose in a sophisticated manner. In particular, the agent who is fully aware of these causal relationships is not precluded from engaging in, but is thereby able to engage in, what Strotz calls "consistent planning." He can choose at the outset of period 1 that overall consumption plan (specifying, among other things, a particular level of consumption for stage 1) that he judges to be most preferred in terms of stage 1 preferences for overall consumption plans, bearing in mind the feasibility constraints that are imposed on such plans by the preferences he will have in subsequent periods (which may, as suggested, be partially determined by consumption in previous periods, including period 1).

13.3 Johnsen and Donaldson

In a more recent article Johnsen and Donaldson consider the case of an agent who draws up a plan for the next two periods of time, where there is no uncertainty in the decision environment in the first period, but any member of a set S of possible states of nature may obtain in the second period.[13] Letting x in X represent a course of action for the first period, and y_s in Y_s a course of action for the second period, given that state s in S obtains, they take (x, y) to be a plan in XxY, where Y is the product of the Y_s's. In effect, they set forth a very simple framework in which a choice node is followed by a set of chance nodes, each of which is followed by a choice node.

The agent's first-period preferences for plans in XxY are described by an ordering R of XxY. His second-period preferences over actions y_s in state s, given past action x and planned action in all the states other than s, are described by an ordering $Q^s[x, y_{-s}]$. Correspondingly, the agent's dynamically defined set of preferences is represented by $\{R, Q\} = \{R, (Q^s): s \text{ in } S\}$.

Suppose now that the agent selects plan (x, y), does x in the first period, and then discovers that s is the state of the world. He is now free to choose any action in the set Y_s. Since, by hypothesis, there is no surprise as to what options remain to him in the second period, if his choice deviates from the original plan, this may be taken, according to Johnsen and Donaldson, as prima facie evidence of "changing tastes." If, however, the original plan is carried through whatever state obtains, one can say that the agent's tastes have remained constant. In such a case the agent's dynamic preferences $\{R, Q\}$ can be said to allow for *time-consistent planning* (TCP).

In more formal terms, let (x^*, y^*_{-s}) be the portion of a plan (x^*, y^*)

that applies to states other than s and designate the restriction of R to Y_s, the agent's ordering of second-period options, given that s is the case, as $R^s[x^*, y^*_{-s}]$. Note that, in principle, R^s can vary as the reference plan varies. That is, R^s is at least potentially a function of what one plans to do in the first period (this is given by x^*) and what one plans to do under each of the contingencies other than s, in the second period (this is given by y^*_{-s}). In terms of these notational conventions:

{R, Q} allows for time-consistent planning (TCP) iff $R^s[x^*, y^*_{-s}]$ = $Q^s[x^*, y^*_{-s}]$ for every s and every (x^*, y^*_{-s}) in XxY_{-s}.

By inspection, TCP can be seen to be a preference version of the dynamic consistency condition DC. Correspondingly, in very general terms, TCP can be satisfied in one of two ways: either by bringing R^s into line with Q^s or by bringing Q^s into line with R^s. Very roughly speaking, the former strategy corresponds to what I have characterized as sophisticated choice; the latter strategy corresponds to resolute choice. Johnsen and Donaldson themselves clearly have in mind such a very general interpretation of TCP, for they proceed to observe that TCP can be satisfied if each second-period ordering Q^s depends on everything that the first-period restricted ordering R^s depends on outside Y_s. In particular, they note, if second-period preferences are allowed to depend also on unrealizable actions – that is, on parts of the agent's original plan that do not now apply, given that the state of the world has turned out to be s – then any initial order R can figure in a dynamic preference set {R, Q} that satisfies TCP. As they explicitly note, the agent has only to let the induced ordering R^s also constitute Q^s (for each state s). That is, TCP can be satisfied by bringing Q^s into line with R^s. This is, of course, a preference ordering counterpart to choosing in a resolute fashion – to choosing so that second-period action conforms to what the agent's initial plan specified he was to do, if and when he arrives at that choice point.

As it turns out, however, the authors move immediately to embrace the more traditional interpretation of such a consistency condition. Observing that regimenting Q^s to R^s leaves open the possibility that second-period preferences themselves will depend on what action was planned for states that did not obtain, that is, that they will depend on "unrealized" alternatives, they proceed to argue that in the usual case one would not want this sort of dependency. This leads them to explore a variety of increasingly stronger separability conditions on Q^s that, in the presence of TCP, set constraints on R^s and hence on R. Thus, they end up doing little more than recognizing the logical possibility of a form of resolute choice.

13.4 Schelling

A preoccupation with sophisticated choice is also characteristic of Schelling's important and influential studies on self-command and self-control.[14] What Schelling presupposes is that except in very rare cases, one can overcome dynamic inconsistency only by employing some version of sophisticated choice. This is because weakness of will is a pervasive feature of the human condition. Thus, what purports to be a general study of egonomics – the science of "self-management" – ends up being particularized to a study of *strategic* egonomics, to cases in which one consciously tries to cope with one's own projected behavior by adopting some version of a sophisticated approach.

What Schelling brings to this subject is, to be sure, a remarkable conceptual eye for all the manifold forms of sophisticated choice that persons can and do employ to protect against themselves. Schelling distinguishes all these devices, however, from the "device" of genuine self-control or self-discipline. This he interprets as a matter of "inner strength, character, or moral fiber, or the change of values that goes with religious conversion."[15] He mentions such forms of self-control, however, simply *en passant,* in order to distinguish them from devices that are realistically available to the typical agent.[16]

13.5 Thaler and Shefrin

A somewhat different perspective is to be found in an article by Thaler and Shefrin.[17] The model they develop is predicated on the notion that over and above the various time-defined selves (the doers), each with its own (consumption) interests, there is an executive or management self, a being who has continuing identity over time and who makes plans (the planner). The planner is concerned with "lifetime" utility, whereas each doer exists for only one time period, has direct control over consumption during that period, and is "completely selfish, or myopic."[18] Within this framework, the authors conclude, the planner has available two basic kinds of management techniques, by means of which he can affect the behavior of each doer. He can (1) modify the preferences (or incentives) of the doers or (2) restrict each doer's opportunities by "imposing *rules* that change the constraints that doer faces."[19] The ideal rule, presumably, would be one that constrains each doer in such a manner that the doer ends up choosing as the planner would have him choose.[20]

In such an extreme case, rules eliminate all discretionary choice by the doer whatsoever; they then function somewhat like precommitment devices. Less extreme rules amount to "internal and self-imposed rules of thumb." More specifically, such rules have the following three characteristics: (1) They are often learned rather than chosen; (2) they are likely (whether learned or chosen) to become habits; and (3) to the extent that they do become habits, there will be rigidities built into the individual's behavior. This classification of techniques cuts squarely across the one Schelling develops. Like Schelling, Thaler and Shefrin treat precommitment as a basic technique, but unlike him, they seem to regard it as simply an extreme form of self-discipline. Now it is central to the more general economic model within which Thaler and Shefrin work that modifying preferences, and/or incentives, is costly. Thus, they suggest, the imposition of rules will prove attractive under certain conditions. As it turns out, however, available rules are imperfect or second-best. Typically, then, there is a trade-off between alternative costs, with the optimal arrangement consisting of some mixture of rules and preference or incentive modifications.

In the end, however, it seems that using various devices to modify preferences and/or incentives and imposing rules both amount to sophisticated approaches to choice. Nowhere does one find mention of the possibility of the planner negotiating with the doers to avoid the costs inherent in all such devices. That is, there is no recognition of any form of resolute choice.

13.6 Bratman

Bratman's recent book, *Intentions, Plans, and Practical Reason,* can be sharply contrasted with all the work discussed so far. The focus is on deliberation and intention that explicitly involve a temporal spread, that is, on future intention: the intention now to do something later. This is interpreted as a matter of settling on a plan. Thus, the notion of a plan is given a central place. Making plans or having intentions about future actions, on this account, involves commitment, which provides an element of stability or inertia. The need for plans, Bratman argues, is rooted in two considerations: Deliberation involves an expenditure of scarce resources, so that there is a limit to the returns that can be expected from deliberating at every choice point, and the pursuit of complex goals requires coordination between present and future activities, as well as coordination between oneself and others.[21]

Bratman's book is ambitious. What he attempts, among other things, is a very general characterization of conditions under which action undertaken in order to execute a plan is rational and conditions under which it would be rational to reconsider or revise one's plans. My preoccupation here, in contrast, has been much more limited. I have been concerned to identify one particular class of situations in which it would be rational to intend to do something in the future and subsequently do that thing. In the main, however, I take my conclusions to be supportive of his. The cases I have discussed in this work seem to me to be clear cases in which it is rational to settle on a plan and then execute it. Moreover, the argument I have tried to make for carrying through on plans, though it does not appeal to decision-making costs, does appeal to the other consideration mentioned by Bratman: the gains to be secured by effective coordination of choice.

Bratman's and my own conclusions perhaps do diverge in one important respect, however. What is at issue between us can be illustrated in terms of an interesting problem posed some years ago by Kavka and discussed at length by Bratman:

You have just been approached by an eccentric billionaire who has offered you the following deal. He places before you a vial of toxin that, if you drink it, will make you painfully ill for a day, but will not threaten your life or have any lasting effects. . . . The billionaire will pay you one million dollars tomorrow morning if, at midnight tonight, you *intend* to drink the toxin tomorrow afternoon. He emphasizes that you need not drink the toxin to receive the money; in fact the money will already be in your bank account hours before the time for drinking it arrives, if you succeed. . . . All you have to do is sign the agreement and then intend at midnight tonight to drink the stuff tomorrow afternoon. You are perfectly free to change your mind after receiving the money and not drink the toxin. (The presence or absence of the intention is to be determined by the latest "mind-reading" brain scanner and computing device [which you yourself believe to be thoroughly reliable].)[22]

Kavka himself suggests that intentions are best viewed as "dispositions to act which are based on *reasons to act* – features of the act itself or its possible consequences that are valued by the agent."[23] On this account of intentions, you face a real difficulty: Tomorrow afternoon you will have no reason to drink the toxin, indeed, very good reason for not drinking it. Thus, he concludes, you cannot intend tonight to drink it tomorrow. Kavka acknowledges that it is always open to the agent to precommit in some fashion or other, that is, make some irreversible arrangement that gives him independent incentive to drink, or hire a hypnotist, and so on. He short-circuits this maneuver, however, by stipulating that the contract you sign rules out such strategies. Alternatively, of course, one might argue that the use of such precommitment devices precludes having the requisite sort of intention: Precommitment at midnight ensures that you will drink the toxin tomorrow; but it does not ensure that you intend to drink the toxin.

To be sure, Kavka is prepared to recognize that matters are a bit more complicated than this. The person does, after all, have every reason to intend to drink the toxin, even if he does not have a reason to drink it:

When reasons for intending and reasons for acting diverge, as they do here, confusion often reigns. For we are inclined to evaluate the rationality of the intention both in terms of its consequences and in terms of the rationality of the intended action. As a result, when we have good reasons to intend but not to act, conflicting standards of evaluation come into play and something has to give way: either rational action, rational intention, or aspects of the agent's own rationality (e.g., his correct belief that drinking the toxin is not necessary for winning the million).[24]

Now Bratman appears to share Kavka's belief that whatever else is true, it cannot be rational of you to drink the toxin intentionally. But whereas Kavka holds that this implies that you cannot intend tonight to drink the toxin tomorrow afternoon (and so cannot secure the million dollars), Bratman is content to argue that even if it were rational of you to adopt at midnight the intention to drink the toxin the next afternoon, it does not follow that it will be rational of you to drink the toxin intentionally. This requires him to argue against what some have taken to be a basic principle governing future intention: If it was rational at t_0 to adopt the intention to A at t_1, and if at t_1 the conditions are just as you expected them to be, then it is rational not to abandon the intention to A at t_1.[25] Applied to the present problem, the claim would be as follows: If it was rational of you at midnight to adopt the intention to drink the toxin the next afternoon, and if the next afternoon the conditions are just as you expected them to be, then it is rational of you the next afternoon not to abandon the intention to drink the toxin. In rebuttal, Bratman argues that "adopt" here is subject to two very different readings. On one, the principle is plausible enough but the inference to the conclusion that it is rational to drink the toxin intentionally does not go through. On the other, the inference goes through but the principle is not plausible. If "adopt" is read as "adopt on the basis of deliberation about whether to so act," the principle is plausible but the inference does not go through, for by hypothesis (a hypothesis that he shares with Kavka) this is a case in which deliberation about whether to act intentionally (as opposed merely to intend to act) leads to the conclusion that you should *not* intentionally drink the toxin. Once again, the money is now in the bank, and you have the best of reasons, given the unpleasant effects of the drink, to refrain from drinking. If "adopt" is read in a more inclusive sense, as comprehending, among other things, "causing" yourself to have an intention (say, by hypnosis), the principle would sanction the inference in question, but the principle is doubtful:

Even if it was rational of you to acquire a new intention by way of such non-deliberation-based processes, and even if circumstances develop as expected, it might be incumbent on you to reconsider if the opportunity arises. There is no guarantee that in acquiring an intention by way of such non-deliberation-based processes you acquire an intention that would match a decision based on deliberation. . . . Even if it is rational of you [the night before] to acquire and have the intention to drink toxin [that afternoon], when [that time] arrives you will have ample opportunity to reconsider and to deliberate about whether to drink. It will be obvious to you then that you have nothing to gain and much to lose from drinking the toxin.[26]

I am not at all sure that I want to disagree with Bratman's diagnosis of the toxin case as presented by Kavka. But this is in part because I am not altogether sure what Bratman's position is. He allows for the possibility that the agent might rationally adopt (on the basis of something other than deliberation about whether to drink the toxin) an intention to drink the toxin – but he also suggests that it will be incumbent on the agent to reconsider if the opportunity arises. This implies that the agent might well have the requisite intention at midnight, but reconsider the next day. In this case, contrary to what Kavka clearly suggests, the agent could expect to collect the 1 million dollars and get away without drinking the toxin. Since I share Bratman's pragmatic perspective, I would agree that were such a strategy available, it would be rational to pursue it.

Consider, however, the following modified version of Kavka's problem: You *can* fulfill the terms of the contract by employing a precommitment device that ensures that you will drink the toxin the next afternoon, but such precommitment will cost you $500,000. Alternatively, you can forgo the precommitment device, settle on the plan of drinking the toxin, and stand to be tested by the brain–mind machine to see if you have the *capacity* to act on such a plan. Thus, if you do not believe that you have the capacity to carry out such a plan, you can sacrifice half your winnings and tie your hands in advance.

This is not Kavka's problem. I suspect, however, that Kavka would hold that the rational agent in this situation must precommit. On the account he gives, there is a link between deliberation in the afternoon of the next day about whether to drink and the possibility of forming a sincere intention the midnight before. Since, then, the agent will deliberately not drink the toxin the next day, he cannot sincerely intend to drink it the evening before. Recasting this in terms of plans and the capacity to act on them, the agent's capacity today to carry out a plan tomorrow is dependent on his being able to ratify the plan tomorrow. But, by hypothesis, when tomorrow comes, the agent will not ratify the plan. The brain–mind machine, then, will find the agent out. Thus, the agent does better to precommit so as to secure at least $500,000.

What would Bratman say about this case? I suspect that he would argue that even if you could cause yourself to intend at midnight to drink the toxin the next day, you would still, once the money were in the bank, reconsider. But this means that you do not have the capacity to carry through on the plan to drink the toxin. He should conclude, then, that your best strategy is to precommit.

This much, at least, is clear. Both Bratman and Kavka presuppose that you will not deliberately drink the toxin the next afternoon – you will either precommit, and hence have no choice but to drink the toxin, or deliberately not drink the toxin. In particular, both presuppose that whether the money is in your bank account or not, deliberation the next afternoon (if it does take place) will take place just by reference to the prospects that still lay open to you: a painless afternoon versus much pain and discomfort during the afternoon.

This, however, amounts to invoking implicitly a separability principle with respect to the deliberation and choice that take place that afternoon. That is, both Kavka and Bratman have taken it for granted that the best you are capable of is a sophisticated approach in which you anticipate your own (separable) dispositions with respect to deliberation and choice in the future and plans accordingly. And for those who take this approach, the following puzzle remains: How can it be rational to settle for $500,000, when all that stands between you and $500,000 is your own inability to decide on a plan and then follow through on it? If you are really prepared to precommit, for example, to have someone else constrain you to drink the toxin, why not "mentally" constrain yourself and save the precommitment costs?

In the end, it appears that Bratman, no less than others, has opted for the view that a rational approach to sequential choice is constrained by a separability requirement. That is, he assumes that at each point in the decision tree the agent, as rational chooser, will reconsider and reevaluate the options still open to him just by reference to (then) possible, as distinct from counterfactual, consequences. Such an agent will, of course, be able to adopt maxims or general policies and generally act upon them, but given his fixed predisposition at any given point to reconsider planned choice by reference to what still lies in the future, it can be said, I think, that Bratman's agent does not take plans as seriously as would a resolute chooser.

Yet it is not clear to me that the framework that Bratman develops forces him to side with sophisticated, as distinct from resolute, choosers. The possibility of an alternative, if only implicit, position is to be found by considering carefully what appears to be pushing his conclusion that "you have nothing to gain and much to lose from drinking the toxin." What he believes is that reasonable habits of nonreconsideration would not inhibit reconsideration in such cases. Must he believe this?

Reasonable habits of nonreconsideration, according to Bratman, are based on a consideration of the impact of a habit of nonreconsideration on the agent's long-term prospects of getting what he wants. When the expected impact exceeds an appropriate threshold, the habit is reasonable. One way in which such a habit can have a favorable impact on long-term prospects concerns savings with respect to decision-making costs. Reconsideration is costly in terms of scarce resources (time, energy, etc.). But a habit of nonreconsideration may also be grounded in a quite different consideration altogether, namely, the need to coordinate. Coordination can bring benefits over and above those associated with reduced decision-making costs. This is true not only with regard to plans that involve a number of agents, but also, as Bratman makes clear, when the single agent must coordinate with his own future selves.[27] Now the modified version of the toxin puzzle presents the agent with just such a coordination problem. This evening it is distinctly in his interests not only to plan to drink the toxin the next afternoon, but to have the capacity to execute that plan. From the perspective of his future self – the self of the next afternoon – however, it is not in his interests to drink the toxin. If he can resolve this coordination problem, he stands to gain an additional $500,000.

Thus, it would appear that Bratman's framework can be employed to rationalize a policy of nonreconsideration that would apply to the modified version of the toxin example. The modified puzzle serves, in effect, as a reminder that a policy of nonreconsideration can be rationalized by reference to the gains to be had from being able to coordinate the decisions of different time slices of oneself. Correspondingly, when Bratman concludes that reasonable habits of nonreconsideration do not support nonreconsideration in the case of Kavka's original puzzle, perhaps this is because he defines the problem in such a way that only considerations of limited resources appear to be relevant.

13.7 Elster

There is perhaps no one who has made a more sustained and imaginative contribution to the literature on dynamic choice theory than Elster. Of particular note here is his book *Ulysses and the Sirens*. A central thesis of that work is that *perfect* rationality involves a capacity to relate to the future, not simply in the sense of being able to look farther ahead, but also to wait and employ indirect strategies. Alternatively put, it involves being able to say no to an attractive short-run advantage (a local maximum) in order to achieve something even better (a global maximum). Elster also argues, however, that human beings manifest this capacity only imperfectly, owing to weakness of will, and that typically, then, they have to settle for a second-best strategy of precommitment.

The story of Ulysses and the Sirens serves as a metaphor for all of this. Simply to sail on toward the island, taking no precaution, and then choose to follow the Sirens would be to act in a purely myopic, "local-maximizing" manner. Global maximization, in contrast, would call for Ulysses to sail by the island and ignore the Sirens. But, so the story goes, Ulysses realizes he faces a problem of weakness of will: When the time comes, he will be beguiled by the Sirens' song into changing his course and heading for the island. Thus, he does the next best thing: He has himself bound to the mast and arranges for the crew to serve as agent (to his present wishes). In so doing, Elster argues, Ulysses reveals himself to be less than perfectly rational since "a rational creature would not have to resort to this device." At the same time, he is no mere "passive and irrational vehicle for his changing wants and desires," for he is "capable of achieving by indirect means the same end as a rational person could have realized in a direct manner."[28] Recasting this in terms of the distinctions developed in Chapter 9, perfect rationality points toward what I have characterized as being resolute, while an imperfectly rational being (such as Ulysses) must settle for some version or other of sophisticated choice.

Ulysses and the Sirens, then, presents a theory of *imperfect rationality,* suited to agents who face a problem of weakness of will. The basic strategy recommended is that of binding oneself in advance – of precommitting. Precommitting, on Elster's account, involves deliberately carrying out a certain decision at time t_1 in order to increase the probability that one will carry out another decision at time t_2. In the analysis that follows, Elster reveals an unusually fine-tuned and imaginative sense of the range of strategies that could qualify, or in some cases almost qualify, as precommitment. In summary, these include (1) manipulating the feasible set by either (a) restricting the set of physically possible actions or (b) changing the reward structure by public side bets; (2) manipulating one's own character by either (a) strengthening one's willpower or (b) changing one's preference structure; (3) manipulating information by either (a) changing one's belief system or (b) avoiding exposure to certain signals; and (4) rearranging "inner space" by, for example, either (a) using private side bets or (b) employing Strotz's technique of consistent planning.[29]

Precommitment, according to Elster, involves utilizing some sort of causal process in the world: "Our intuitive notion of what it is to bind oneself seems to require that we temporarily deposit our will in some external structure; that we set up a causal process in the external world that after some time returns to its source and modifies our behavior."[30] This is true even in the case of the manipulation of one's own "character." By reconstructing a series of quotations from Pascal,

Elster connects strategies of type (2) with Aristotle's theory of moral education, in which one becomes a good person by performing good actions. Initially, being virtuous requires much effort, but repeatedly doing the right thing results in the formation of a *hexis* (habit) from which subsequent virtuous actions flow smoothly. Elster also finds in Descartes a parallel argument to the effect that passion can be used to overcome passion. The suggestion is that even very small amounts of willpower can suffice for the most extraordinary feats of self-control if only one has an understanding of the physiological mechanisms by which habits are formed and changed.[31] An implication of these interpretive explorations seems to be that there is a connection between strategies of type (1) and (2): Successful manipulation of character can be facilitated in part by the utilization of more prosaic forms of precommitment. For example, by tying one's hands or making public side bets, it becomes possible to act in a certain manner, and repeated actions of the type in question lead to the development of the appropriate habit.

In all such cases, Elster argues, one does not rely just on future intention, that is, on deciding how to decide in the future. Precommitment involves engineering, not simply deciding on, a change in the set of options or one's future preferences or one's beliefs. This, in turn, means that strategies of type (4) fail to qualify, strictly speaking, as forms of precommitment, even though they can be regarded as an alternative way of dealing with weakness of will. Deliberate rearrangement of inner space – intentional shaping of desires or preferences – is characterized by Elster in his later work, *Sour Grapes,* as a matter of "character planning," and this includes, besides the technique of making private side bets or anticipating one's own future behavior, the much more comprehensive strategies advocated by, for example, Stoic, Buddhist, and Spinozistic philosophies.[32] In *Ulysses and the Sirens,* this sort of approach is also associated with the "responsibility for self" view to be found in Sartre and Charles Taylor, according to which one can effect change (at least in certain cases) by redefining oneself. Elster interprets this as a view to the effect that thinking that something is so can make it so. That is, redefining oneself is presumed to function as a self-fulfilling prediction: Redefining oneself can suffice to bring it about that one becomes the sort of person that meets the new definition one has projected.[33]

On one reading, the notion that precommitment involves setting into motion some causal process in the external world is merely a matter of definition. That is, noncausal, intentional self-definition is still possible. Indeed, at one point Elster suggests that the two processes – of self-definition and precommitment – do not contradict but rather supplement each other.[34] The point is that although intentional self-definition is possible, there are real and significant limits to this sort of strategy. In many cases, transformation can be effected only by the use of more prosaic precommitment devices. It seems clear, however, that Elster finds the engineering/Aristotelian model much more plausible than the self-definition/Sartrian model. Moreover, the prefatory remarks in *Sour Grapes* suggest a retreat even from this position: There he expresses a more cautious view about the possibility of employing engineering strategies of type (2).[35]

Elster's concept of perfect rationality as global maximization points directly to what I have characterized in this work as resolute choice. I suspect, however, that what he means by global maximization falls somewhat short of resolute choice of the sort I have been exploring. However global maximization is defined, it is clear that we disagree over its feasibility. Elster sees this sort of perfect rationality as typically beyond the reach of human beings, and this explains his preoccupation with differentiating among various "second-best" (sophisticated) strategies. In contrast, I have been preoccupied with making the case for the real possibility of being resolute in certain circumstances. Despite the creative and imaginative nature of Elster's exploration, I am not altogether persuaded by his classification scheme or his conclusions. On a different interpretation of alternative strategies, I believe, perfect rationality as resolute choice can be seen to be within the reach of the representative individual. Moreover, even on Elster's own account, there is something bothersome about his assumption that humans can typically hope to achieve no more than imperfect rationality.

Consider first the manner in which he interprets alternative versions of sophisticated choice. The metaphor of Ulysses is extended to cover not only prosaic cases of precommitment – tying one's hands, making public pronouncements from which it would be embarrassing to back down, and so on – but subtle and complex processes of the sort with which Aristotle was preoccupied, in which the self is gradually redefined by an incremental process of doing. Against these, he groups together an equally disparate collection of strategies, ranging all the way from Strotz's method of consistent planning to that of existential self-definition. Between these two groups, the implicit differentia appears to be *doing*, which sets in motion some sort of causal process in the world, versus merely *thinking* or *intending*. As illuminating and as important as this is, to make it the organizing distinction obscures an important link between, for example, prosaic forms of precommitment and Strotz's method of consistent planning. In a revealing footnote Elster himself notes this connection: Consistent planning, he remarks, is sophistication within the limits of the feasible: precommitment is sophistication amounting to a modification of the limits.[36] In either case, however, being sophisticated involves coming to realize one's own limits – the constraints that one's own future selves place on the present self. That is, neither form of sophisticated choice involves any attempt to modify the dispositions of one's future selves: Each takes one's own future selves as having behavioral dispositions that can be predicted and made the object of strategic maneuvering, but not altered.

This contrasts sharply with what happens in all of the other cases marked out by Elster. Specifically, strategies of type (2), manipulation of character – either by strengthening one's willpower or by changing one's preference structure – and of type (4a) – private side bets, as well as the Sartrian technique of self-definition – are all linked in an important respect. Each presupposes a rejection of the view that the dispositions of one's own future selves are something given – something to be predicted and strategically contended with, but not altered. Each, then, is committed to the view that the self can be transformed (if only very gradually). This, I want to suggest, is perhaps the more useful distinction to make: between strategies presupposing that the dispositions of one's own future selves are givens that set real constraints on what can be done, and those presupposing that the dispositions of one's future selves can be reshaped or managed, at least to some degree.

On this different reading, most of Elster's strategies for the "rearrangement of inner space," including the more extreme views of Sartre and other existentialists, connect naturally with Aristotle's notion of character development. Indeed, Sartrian self-definition can perhaps best be understood as the limiting (and ideal) case of the Aristotelian program for the *construction* of the self. Elster himself takes cognizance of this connection when he speaks of the psychologist Ainslie's "profound suggestion that strategies (4a) and (2a) may be closely connected (i.e. that the technique of private side-bets may involve a general strengthening of will-power."[37] Unfortunately, his own interpretation of alternatives drives a wedge between these two types of technique.

I do not mean to suggest that the key to understanding the possibility of achieving perfect rationality lies simply in emphasizing the distinction among techniques for transforming, as distinct from strategically anticipating, the dispositions of one's own future selves. What is needed, I think, is a sense of the fuller range of techniques that this reinterpretation suggests. One's own future dispositions are not just the object of prediction, manipulation, or transformation: They can also be the object of executive management, as it were. This, I suggest, is just the sort of conception of the choosing self that I outlined and sought to defend in the preceding chapters, in connection with the discussion of the conditions under which resolute choice would be possible. There I argued not simply that the self must settle on a plan and then carry it out resolutely, but that the very possibility of doing this hinges on the self assuming what amounts to an executive role – that of impartial manager of the manifold of time-defined preferences or interests.

The self as executive manager is to be understood as being concerned with what works to the mutual advantage of all the relevant time-defined selves. The appropriate analogy here is to the theory of social interaction – of the coordination of choices with a view to what is mutually beneficial. To be sure, the appeal to what is mutually beneficial suggests a sense in which being resolute can be rationalized by reference to considerations of "long-term gain" – but this is a form of "long-term gain" that cannot be subsumed under the traditional notion of "expected gain," as judged from some particular time-defined perspective. The metaphor of a failed coordination scheme remains the appropriate one here: No particular individual can suppose that his decision to defect really causes the scheme to fail or even significantly increases the probability of such a failure; what generates failure (or increases its probability) is the macro or cumulative effect of many micro choices.[38] Similarly, the problem that the individual faces vis-à-vis his own future selves is that failure to coordinate effectively can result in losses, even though any particular subsequent time-defined self, contemplating the expected value of departing from, say, some plan previously settled on, may reasonably conclude that departure is justified.

All of this suggests a much more ambitious notion of global maximization. The global maximizer is to be understood not simply as one who has developed a capacity to say no to short-run considerations and yes to "long-run" expected return, as judged from some time-defined perspective. A global maximizer must also be able to say no in an even more sophisticated manner: He must be a resolute chooser. Global maximization, then, includes rejecting strategies that work to the mutual disadvantage of all the time-defined selves. This, in turn, is something that can be effected only by a self that assumes the role of manager, not manipulator, of future preferences.

Elster does not press the concept of global maximization in this direction. In fact, he does not explicitly suggest a perspective that transcends that of simply anticipating future contingent possibilities from a time-defined perspective. But without that sort of conception of global maximization, one is driven to just the position that Elster appears to hold, namely, that the global capacity involves either the rigid imposition of rules or the transformation of what would otherwise be the preferences of one's future selves. In order to pass between the horns of that dilemma, I suggest, one needs a theory of the self as an executive manager, and not merely as a predictor and/or manipulator of future preferences.

This concept of self-management opens the door to a very different way of looking at, among other things, willpower. Elster's own view of this is revealingly uncomplimentary:

When the subject rearranges his inner space and reward system, so that a failure to follow up on one decision (e.g. the decision to stop smoking) has negative implications for other decisions (e.g. the decision to diet), the inter-related system of goals and desires may come to exhibit the rigidity and inflexibility often associated with the notion of will-power.[39]

The problem, it seems, is that within Elster's basic model, the preferences of future selves cannot be intentionally managed but only artificially thwarted (by some "tying of the hands" device) or completely transformed (by becoming a different person). But whether it is a matter of thwarting or transforming, on the account that Elster gives this must amount to the *imposition* of the values of the present self on one's future selves, and this, I think, is what accounts, beyond his pessimism concerning the possibility of transformation, for his negative view of the same: In the last analysis, even transformation appears to be a form of "self-enslavement."

All of this comes to a head, at the end of the section on the logic of imperfect rationality, in his comments on a remark of William James to the effect that "the *highest* ethical life . . . consists of all times in the breaking of rules which have grown too narrow for the actual case."[40] Elster supposes that James is here referring to a higher form of life than that characterized by "self-imposed rules or strategies of pre-commitment," that is, to something other than what can be achieved by various forms of sophisticated choice. The suggestion, then, is that the even higher form of life involves flexibility with regard to rules, the achieving of control without rigidity. Elster's problem, however, is that his basic model of precommitment provides him with few clues as to what would count as control without rigidity. Once again, my own sense is that this problem can be resolved only within a framework that invokes the conception of a hierarchical self as sympathetic and committed manager of the manifold distinguishable interests of the person. This, it seems to me, is what is lacking in Elster's account.[41]

Finally, there is an unresolved problem lurking in the background of the entire conceptual scheme that Elster has set up. We are told, at the outset, that there is something that could be characterized as perfect rationality, but it is not vouchsafed to humans. Humans are capable only of imperfect rationality. Why? Because of weakness of will. But what accounts for the latter? Elster, following Davidson, is content to take weakness of will as a *surdity*.[42] Nonetheless, he insists that the presumption of rationality is fundamental for understanding

human behavior. Global maximization or strategies of precommitment – first-best or second-best rationality – are, he argues, natural
forms of behavior that do not require any further explanation. An
explanation is required, however, when deviations from perfect and
imperfect rationality are observed.[43] If this is true, it seems that Elster
has failed to meet the demands he himself has set for a theory of
human behavior. Imperfect rationality involves, by definition, a deviation from perfect rationality, and thus we require, on his own
account, an explanation of why we are typically limited in this fashion.
On my reading, however, *Ulysses and the Sirens* does not offer such an
explanation.

Let me close on a more conciliatory note. Elster's remarks about
strategy (2a) – manipulating our character by strengthening our
willpower – provide a natural introduction to the problem of developing a capacity for being resolute. Viewed in that way, the Aristotelian line he takes is highly plausible. As in so many other areas
involving the mastery of a skill, practice makes perfect: We learn by
doing. And viewed in this way, the whole of what I have said in this
work and what I understand Elster to be saying in *Ulysses and the Sirens*
are altogether compatible with one another. To borrow from Elster's
reading of Pascal, what we need is a two-barreled approach: Only
reason can arrive at the intellectual insight that practical reason involves more than "local maximizing," but reason also suggests that
intellectual insight is not enough – that we need to practice adopting
a global perspective in our practical affairs if it is to take hold and
regulate our way of making decisions. In this work I have tried to
make the intellectual case for a genuinely "global" approach to dynamic decision making; what Elster can be construed as doing is re-
minding us that we also need to attend to the way we should act so as
to develop this capacity fully.

14

Conclusions

14.1 The standard theory of rationality

At the outset of this work I posed the question of what kind of support can be offered for the weak ordering and strong independence principles – the principles that form the cornerstone of the modern theory of expected utility and subjective probability. The various pieces of my answer are now in place, but the telling has required a series of explorations that have occupied many chapters. Let me try, now, to consider all of the pieces together and focus on what they imply with regard to the status of the two principles in question.

Recall, first of all, that although as a matter of logic the conjunction of PR, DC, and SEP entails both CF and CIND, that formal result does not provide much grounding for the principles in question. Those who find certain violations of CF or CIND plausible can argue from that conviction (via modus tollens) to the conclusion that not all of PR, DC, and SEP are acceptable. In particular, those who find SEP to be plausible can defend violations of either CF or CIND by accepting modifications of the underlying presupposition concerning what plans are feasible – adopting VSF – and, correspondingly, qualifying NEC and, hence, PR. As detailed in Section 8.7, the resulting weakened set of postulates does not suffice for the derivation of either CF or CIND.

I must confess that for my part I began by being skeptical about the principles of the received theory of rational choice, and it is the mark of the skeptic that he tends to favor arguments that proceed in the manner of modus tollens rather than those that proceed in the manner of modus ponens. Given what seemed to me an implausibly strong conclusion, namely, that rational choice consists in the maximization of expected utility, I responded by questioning the premises. But whether one is a believer or a skeptic, it is clear that logic alone cannot do the job. In this regard, one can hardly improve on a remark that Savage (a believer) makes in *The Foundations of Statistics:*

In general, a person who has tentatively accepted a normative theory must conscientiously study situations in which the theory seems to lead him astray; he must decide for each by reflection – *deduction will typically be of little relevance* – whether to retain his initial impression of the situation or to accept the implications of the theory for it.[1]

If what is sought is a derivation of the principles of expected utility and subjective probability from a *secure* set of conditions on dynamic choice, the formal constructions presented in Sections 8.2 and 8.3 do not suffice. What is needed, in addition, is some independent argument in support of the conditions invoked. Now Hammond presumably finds such support in the consideration that the conditions in question can be associated with what he terms a plausible consequentialist principle. But as I argued in Section 8.10, I do not think he is successful. By his own admission, SEP is conceptually distinct from consequentialism, and consequentialism itself is plausible only if it is permissive with respect to what can count as a consequence. This poses a real dilemma, however, since on my reading a catholic criterion of consequences seriously narrows the scope of SEP.

I went on to argue that even if the constructions presented at the beginning of Chapter 8 are not dispositive with regard to the status of CF and CIND, they are still useful for diagnostic purposes. They do serve to establish that one who is committed to methods of evaluation that relax either CF or CIND will not be able to satisfy all of PR, DC, and SEP in certain specific dynamic choice settings. This led me in Chapter 9 to the suggestion that in such cases the agent has three degrees of freedom: He can take a myopic approach, maintaining a commitment to both PR and SEP but relaxing DC; a sophisticated approach, maintaining a commitment to both SEP and DC but relaxing PR; or a resolute approach, maintaining a commitment to both PR and DC but relaxing SEP. The question then became: What argument, if any, could be offered for opting for one, as opposed to another, of these approaches? In Chapters 10 and 11 I sought to answer this question by appealing to the pragmatic conception of rationality first articulated in Chapter 5. I concluded that although pragmatic objections can be raised to the first two approaches – the agent can typically be maneuvered into violating DSO, the principle of dominance with respect to sure outcomes – no such objection can be raised to resolute choice. Translated into the terms of the formal constructions explored in Chapter 8, this means that SEP is suspect.

The conclusion to be derived from all of this, however, is that CF and CIND – alternatively, WO and IND – cannot be secured by any of the versions of the pragmatic arguments I have explored. That is, their derivation proceeds by way of an appeal to a condition – SEP – that is not mandated by pragmatic considerations pertaining to dynamic choice. And this means, in turn, that both the expected utility theorem and its correlative, the theorem concerning the existence of well-defined subjective probabilities, cannot be neatly grounded in a set of postulates that can themselves be defended by appeal to pragmatic considerations.

Of course, those who accept WO and IND (and the conclusions that follow when these postulates are combined with other assumptions) are not thereby shown to be irrational in any sense. The received theory describes *one* way of evaluating risk and uncertainty that satisfies the requirements of rationality; but it is not the only way. My conclusions in this regard, like Hume's, are permissive. A wider class of evaluative methods qualify as rational than the standard theory would allow. However, this in turn puts one in a position to challenge the claim that there is a clear argument against the various revisionist proposals that I have discussed in the course of this work – proposals such as Levi's theory of E- and S-admissibility for choosing among uncertain prospects, the minimax risk theory, Ellsberg's ambiguity measure, Allais's proposals concerning the need to develop measures that take into account dispersion considerations, Machina's proposal for a utility theory without the independence axiom, and so on.

To be sure, certain proposals for modifying the expected utility approach can be shown to be pragmatically troublesome. As others have already noted, for example, Kahneman and Tversky's "prospect theory" permits violations of DSO. Since I think this principle does give expression in a nonproblematic manner to a pragmatic perspective, I find prospect theory unacceptable from a normative point of view. However, as I have tried to show in this work DSO does not provide a blanket argument, deductive or pragmatic, against any relaxation of either WO or IND.[2]

14.2 A possible fallback position

Some, no doubt, will want to cling to SEP and the sophisticated approach, although the grounds for this, particularly given what I have tried to argue in Chapters 10, 11, and 12, escape me. Those who insist on SEP can, of course, take comfort in the thought that from its perspective a resolute approach is simply not possible and that, consequently, it can be no criticism of a sophisticated approach that the plan it selects will typically be dominated with respect to sure outcomes by the plan selected by a resolute approach. Those who accept SEP will insist that the pragmatic arguments require an appeal to feasible plans. Granting this, sophisticated choice will qualify as a pragmatically impeccable way to deal with the relevant dynamic choice problems. If, then, I have failed to convince the reader of the plausibility of a resolute approach, this will simply strengthen the case for the pragmatic defensibility of a sophisticated approach. Translating this into the formal constructions examined in Chapter 8, this amounts to an argument for SEP and DEC, but against the NEC factor of PR. Within the framework in question, however, NEC is needed for the derivation of both CF and CIND. Thus, although the critique in this case proceeds differently – it is NEC rather than SEP that is suspect – still the conclusion is the same: The expected utility and subjective probability theorems I have been exploring are secured by appeal to postulates that cannot themselves be securely grounded in pragmatic considerations.

In this respect, then, the dispute over whether resolute as well as sophisticated, or only sophisticated, choice is feasible amounts to an in-house debate among those who reject the standard theory. That is, those who find themselves adversaries on this issue may still be able to agree that the various deductive and pragmatic arguments for CIND and CF that I have explored here are unsound. I believe, however, that the quick dismissal of resolute choice on the grounds of feasibility is simply question begging in favor of SEP and against PR (and, more specifically, NEC). One cannot decide the issue in favor of SEP and sophisticated choice by appeal to a criterion of feasibility that presupposes SEP. My own view is that once one sees this, the presumption against resolute choice drops away, and the *pragmatic* argument discussed in Chapter 11 makes a serious case for being resolute rather than sophisticated.

Once again, of course, it is open to those who want to defend SEP to try to construct some nonpragmatic argument for SEP. But even if one comes up with a convincing argument of this sort, two deep problems remain. First, in the spirit of the strong version of Hume's test, others may well ask what makes this (nonpragmatic) consideration regulative for them (as well as those who put it forward). There remains, in effect, the vexing problem of whether any such consideration will prove to be interpersonally transferable. Second, such a line of reasoning must still compete with the pragmatic considerations presented in Chapter 11. Those who manage to be unimpressed by this alternative argument and who proceed to choose in a resolute fashion will end up doing better than their sophisticated counterparts. And this will surely incline them to remark to their sophisticated counterparts, "If you're so smart, why ain'cha richer than us?"[3]

14.3 Consequentialist choice

Even though I am unable to share Hammond's conviction that consequentialism leads to the acceptance of both CF and CIND, it is still the case, as Chapter 9 seeks to make clear, that each of the modified approaches I have explored – sophisticated and resolute choice – retains much of Hammond's framework. Moreover, the pragmatic tests that I have made central to this work are clearly in the spirit of his consequentialist principle.

Sophisticated choice expresses an incrementalist version of a pragmatic or consequentialist perspective. Judged from its perspective, resolute choice can be said to be nonconsequentialist in the following sense: At any given choice point, the resolute chooser looks to more than just what prospects still lay open to him – choice is based on considerations pertaining to plans, sequences of choices conceived as wholes, and hence, characteristically, on something that was initiated in the past.

As I argued in Section 12.6, however, I have sought to defend only a restricted version of resolute choice, namely, being resolute when this can be shown to satisfy a condition of intertemporal (or intrapersonal) efficiency – that is, to serve the continuing interests of the agent. Under such conditions, I went on to suggest, resolute choice can be said to express a consequentialist perspective, albeit one that is defined holistically rather than incrementally. That is, the case for being resolute under certain circumstances is precisely a consequentialist case: By being resolute the agent gains with respect to his own continuing interests. Thus, although I have argued in this work that a properly articulated consequentialist perspective does *not* yield a defense of either CF or CIND, I have also argued, more positively, that it does yield an argument for why, under certain circumstances, it makes sense to be resolute and follow through on the plan adopted.

Since the myopic agent exposes himself to losses that both the sophisticated and the resolute agent can avoid, the myopic approach, despite its commitment to a form of incremental consequentialism, cannot be rationalized from a carefully defined intertemporal (intrapersonal) consequentialist perspective. And I have tried to suggest, in Chapter 11, why I think that sophisticated, no less than myopic, choice must be judged unacceptable from that very same perspective. Yet if a resolute approach were judged to be impossible, then a sophisticated approach would emerge as defensible from the perspective of an intertemporally defined version of consequentialism. Notice, however, that just as in the case of resolute choice, the intertemporal perspective cannot be used to provide a blanket defense of sophisticated choice. In particular, the "sophisticated" strategy of precommitment will not always be defensible from that perspective, since it is quite possible that what precommitment achieves is to secure the interests of the ex ante self at the expense of the interests of the ex post self.

14.4 Symmetry of the arguments presented

The line of argument I have pursued has an additional implication of some importance. Among critics of the received theory there has been a tendency to argue in favor of holding fast to one or the other of CF and CIND and relax the other. Levi, for example, focuses on the context-free principle (as well as the issue of the completeness of the ordering), whereas Allais, Ellsberg, and Machina have no quarrel with that principle but argue that the independence axiom should be relaxed.[4] I myself am among those who have tended to ignore the issue concerning the context-free conditions on orderings and who have focused instead on the independence principle.[5]

The thrust of the formal results in Chapter 8, however, is that CF and CIND stand on a par with each other. Within the framework of DC, PR, and SEP, what distinguishes the derivation of CF from the derivation of CIND is simply the assumption in the latter case that decision trees can involve chance as well as choice nodes and that choice at some point n_i is as much separable from counterfactual events (from events that might have taken place) as it is from counterfactual choices (from options that were previously available, but are no longer, in virtue of choices made). Even when that formal structure is weakened by the introduction of the more restrictive feasibility condition SF, parallel derivations of important factors of CF and CIND respectively are still possible. When SF is replaced with VSF, neither principle is any longer derivable. Similarly, the pragmatic arguments considered in Chapters 10 and 11 clearly work or, as the case may be, fail to work, in a very evenhanded manner. A myopic approach to violations of CF no less than a myopic approach to violations of CIND lands the agent in pragmatic difficulty. I have been unable to find, then, a convincing version of a pragmatic argument for weakening the ordering assumption but not the independence principle.

14.5 The issue of choice versus preference

The thrust of the argument in Chapter 10 is that agents who employ methods of evaluation that violate either CF or CIND may be subject to pragmatic difficulties if they do not adopt the appropriate stance toward the dynamic problems with which they can be confronted. Now CF and CIND are conditions not on picking some unique element from among those judged to be equally acceptable but on acceptable sets. Correspondingly, the focus of Chapters 10 through 12 has been the sort of pragmatic liability the agent is exposed to insofar as his acceptable sets fail to satisfy these two conditions. In particular, I have supposed that the manner in which the agent *picks* (as distinct from the manner in which he chooses) raises no pragmatic issue at all.

Notice that within the framework adopted here, picking will violate both CF and CIND. To take the simplest example, consider a situation in which the agent's method of evaluation satisfies CIND with respect to acceptable sets. If the agent ranks gambles x and y in such a manner that both are in $D(\{x, y\})$, it will also be the case that both $g_x = [x, p; z, 1 - p]$ and $g_y = [y, p; z, 1 - p]$ are in $D(\{g_x, g_y\})$. Given the distinction between picking and choosing, moreover, nothing precludes the possibility that the agent picks x and also picks g_y. Could picking behavior of this sort be exploited by an entrepreneur, unless the agent were to adopt, say, a resolute approach? More specifically, suppose the agent approaches such picking situations myopically. Is he then subject to violations of dominance with respect to terminal outcomes?

The essence of the argument against myopia is that it involves a situation in which all of the following conditions obtain: Some plan s is preferred to another plan $r(+)$, which dominates a third plan r; the structure of the decision tree is such that choice between s or r, on the one hand, and $r(+)$, on the other, is forced at the outset; and at the point where the agent must choose between s and r, he no longer prefers s to r and, thus, may choose to implement r. The argument, then, turns on much more than assuming that there is a situation in which the agent adopts one plan at the outset and later "shifts" and selects another plan. For the myopic chooser to get into trouble, this reversal must take place against the background of a foregone plan, $r(+)$, that now emerges as superior to the one that does get implemented. I see no foothold here for the conclusion that those who violate CF or CIND in picking will thereby face pragmatic difficulties.

At the same time, however, I cannot find any pragmatic basis for the sort of line drawn recently by Levi. The suggestion, in effect, is that the agent who has full-blown preferences that violate the strong independence principle IND will be liable to difficulties, whereas the agent who violates only the choice-set version CIND will not. Now I have focused in this work on CIND rather than IND. Of course, that the *formal* results of Chapter 8 can be couched in terms of principles governing the composition of acceptable sets settles nothing. Anything can be exhibited as a deductive result if one is prepared to make the appropriate assumptions. Since Levi is disinclined to accept CF and CIND as normative for acceptable sets, he will not be disposed to accept any set of conditions that entail those two principles. On this point, of course, there is no quarrel between us. Like Levi, I am prepared to judge the deductive approach taken in Chapter 8 to be less than successful. The argument of Chapter 10, however, seems to me to work against his suggestion. Agents become liable to pragmatic difficulty (albeit this is a liability from which they can escape) long before they arrive at the point of employing methods of evaluation that could be said to give rise to well-behaved binary-based preference orderings. That is, from a purely pragmatic point of view, the line between full-blown preferences and relatively unstructured accept-able sets does not appear to have any significance.[6]

14.6 Final remarks about dominance arguments

The argument of Chapters 10 and 11 turns on an appeal to the simple dominance principle DSO – dominance with respect to sure out-comes. As I pointed out in Chapter 3, however, within a framework in which the agent is presupposed to be concerned only with terminal payoffs and probabilities, the much stronger dominance principle GDE is essentially equivalent to the strong independence principle, a principle that, I have been intent on arguing, is suspect as a rationality condition. It is essential to my whole argument, then, that one can plausibly appeal to DSO without thereby committing oneself to the much stronger condition GDE.

One way in which to understand the ready acceptance of the ex-pected utility and subjective probability constructions lies in the con-sideration that one has here a remarkable *convergence* between what is needed from the point of view of a formal theory of the measurability of utility or value and a relatively simple intuition. The formal work over the past few decades in the theory of measurement – as encap-sulated, for example, in Krantz, Luce, Suppes, and Tversky, *The Foun-dations of Measurement* – makes it clear that *some* sort of independence principle is pivotal for any theory that aspires to provide a quantita-tive measure of preference or value – as distinct from a theory that is content to take preference as measurable only on an ordinal scale. Against this background, Savage's suggestion that an independence condition of the requisite sort can be secured (at least in the presence of other allegedly plausible assumptions) by means of the sure-thing principle was bound to meet with great enthusiasm. All that Savage really required was that one accept the extension of sure-thing rea-soning from DSO to GDE – from cases in which dominance obtains for a partition framed with respect to sure outcomes to cases in which dominance obtains with respect to some (arbitrarily defined) partition of "outcomes."

Still, the extension required critical examination. That began, of course, in effect with the work of Allais and, somewhat later, with that of Ellsberg. Allais was prepared to grant the intuitive plausibility of DSO but not IND (and, hence, not GDE).[7] Ellsberg objected to SI, Savage's version of the independence principle for choice under con-ditions of uncertainty, and hence also to GDE.[8] The concern of both of these critics, however, was with the plausibility of such conditions as descriptive of, rather than normative for, choice. Moreover, in their case, and in the case of virtually all those who have followed their lead, the argument proceeded in very large part by an appeal to allegedly clear counterexamples.

That discussion tended to proceed by way of counterexamples is particularly relevant because the challenged principles had become enormously useful not only (as mentioned above) for a formal theory of the measurability of preference and subjective probability, but also for theory construction in microeconomics and in the newly emerging and enormously powerful theory of games. In short, what the counterexamples had to confront was not a working hypothesis, but a paradigm. All of this has tended to obscure what I think to be the basic issue at the level of a *normative* theory, namely, whether there is any justification for extending DSO to GDE. I propose to bracket the issue of the usefulness of the principle for a variety of formal constructions and representation theorems and focus once again on the specific issue raised in Section 4.7, namely, on the issue of what warrant there is for an extension of DSO to GDE within a normative theory of rationality.

It is instructive, in this regard, to consider once again the first of the articles in which Savage appeals to the sure-thing principle. Sure-thing reasoning is there introduced explicitly in a setting in which the agent is presumed to be interested only in *expected* income: "If for every possible state, the expected income of one act is never less and is in some cases greater than the corresponding income of another, then the former act is preferable to the latter."[9] In this setting, of course, at least in the presence of probabilistic independence of the appropriate sort, a commitment to choosing in terms of expected income virtually commits one to GDE. Regardless of what probability distribution is assigned to the elements in the partition of uncertain events, the "sure-thing" option will bear a greater expected return. Sure-thing intuitions, then, slide smoothly into place on the heels of the assumption that the agent has no interest in anything but expected income. In this case, the dispositions of the agent have been characterized in such a manner that dispersion considerations and considerations of ambiguity or uncertainty already seem out of place.

In the article jointly authored by Savage and Friedman, the setting is changed; there is no explicit assumption that the agent is concerned only with expected return.[10] But the example offered, that of a doctor, seems intuitively secure. The doctor is presumed to be concerned with improving the condition of his patient. He does not know which of a number of possible diseases his patient has, but he does know that regardless of which disease he has, bedrest will improve his condition. So he prescribes bedrest. If the background to be provided here is that the doctor is concerned only with increasing his patient's chances

of recovery or improvement – with expected recovery or improvement – then, of course, sure-thing intuitions slide into place for the
reasons given earlier. If the background provided is the assumption
that for each of the possible diseases, bedrest *in fact* will improve the
condition of the patient (as distinct from merely increasing his chances
of recovery), then the example illustrates the simple dominance condition DSO.

The formulation presented immediately after the bedrest example
neatly embraces these two distinct types of case. The "outcomes" $f(a)$,
$f(b)$, and so on are explicitly taken to be *gambles*, but no stipulation is
made that the agent is concerned only with expected values. The
formulation, however, embraces a good deal more. What is formulated is a significantly stronger principle – namely, GDE rather than
DSO – that takes one well beyond the intuitions of either the case of
the expected-income maximizer or the reasoning of simple dominance with respect to terminal outcomes.

No defense is offered for this extension. Indeed, as far as I have
been able to determine, only one serious argument has been offered
for the extension. This is the one presented by Savage and mentioned
in Section 4.7, according to which it is justified because it is
unavoidable.[11] Savage argued that accepting DSO but rejecting GDE
presupposes that one can distinguish gambles whose outcomes involve no risk from those whose outcomes do involve further risk –
that is, distinguish between probability distributions over *sure*
outcomes and probability distributions over probability distributions.
However, as he saw the matter, that distinction cannot be drawn: It is
risk all the way down. There being no distinction to be drawn, Savage
apparently found no trouble in supposing that as DSO is transformed
into GDE its intuitive plausibility remains intact.

I initially responded to this by pointing out that one could take the
argument to cut the other way. If there are no terminal outcomes, one
might choose to conclude that there is no place for "sure-thing" reasoning to secure a foothold. But to argue no more than this would
leave the thesis of this book on very insecure footing. I have insisted
that by appeal to DSO one can argue against a myopic (and also a
sophisticated) approach to certain dynamic choice situations. If it is
risk all the way down and no bedrock level can be identified, and if
one concludes from this that no version of dominance can work, then
there is no longer a basis on which to argue for the comparative
advantages of a resolute, as opposed to myopic (or sophisticated),
approach. In effect, I no less than Savage have an interest in maintaining the plausibility of DSO, but unlike Savage, my argument also
presupposes that a distinction can be maintained between DSO and
GDE.

I suggested in Section 4.7 how I believe the distinction can be maintained. Oddly enough, it is precisely Savage's notion that probability as well as preference is best understood in a subjective (or "personalist") framework that seems to me to provide the key. Preference, on any intelligible view, seems clearly to be a matter of attitudes. Moreover, the object of a preferential attitude is not simply some state of the world, but a state of the world under a certain description. Thus, what we prefer and endeavor to realize is very much a function of our beliefs about the character of our actions and their consequences. Now on a subjective view of probability, probability is also a matter of attitude – and once again an attitude that takes as its object not a state of the world but a state under a certain description.

From this perspective, the appeal to the notion of a terminal outcome and, correspondingly, of a bounded decision tree does not involve a falsification of the nature of the reality we face. The concept of a terminal outcome seems rather to be a natural and inevitable component of any evaluative procedure. If the world in fact opens to endless possibilities, still evaluation of risks and uncertainties requires some sort of closure. Whether one approaches evaluation by the folding-forward perspective implicit in PR or by the folding-backward perspective implicit in SEP, one can project forward only so far into what, by the line of reasoning pursued by Savage, must be seen as a Chinese puzzle box. What lies beyond what one is able to describe lies beyond what is relevant to evaluation and deliberation at that point in time, *and* what lies within the range of one's description is always at least potentially relevant to evaluation. Wherever the agent sets his horizons, it is there that he will have to mark outcomes as terminal outcomes – as having values that may be realized by deliberate choice, but nevertheless as black boxes whose contents, being undescribed, are evaluatively irrelevant. If the agent is concerned about more than expected values – if dispersion considerations are of importance to him – he cannot meaningfully react to the dispersion of "values" that lie beyond his descriptions; but by the same token, it lies open to him to be concerned with the value dispersion of those possibilities that he can describe.

On this view of the matter, there could be no relevant risk all the way down, because there is no relevant risk beyond the reach of attitudes and descriptions. The world continually opens up new possibilities, and when it does, plans must be revised. But relative to any problem calling for deliberation and choice, possibilities are bounded, and risk (in what I take to be its only meaningful sense – the phenomenological sense) bottoms out. Thus, for the deliberative mind, I suggest, there is a bedrock.

Suppose, then, it can be shown that a certain proposed course of action has the following great disadvantage: *As best as one can ascertain,* it will yield the agent less of what he wants, regardless of the turn of events, than some other course of action open to him. This is a cogent reason for him not to pursue that course of action. But suppose now, to the contrary, some course of action is *not* dominated in this sense (i.e., with respect to what he takes to be terminal outcomes) by another course of action, at least *as best as he can ascertain.* In this case, the options of one who thoughtfully deliberates are, at least in principle, open to treatment in terms of *all* of the features of the distribution of possible values to be realized thereby – including the dispersion as well as the mean value of each such prospect.

Recall once again the Kahneman and Tversky case as presented in Section 4.5. When the prospects are presented to you as they are given in Figure 4.3, you find yourself inclined to choose g_1 over g_2, but also to choose g_4 over g_3. Suppose that I come along and point out to you that for the second choice problem I can repartition the conditioning states in such a way that relative to that partition, GDE will apply – that the prospects corresponding to this partition are ranked by you in such a way that g_3 dominates g_4. In particular, I point out to you that under the alternative description of these options as $g_3^* = [g_1, .34; \$0, .66]$ and $g_4^* = [g_2, .34; \$0, .66]$, by your own account you would choose g_1 over g_2 if offered just those two components as options. Does this now count as a cogent reason for reversing your initial decision and choosing g_3^* instead of g_4^*? I think not. Relative to the fullest amount of information available to you – as expressed in terms of the notion that g_4^* exposes you still further down the line to getting either \$2500 or \$0, and g_3^* exposes you to getting either \$2400 or \$0, the latter does not dominate the former. That consideration, I suggest, undercuts the appeal to GDE. Notice, in particular, that if you do choose g_4^* and fortune smiles upon you – events transpire to yield you the \$2500 payoff – I surely cannot admonish you with the thought that had you chosen differently you would now have even more money!

In the beginning of the debate between those who advocated the expected utility result and those who had questions about it, advocates were inclined to dismiss violations of the independence condition on the grounds that these could typically be explained as cases in which the agent was "taken in" by what were essentially irrelevant features of the problem. I suggest that one can reply in a similar way to the argument discussed in the preceding paragraph. Against the background of an explicit representation of a *finer* partitioning of events and outcomes in terms of monetary payoffs for g_3 of either \$2400 or \$0 and for g_4 of either \$2500 or \$0 – payoffs by reference to which no dominance relation can be established between the two options – the appeal to the *coarser* partition in question is an appeal to an irrelevant feature of the problem. That is, I would suggest that in this instance it is the advocates of GDE, not the critics, who are taken in by an irrelevant feature of the problem. All are inclined to insist that the sort of excitement or anxiety that one experiences in the course of the running of a multistaged lottery should not count in the rational evaluation of such an option. Consider, then, the anxiety you might experience, having selected g_4 over g_3, at the thought that regardless of the course of events, you will be exposed, *en passant*, to a prospect you would disprefer to the prospect you would then face had you chosen g_3 instead. Might not it be argued that this sort of anxiety is at best irrelevant to rational choice?

14.7 The demand for a determinate theory

The line of argument I have pursued here neatly intersects, as I have noted, with the one taken by David Hume in the passage quoted at the very outset of this book. Hume's position is that to show that a particular choice is irrational or unreasonable, one must show it to be choice that is insufficient to bring about the desired ends (or that it rests on false beliefs). Thus, choice that is sufficient to one's ends and does not rest on false beliefs cannot be faulted as irrational. That is, Hume's test in virtue of being demanding about what can count as irrational is permissive about what can count as rational. My conclusion is that the principles of the received theory – specifically the context-free condition CF and the independence principle for choice CIND – cannot pass this test. Failure to satisfy these principles in one's choice behavior need not imply that such choice fails to be as effective as it might. From the perspective of Hume's pragmatic test, quite a range of possible revisionist theories deserve to be given a serious hearing. In this respect, it must be concluded that the received theory of rationality is too restrictive.

It is my hope, of course, that if the arguments developed in this work are correct, they will encourage inquiry into less restrictive theories of rationality. But I operate under no illusions here. The disposition to cling to an overly restrictive concept of rationality is due not simply, I think, to an excessively optimistic sense of the dispositive nature of the pragmatic arguments for the received theory, but also in no small part to two powerful habits of thought – habits that one would do well to pause and reconsider. One is a tendency to formulate the requirements of an adequate normative theory on the model of requirements for an adequate positive (i.e., descriptive and predictive) theory. The other is a tendency to blur the line between criteria of rationality and those pertaining to principles of public policy (and morality).

Consider first the tendency to take positive theory as providing a model for normative theory. It is an ideal of positive inquiry that theories be found that have a high degree of explanatory and predictive power (as distinct from predictive accuracy). It is judged to be a defect of a positive theory if it fails to explain or fails to yield determinate predictions (which could then be used to test the theory in some situation). Other things being equal, one theory is to be judged superior to another if the former explains more phenomena, or if the former is more determinate in its predictions. It seems quite natural, then, to ask whether a normative theory might not be subject to a similar appraisal. Of course, the objective of normative inquiry is not a theory that explains or predicts, but rather one that prescribes. But there might still seem to be an analogue. One might try to argue that the ideal normative theory should be able to give direction to choice in a wider rather than narrower set of circumstances. Thus, one normative theory might be said to be superior to another if, other things being equal, the former gives direction to choice in a wider range of cases than does the latter.

On further reflection, however, this is an unacceptable test for a normative theory. One need only be put in mind here of the trichotomous nature of all *modal* concepts. Normative theory is concerned not only to prescribe (mark out the region of the required or the necessary) and proscribe (mark out the region of the forbidden or the impossible), but also to say what may be done (mark what is permissible or possible). In the case of a judgment of permissibility, normative theory remains silent as to whether the agent should, or should not, take the action in question. But silence in such a case can hardly be construed to be the analogue of silence in the case of a descriptive theory, that is, the analogue of a case in which a descriptive theory fails to explain or render a determinate prediction concerning whether a given event will take place. A theory that marks out a nonempty region of the permissible is not thereby shown to be less adequate than a theory for which everything is either prescribed or proscribed.

Those who come into normative inquiry from a study of the sciences do not always avoid this trap. The presumption for some, it would seem, is that one should seek a theory that yields more directions rather than fewer. If it is proposed that a particular constraint on rational choice should be dropped, one hears the complaint that the theory that will result is indeterminate: It does not instruct the rational agent as to what in particular he should do in that situation. But although the more general theory is clearly indeterminate in that sense, it is not indeterminate in the appropriate sense: In terms of the trichotomous division into required, permissible, and forbidden, the theory need not be seen to be indeterminate. It does tell the rational agent something about the action in question, namely, that the action is permissible.

The problem here has perhaps even deeper roots. The whole of the positive theory of microeconomics rests on the notion that economic agents are rational in a sense that has some determinate content. The more permissive the conception of rationality, the less predictive power there will be in any positive theory that seeks to characterize how agents will in fact interact. Moreover, from a pragmatic perspective there is bound to be a deep interest in the creation of theories that leave less in the region of the permissible-but-not-required. One seeks in a normative theory not only a guide to choice for oneself, but a basis for predicting how other agents with whom one must interact will themselves behave. If the theory of rational choice leaves choice between two options a matter of personal, and essentially idiosyncratic, preference and you confront an agent who faces a choice between these options, you may not be able to predict how he will choose, and this uncertainty may be costly to you. In particular, you may not be able to come to any reasoned decision yourself as to how to choose, unless you can predict his choice.

Despite these pressing interests in a more determinate theory, microeconomics and game theory can manage to survive with a more general theory of rationality, particularly in view of the consideration that the predictive power of the more restrictive theory of rationality associated with modern economic thought is surely not very profound: What gives microeconomic theory its predictive power appears to be various supplementary assumptions – for example, the assumption of diminishing marginal rates of substitution. And although it may be true that an adequate theory of games as a tool for strategic decision making presupposes a fully determinate theory of individual choice, the need for such determinacy can hardly be dispositive: It may simply happen that no such fully determinate theory can be constructed.

Consider now the matter of the relationship between norms of rationality and those belonging to the sphere of public policy (and morality). It may well be that in some domain the demands of public policy and those of rationality can come into conflict. Here the problem is not so much that rationality is permissive whereas principles of public policy are not. Rather, the problem is that Hume's theory of rationality is structured around the notion of means appropriate to chosen ends. This implies that a given course of action may well be required from the perspective of rationality – it being the most efficient means to the chosen end – and yet still be one that, from the perspective of the study of public policy, should be discouraged. But to admit this is to find oneself in a deeper dilemma. The concept of rationality is a normative concept in the sense that to say that a given course of action is the most rational course of action is to recommend it – to imply that it is the course of action the agent ought to undertake. But it is usual also to take the principles of settled public policy (and morality) as normative in the same sense. To say that a course of action is prescribed by such principles is to recommend it, to imply that it ought to be undertaken. Hume's theory allows, then, for at least the possibility of open warfare between the region of what is rationally required and the region of what is required as a matter of public policy (or morality). Many find this intolerable and, hence, are driven to try to reinterpret the norms of rationality in such a way that they do not conflict with those pertaining to at least settled principles of public policy (and morality). One natural result is that one may be led to ignore Hume's injunction that the region of the rational pertains to just what is or is not appropriate with respect to given ends and to insist that ends, and not just means, can be judged rational or irrational.

Those who come to this subject from the disciplines of economics and decision theory are perhaps less likely to end up legislating in this way, but even those who pride themselves on their clear sense of the distinction between fact and value do not always manage to avoid confusing the region of the rational with the region of public policy and morality. Virtually any viable private-property-based market economy requires much from its participants – in particular, a capacity for deferred gratification and willingness to risk a certain degree of disinterestedness on the part of interacting agents and, as Hirschman suggests, a general orientation to the interests rather than to the passions.[12] But it would appear to be an open question whether requirements of this sort can be derived from the purely instrumentalist conception of rationality espoused by Hume.

To close with an observation on one such issue – one that takes me back to a central theme of this work, namely, attitudes toward risk and uncertainty, it is hard to avoid the sense of a special congruence between the modern theory of expected utility and the ideals of investment-oriented capitalism. It is surely no accident that the modern theory of rationality has its roots in the suggestion that expected monetary return can serve as a sufficient criterion for choosing among gambles. That principle requires of the agent what is formally characterized as an attitude of "neutrality" toward risk; that is, what is important is not the dispersion of payoffs, but the expectation. But the typical mortal, with limited stakes and limited opportunity to let the law of averages work, is bound to see this for what it is, as a demand that he be willing to take risks, and this, I should suppose, is what the ethics of venture capital is all about. This part of the case for a pure free-market approach, then, rests on a series of conclusions about what the average person can *expect* and what will be the case in the *long run*. But the typical citizen is likely to be more concerned with what *might* or *could* happen to him in the *short run*.

The principle that one should maximize monetary expectation did not survive Bernoulli's St. Petersburg paradox, according to which a "rational" agent should be prepared to pay any sum of money he can lay his hands on to play in a particular one-shot gamble. The gamble in question is run by the repeated flipping of a fair coin until heads comes up, and its payoff is set by the following formula: $(\$2)^n$, where n is the trial on which heads finally comes up. As the story is usually told, the modern theory of expected utility is indebted to this paradox, which forced Bernoulli, in trying to resolve it, to introduce the notion of "value" (i.e., *utility*) as distinct from monetary return. But it is worth reflecting on the fact that Bernoulli moved toward the modern notion of "value" precisely in order to save the expectation hypothesis, that is, the hypothesis that some sort of straight expectation rule suffices as a criterion for choosing among (well-defined) gambles. One would hope that perhaps the time has finally come to stop trying to save this hypothesis. What should prove useful now, among other things, I believe, is a much more careful and sympathetic exploration of alternative approaches to decision making, particularly under conditions of risk and uncertainty.

15

Postscript: projections

I have now completed the task of exploring just what sort of case can be made, from a pragmatic perspective, for the various axioms that form the cornerstones of the modern theory of individual rationality. Although my conclusion has been essentially negative, the route I have taken to that conclusion, involving as it has an appeal to the strategy of resolute choice, turns out to have some constructive implications with regard to at least two other areas in which more traditional models of rational choice have generally been perceived to generate rather problematic results: the theory of games, on the one hand, and the theory of moral choice, on the other. I cannot hope to do any more than sketch, in the very briefest terms, what the issues are, but I hope that my remarks will give the reader a sense of how one could proceed, with the concept of resolute choice in hand, to make some constructive advances in each of these two areas.

15.1 Resolute choice and game theory

There is an obvious and important analogy between the single decision maker faced with making a sequence of decisions over time and a group of persons faced with coordinating their actions. The situation analyzed in Section 12.6 is the *intra*personal counterpart to one that is the focus of the theory of *inter*personal interaction, that is, game theory. In the latter situation, different individuals have different preference orderings over various possible jointly attainable outcomes, and the task becomes, given the strategic structure of the game in which they are participants, to determine a rational choice for each, on the assumption that each other participant also chooses rationally.

More specifically, given the temporal structure of intrapersonal problems, the closest analogy is to interaction in an *ultimatum* game, in which one player selects a strategy and then the other player chooses in full knowledge of what the first player has selected.[1] On the standard account, if player 1 (who goes first) knows that player 2 (who goes second) is rational, then the rational choice for player 1 is to select a strategy whose expected return to himself is maximum, on the assumption that player 2 will respond by choosing a strategy that, given the initial choice by player 1, maximizes expected return for player 2. On this account, player 1 should view player 2 not as a potential collaborator in a coordination scheme but rather as a partially dependent variable – as a factor to be reckoned with, if he, player 1, is to maximize his own expected return. Such a strategic approach, of course, is the analogue to a sophisticated approach to intrapersonal choice.[2]

More generally, the theory of sophisticated choice can be thought of as providing an intrapersonal analogue to the standard theory for noncooperative games. On that theory, once again, each person is a participant in a situation of *strategic* interaction in which one's task is not to coordinate one's choice with that of the others, but merely to anticipate correctly the moves of each other (rational) participant and then choose one's own strategy so as to maximize expected return against that prediction. On such a view, the choice behavior of each other agent is a parameter whose value is to be estimated, just as one tries to estimate the value of the other parameters that condition one's prospects in any choice situation.

Curiously, however, if one traces the modern theory of games back to its source, in von Neumann and Morgenstern, one finds a remark to the effect that a game is a situation in which a player is not in a position to treat the choice behavior of the other player in the same way he treats the natural environment, namely, as a parameter whose value is to be estimated:

... every participant can determine the variables which describe his own actions but not those of the others. Nevertheless these "alien" variables cannot, from his point of view, be described by statistical assumptions. This is because the others are guided, just as he himself, by rational principles – whatever that may mean – and no *modus procedendi* can be correct which does not attempt to understand those principles and the interactions of the conflicting interests of all participants.[3]

The authors then proceed to elaborate on this by distinguishing between what they term "dead" variables, which refer to the "unalterable physical background of the situation," and variables that "reflect another person's will or intention of an economic kind – based on motives of the same nature as his own." Kaysen, in a very early review of von Neumann and Morgenstern's *Theory of Games and Economic Behavior*, comes perhaps closer than anyone to capturing this distinctive feature of interaction between rational agents:

The theory of such games of strategy deals precisely with the actions of several agents, in a situation in which all actions are interdependent, and where, in general, there is no possibility of what we call parametrization that would enable each agent (player) to behave as if the actions of the others were given. In fact, it is this very lack of parametrization which is the essence of a game.[4]

What von Neumann and Morgenstern proceed to do, however, and what other theorists have done ever since, is build a theory based on denying, in the end, that the behavior of each other rational player cannot be parametrized. In effect, what they do is reduce the problem for each participant to that of a standard maximization problem. For von Neumann and Morgenstern, the reduction of the two-person game problem is effected by an ingenious extension of the ultimatum game framework mentioned earlier. They suppose that if there is a rational way for player 1 to choose, then player 2 (who is presumed to know that player 1 is rational) will be able to anticipate correctly just how player 1 will choose. But taking that choice behavior on the part of player 1 as given, player 2 can then respond so as to maximize his own (expected) return. And player 1, in turn, can take this maximizing disposition on the part of player 2 as a given and adjust his own choice accordingly. That is, player 1 can choose a strategy whose return to him is maximum, given his expectation that player 2 will maximize in response to whatever he, player 1, does.[5]

Luce and Raiffa offer a related but distinct argument – one that leads directly to the standard equilibrium condition. If there is a theory of how rational players will choose and if each player knows that theory, knows the strategy and payoff structure of the game, and, finally, knows that each other player is rational, then each player will know how each other player will choose. But given that information, each player's task reduces to choosing a strategy for himself that maximizes his own expected return. This, they argue, leads directly to the following necessary, but not sufficient condition on an adequate theory of games: If there is an adequate theory of how rational players should choose in a two-person game, and if that theory prescribes that player 1 choose s_1 and that player 2 choose s_2, then it must be the case that s_1 is a utility-maximizing response for player 1 against an expected choice of s_2 by player 2, and s_2 must be a utility-maximizing response for player 2 against an expected choice of s_1 by player 1.[6]

The past forty years have witnessed an extraordinarily sophisticated exploration of these and other related models, each predicated on the implicit or explicit use of such an indirect form of reasoning, in which strategic interaction is reduced to a parametric situation for each player via the assumption of the existence of a determinate theory of rational choice. Consider more closely, however, the logic of this form of argument. What von Neumann and Morgenstern originally argued, in the quote given earlier, is that no rational player is in a position to predict the behavior of any other rational player except by reference to a satisfactory theory of rational interactive choice. The indirect argument purports to establish at least some of the features of that theory by supposing the theory exists and then determining how a given player would be inclined to choose, given that the choice behavior of others can be parametrized by reference to that theory. In fact, however, what is supposed is that the theory of rationality, which is presumed to exist and which anchors the choice of all other players, does not anchor the choice of the player under consideration: that player is taken to be an expected utility maximizer. But, then, the argument does not simply conclude something about the content of the theory in question; rather, it starts out *presuming* something about the theory, namely, that the theory must generate prescriptions for choice that are fully consistent with each player being an expected utility maximizer.

Now it may well be that in the final analysis, no theory of rational interactive choice that failed to square with the assumption that individual players are utility maximizers would be satisfactory. But surely such a thesis should be defended, not simply taken for granted. After all, as von Neumann and Morgenstern's remark (and Kaysen's remark) clearly suggest, the interactive situation is rather special. It is, then, not obviously implausible that it calls for a special theory of rationality. Some years ago I argued that the presupposition that rational players are nonetheless bound by the principle of the maximization of expected utility proves highly questionable even in the context of that class of games for which one might have expected the principle to be most plausible, namely, strictly competitive games.[7] These are games in which there is no possibility of mutual gain, and hence no reason, it would seem, for players to try to coordinate their choices with one another. When one turns to consider non-strictly-competitive games, however, the assumption that rational players are bound by the principle of the maximization of expected utility proves to be quite paradoxical. Except under very special circumstances, it ensures that rational interaction will fail to satisfy the criterion of Pareto optimality. That is, it ensures that rational players who know each other to be such will have to settle for outcomes that are mutually disadvantageous relative to other outcomes that are, at least in principle, open to them.[8]

The usual way to deal with this well-known implication of the standard theory of non-strictly-competitive games is to suggest that rational players will typically be able to devise mechanisms that will motivate them to keep their agreements with one another and thereby realize the fruits of cooperation. And, of course, as utility maximizers they will want to employ such mechanisms. Such mechanisms, of course, are analogous to precommitment devices. Moreover, as such, they are subject to an objection that is the counterpart to the objection that I leveled against sophisticated choice from the perspective of resolute choice. Such mechanisms can rarely be utilized without the expenditure of at least some of the surplus that cooperation makes possible. But then the paradox remains unresolved. That is, it is paradoxical to argue that it is rational for members of a group to employ such mechanisms so as to secure mutual gains, but then deny that it would be rational for them to agree simply to coordinate their actions (without threats of punishment and the like) and then act accordingly. Why, if the possibility of gain drives them to enforcement devices, does it not also drive them *beyond,* to an even more efficient form of coordination?

Now the alternative theory for which I have argued – the theory of resolute choice – is predicated on the notion that the single agent who is faced with making decisions over time can achieve a cooperative arrangement between his present self and his relevant future selves that satisfies the principle of intrapersonal optimality. The question naturally arises, then, whether the theory of resolute choice might not be extended to the case of interaction among rational agents who know each other to be such. If the single agent is able to coordinate with his own future selves, might not he also be able to coordinate his actions with the actions of other agents, at least if and when this could be shown to serve both his own interests and those of the others involved?[9]

Such a theory, of course, concerns rational interactive choice under ideal conditions of common knowledge of the strategy and payoff structure of the game and the rationality of all the participants. With regard to real-world interactions, one will have to recognize that some will not do their part and to consider ways in which such defections can be minimized. These are obviously pressing matters; but they are matters that belong to a theory of *imperfect* rationality – a theory concerning what persons should do when they cannot count on others (or themselves!) to be fully rational.

What stands in the way of such a theory of non-strictly-competitive games is an assumption that is analogous to the separability assumption for the theory of rational dynamic choice. The standard theory presupposes that each player must choose so as to maximize his expected return, as judged from his own separable perspective and according to his estimate of the choice behavior of each participant, regardless of what he might be able to achieve by cooperating with those others. Moreover, it is held that this is a constraint on an agent's choice behavior, regardless of any agreement that the participants did in fact reach about how to coordinate their actions, so long as the agreement is not binding, that is, so long as the agreement can be violated with impunity. Alternatively put, an agreement on a coordination scheme has no inertial force; the rational agent will always assess each such situation from his own separable perspective. This, I want to suggest, is just what drives the argument for the equilibrium condition.[10]

There is, to be sure, in the modern theory of games, one line of research that presupposes a somewhat different perspective. This is the theory of bargaining, a central feature of which is that rational negotiators will not settle for an outcome that fails to be Pareto optimal. But it is customary to suppose that bargaining theory applies only on the asumption that mechanisms of one sort or another have been put in place to ensure that the agreement is binding. Moreover, even in the context of that theory, the concept of strategic interaction – with its presupposition that rational choice involves effectively maximizing with respect to separable defined preferences for outcomes, given the expected behavior of others – continues to play a controlling role. On the received version of bargaining theory, a rational division of the gains that cooperation makes possible is ultimately a function of the relative bargaining power or threat advantage of the interacting participants.[11]

Of those who have contributed to the theory of bargaining, only Gauthier has managed to break away from both of these essentially constraining perspectives. The normative theory of interaction that he espouses is predicated on the assumption that (1) rational participants who know each other to be such will constrain their disposition to maximize against the expected behavior of others and choose rather in accordance with plans that can be understood to be the outcome of a rational bargain, and (2) the terms of the bargain itself are not determined by reference to the equilibrium of bargaining or threat advantage.[12] Gauthier's own argument for this theory is predicated, however, on assuming that the standard version of expected utility theory holds for the case of individual decision making under conditions of risk and uncertainty. I have argued, in reply, that he cannot hope to sustain his theory of rational interactive choice without also evaluating the theory of individual decision making. My sense is that the theory of individual dynamic choice that I have put forward in this book may provide a foundation for his own theory of interactive choice.[13]

15.2 Resolute choice and morality

The possibility of revising the theory of rational interaction in the manner sketched in the preceding section also proves suggestive with regard to an unresolved problem in the history of ethics, namely, the relation between rational choice and moral principles. The problem is posed at the very beginning of the history of philosophizing about the justification of moral rules, in Plato's *Republic*. Glaucon acknowledges that agreement on certain moral rules can serve the mutual interests of those who are parties to the agreement. That is to say, if two or more persons can agree to abide by certain rules in their dealings with one another, this can work to their mutual advantage. But he goes on to argue, by appeal to the story of the ring of Gyges, that the ways of morality cannot be fully justified in terms of rational self-interest. If one did in fact possess a ring that made one invisible, it would be in one's own interest to use it to secure one's own ends, even though this would clearly mean violating the usual moral constraints. Gyges used the ring in just this way: He seduced the queen, killed the king, and seized the throne for himself.[14]

What the story of the ring of Gyges appears to do is drive a wedge between the concept of rational choice and that of choice that respects the usual kinds of moral constraints. Granted that those who interact stand to benefit mutually by having certain moral constraints in place, still (to see matters from the perspective of the strategic theory of games) each person stands to gain, not from imposing those constraints on his own actions, but from others imposing them on their actions. Thus, insofar as any one person can count on morally constrained behavior from others, but avoid imposing the same constraints on his own behavior, he will be the gainer for doing so: He will derive the benefit of the cooperative arrangement without having to share in its costs. This, it is usually argued, means that he will have a rational basis for defecting, when he can do so with impunity.[15] The rational injunction, then, with respect to moral rules is highly conditional: Follow these rules unless it is in your interest to violate them.

Moral rules, however, are supposed to be constraints on an individual's choice that cannot be set to one side by considerations of what would serve the rational interests of that individual. From this it is usually taken to follow that what is needed is a different sort of justification of moral rules altogether – one that proceeds by reference to something other than the rational interests of the agent whose behavior is thereby to be constrained. For some, like Bentham and Mill, appeal is made to a generalized principle of interest – doing what serves the interests of the greater number; for others, like Kant, appeal is made to some allegedly non-interest-based principle (e.g., the categorical imperative).

Glaucon fails to note, however, the symmetry of the situation: All do, in fact, possess the ring of Gyges, since for each there are occasions on which some moral rule can be violated with (relative) impunity. Moreover, it is plausible to suppose that all would do better if all were to accept the moral constraints as binding than if all were to defect whenever this could be done with impunity. This can be the case even though it is also true that holding the behavior of all others as constant, each is better off defecting. All of this, of course, suggests that an agreement to abide unconditionally by at least certain moral rules would be mutually advantageous, even though, of course, such an agreement would be unstable, as judged from the perspective of the traditional way of thinking about non-strictly-competitive games.

As I argued in the preceding section, however, I believe the time has come to reconsider the traditional solution concept for non-strictly-competitive games. Adapting the point I sought to make there to the matter at hand, one need not suppose that a gap exists between rational pursuit of interest and commitment to moral principles. That gap exists only for those who persist in conceptualizing rational interactive choice in terms of the principle that each should maximize with respect to his own interests, as characterized in terms of his own separably defined perspective. On the alternative view of interactive rationality, according to which it is at least prima facie rational for each individual to do his part to maintain a mutually advantageous arrangement, the gap disappears.

To put this point in a slightly different way, but one that should be familiar to philosophers, such a revised conception of rationality can provide a grounding for the notion that moral rules constitute practices (in a technical sense of that term introduced by Rawls). These practices may themselves be rationalized by reference to the interests of those who participate in them, but this consideration does not apply directly (at least under ordinary circumstances) to the actions the practices are supposed to govern. The practices themselves serve as (partial) criteria for the rightness of actions falling under them. Thus, although the ultimate standard for the evaluation of the agent's action remains the rational pursuit of his interests, this standard has to be understood as applying to the practices in which the agent participates and not directly to his choice of action *qua* participant.[16]

Looking back at the history of the controversy over the relation between the rational pursuit of interest and moral rules, it is no wonder that the problem of the justification of moral rules has seemed so intractable. If rational interest requires one to violate moral side constraints when this can be done with impunity, then it is understandable that theorists have been driven to seek some other way to justify such rules. It is instructive, in this regard, to consider that Plato himself, in the main argument of *The Republic*, never challenges Glaucon's characterization of rational choice in terms of the pursuit of separable interests. It is this, together with his belief – characteristic of Greek thought – that morality is intimately connected with the interests of the agent to whom its constraints apply, that, I suggest, leaves him no alternative but to reconceptualize radically the "true" interests of the agent.

The history of this justificatory problem is, as a matter of fact, a series of dialectical encounters between those who, like Hobbes and Hume, attempt to make the notion of rational interest central and those who, like Kant, sensing the inadequacy of any such account, are driven to postulate that moral rules must be grounded in some radically different fashion. For the former group, the organizing presupposition is that rationality provides an unproblematic basis for the justification of moral rules; but the residual problem they are unable to resolve is simply that this form of justification, *as it has traditionally been construed*, cannot be stretched far enough.[17] For the latter group, the organizing presupposition is that moral rules must be shown to be more than simply conditionally binding; but the residual problem that they are unable to resolve is simply that nothing they have tried to offer in place of a theory of rational interested choice seems very compelling. At root, these two traditions face a common problem, for both have saddled themselves with one and the same limited incrementalist theory of rationality. An alternative theory of rational interactive choice, based on an extension of the strategy of resolute choice, might, one would hope, provide a way to bridge the gap between moral choice and rational interested choice. I have, of course, only suggested, not demonstrated, that such a bridge can be constructed and have said very little about what the resultant theory of morality might be. In this last regard, indeed, to give credit where credit is so clearly deserved, my brief remarks here do no more than point in the direction of a certain kind of theory, the kind that Gauthier has already carefully worked out in *Morals by Agreement*.

Notes

1. Introduction and sketch of the main argument

1. The literature here is extensive, but for some relatively elementary expositions of the weak ordering and independence principles and their role in the construction of a theory of utility see Friedman and Savage (1952), Alchian (1953), and Luce and Raiffa (1957, Chap.2). For more technical expositions see von Neumann and Morgenstern (1944 [1953], in particular, Chap. 3 and App.), Herstein and Milnor (1953), Arrow (1972), Harsanyi (1977, Chap. 3), and Fishburn (1982).
2. Again, the literature here is extensive. Helpful elementary expositions are virtually nonexistent. Luce and Raiffa (1957, Chap. 13) is a good place to start. Axiomatic treatments are to be found in Ramsey (1931), Savage (1954 [1972]), Anscombe and Aumann (1963), and Arrow (1972). Kyburg and Smokler (1964), and more recently Gärdenfors and Sahlin (1988), contain important articles on subjective probability.
3. See Rubin (1949), Pratt, Raiffa, and Schlaifer (1964), Savage (1954 [1972]), Jeffrey (1965), Luce and Suppes (1965), Arrow (1972), and Fishburn (1981).
4. Given its importance, it is remarkable how little useful literature there is on the distinction between foundationalist and coherentist approaches to the justification of normative principles. Concerning the distinction in the context of the justification of moral principles, Rawls (1951) appears to defend a foundationalist approach, but the argument to be found there is adapted and put to use in Rawls (1971, Sec. 87) in support of what seems clearly to be a coherentist position. White (1956) and Daniels (1979) explicitly defend a coherentist view. For a more recent review of the issue see Timmons (1987).
5. For a representative sample see Allais (1953, 1979), Ellsberg (1961), Levi (1974, 1980, 1986a, b), Hansson (1975), Tversky (1975), McClennen (1983b), Sen (1985). Allais and Hagen (1979) contains a number of relevant articles. Gärdenfors and Sahlin (1988) reprints many of the important critical papers, along with a very comprehensive bibliography and helpful introductory remarks.
6. Hume (1739–40 [1888], Bk. 2, Pt. 3, Sec. 3).
7. Friedman and Savage (1952); see also Savage (1951).
8. See, e.g., Davidson, McKinsey, and Suppes (1955), Raiffa (1968, pp. 77–80), and Yaari (1985).
9. Ramsey (1931), de Finetti (1937), Shimony (1955), Lehmann (1955), and Kemeny (1955). See also Yaari (1985) and Green (1987).

10. Hammond (1976, 1977, 1982a, b, 1988a, b).
11. Roughly speaking, one needs to assume in addition that the agent is (1) concerned just with (possible) monetary payoffs and their respective probabilities and (2) indifferent, in a dynamic context, between any two courses of action that offer him the same monetary payoffs with the same probabilities. Assumption (2) means, in particular, that the sequential order of events that take place and choices to be made is irrelevant. This assumption turns out to be more controversial than one might at first suppose. I return to discuss various versions of this assumption at great length in Chapters 7 and 8.
12. If g_4 is really strictly preferred to g_3, then very marginal improvements in g_3 will presumably still result in a prospect that is dispreferred to g_4.
13. I am indebted to Hanan Polansky for suggesting how a "dashed-line" notation can be used to clarify the situation the agent faces at each choice point in a sequential choice problem.
14. Quite distinct versions of this type of argument, invoking somewhat different presuppositions, are to be found in Raiffa (1968, pp. 83–6), Yaari (1985), and Seidenfeld (1988a, b).
15. See Schick (1986), but also Strotz (1956), Hammond (1976, 1977), and Yaari (1977).
16. Hammond (1988b, pp. 28, 33–6) and Seidenfeld (1988a, pp. 276–8), in particular, explicitly invoke just such a separability condition. I discuss Hammond's formulation of this as a "consistency" condition in Section 8.1 and Seidenfeld's formulation in Section 10.5.
17. Seidenfeld (1988a, pp. 276–8) provides a very clear statement of this line of reasoning. There is an important parallel between this sort of view and the standard equilibrium requirement of game theory. I return to this point in Section 1.10 and again in the Postscript.
18. This marks a conclusion that is broader than, and contains a radically different prescription from, the one arrived at by Schick (1986) and Levi (1986a, b, 1987). They limit themselves to questioning the pragmatic credentials of certain features of the weak ordering principle, and they believe that a sophisticated choice approach will suffice to ensure that pragmatic difficulties are avoided. In addition, Levi insists, following Seidenfeld (1988a, b), that one can construct a pragmatic argument against relaxing the independence axiom. See, in particular, Levi (1986a, p. 45, fn. 6; 1986b, pp. 144 and 235, fn. 21).
19. I am indebted here to Yaari (1977), although, it should be noted, he explicitly rejects this conclusion.
20. Bratman (1987).
21. There are obvious connections here to the recent work of Schelling (1978a; 1984, Selections 3 and 4) and Elster (1982, 1983). I shall explore these connections in Chapter 13.
22. See Hume (1739–40 [1888], Bk. 1, Pt. 4, Sec. 6).
23. See in particular Arrow (1959) and Sen (1970, 1971, 1973). Sen (1982) contains reprints of Sen (1971, 1973) and includes a useful introduction that updates the relevant literature. See, in particular, pp. 1–5.
24. I build here, in particular, on the literature dealing with dynamic con-

sistency and changing preferences, including Strotz (1956), the papers by Hammond cited in note 10 above, Yaari (1977), and Johnsen and Donaldson (1985).
25. I find Chapters 2 and 13 of Luce and Raiffa (1957) most helpful in this regard.

2. The ordering principle

1. Given the usual definition of strict preference P and indifference I in terms of R, full transitivity immediately implies all of the following conditions: (a) If $x P y$ and $y P z$, then $x P z$; (b) if $x I y$ and $y I z$, then $x I z$; (c) if $x P y$ and $y I z$, then $x P z$; and (d) if $x I y$ and $y P z$, then $x P z$.
2. A strict order, by contrast, is one in which distinct elements, insofar as they are ranked at all, are ranked strictly – either the first is ranked over the second or the second is ranked over the first. As an example of a strict and connected ordering, consider the set of real numbers. For any two distinct real numbers, either the first is larger than the second or the second is larger than the first.
3. See, e.g., Sen (1970, Secs. 1*3 and 1*4) and the references therein.
4. See, e.g., Arrow (1959) and Sen (1970, Chap. 1*, 1971, 1973). The latter two articles are reprinted in Sen (1982), the introduction to which (pp. 1–10 in particular) provides a valuable overview and updating of the relevant literature.
5. See, in particular, Sen (1970, Sec. 1*2, p. 10).
6. To be sure, if one assumes that there is some underlying weak ordering R defined on X, but that an observer does not know just how the options in the set are ordered by that agent, the actual choices made by the agent from various possible subsets S of X (something that is observable) *may* provide the observer with evidence concerning this ordering. For example, if the agent chooses x, when confronted with a set consisting of just x and y, one may be able to infer that with respect to the segment of the ordering defined over X that pertains just to x and y, it is the case that $x R y$. That is, the agent's choice behavior may reveal, in the sense of serving as evidence for, various segments of his preference ordering over X. Given enough experiments (observations), it may even be possible to reconstruct the whole underlying ordering (as least if X is finite). That one can effect some such reconstruction of the underlying ordering by observing the actual choices made by the agent under various conditions is regarded by Sen as the correct way to understand revealed preference theory. See, in particular, Sen (1973). In the explorations to follow, this viewpoint (and the issues that it raises) plays no role whatsoever. My concern is solely with various proposals concerning how preference orderings and choice sets can be related in a purely formal or conceptual manner, not with proposals for operationalizing either of these concepts in behavioral terms. Moreover, for reasons that will shortly emerge (see Section 2.5 and subsequent sections), choice behavior with respect to various subsets of X may not reveal anything about the agent's ranking over any given fixed set X of options.

7. See, in particular, Sen (1971, Sec. 2).

8. Notice, once again, that since there is no assumption that these choice sets are unit sets, there is nothing that requires one to think of this as a more behavioristically oriented view. To be sure, this notion of preference does entail a certain formal connection between preference and choice *behavior* (as distinct from choice sets): If x is actually chosen in the presence of y, then $x R_c y$. Recall also that from the viewpoint of the preference-based choice concept discussed earlier, if x is chosen from the pair set containing both x and y, then one may be able to infer from this that $x R y$. The difference is simply that in the present case, the if – then statement is licensed by a definition, whereas in the case discussed previously it rests on an implicit evidentiary criterion for preference (that the agent chose x in the presence of y is evidence that the agent regards x as at least weakly preferred to y). It is also, of course, possible within a probabilistic model of choice behavior to relate a nonunit $C(S)$ to observable choice. One can think of a claim that $C(S)$ has more than one element as a claim to the effect that the agent is just as likely to choose one of these elements as another. For example, if $C(S) = \{x\ y,\ z\}$, then the claim might be that the agent is equally likely to choose any one of these. But once again, for what is to follow, the important connection is that which obtains between preference and choice sets, not choice behavior.

9. See Sen (1970, Chap. 1*) for a more thorough treatment of these conditions. See also Arrow (1959) and the very comprehensive discussion in Herzberger (1973).

10. Sen (1970, Lemma 1*j, p. 14).

11. Sen (1970, Lemmas 1*m, p. 17, and 1*q, p. 19). Lemma 1*m suffices to establish that if the underlying ordering R is weak, then the choice function $C(\cdot, R)$ will satisfy Alpha, and Lemma 1*q implies, among other things, that if R is a weak ordering, then $C(\cdot, R)$ will satisfy Beta.

12. See Sen (1971, corollary to Theorem 8). The choice-constructed ordering in this instance is based on pair sets, as given in the definition at the end of Section 2.2. But as Sen's corollary to Theorem 8, with its reference to Theorem 3, makes clear, if $C(\cdot)$ satisfies CF, all the possible choice-constructed preference relations will coincide, and the implied ordering will satisfy the conditions of being a weak ordering.

13. See, e.g., Sen (1971), especially the results for normal choice functions and Theorem 3.

14. The rule is credited to Savage (1954 [1972], Chap. 9). See also Luce and Raiffa (1957, Chap. 13), and Milnor (1954).

15. For simplicity, I assume that the value an agent attributes to various sure amounts of money is linear with respect to the corresponding monetary amount, so that monetary amount can be taken as a simple measure of value.

16. See Milnor (1954) and also Luce and Raiffa (1957, pp. 297–8).

17. Arrow (1972, p. 22).

18. The proof of Proposition 2.6 is straightforward. See Lyon (1980, Prop. I.5, p. 27).

19. To see what can happen when the underlying choice function does not

satisfy CF, consider the following case: Suppose that $C(\{x, y\}) = \{x\}$, $C(\{y, z\}) = \{y\}$, $C(\{x, z\}) = \{z\}$, but $C(\{x, y, z\}) = \{x, y, z\}$. Then $C(\cdot)$ is defined over the triplet, although Alpha, and hence CF, is violated. By definition of R_c we have $x\,R_c\,y$, $y\,R_c\,z$, and $z\,R_c\,x$. Then R_c fails to be acyclic over the triplet in question, and from this it follows that $C(\{x, y, z\}, R_c) = \emptyset$. In this case, however, not only do $C(\cdot)$ and $C(\cdot, R_c)$ fail to coincide; $C(\cdot, R_c)$ does not even exist.

Coincidence of these two sets is characterized by Sen (1977, Sec. 4, pp. 63–71) as *basic binariness*. This is equivalent to the conjunction of Alpha and Gamma2. The latter requires that if $x\,R_c\,y$ for all y in S, then x is in $C(S)$. Gamma2 is independent of Beta. If a choice function satisfies basic binariness, then it is determined by a single binary relation in a way that is not affected by the presence or absence of other alternatives. The conjunction of Alpha and Gamma2, then, may be thought to capture at the level of choice function conditions what CFO captures at the level of orderings. All of this should serve as a reminder that CF is not the appropriate counterpart to CFO: The former is a much stronger condition, for it ensures that the induced relation R_c not only orders a feasible set in a context-free manner, but constitutes a weak ordering. I am indebted to John Bennett for help in clarifying these points.

20. See Sen (1970, Lemma 1*k, p. 14). Reflexivity of R, it should be noted, is essentially a "don't care" matter from the perspective of choice. It ensures that $C(S, R)$ is nonempty for every singleton set S; but singleton sets do not define occasions for choice.
21. Sen (1970, Lemma 1*1, p. 16).
22. Ibid.
23. This would, of course, be a rather odd sort of ranking. I have not been able to think of an evaluation rule that would behave in this way.
24. See Sen (1970, pp. 9–10).
25. More carefully, $M(\{x, y\}) = \{x, y\}$ under the stated conditions and on the plausible assumption that no element is strictly preferred to itself.
26. Suzumura (1976) has explored the properties of maximal set functions.
27. Levi (1974). The suggestion made there is developed at much greater length in Levi (1980, 1986b, Chap. 7). Discussion of indeterminate probabilities can be traced back at least to Schick (1958) and Kyburg (1961). See also Schick (1979, 1984).
28. See Lyon (1980, Prop. I.18, p. 95) for a substantiation of this conjecture.
29. Of course, one might take the agent's tossing a coin and saying "Heads, I take x; and tails, I take y" as evidence of a nonunit choice set; but then it could also be taken as evidence that the agent prefers the mixed option $(x, \frac{1}{2}; y, \frac{1}{2})$ to either option taken by itself!

3. The independence principle

1. This formulation of the independence principle is essentially the one to be found in Samuelson (1952). Closely related versions can be found in, e.g., Rubin (1949), Marschak (1951), and Markowitz (1959).
2. Notice that IND directly implies that if $x\,P\,y$, then $g_x\,R\,g_y$; and also that if

$x I y$ then $g_x R g_y$. As these versions suggest, under particularization of the antecedent condition, the weak ordering relation can be plausibly retained in the consequent term only if the biconditional is changed to an "only if." But if a corresponding particularization of the consequent relation is also introduced, the full biconditional form can be recovered: $x P y$ iff $g_x P g_y$; $x I y$ iff $g_x I g_y$. Again, any one of these versions can be weakened by reducing "if and only if" to either just "if" or just "only if."

In the original work of von Neumann and Morgenstern (1944), which provided the major impetus to the axiomatic treatment of utility theory, the independence principle is partially captured in a condition on indifference relations. However, this part of the condition is not given an explicit axiomatic formulation. It is buried in the definition of an operation on equivalence classes (see von Neumann and Morgenstern [1944, Sec. 3.6, p. 26], as pointed out by Malinvaud (1952).

In the context of certain axiomatic treatments, it suffices to particularize IND to just the case where $p = \frac{1}{2}$, that is, as a condition on the ordering of even-chance gambles. For example, in Herstein and Milnor (1953), one finds the following version (credited to Debreu): "If x is at least as good as y, then for any z, $[x, \frac{1}{2}; z, \frac{1}{2}]$ is at least as good as $[y, \frac{1}{2}; z, \frac{1}{2}]$."

3. See, e.g., Luce and Raiffa (1957, p. 27).
4. So formulated, IND is closely related to what Luce and Raiffa (1957, p. 290) characterize as Rubin's axiom for decision making under conditions of uncertainty.
5. Savage (1954 [1972], pp. 22–3). In effect, the consideration that preference should be constrained by IND when probabilities are fixed leads naturally enough to a more general principle. If certain preference relations are mandated simply in virtue of fixing the probabilities, then it makes no difference what values they are fixed at; hence, one might also suppose that it makes no difference whether one knows the probability values, so long as one is assured that they are fixed. The version that applies to cases in which the agent faces uncertain as distinct from well-defined risks is indispensable in view of the objective of Savage's work, namely, to develop a theory of personal or subjective probability.

As it turns out, Ramsey (1931) offered the earliest version of an independence principle for the case of uncertainty. There the principle is introduced as a constraint on preferences for gambles predicated on what Ramsey characterizes as "ethically neutral events which are believed to degree $\frac{1}{2}$." For Ramsey, E is such an event if the agent regards two possible worlds that differ only with regard to the truth of E as of equal value. Alternatively put, E is an event the truth or falsity of which in and of itself (i.e., independently of what consequences might be conditioned by that event) is not the object of any desire of the agent. An ethically neutral event E that is believed to degree $\frac{1}{2}$ is one such that the agent is indifferent between a gamble in which he gets some consequence x if E and y if not $-E$ and a gamble in which he gets y if E and x if not $-E$. Somewhat more informally stated, it is an ethically neutral event such that the agent assigns a subjective probability of $\frac{1}{2}$ to it and $\frac{1}{2}$ to its negation. Given these definitions, Ramsey's version of the independence principle can be formulated as follows: If E is an ethically neutral event believed to degree $\frac{1}{2}$ and if the gamble $[x, E; y, -E]$ is indifferent to the gamble $[z, E; w, -E]$, then x is at least as good as z iff w is at least as good as y. Of course, the drawback of this approach is that it presupposes there to be at least some event the probability of whose occurrence is well-defined. But it does permit a very simple and intuitively clear presentation of the theory of subjective probability, as can be seen in the more recent work of Anscombe and Aumann (1963) and Harsanyi (1977, Sec. 3.4, pp. 41–6).

6. See, e.g., Luce and Raiffa (1957, p. 26, Assum. 2), Harsanyi (1978, Ax. 3: Probabilistic Equivalence), and Friedman and Savage (1952, p. 467).

7. Samuelson (1952, pp. 672–3). Samuelson's point here echoes a similar one made somewhat earlier by von Neumann and Morgenstern (1944 [1953], pp. 17–18): "By a combination of two events we mean this: Let the two events be denoted by B and C and use, for the sake of simplicity, the probability 50% – 50%. Then the 'combination' is the prospect of seeing B occur with probability 50% and (if B does not occur) C with the (remaining) probability of 50%. We stress that the two alternatives are mutually exclusive, so that no possibility of complementarity and the like exists." See also ibid. (p. 27).

8. See, e.g., the ubiquitous appeal to this sort of assumption in the constructions found in Krantz, Luce, Suppes, and Tversky (1971).

9. The earliest reference to the sure-thing principle, as far as I have been able to determine, occurs in a discussion by Savage (1951, p. 58) of a decision situation in which risk is not well defined – what has come to be known as a situation of decision making under conditions of uncertainty. Savage imagines an agent who is interested simply in maximizing *expected* income but who is faced with a situation in which he cannot appeal to well-defined probabilities. Under such circumstances, Savage argues, "there is one unquestionably appropriate criterion for preferring some act to some others: If for every possible state, the expected income of one act is never less and is in some cases greater than the corresponding income of another, then the former act is preferable to the latter. This obvious principle is widely used in everyday life and in statistics, but only occasionally does it lead to a complete solution of a decision problem." Neither in this article nor in the one he wrote with Friedman a year later does Savage characterize the principle in question as the "sure-thing principle": That term appears to occur for the first time in *Foundations of Statistics* (1954 [1972], pp. 21–6).

10. Friedman and Savage (1952, pp. 468–9).

11. Savage (1954 [1972], p. 114).

12. See, e.g., Jeffrey (1965, pp. 8–10). It should also be noted that the appeal to sure-thing reasoning must also be made with great care in cases in which there is probabilistic dependence among the distributions involved in the compound lotteries. Suppose a coin of unknown bias is to be flipped twice. Let x be the gamble that yields \$5 if the second flip lands heads and \$0 if it lands tails; let y be the gamble that yields \$0 if the second flip lands heads and \$5 if it lands tails; and let z be the "gamble"

of getting $0 for sure. It is plausible to suppose that a typical agent will be indifferent between x and y if choice must be made in the absence of any evidence as to the bias of the coin. Consider now the compound gamble g_x = [z if the first flip lands tails; x if the first flip lands heads] and the compound gamble g_y = [z if the first flip lands tails; y if the first flip lands heads]. Sure-thing reasoning requires that the agent be indifferent between g_x and g_y. One is, presumably, indifferent between the outcomes (z in each case) of g_x and g_y, given that the first flip lands tails; and, by hypothesis, indifferent between x and y, the outcomes, respectively, of g_x and g_y, given that the first flip does not land tails, that is, lands heads. But learning that the first flip has landed heads is evidence that the bias, if any, is in the direction of the coin landing heads, in which case the agent will presumably prefer g_x to g_y. I am indebted to T. Seidenfeld for this point.

In cases such as this, sure-thing reasoning can still be employed, so long as (1) a distinction is drawn between preferences for consequences and preferences for acts, conditional upon some event taking place – which both Savage (1954 [1972]) and Arrow (1971) do – and (2) the sure-thing principle is formulated in terms of preferences for the latter, i.e., conditional acts. In the above example, the agent is presumed to be indifferent between the gambles x and y, abstractly considered, but a different account can be given of preferences for conditional acts, i.e., of preferences between g_x and g_y, given various possible events. By construction, if the agent learns that the first flip of the coin is heads, he will plausibly prefer the situation he then faces, in the event he has chosen g_x, to the situation he then faces, in the event he has chosen g_y. That is, on the very account given above, he prefers g_x to g_y, given that the first flip comes up heads, and he is indifferent between g_x and g_y, given that the first flip is tails. Thus, once again by appeal to the sure-thing principle, he should prefer g_x to g_y.

Both types of probabilistic dependence discussed above should be much more fully explored if one is to appreciate the implicit limits of the independence principle, particularly as it has figured in axiomatic treatments of utility theory. My concern, however, is with the question of the appropriateness of the principle as normative for paradigmatic cases in which the issue of probabilistic dependence does not arise.

13. The seminal article here is that of Gibbard and Harper (1978). For a recent overview of the issues involved, as well as reprints of some of the most important articles, see Campbell and Sowden (1985).

14. Friedman and Savage (1952, p. 469).

15. For the two quotations given and the proof, see Arrow (1972, pp. 23–6).

16. In Savage (1954 [1972], pp. 21–2), discussion of the independence postulate is prefaced by the following remarks:

A businessman contemplates buying a certain piece of property. He considers the outcome of the next presidential election relevant to the attractiveness of the purchase. So, to clarify the matter for himself, he asks whether he would buy if he knew that the Republican candidate were going to win, and decides he would do so. Similarly, he considers whether he would buy if he knew the Democratic candidate were going to win, and again finds that he would do so. Seeing that he would buy in either event, he decides he should buy, even though he does not know which event obtains or will obtain, as we would ordinarily say. It is all too seldom that a decision can be arrived at on the basis of the principle used by this businessman, but, except possibly for the assumption of simple ordering, I know of no other extralogical principle governing decisions that finds such ready acceptance.

Having suggested what I shall tentatively call the *sure-thing principle,* let me give it relatively formal statement thus: If the person would not prefer f to g, either knowing that the event B obtained, or knowing that the event $-$B obtained, then he does not prefer f to g. Moreover (provided he does not regard B as virtually impossible) if he would definitely prefer g to f, knowing that B obtained, and, if he would not prefer f to g, knowing that B did not obtain, then he definitely prefers g to f.

His next remarks, however, seem to amount to a retreat from this appeal to sure-thing reasoning:

The sure-thing principle cannot appropriately be accepted as a postulate in the sense that P1 [the weak ordering principle] is, because it would introduce new undefined technical terms referring to knowledge and possibility that would render it mathematically useless without still more postulates governing these terms. It will be preferable to regard the principle as a loose one that suggests certain formal postulates well articulated with P1.

What technical interpretation can be attached to the idea that f would be preferred to g, if B were known to obtain? Under any reasonable interpretation, the matter would seem not to depend on the values f and g assume at states outside of B. There is, then, no loss of generality in supposing that f and g *agree* with each other except in B, that is that $f(s) = g(s)$ for all s in $-$B. Under this unrestrictive assumption, f and g are surely to be regarded as equivalent, given $-$B; that is, they would be considered equivalent, if it were known that B did not obtain. The first part of the sure-thing principle can now be interpreted thus: If, after being modified so as to agree with one another outside of B, f is not preferred to g; then f would not be preferred to g, if B were known. The notion will be expressed formally by saying that $f \leq g$ *given* B.

It is implicit in the argument that has just led to the definition of $f \leq g$ given B that, if two acts are so modified in $-$B as to agree with each other, then the order of preference obtaining between the modified acts will not depend on which of the permitted modifications was actually carried out. Equivalently, if f and g are two acts that do agree with each other in $-$B, and $f \leq g$; then if f and g are modified in $-$B in any way such that the modified acts f' and g' continue to agree with each other in $-$B, it will also be so that $f' \leq g'$.

What follows this is a formal presentation of the independence postulate discussed at the end of Section 3.1 – a version of common outcomes independence (ICO) framed to apply to situations in which well-defined probabilities are not presupposed.

Does this mean that the sure-thing principle is thus to be understood as serving no more than a heuristic purpose? On the contrary, the deemphasis of the sure-thing principle seems to reflect no more than a formal concern on Savage's part that the *axiomatic* presentation of the theory minimize the number of primitive concepts and basic axioms. In other words, from the perspective of the formal derivation of the theory of utility and subjective probability, Savage thinks it more convenient and parsimonious to postulate directly the independence version of the principle. But as I shall explore in somewhat more detail in the next chapter, he continues to treat the sure-thing formulation as providing an intuitive grounding for the independence principle.

17. Luce and Raiffa (1957, p. 28).

18. For a recent review of the literature on stochastic dominance, see Machina (1983); many of the relevant papers are to be found in Diamond and Rothschild (1978).

19. In the case of the principal constructions with which I have been concerned, in particular those of von Neumann and Morgenstern (1944), Friedman and Savage (1952), Savage (1954 [1972]), Herstein and Milnor (1953), Arrow (1972), and Harsanyi (1977), the above framework assumptions hold. All of them introduce some reduction postulate that ensures that the agent will regard gambles that yield the same outcomes with the same probabilities as essentially equivalent to each other, and all assume transitivity of weak preference.

20. This turns out to be essentially the approach taken in Chernoff (1949), which contains one of the very earliest treatments of independence. His version is more general with respect to choice conditions (he does not limit the principle to choice from pair sets) and more particular with respect to probabilities. Adapted to the notation of this work, his principle reads: "If the feasible set of gambles in one problem is G, and $D(G)$ is the choice set for G, and the agent is now confronted with a modified problem in which the set G' of feasible gambles is defined as follows: $G' = \{[x, \frac{1}{2}, z, \frac{1}{2}]$, for all x in G, and constant $z\}$, then x is in $D(G)$ iff $[x, \frac{1}{2}; z, \frac{1}{2}]$ is in $D(G')$."

21. It should be noted that some, such as Levi (1986b), have argued that these two versions are not interchangeable – that independence as a rationality condition on preference is plausible enough, whereas the counterpart condition on choice is not. For example, Levi is prepared to sanction violations of CIND in contexts in which, on his account, agents do not have well-defined preferences and/or well-defined probabilities but are still faced with making choices. He does, however, insist that IND is a plausible condition in any context in which agents can be said to have both well-defined preferences and well-defined probabilities.

This raises an interesting set of issues that I will not be able to resolve fully until I have worked through the material presented in Chapters 8, 9, and 10. For the next few chapters, where I shall be concerned for the most part with exploring a framework that includes conditions strong enough to yield both CF and CIND, CIND will clearly suffice. That is, in the presence of CF, one will be able to get from CIND to IND, the preference version of the independence principle. In later chapters, where I shall explore considerably weaker frameworks, it turns out that agents who relax CIND will be liable to certain problems, regardless of whether they accept CF.

Let me also note that one must carefully distinguish between choosing in the sense of marking out options that are acceptable and choosing in the sense of picking among those that are judged to be acceptable. I would agree that once an agent has narrowed the set of feasible options to those that are acceptable, the choice he then makes from that set is not one that is appropriately thought of as constrained by CIND. To speak of principles governing sets of acceptable choices is to speak of principles governing the methods of evaluation used; it is not to speak of principles governing picking – what is left to be done when the results of evaluations have been registered and the selection process has narrowed things down to a set of acceptable alternatives. For reasons that will emerge subsequently, I remain unpersuaded by Levi's attempt to apply the distinction more generally to the processes by which options are evaluated and subsequently judged acceptable or unacceptable.

22. Luce and Raiffa (1957, p. 27).
23. See, e.g., Herstein and Milnor (1953, p. 292), where this is effected by supposing that the axioms apply to a "mixture set" of options. See also Harsanyi (1977, pp. 22–6), where the notation makes it clear that the axioms apply to "composite" risky prospects, i.e., prospects some of whose components are themselves risky prospects, and Arrow (1972, p. 28), where the interpretive remarks make clear that the proof proceeds by establishing a result for "probability distributions of probability distributions."
24. Von Neumann and Morgenstern initiate this tradition (e.g., 1944 [1953], p. 18, fn. 10); see also Alchian (1953, pp. 32–3).
25. Savage (1954 [1972]) is very clear about this. See his Section 5.6 and, in particular, p. 99; but see also below, Section 4.7.

4. The problem of justification

1. This is known as the Cartesian view of justification. For discussions of its application to normative theory see, e.g., Hare (1952, Ch. 3) and Rawls (1971, Sec. 87).
2. For example, Friedman and Savage (1952, p. 468) are content to announce that they find both the sure-thing principle and the weak ordering assumption to be extremely plausible. See also Marschak (1968).
3. Samuelson (1952, pp. 672–3).
4. See, e.g., Rawls (1951, 1971, Secs. 9 and 87) and Daniels (1979).
5. Of particular note here are the articles in *Econométrie* (1953) that constitute the proceedings of a conference organized in Paris in 1952 to discuss the foundations of expected utility theory. The articles, including ones by Savage and Arrow, are in French, and most have never been translated. Allais's own contribution to this volume has been translated, however. See Allais (1979); see also Friedman and Savage (1948, 1952), Samuelson (1950), Baumol (1951), Malinvaud (1952), Allais (1953), Ellsberg (1954, 1961), Fellner (1961, 1963), Raiffa (1961), Brewer (1963), and Allais and Hagen (1979).
6. Levi (1974) and Schick (1979) are particularly important here. For a more recent and much more comprehensive statement, see Levi (1986b). For the earlier debate that arose concerning a related condition on social choice functions see, e.g., Sen (1970) and the references therein to the independence of irrelevant alternatives condition.
7. All of this became abundantly clear at the First International Conference

on Foundations of Utility and Risk Theory, which was held in Oslo in 1982. Machina presented his view that utility theory could do without the independence axiom and effectively won the day on the issue of the descriptive inadequacy of the standard theory of expected utility. At the final plenary session, however, a number of the speakers, after acknowledging the importance of Machina's findings for descriptive theory, insisted that the independence axiom was still secure as a normative principle. For the papers read at this conference, see Stigum and Wenstop (1983).

8. Gärdenfors and Sahlins (1988, Pts. 2 and 3) contains reprints of some of the most important contributions; it also contains an excellent bibliography. See also in this regard Allais and Hagen (1979).

9. See, in particular, Harsanyi (1978, pp. 224–5). Harsanyi does not always argue for the reduction principle in this manner. In Harsanyi (1977, Chap. 3, pp. 22–47), the reduction assumption is tacitly incorporated by means of a series of "notational conventions."

10. Von Neumann and Morgenstern (1944 [1953], p. 28).

11. See, however, Kahneman and Tversky (1979) and Kahneman, Slovic, and Tversky (1982), and the bibliography therein, for surveys of attitudes toward risk exhibited by experimental subjects.

12. Arrow (1972, p. 22).

13. Sen (1970, p. 3).

14. In the case of the minimax risk criterion, indeed, the ranking over any fixed set of feasible alternatives is otherwise very well behaved, i.e., connected and fully transitive.

15. Broome (1988, Part 2).

16. Ibid. (p. 8).

17. See, e.g., Quine (1951).

18. See von Neumann and Morgenstern (1944 [1953], pp. 17–18), Marschak (1951, pp. 502–3), and Samuelson (1952, p. 672).

19. The possibility of complementarity is discussed in Manne (1952), Allais and Hagen (1979, p. 80–106), McClennen (1983), Loomes and Sugden (1984), and Sen (1985). Broome (1988, pp. 37–8, fn. 13) has complained that I do not understand that "complementarity" is a term (as used by economists) that applies just to the context of conjunctive bundles of commodities. I am prepared to yield to Broome with regard to a point of terminology; but terminology, it seems to me, is not the issue. As the examples to be discussed in this section show, I believe, the considerations that undercut the application of the independence condition to certain cases of choice under conditions of risk and/or uncertainty closely parallel the considerations that undercut the application of an analogous independence condition to certain cases of choice among commodity bundles.

20. See Allais (1953, 1979) and Allais and Hagen (1979).

21. Empirical findings are surveyed in, e.g., Kahneman and Tversky (1979), MacCrimmon and Larsson (1979), and Schoemaker (1980). Savage himself, who was firmly committed to IND, admitted that on first consideration these were his preferences. See Savage (1954 [1972], p. 103).

22. Savage (1954 [1972], p. 103).
23. Kahneman and Tversky (1979).
24. Again, for the sake of the example, I assume that the agent is concerned simply with monetary payoffs and probabilities (including, of course, in this case the dispersion features of the probability distributions) and that he treats the value of sure amounts of money as a linear function of monetary amount. Similar results can be obtained if shortfall and, more generally, dispersion are measured in terms of, e.g., the Gini coefficient.
25. Ellsberg (1961). See Postulate 2 in Savage (1954 [1972], pp. 21–6).
26. Samuelson (1952, pp. 672–3).
27. See Ellsberg (1961). That they are uncertainty *averse* is not essential; a similar violation will occur for those who are attracted to uncertainty.
28. A closely related case is discussed by Ellsberg (1961, p. 654, fn. 4), who attributes the example to Arrow.
29. Broome (1988, pp. 15–16).
30. Ibid. (p. 18).
31. Broome carefully distinguishes between preference, abstractly considered, and "practical" preference. For a given agent to have a practical preference for *x* over *y*, it must be possible that the agent be faced with choosing between *x* and *y*. See ibid. (p. 2).
32. Ibid. (p. 27).
33. See Friedman and Savage (1952, pp. 468–9).
34. Even if GDE seems plausible, its implications with regard to IND can be used to argue against it. That is, if GDE together with a plausible reduction assumption implies IND, and IND is, as suggested in Section 4.5, too restrictive, then this counts as an argument against GDE.
35. Savage (1954 [1972], p. 99).
36. This undercuts, I think, one version of an argument that Seidenfeld (1988a, b) and, following him, Levi (1986a, p. 45, fn. 6; 1986b, p. 144 and p. 235, fn. 21) have offered. Both appear to make no distinction between FSD and GFSD. I return to this matter in Section 10.5; see, in particular, Chapter 10, note 9.

5. Pragmatic arguments

1. See, in particular, Hammond (1988a, b).
2. Ramsey (1931) and de Finetti (1937).
3. Hammond (1988b, p. 25).
4. If one mistakenly supposes Hume to be putting forth a criterion for what preferences and choices are to count as *morally* acceptable, one is bound, of course, to recoil from this. But even those who do not misread Hume in this manner are likely to resist his suggestion. All are prepared to accept the notion that one appropriate basis for judging the rationality or reasonableness of a choice is in terms of the contribution it can make to the realization of desired ends; perhaps only a few are prepared to allow that this is the only appropriate test of rationality.
5. I use the term "thin" here in something like the way Rawls employs it in his account of goodness as rationality in (1971, Ch. 7, esp. p. 396, and Sec.

61). Elements of this sort of theory of rationality are to be found quite early in Plato's dialogue *The Protagoras* and in Aristotle's brief remarks in the *Nicomachean Ethics* and in *De Anima* concerning the "practical syllogism." It is also, of course, central to the way that philosophical pragmatists have conceived of rationality. See, in particular, C. I. Lewis (1946, Chap. 12). A commitment to such a minimalist notion of rationality is also, of course, central to much contemporary microeconomics and decision theory. My quarrel is not with this sort of commitment, but with the failure of many economists and decision theorists to stay within its bounds. They have managed, I believe, to incorporate more into a minimalist view than is warranted.

6. Recall here the discussion in Section 4.2. Both Broome and Hammond have addressed this issue, and both have concluded that a pragmatic (or consequentialist) perspective does not preclude having preferences with regard to features of gambles other than "outcomes" and probabilities. On their account, preferences with regard to, say, structural features of gambles can be reinterpreted as preferences with regard to a special class of consequences. I shall subsequently argue that this represents an important qualification in the characterization of a pragmatic or consequentialist perspective and one that in the end undermines Hammond's constructive project. See Section 8.10.

7. Davidson, McKinsey, and Suppes (1955, p. 145).

8. Ibid. (p. 146).

9. A similar argument can be constructed for cases in which the agent's preference ordering does not satisfy transitivity of indifference, that is, $x\,I_c\,y$, $y\,I_c\,z$, but $x\,P_c\,z$ (or $z\,P_c\,x$)

10. Yaari (1985, pp. 9–11) offers a somewhat analogous argument in support of the strong independence principle IND and its choice counterpart CIND. Suppose, he suggests, the agent prefers the gamble $g_x = $ [\$x, p; \$0, $1 - p$] to the gamble $g_y = $ [\$y, q; \$0, $1 - q$] but, in violation of the independence principle, prefers the gamble $g_y^* = [g_y,\,H;\,\$0,\,T]$ to the gamble $g_x^* = [g_x,\,H;\,\$0,\,T]$, where "H" and "T" designate the outcomes of a flip of a fair coin. Suppose now the agent comes into possession of g_x^*. For a small positive fee, he should be willing to exchange g_x^* for g_y^* (since, by hypothesis, the latter is strictly preferred to the former). But once in possession of g_y^*, the agent is now made the following offer: For a small fee, he will be provided with the option, if H comes up, of exchanging g_y for g_x. Since by hypothesis, he prefers g_x to g_y, he should accept this offer. But now, once he accepts this offer, and before the flip of the coin, he finds himself just where he started, in possession once again of what amounts to g_x^*, but poorer by a small amount of money. There are, however, ambiguities in Yaari's account that seriously undercut the force of his argument. I return to this matter in Section 10.3, note 4.

11. Raiffa (1968, pp. 83–5).

12. Ibid. (p. 83).

13. There are two other possibilities. The first is that he is asking you to *predict* at the outset what you would choose once the coin has been tossed.

This is not a promising interpretation. By hypothesis, you have already indicated that you would choose g_1 over g_2^* and g_3 over g_4^*, hence predicted such conditional choices. The other possibility Raiffa might have in mind is that you have the opportunity to make a choice between plans at the outset, but you have reconsideration rights after the coin is tossed. This, however, is really not distinct from the first of the interpretations mentioned before. Being able to "choose" now but reconsider later is not really distinct from being in a position to "settle in your own mind upon a plan of action" and then being faced later with actually implementing one rather than another of these plans.

14. Raiffa (1968, p. 84).
15. See Section 1.6.
16. Ramsey (1931, p. 182).
17. Kemeny (1955), Lehmann (1955), and Shimony (1955). More recent appeals to this sort of argument are to be found in Yaari (1985) and Green (1987).
18. I adapt here a more general example found in Schick (1986).
19. See Kyburg (1978) and Schick (1986).

6. Dynamic choice problems

1. This is consistent with the suggestion made in Section 4.7 to the effect that despite the correctness of Savage's claim that it is risk all the way down, what is relevant to the agent's evaluation of plans is how he describes the outcomes. What makes an outcome terminal is at least partly a matter of there being deliberately set planning horizons and partly a matter of there being natural limitations on the ability of any agent to anticipate the future.
2. Unless otherwise noted, I shall assume that a plan always specifies some unique choice to be made at a given choice point. See, however, Section 6.7 and the discussion of feasibility in Sections 8.5 through 8.7.
3. Notice, for example, that in the decision tree given in Figure 6.2, the agent has a total of four possible plans. Plans s_1 and s_3 coincide with respect to what is to be chosen at n_1; plans s_2 and s_4 coincide at n_1; plans s_1 and s_4 coincide at n_2; and plans s_2 and s_3 coincide at n_2. Plans s_1 and s_2 are disjoint, as are plans s_3 and s_4.
4. See Sections 8.5 through 8.7.
5. In Chapters 3 and 4, I made extensive use of RD together with WO to establish the relationship between various versions of the independence principle. Here, however, where dynamic choice foundations are to be provided for both WO and IND, it is important to be as parsimonious as possible in the use of supporting assumptions. The text reflects this. It is not necessary to assume that the agent's ordering is fully transitive with respect to indifference. All that is required here is that transitivity of indifference hold with respect to a specific class of gambles, namely, the set of gambles that all reduce to the same probability distribution over the

same set of outcomes. Alternatively put, all I am assuming here is that any such set of gambles forms an *equivalence* class. See, e.g., Krantz, Luce, Suppes, and Tversky (1971, pp. 15–16).

6. For applied work, see in particular Raiffa (1968) and references contained therein.

7. In recent years there have been a number of other important contributions. See, in particular, Kreps and Porteus (1978, 1979) and Johnsen and Donaldson (1985).

7. Rationality conditions on dynamic choice

1. See Sections 8.5 through 8.7.

2. See, e.g., Luce and Raiffa (1957, Chap. 3).

3. See Strotz (1956), Pollack (1968), Peleg and Yaari (1973), Hammond (1976, 1977), and Yaari (1977).

4. Hammond opts, in effect, to treat what I have characterized as dynamic consistency in this manner, and thus concludes that this type of consistency places no constraint on the agent's choice behavior. This is explicitly discussed in the earlier version of his argument. See Hammond (1982a, pp. 3, 5). In Hammond (1988b), the consistency condition to which he appeals (see, in particular, pp. 28, 33–6) is something quite different: It appears, at the very least, to imply the separability condition that I discuss in Section 7.5.

5. Note that all that is required here is that there be some plan in S whose plan continuation at n_i is equivalent to $r(n_i)$.

6. Notice, however, that for any tree T and any node n_i, the ranking between $g_{s(n_i)}$ and $g_{r(n_i)}$, which is determinative of the ranking between $s(n_i)$ and $r(n_i)$, is to be understood here as fixed with reference to the set $G_{s(n_i)}$ – the set of all prospects still open to the agent at n_i. That is, in treating $T(n_i)$ as if it were a tree that begins de novo at choice point n_i, one fixes the set of prospects within which $g_{s(n_i)}$ and $g_{r(n_i)}$, as members of that set, are to be compared. Care must be taken, however, in interpreting this conclusion. Consider a modified version T' of the tree in Figure 6.1, in which one faces at n_2 not only $s(n_2)$ and $r(n_2)$ but also some third truncated plan, $t(n_2)$. TR does *not* imply in this case that $s(n_2)$ and $r(n_2)$ must still be ranked vis-à-vis each other in the same manner they are ranked at $T(n_i)$. The presence of the third truncated plan $t(n_2)$ can affect how $s(n_2)$ and $r(n_2)$ are ranked vis-à-vis each other. Thus, although TR rules out any influence by counterfactual possibilities (forgone opportunities), it does not rule out influence by feasible possibilities (opportunities not yet forgone). In particular, then, TR does not rule out a context-dependent ordering of outcomes or prospects. What this suggests, and what I will shortly explore more fully, is that within the present framework DC must be added to TR in order to ensure the context-free conditions on orderings.

7. SEP is closely connected with the conditional preference postulate (CP) that Arrow (1972, pp. 23–4) employs and to which reference was made in Section 3.5. Arrow formulates his postulate explicitly in terms of a requirement on the ordering of acts conditional upon some event taking

place – where the event is presumed to be one that conditions the outcome of the act chosen and that has assigned to it some (more or less determinate) probability. Arrow was not explicitly concerned in that treatment of utility theory with dynamic or sequential choice, but SEP provides a natural extension of CP to such problems. In the dynamic setting, moreover, the conditioning event can be conceived in somewhat more general terms, as any prior chance event or choice made by the agent himself, that conditions his being at the choice point in question.

8. Notice that in virtue of (4), the agent must at n_0 choose to head toward n_1, in the event that chance takes him to n_2 to select $r(n_2)$. But it can be argued that in virtue of (2), the agent cannot expect to execute plan r – for he must expect that upon arriving at n_2 he will select $s(n_2)$ instead. It would seem, then, that r is not really a plan available to the agent, given all the acceptable sets as specified. That is, only s and t are available, or feasible, plans. If NEC is reformulated so as to take this into account, i.e., taken to apply only to feasible – as opposed to all logically possible – plans, then the possibility just considered collapses: We cannot have that just $s(n_2)$ is in $D(S(n_2))$, while just r is in $D(S)$. But, of course, to restrict NEC in this way is to assume that whatever else happens, DC must be satisfied, and so the collapse is not surprising at all. One cannot have that all of RD, NEC, SEP, and DC are satisfied, yet DC is not satisfied! See Sections 8.5 through 8.7 for a much fuller exploration of problems posed by alternative characterizations of feasibility.

9. See Hammond (1988b, pp. 46–50) and Section 8.1 of this volume. Strictly speaking, SEP follows not from Hammond's consequentialist principle itself, but from what he characterizes as a "consistency" principle; but his Theorem 8 establishes the existence of a consequentialist norm that also satisfies the consistency condition. See, in particular, Hammond (1988b, p. 34).

8. Consequentialist constructions

1. The most complete exposition of this is to be found in Hammond (1988b).
2. Ibid. (p. 25).
3. Ibid. (p. 38).
4. Ibid. (p. 26).
5. Ibid. (pp. 28, 34).
6. Ibid. (p. 28).
7. See Section 7.4 and note 4 of Chapter 7. Hammond occasionally strays from his rigid behavioral approach. In Hammond (1982a, p. 29), he speaks of an agent who plans to make a certain choice, only subsequently to choose otherwise. The implications of his behavioral view emerge clearly in his discussion (Hammond, 1976, pp. 161–3; 1988b, pp. 35–6) of the difference between a myopic and a sophisticated potential drug addict. Whereas I diagnose the myopic agent as violating DC and the sophisticated agent as violating NEC, Hammond insists that both the myopic and the sophisticated potential addict exhibit consistent behavior, and, correspondingly, both violate NEC.

It also appears, if I have interpreted his notation correctly, that Hammond has an odd notion of a strategy (plan, behavioral norm): It specifies choice behavior for *every* choice node in a tree. See Hammond (1987, Sec. 3, and, in particular, p. 9). By way of contrast, I have sought to remain faithful to the ordinary notion of a plan, which specifies choices to be made at each choice point that can be reached by implementation of earlier stages of the plan in question. It is for this reason that I require, and Hammond does not, a qualifier with respect to the required coincidence between $D(S)(n_i)$ and $D(S(n_i))$, namely, that $D(S)(n_i)$ be nonempty.

8. In subsequent chapters I shall argue that TR, with its presupposition of SEP, provides only one, and by no means the most plausible, way in which to articulate a consequentialist perspective.

9. Hammond (1988b). See, in particular, Theorems 5.4, 5.6, and 5.7.

10. The four conditions SR, NEC, DC, and SEP can also be employed to characterize the folding-forward and folding-backward techniques for evaluating options in a sequential decision problem. The folding-forward method is characterized by SR, NEC, and DC; the folding-backward method is characterized by SR, SEP, and DC. For an account of these methods, see Raiffa (1968). The combination of SEP and DC also characterizes what is known as Bellman's (1954) optimality principle.

11. Note, more generally, that if DC and any condition that functions like the conjunction of SR, SEP, and preferences with regard to prospects open at n_i are taken as given, then it might seem that a question can be raised about the plausibility of supposing that all logically possible plans are feasible. Suppose for the moment any dynamic choice condition C that permits that $D(S(n_i))$ be determined independently of the application of any criterion of acceptability of whole plans to the choices to be made at n_0. For this more general class of cases, once again there will be a potential conflict between the presupposition that all logically possible plans are feasible and the assumption that C holds. The reason for this is that given condition C, the agent may be able to ascertain what would be acceptable from the vantage point of n_i. From the vantage point of n_0, however, these applications of C to n_i also have implications of a projective sort: The agent who is committed to C will expect that he will evaluate choices at n_i in conformity with C and choose accordingly. Thus, what is prescriptive from the standpoint of n_i carries predictive implications from the standpoint of any ancestor of n_i, hence from the standpoint of n_0. But these predictive implications, in turn, are naturally taken as having implications for what is *feasible* at the ancestral node. If C implies that some strategy $s(n_i)$ is not in $D(S(n_i))$, then the agent will expect that if and when he arrives at n_i, he will not choose $s(n_i)$. But this directly implies that s is not a feasible plan: It calls upon the agent to make a choice at some subsequent choice node that he fully expects he will not make.

12. Of course, there is no reason to particularize this requirement to just n_0 and its successors. More generally, then, letting n_{i+} designate any successor of n_i, the strong truncated plan condition TR can be modified to the following:

Restricted truncated plan reduction (RTR). For any $s(n_i)$, such that for all n_{i+}, $s(n_{i+})$ is in $D(S(n_{i+}))$, $s(n_i)$ is in $D(S(n_i))$ iff $g_{s(n_i)}$ is in $D(G_{S(n_i)})$.

This amounts to requiring that a plan's (or truncated plan's) being a "winner" at every successor node n_{i+} to n_i is a necessary condition for that plan (or truncated plan) to be feasible at n_i.

13. For a more comprehensive treatment of dynamic choice, VSF must be generalized to cover the case in which more than two plans satisfy the "only if" part of SF and are all defined at some choice point n_i. The condition as formulated, however, will suffice for present purposes.

14. There has been a tendency for theorists to focus on strict preference and to more or less ignore issues that arise concerning indifference relations. In McClennen (1972, 1975, 1978) I argue that fully attending to both relations poses serious problems for the traditional equilibrium theory of noncooperative games.

15. It might even be possible to recast this story in terms of a more restrictive criterion of feasibility as it would apply, in this case, to SEP. The notion would be that an agent who has decided on a certain plan might view a particular truncated plan as simply not feasible – it being incompatible with what he intends to do – even though, abstracting from the background assumption that he has made a commitment to a plan, he would be disposed to choose that truncated plan.

16. Hammond (1988b, p. 26).

17. Ibid. (pp. 26–7).

18. See, in particular, Hammond (1988b, pp. 28, 34–6).

19. More specifically, it casts doubt on what is an explicit, and required, presupposition of Hammond's construction, namely, that there is an unrestricted domain of consequential decision trees. See, in particular, Hammond (1988b, p. 27). Note that on p. 76, fn. 4, Hammond acknowledges that if the consequence domain is expanded to include counterfactual possibilities and the like, the assumption of an unrestricted domain of consequential decision trees may be "restrictive."

20. See Luce and Raiffa (1957, Sec. 2.5) and Herstein and Milnor (1953).

9. Reinterpreting dynamic consistency

1. Strotz (1956, p. 165).

2. Hammond (1988a, b).

3. Recall (Section 8.1 and note 7) that, unlike Strotz, Hammond does not diagnose the "myopic" agent (or naive agent, as he chooses to characterize him) as a violator of DC. The formal framework developed in Chapters 6 and 7, then, more closely accords to the framework implicit in Strotz, and the diagnosis of myopia that I favor coincides with his: The myopic agent adopts plans only to abandon them subsequently and thus fails to choose in a manner that satisfies DC. The cases that I want to examine, however, are those about which Hammond is concerned, namely, cases in which the agent's preference ordering of prospects gives rise to acceptable sets that fail to satisfy CF or CIND.

4. Strotz (1956, p. 173). Hammond (1976, p. 162, and 1988b, p. 35) illustrates this type of sophisticated strategy with the example of the potential drug addict. The potential addict prefers moderate use to abstention, and both of these to heavy use in virtue of the addiction it implies. The myopic chooser in this situation is one who, on the basis of this evaluation, plans to continue to take the drug in moderate doses. Subsequently, however, he comes to prefer heavy use to moderate use and thus ends up being addicted. By contrast, the sophisticated chooser projects that were he to take the drug he would not be able to stop short of heavy use and addiction. That is, he anticipates that he will subsequently prefer heavy over moderate use. Since he now does not want to become addicted, he chooses to abstain altogether.

5. Strotz (1956, p. 173). For Strotz, Ulysses personifies this sort of sophisticated approach. Anticipating that he will want to follow the Sirens once he hears their song, he has himself bound to the mast of his ship and gives instructions to his crew not to untie him until they are past the Sirens' island. Ulysses manages to carry through the plan he adopts at the outset, by means of the device of precommitment. By contrast, presumably, the many who litter the beaches of the cursed isle were myopic choosers – persons who sailed on toward the island, intending to resist the Sirens' song, but who in the end (predictably) failed to do so.

6. At least on the presupposition that the agent regards g_4 as sufficiently more attractive than g_3 that he would be willing to pay \$1 to trade up from the latter to the former.

7. A similar story can be told of the sophisticated approach to choice in the Kahneman and Tversky example presented in Section 9.2 (see Figure 9.2). The sophisticated agent ranks the prospect associated with plan s (to choose $s(n_3)$ if and when the opportunity presents itself) over that associated with plan r, but since also, by hypothesis, he ranks the prospect associated with $r(n_3)$ over that associated with $s(n_3)$ were he to face those two options de novo, he projects that he would choose $r(n_3)$ – not $s(n_3)$ – if and when the opportunity presents itself. Given that projection, he regards plan s as not feasible, and $(r+)^n$ emerges as the best of the feasible options. Once again, however, the agent's choice dispositions violate NEC. The agent would choose s^n over $(r+)^n$, that is, would choose differently, if all plans were in normal form.

8. The concept of a sophisticated approach actually requires, I think, commitment to VSF and, correspondingly, VRPR. The sophisticated agent is required to make a prediction concerning his own future behavior, and as such he must project not simply which are the plan continuations he will not choose, but how he will resolve cases in which more than one truncated plan will be judged equally acceptable.

9. The one exception, to the best of my knowledge, is Johnsen and Donaldson (1985). See Section 13.3.

10. Elster (1979, p. 43) is responsible for the metaphor of "depositing one's will." See also Section 13.5. A similar contrast between sophisticated and resolute strategies could be drawn in connection with Ulysses and the potential drug addict. Sophisticated Ulysses precommits; the sophisti-

cated potential drug addict abstains altogether. Both regiment their plans to avoid situations in which they project they would choose in a manner that they now prefer not to. However, in each case the agent chooses an alternative whose outcome is judged inferior to the outcome of some other logically possible course of action: taking the drug in moderate amounts; sailing by the island and ignoring the song of the Sirens. Imagine now that the potential drug addict, upon contemplating the costs to himself of protecting against his own future choice, resolves to take the drug in moderation and then proceeds to act on that resolve. Similarly, imagine that Ulysses, on contemplating the costs of hemp, wax, and agency arrangements, resolves to sail by the island and pay the singing sisters no mind and then proceeds to do just that. I do not mean to suggest here that there is nothing problematic about being resolute in such situations. These two examples are introduced here purely for the sake of illustration – and to make a connection with earlier discussions in the literature. They merely indicate what it *would* be to be resolute in such situations if resoluteness *were* possible. I shall argue in Chapter 12 that Ulysses and the potential drug addict are perhaps best treated as agents for whom a resolute approach is not possible, or at least very problematic.

11. Notice, for example, that since the plan that he adopts at the outset is responsive to a wider set of prospects, it is possible that if the decision problem were altered in some fashion or other that still left unchanged the prospects to be faced at some point, n_i, $i \neq 0$, within the tree, his initial choice of a plan would be altered. That is, he might well find himself, upon arriving at n_i, prepared to choose differently than he was prepared to do in the original, unaltered version of the problem, even though, from the point n_i onward, he faces the same set of prospects. Thus, one must conclude that what might have been the case under conditions that will not in fact obtain can make a difference to how such an agent chooses ex post, i.e., and once again this implies choice behavior in violation of SEP.

12. As I hope will become clear in Chapters 11 and 12, I do not intend the appeal to "commitment" to be final. That is, I am not proposing here that choice of some option at n_i, $i \neq 0$, be rationalized simply in virtue of the agent having earlier as a matter of fact resolved to choose at n_i. To do so would be to develop a "deontic" theory of resolute choice that would form the analogue to, say, a theory of morality in which the fact of having promised was taken as sufficient to establish an obligation. This would be to unhinge resolute choice from what I take to be its basis, namely, pragmatic considerations. Moreover, I also want to leave open the possibility that even if the agent did not as a matter of fact resolve at some point before n_i to choose in a certain fashion at n_i, still one can consider as relevant to the question of what is to be chosen at n_i what one would have resolved to do at some antecedent point if one had (counterfactually) considered the matter.

13. It is interesting that SR is nowhere at issue among the three approaches. This is not surprising, for, as I have argued throughout, the "unortho-

dox" methods of evaluation that I have explored do not imply any violation of SR.

10. A critique of the pragmatic arguments

1. To see this, note that each of x, y, and z is rejected in one of the three possible pair sets; thus, if Alpha is satisfied, none of x, y, or z can be in $D(\{x, y, z\})$, i.e., $D(\{x, y, z\})$ is empty; hence, there is no acceptable-set function defined here.

2. I leave it to the dedicated reader to work out comparable analyses for the other six cases.

3. For the discussion in the text, I have assumed that the agent is fully aware, at the outset, that the entrepreneur will attempt to work his way through at least one full cycle, and perhaps more. Suppose, for the sake of argument, that the agent is not aware of this. In the case of a myopic agent, it makes no difference, since he chooses in an incremental fashion and does not take into account his own future behavior. For the sophisticated agent, by contrast, lack of information proves disadvantageous. If he does not believe that certain options will be presented to him in the future, he cannot make predictions about how he will choose and then fold this information back to sort out, at n_0, what plans are and what plans are not feasible. This means that the sophisticated agent can be exploited – but only in a very limited manner, assuming at any rate that he has a memory. Once he has been run through one cycle, he will then be on his guard.

   What about the resolute agent? In order to exercise his capacity to form, and then act on, a resolve, we must suppose that he expects that he can trade three rounds – so that plans s_1 through s_4 are available to him – i.e., we must suppose that he expects to face choices up through n_2. If he initially supposed that only the choices at n_0 and those at n_1 were open to him, how are we to expect that he would react were he to arrive at n_1 and then be informed that another choice awaited him at n_2? One seemingly plausible answer would be for him to reflect, at that point, on what he would have resolved to do if he then had the information now available to him, and choose accordingly. On that interpretation, he faces no problem at all. That is, he cannot be exploited for even a single round. At the worst, however, he would not appear to be subject to any more exploitation than that to which the sophisticated chooser is subject.

4. Similar conclusions can be drawn with regard to the argument of Yaari's mentioned in note 10, Section 5.4, to the effect that the agent who violates IND (or CIND) can be turned into a money pump. Yaari's hapless agent faces the dynamic choice problem shown on p. 287. At n_0 the agent has to choose between plan t, which consists in retaining g_x^*; plan s, which involves trading that prospect together with \$$e$ for prospect g_y^*, which he accesses by making a choice of $s(n_3)$ if and when the opportunity arises, thereby exposing himself to the prospect g_y; or plan r, which coincides with s at n_0 but calls for trading again at n_3 and securing rights to g_x, for another small sum of \$$d$. If he adopts either s or r and chance at n_1 takes

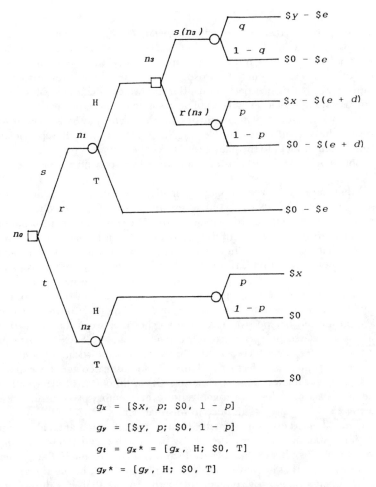

$$g_x = [\$x, \ p; \ \$0, \ 1 - p]$$

$$g_y = [\$y, \ p; \ \$0, \ 1 - p]$$

$$g_t = g_x{}^\star = [g_x, \ H; \ \$0, \ T]$$

$$g_y{}^\star = [g_y, \ H; \ \$0, \ T]$$

him to n_3, then he will face another choice – between standing pat or trading the balance of his rights to $g_y^\star$, together with a small amount of money $\$d$, for g_x.

Now Yaari describes the problem as if the agent at n_0 thinks just about the choice between s and t, without reference to the choice that will subsequently have to be made at n_3, i.e., without reference to the alternative plan r, and as if he thinks at n_3 (if and when he arrives at that point) just about the choice between $s(n_3)$ and $r(n_3)$, with their associated prospects g_x and g_y, without reference to any decision he made at n_0. In short, each choice point is treated as presenting a new problem. Feasibility considerations stemming from projected future choices are ignored, and past decisions are ignored.

Behavior of this sort characterizes the myopic chooser, who is committed to SR, NEC, and SEP and who thus ends up violating DC with respect to plans and DSO with respect to associated prospects. A sophisticated chooser, by contrast, will anticipate, given his commitment to SR and SEP, that he will trade at n_3 and thus, in accord with SF, will regard plan s as not feasible. Of the remaining plans, t is clearly superior to r by appeal to RPR (or VRPR) since its prospect dominates, by reference to sure outcomes, plan r's prospect. Thus, the sophisticated chooser will select t and avoid any violation of DSO. The resolute chooser, however, will, by appeal to PR, adopt plan s and then, in the event that he arrives at n_3, refuse the second trade by selecting $s(n_3)$ instead (and thereby violate SEP). Commitment to the plan he adopted, then, enables him to avoid the problem of dynamic inconsistency and thereby also avoid any violation of DSO.

What happens if Yaari's agent is made aware of the possibility of a second trade only at n_3, if and when he arrives at that second choice point? Here, as in the case of violations of CF, changes in the information available to him make a difference. If he is not informed at n_0 of the choice that will be open to him at n_3, then, of course, the problem he faces at n_0 is not fully defined. If, upon ex post reflection, the agent insists he would not have traded at n_0 had he known what he was going to face at n_3, this would suggest that he was a sophisticated agent. But, of course, the past decision is (now) irrevocable, and what he now confronts (from a sophisticated perspective) is a de novo choice between $s(n_3)$ and $r(n_3)$, whose associated prospects are, respectively, g_y and g_x. Since, by hypothesis, the latter is preferred to the former, the sophisticated agent will choose to trade, i.e., select $r(n_3)$. Thus, the sophisticated agent is exploitable in a very limited sense. By the selective withholding of information, he can be manipulated. Presumably, however, memory protects him from being exploited more than once in this manner.

What about the resolute agent? If he is not informed at n_0 about the options awaiting him at n_3, he will, by hypothesis, prefer to trade at n_0. What happens, then, if he does trade and is then informed, if and when he reaches n_3, that he may choose either g_y or g_x? Since he has not settled yet on a plan calling for resolve, are we to suppose that, like the sophisticated chooser, he will choose g_x? If so, like the sophisticated chooser he can be exploited – at least for a round. Alternatively, he might reflect upon what he would have resolved to do had he been in possession of the information he now has, and act accordingly. In this case, he will not be subject to even one round of exploitation.

5. See Raiffa (1968, p. 83), and also Section 5.5.

6. Seidenfeld (1988a, p. 273). The mixture-dominance version of independence is violated by those who, following Ellsberg, would disprefer symmetric uncertain prospects of getting either $0 or $100 to an even-chance prospect of getting $0 and $100 (see the discussion of this example in Section 4.5). The other examples discussed by Seidenfeld appeal to closely similar arguments, so discussion of the one case here should suffice.

7. By assumption, these preferences respect stochastic dominance in dollar payoffs, so there is no "incoherence" in choice among these ("static") options.

8. Seidenfeld (1988a, p. 278).

9. Seidenfeld (1988a, p. 275). In a gloss on the principle that he formulates there, Seidenfeld suggests that although choice rules do not have to induce orderings, when they do so with regard to "terminal decisions" (i.e., static choices) condition (ii) adds nothing to condition (i). Seidenfeld's point here, I take it, is that to the extent that "static" alternatives are preferentially comparable, and some lottery g_1 is judged inadmissible by reference to some other lottery g_2, which stochastically dominates it, then anything else that is judged indifferent to (the rejected) option g_1 will also be judged inadmissible. That is, the assumption that the agent has an ordering over various alternatives does the work. As the rest of the argument makes clear, however, the case in which Seidenfeld is interested is one involving a sequence of choices to be made. In that context clause (ii) does add something to (i).

10. See Seidenfeld (1988a, p. 279). I have adjusted the notation to conform to that used in the present work. As in the case of Raiffa's argument, there are ambiguities here. The argument quoted above is preceded by the following somewhat more informal remarks (once again adjusting the notation):

> At choice nodes n_3 through n_6, regardless of the fall of the coin, the agent prefers the choice he makes under plan s_1 to what he chooses under plan s_2.
> If the coin lands heads-up, the choice under s_1, at n_3, \$5.50 is preferred to the choice under s_2, at n_5, the lottery $g_1 - \$e$. Likewise, if the coin lands tails-up, the choice under s_1, at n_4, \$5.50 is preferred to the choice under s_2, at n_6, $g_2 - \$e$. Therefore, though the agent prefers plan s_2 to plan s_1 initially (at n_0), he knows that this preference is reversed at nodes n_3 through n_6, regardless of how the coin lands (pp. 278–9).

This, Seidenfeld suggests, makes the preference for plan s_2 over plan s_1 embarrassing. What, precisely, is the embarrassment, and what does it presuppose? The remarks just quoted suggest that one could, by considering just the decision tree in Figure 10.6, see that something is odd, that there is, as he puts it, a "contradiction" in the assessment of this sequential decision problem.

Let us follow this line of reasoning out. Notice, first of all, that this portion of his argument proceeds by reference to preferences across choice points in the tree. We are to suppose that after the coin is flipped the agent who embarks on plan s_2 and, for example, finds himself at n_5 will conclude that (given that flip of the coin) he now prefers that he would have chosen plan s_1 instead, which would have placed him at n_3, etc. Now what accounts for this regret? Again, of course, what we have is that Seidenfeld has simply assumed SEP to hold – and not simply with respect to choices at some point *in* the tree, but *across* different choice points. All such preferences, on this account, are simply to be read off the basic ordering of the original set of (static) lotteries. Note in particular the wording of the crucial set of claims: "If the coin lands heads-up, the choice under s_1, at n_3, \$5.50 is preferred to the choice under s_2, at n_5, the lottery $g_1 - \$e$ ... etc." Now suppose that the propriety of preference comparisons across choice points is granted and, further, that these comparisons should respect SEP. Still, the conclusion of the first paragraph does not follow. The conclusion reads, in effect, that there is an embarrassment here because, although the agent prefers plan s_2 to plan s_1 initially (at n_0), he knows that *this preference* is reversed at nodes n_3 through n_6, regardless of how the coin lands. Given the separable perspective that Seidenfeld has presupposed, the choice between plan s_1 and plan s_2 is now "water under the bridge": With what propriety, then, does Seidenfeld assume that *this preference* for plan s_2 over plan s_1 is now reversed, that he now prefers plan s_1 to plan s_2? Presumably, the question here must be one of regret again – that from the vantage point of, say, n_6, the agent now wishes that he had chosen plan s_1 – for that would have put him at n_4, etc. That is meaningful enough, but the embarrassment presumably cannot derive simply from there being some outcome that provokes such regret: Rather, the embarrassment must derive from it being the case that regret is felt regardless of what eventuates. (Any gamble – as that term is usually understood – involves some outcome such that, after the fact, the agent will regret having chosen to gamble.) Now *that* condition would seem to be satisfied: Seidenfeld is entitled to insist that the agent will experience such regret regardless of the outcome of the coin flip. On this reading, Seidenfeld's argument turns on appeal to (a sequential version of) a dominance principle. Does this mean that the argument goes through? I think not. Note, first of all, that although we are not informed as to what the composition of the gambles g_1, etc., is, we must assume (if all of this is diagnosis of the trouble that Allais, Machina, and I get into) that g_1 and g_2 are bona fide gambles that offer the possibility of some prize worth more, and some prize worth less, than not only $5 (this being, by hypothesis, the sure-dollar equivalents to these two lotteries), but of $5.50 as well (the amount the agent could have guaranteed himself had he chosen s_1 instead of s_2). But, then, although it may be true that *after* the toss of the coin, and *before* the running of the events that condition the outcomes of g_1 and g_2, the agent experiences regret, still that regret *may* be short-lived. That is, once the remaining conditioning events have been run, the agent may well be pleased with his decision to gamble on g_3 (the combination of g_1 and g_2) rather than accept $5.50 outright. But this means that he does not violate dominance with respect to what he takes to be the terminal outcomes (the outcomes that result from running the events that condition g_1 and g_2). Thus, the remarks made in Section 4.7 apply: The agent moves through a state in which a dominance relation obtains, but this is simply something he experiences *en passant*.

Alternatively put, on this interpretation of Seidenfeld's argument, the argument must appeal to GDP rather than DSO. And since, per the analysis of Chapter 3, GDP is essentially equivalent to IND, this would amount to subtly begging the issue. Levi (1986b, see, in particular, p. 144 and fn. 21, p. 235) appears to endorse this interpretation of Seidenfeld's argument when he offers an example of how the argument would run against an agent with Allais-type preferences. Incidentally, both Seidenfeld and Levi appeal to stochastic dominance in this connection, although in terms of the distinctions made in Chapter 3, it seems clear that both appeal to dominance with respect to outcomes, not probability distributions. This, presumably, is of no particular moment, however, if, as I have suggested in Chapter 3, GDP and GFSD (not FSD – recall the distinction made in Section 3.6 between FSD and the much stronger condition GFSD!) are essentially equivalent.

11. See McClennen (1988a). Seidenfeld (1988b) has suggested, in rejoinder, that my appeal there (1988a, pp. 305–7) to the condition DYN-SUB* is "question begging." I can only observe that if DYN-SUB* begs the issue of transitivity for nonsequential choice, his principle D-SUB begs the issue of substitution for nonsequential choice. The conclusion I draw from this, of course, is that *neither* condition is plausible.

12. See Seidenfeld (1988b, p. 314). In invoking the condition of "stability of values," Seidenfeld makes explicit, if I understand him correctly, something that is only implicit in my account, namely, that for the kinds of decision problem here under consideration, any given *prospect* or *consequence* is presumed to have the same value, when abstractly considered, regardless of the time at which it is being contemplated. In particular, if the agent is indifferent between g_1 and g_2, when these consequences are considered ex ante, he will still be indifferent between them when they are considered from the ex post perspective. See note 15 for more on this issue.

13. See Hammond (1988c, Sec. 2).

14. Seidenfeld has offered some additional comments in private correspondence, but I confess I am still unpersuaded. It is my expectation, and hope, that future public exchanges between us will place other interested researchers in a position to form their own judgment as to the plausibility of each of our positions on what are appropriate conditions of feasibility for those who accept a framework in which SEP holds.

15. In (1988a, p. 277, fn. 8), Seidenfeld raises a number of questions about resolute choice. It is my hope, of course, that the discussion in Sections 9.6 through 9.8 and in Chapter 12 will allay Seidenfeld's concerns about resolute choice. Let me say something here, however, specifically in response to the three sets of problems that he raises in footnote 8.

With regard to the first set of problems (I presume here that the reader is familiar with his comments), Seidenfeld incorrectly interprets my resolute chooser as having preference changes for basic lotteries at (i.e., consequences associated with) nodes. For the cases under consideration, I assume that the agent's preferences for basic lotteries do *not* change across nodes in a sequential decision tree. See the comments above in note 12 of this chapter. There is, in fact, no preference *change:* only a difference in the preferences the agent now has with respect to certain plan continuations and those he would have were he to face the same sort of situation de novo. I reject, then, Seidenfeld's inference that the resolute chooser will place a value of $6 on L_1 at (a). By hypothesis, of course, the resolute agent does value the *plan* he will finish up executing, if and when he arrives at (a), at $6 – for that plan has associated with it the consequence of L_3, which he values at $6. Seidenfeld is correct, however, when he observes that the resolute chooser does behave in *sequential choice situations* as if he were adhering to an independence requirement (albeit one framed with respect to plans and plan continuations, not outcomes). In terms of Seidenfeld's example, if at n_0 the resolute chooser prefers the plan whose associated prospect is g_3 to the plan whose associated prospect is \$5.50, then he must, if and when he arrives at n_3, prefer the plan continuation whose associated prospect is g_1 to the one whose associated prospect is \$5.50. But note that this does not commit him to the much more crucial requirement that if he prefers a de novo plan whose associated outcome is \$5.50 to one whose associated outcome is g_1, and if he then confronts two sequential plans that differ only in that at some subsequent point the first requires the choice of a plan *continuation* whose associated outcome is \$5.50, whereas the second requires choice of a plan *continuation* whose associated outcome is g_1, then he must prefer the first plan to the second.

His second set of objections, concerning the implications of resolute choice for a sequential version of an Ellsberg-type situation, are predicated once again on his (incorrectly) inferring that the resolute chooser experiences a "preference shift" with respect to outcomes. What justifies choice of the plan continuation, "take the contents of the right pocket" once the coin lands heads up, is simply that by so choosing, the agent completes the execution of that plan whose associated prospect he most prefers (i.e., $[g_1, .5; g_2, .5)$.

His third concern has to do with how resolutions are to be "ratified," i.e., by what standards the agent can reassess the merits of a resolution made at an earlier time. In very general terms, I suppose that if the original choice of a plan were justified and if circumstances have not changed, i.e., the agent has not come into possession of new information concerning either outcomes or their likelihood, then the agent is justified in acting on the plan in question. This, I take it, is only a sufficient, not a necessary, condition for ratification. But it does cover, I think, the sorts of cases that both Seidenfeld and I have focused on, e.g., the Allais and Ellsberg cases. In Chapter 12 I take up the important, and distinct, question of when an agent is justified in choosing to adopt a plan.

11. Formalizing a pragmatic perspective

1. Levi (1986b, Chaps. 5 and 6) has pressed the importance of this distinction between preference and choice. I return to this matter in Section 14.5.

2. See Section 8.6 for the characterization of CIND-S.

3. What is at issue here, I take it, is related to whether the preferences of the agent satisfy an Archimedean (or continuity) requirement. See, e.g., Herstein and Milnor (1953, p. 293, Ax. 2), Luce and Raiffa (1957, p. 27), and Seidenfeld (1988a, pp. 268–9).

4. The point is simply that creating pragmatic difficulties for the myopic chooser who violates Alpha may, as in the case of Levi's E- and S-

admissibility rules, require constructing a decision tree in which the agent has some such alternative t available to him at n_0.

5. This will not always be the case. Consider Levi's E-admissibility rule. It treats both $g_s = [\$7, p; \$0, 1 - p]$ and $g_r = [\$3]$ as admissible in pairwise comparison, but g_s is also E-admissible in pairwise comparison with $g_{r+} = [\$4]$. That is, an enhanced version of g_r is not chosen over g_s.

6. As I shall shortly illustrate, by reference to Levi's E-admissibility rule, transformations of this sort cannot invariably be made.

7. Perhaps it could be argued that E-admissibility by itself is not a plausible way to order uncertain options. It has the bothersome implication that an agent who employs it will not be able to price uncertain prospects. On the account Levi gives, any dollar amount between \$2 and \$7 will be E-admissible in pairwise comparison with $[\$7, p; \$2, 1 - p]$, when p is completely indeterminate, but for no amount in this range will the agent be completely indifferent between that amount and the gamble in question.

8. This particular technique cannot be smoothly generalized. E-admissibility satisfies another version of the independence principle, which is usually characterized as the anticonvexity condition: If a probability mixture of g_s and g_r is admissible, then so also would both g_s and g_r if they were added to the feasible set. That is, one cannot improve the situation by taking probability mixtures of options. (There is also, it should be noted, a counterpart condition, known as convexity, which requires that if both g_s and g_r are admissible, then so also is any probability mixture of these two gambles. Convexity of this sort is closely connected with Seidenfeld's MD version of independence. Levi's E-admissibility rule does not, as a matter of fact, taken by itself or in conjunction with S-admissibility, satisfy convexity. See Levi (1974, p. 411, fn. 14; p. 415, fn. 16).) Suppose that anticonvexity did not hold. Then $g_{\text{mix}(s, r)}$ might well be chosen over both components and, correspondingly, for any rule that respected DSO, $g_{\text{mix}(s+, r+)}^n$ would have to be chosen over $g_{\text{mix}(s, r)}$ – and thus one would not be able to construct a $g_{\text{mix}(s+, r+)}^n$ such that g_s is still admissible and thus leave open the possibility that the agent will head toward n_1. Since what is under consideration here are methods of evaluation that do not necessarily satisfy the independence principle, one cannot assume that anticonvexity (or convexity, for that matter) will hold. Notice, also, that the technique employed in the text also works in this case because of the odd feature of E-admissibility rule mentioned in note 5, allowing for the possibility that g_{r+} can dominate g_r, g_s can be admissible in pairwise comparison with g_r, but yet also be admissible in pairwise comparison with g_{r+}.

9. What seems to frustrate a general argument here is that within the very general framework under consideration, one has to allow for violations of convexity and anticonvexity, and for continuity problems that arise in connection with pricing gambles, etc.

10. Again, problems about pricing gambles and violations of convexity and anticonvexity complicate matters considerably.

11. I remind the reader that this argument is predicated on the assumption that a resolute approach is feasible. The next chapter is devoted to defending this assumption.

12. The feasibility of resolute choice

1. Here the letter "R" designates feasibility constrained by rationality conditions, whereas previously "R" designated simply feasibility in some restricted sense. But the thrust of the discussion is that SF and VSF (as presented in Section 8.5) are defined by reference to rationality conditions that the agent projects will constrain his future choices.
2. See Section 9.3 for an account of these cases as presented, respectively, by Strotz and Hammond.
3. For similar reasons, Schelling's interesting theory of egonomics is perhaps best understood as a theory of second best for akratic, and hence imperfectly rational, agents. See Schelling (1978a, 1984, Selections 2 and 3).
4. The folding-forward and folding-backward techniques for evaluating decision trees, as mentioned in note 10, Chapter 8, and discussed, e.g., by Raiffa (1968), serve as models of how entrenched advocates of sophisticated choice and entrenched advocates of resolute choice might proceed in this regard. The folding-forward approach involves a commitment to PR and DC, the folding-backward approach a commitment to SEP and DC. The folding-forward and folding-backward approaches themselves, of course, are simply techniques for the *evaluation* of alternative plans; under the alternative here being considered they can be taken as models of how to conceptualize the feasible alternatives available to the decision maker.
5. Of particular relevance here are the findings of Grether and Plott (1979) and Tversky and Kahneman (1981).
6. For examples and models of nonseparable preferences, see Machina (1981, pp. 172-3), Loomes and Sugden (1982, 1984, 1986), and Sugden (1986).
7. This, as far as I have been able to discern, is what motivates the introduction of the condition in Hammond's work – see in particular (1988a, b) – and it also seems to be what Arrow (1972, p. 23), e.g., takes as the motivation for his principle of conditional preferences.
8. For endogenous accounts of institutions see e.g., Buchanan and Tullock (1962), Demsetz (1964), Ullmann-Margalit (1977), and Schotter (1980). Yaari (1977) and Elster (1982, 1983) deal with endogenous changes in preferences, but both focus on nonrational processes of endogenous change.
9. I have tried to say something about the analogous problem of justice as a condition for cooperation among different individuals in McClennen (1989). For a parallel, somewhat different, but more carefully worked out account, see Gauthier (1986, esp. Chap. 5).
10. For Hume's worries about the concept of the self, see Hume (1739-40 [1888], Bk. 1, Pt. 4, Sec. 6).
11. See Butler (1726 [1729], esp. Sermon 11).

13. Connections

1. I must acknowledge two serious sins of omission. I have not explicitly addressed an important article by Machina (1989), which I received in

final draft form only after this work had been submitted to the publish-
ers. I have also not addressed D. Parfit's work, *Reasons and Persons* (1984).
To have done justice to Parfit's very thoughtful, but also very complex,
arguments would have required adding a whole new chapter to a work
that was already too long.
2. Strotz (1956, p. 173).
3. Ibid. (p. 172).
4. Ibid. (p. 177).
5. Ibid., emphasis added.
6. Ibid. (pp. 170–1).
7. Strotz (1956) concludes by reflecting on the implications of his analysis
for the issue of consumer sovereignty and, in the process, notes clearly
the parallel here to the problem of social choice:

What becomes of the concept of consumer sovereignty for dynamic decision-
making problems? . . . ought we allow people to behave imprudently? Should we
permit them the strategy of precommitment? . . . And ought we to instruct people
to substitute a log-linear discount function for the true one? . . .
  My view is that these questions are difficult to answer mainly because consumer
sovereignty has no meaning in the context of the dynamic decision-making problem. The individual over time is an infinity of individuals, and the familiar problems of interpersonal utility comparisons are there to plague us. The interpersonal
aspect of the intertemporal problem becomes clear if we think of a similar problem
involving a family of brothers where each has a utility functional depending not
only on his own utility but upon a weighted sum of the utilities of all of them.
Suppose the oldest brother always has the power to allocate the annual proceeds
of an estate, but with it being foreknown that each year one brother will die off, the
oldest next. The shifting of the discount function of the family head gives rise to
the danger of inconsistent planning; and the family head of the moment may
consider the alternative strategies of (a) an irrevocable trust, or (b) playing his
favorites extra heavily now knowing that they will be out of favor at a later date.
What can the detached view of consumer sovereignty be in this context! (p. 179)

  One might have expected that Strotz would make appeal here to the
criterion of Pareto efficiency, which does not presuppose interpersonal
comparisons. That he does not serves to underline a presupposition that
is also expressed in his account of the brothers, namely, that individuals
are capable of strategic interaction, but not cooperation. And this in turn
reveals what is fundamental to Strotz's whole account of dynamic inconsistency: I can strategically interact with my future selves, but I cannot
cooperate with them. Correspondingly, there is no suggestion that a rational approach to planning for the individual who is faced with making
choices over time will consist in rejecting strategies that fail to satisfy an
analogous condition of intertemporal optimality. That sort of criterion,
presumably, applies to those who can cooperate. Since, however, in this
context, a plan is essentially a scheme for cooperation, the implication of
Strotz's approach is that his agents do not really plan.
8. Pollack (1968); Blackorby, Nissen, Primont, and Russell (1973).
9. Peleg and Yaari (1973, p. 395).
10. Yaari (1977).
11. The only problem he finds with this approach is that, as shown by those
who discussed the original Strotz argument, the plan that is optimal in

this sense may not exist. When existence fails, however, one can always show that there exists an optimal equilibrium plan. And again, of course, if the plan that is optimal in the Strotz–Pollack sense does exist, it is an optimal equilibrium plan.

12. Yaari (1977, p. 180).
13. Johnsen and Donaldson (1985).
14. Schelling (1978a, 1984).
15. Schelling (1984, p. 69).
16. There is something odd about Schelling's studied insistence on thinking about these problems from a purely sophisticated perspective. In his original book on game theory, Schelling (1960) calls for a basic reorientation of game theory, with more emphasis on the coordinative (or cooperative), as distinct from the strategic, dimension of interactions. See, in particular, Chap. 4.
17. Thaler and Shefrin (1981).
18. Ibid. (p. 394).
19. Ibid. (p. 397).
20. Ibid.
21. Bratman (1987).
22. See Kavka (1983, pp. 33–4) and Bratman (1987, pp. 101–6).
23. Kavka (1983, p. 35).
24. Ibid. (pp. 35–6).
25. See, e.g., Gauthier (1984, p. 159).
26. Bratman (1987, p. 106).
27. See Bratman (1987, Chap. 7, esp. pp. 107–8).
28. See Elster (1979, p. 36).
29. These strategies are detailed in Elster (1979, Pt. II) and summarized in Sec. II.9 of the same work.
30. Elster (1979, p. 43).
31. Ibid. (Secs. II.3 and II.4).
32. Elster (1983, p. 21).
33. Elster (1979, pp. 105–6).
34. Ibid. (pp. 106–7).
35. Elster (1983, p. vii).
36. Elster (1979, p. 66, fn. 60).
37. Ibid. (p. 104).
38. I borrow Schelling's useful terminology here. See Schelling (1978b, Chap. 1).
39. Elster (1979, pp. 104–5).
40. Ibid. (p. 107).
41. It should not be supposed that self-management, as distinct from manipulation of the feasible set and/or our own preferences, poses no conceptual problem. Elster himself (1979) raises the issue. He speaks of the "spectre of infinite regress that must arise as soon as we introduce the spectre of self-manipulation" (p. 110). To be sure, the appeal here twice over to the notion of a "spectre" is troublesome. Manipulation of the sort that Elster characterizes as precommitment does not seem to raise any specter of a hierarchical infinite regress: It can be accounted for simply

by appeal to the notion of what it is possible for the ex ante self to impose on the ex post self, simply in virtue of the fact that causality operates only forward in time.

If, however, one wants to argue that global maximization presupposes the existence of a higher-order self that manages the preferences of the relevant time-defined selves, then there is no need to suppose that appeal to this sort of self must raise the specter of manipulation. Plato, in *The Republic*, embraces a conception of a "higher" self (reason) that is, of course, frankly authoritarian and manipulative. There is, however, as I have already mentioned, a quite different tradition, finding expression in Bishop Butler's notion of self-love and Freud's notion of the ego (as distinct from the superego!). On this view, the role of the "higher" self is that of a sympathetic manager of our passions and/or affections – of one concerned with organizing actions so as to satisfy as many as possible of our separate interests.

Elster's legitimate concern here, then, is presumably with the problem of how to appeal to the notion of some "higher-order" self (or higher-order preferences) without opening the door, at least in principle, to higher orders ad infinitum. He himself suggests that escape from such a regress may be possible along lines analogous to those employed in game theory in which the apparent regress in reciprocal expectations does not preclude there being a solution to a game. Alternatively, I would suggest, it is open to us to try to account for such a hierarchical structure by reference to evolutionary theory: Beings who are capable of such a form of self-management may plausibly be thought to have a better chance of survival.

42. Elster (1979, p. 52, fn. 37).
43. Ibid. (p. 87).

14. Conclusions

1. Savage (1954 [1972], p. 102), emphasis added. If I have spent a great deal of this work looking at various alleged formal demonstrations, it is precisely because, despite Savage's cautionary remarks, theorem building has been the favored approach.
2. Kahneman and Tversky (1979, pp. 283–4); see also Seidenfeld (1988, p. 274, fn. 6). Once again, however, I remind the reader that, on my reading, neither Seidenfeld (1988a,b) nor Levi (1986b, pp. 144, 235, fn. 21) have managed to show that the agent who violates IND can be caught in a violation of DSO (or FSD). All they have shown is that such an agent will end up violating GDP (or GFSD). Since the latter are essentially equivalent to IND itself, that Seidenfeld and Levi are able to show this is not surprising. See Section 10.5, esp. fn. 10.
3. I adapt this from D. Lewis (1981).
4. Allais (1953, 1979), Levi (1974, 1986b), Allais and Hagen (1979), and Machina (1982, 1983).
5. See McClennen (1983); also McClennen (1981).

6. See Levi (1986a, 1986b, Sec. 7.7, esp. pp. 130–1, and Sec. 7.8, esp. p. 144).
7. See in particular Allais (1979), who argues for the principle of first-order stochastic dominance (which he terms the principle of absolute preference) while still rejecting the independence axiom.
8. Ellsberg (1961).
9. Savage (1951, p. 58).
10. Friedman and Savage (1952, pp. 468–9).
11. Savage (1954 [1972], p. 99).
12. Hirschman (1977).

15. Postscript: projections

1. See, e.g., Harsanyi (1977, p. 186).
2. It is clear that a myopic choice approach does not in general satisfy the analogous requirement on rational ex ante choice, whereas a sophisticated approach does. Indeed, in situations in which there is a divergence between ex ante and ex post evaluations, the distinction between myopic and sophisticated choice of the sort that Strotz characterizes as "consistent planning" is precisely the distinction between an ex ante self that fails to take account of what its ex post self will do (that fails to maximize in the light of what it can expect its ex post self will choose to do, on independent grounds) and an ex ante self that does select its own plan in the light of the future and independently oriented behavior of its own ex post self.
3. Von Neumann and Morgenstern (1944 [1953], p. 11).
4. Kaysen (1946–7, p. 2).
5. Von Neumann and Morgenstern (1944 [1953], pp. 147–8).
6. Luce and Raiffa (1957, pp. 63–4).
7. McClennen (1975, 1978).
8. For very simple situations involving two players, the Pareto criterion can be formulated in the following manner: The strategies that two players choose can be said to be interpersonally optimal iff there exists no alternative way of interacting such that the associated prospect of so doing would be judged preferable by each player. This criterion of interpersonal optimality, it should be noted, applies not only to games in which play is simultaneous but also to games in which play is sequential.
9. I have offered a sketch of such an extension in McClennen (1985).
10. See, e.g., Luce and Raiffa (1957, pp. 63–4) and Nash (1951). Separability in this context, in requiring the agent to maximize against his expectations concerning how the others will choose, also requires choice of dominating over dominated strategies. In this sense, many of those who are not altogether convinced by the equilibrium argument still hold that in the standard Prisoners' Dilemma game, rational players who know each other to be such must defect. But as Howard (1971, esp. the discussion of the "Third" paradox of rationality) showed many years ago, those who approach such games with a heightened sense of the potential for gain through coordination (as expressed by his notion that they will employ meta-game strategies), but who still are committed to dominance argu-

ments, will not do as well as they would have done had they been able to resist the lure of this form of reasoning.

11. See Nash (1953); also Luce and Raiffa (1957, Sec. 6.9, pp. 140–3).
12. Gauthier (1986).
13. I address one aspect of such a defense of Gauthier's position in McClennen (1988b).
14. Plato, *The Republic,* Book 2.
15. Moral rules, in short, exhibit the features of public goods and are thus subject, on the standard account of rationality, to the problem of free riding.
16. For an account of the practice conception of rules, see Rawls (1955) and Harsanyi (1982, pp. 56–60).
17. For a sense of how difficult it is to stretch the concept of self-interest see, e.g., Hobbes (1651, Pt. 1, Chap. 15), who attempts (unsuccessfully) to deal with the "fool who says in his heart there is no justice, . . . that every man's conservation and contentment being committed to his care, there could be no reason why every man might not do what he thought conduced to one's benefit," and Hume (1951, Sec. 9, Pt. 2), who attempts to answer the fool's cousin, the sensible knave.

Bibliography

Alchian, A. (1953). "The Meaning of Utility Measurement." *American Economic Review, 43,* 26–50.

Allais, M. (1953). "Le comportement de l'homme rationnel devant le risque: Critique des postulats et axioms de l'école americaine." *Econometrica, 21,* 503–46.

(1979). "The Foundations of a Positive Theory of Choice Involving Risk and a Criticism of the Postulates and Axioms of the American School." In *Expected Utility Hypothesis and the Allais Paradox,* ed. M. Allais and O. Hagen. Dordrecht: Reidel (translation of a paper originally published in 1953, in *Econometrie,* Vol. 40).

Allais, M., and Hagen, O., eds. (1979). *Expected Utility Hypothesis and the Allais Paradox.* Dordrecht: Reidel.

Anscombe, F. J., and Aumann, R. J. (1963). "A Definition of Subjective Probability." *Annals of Mathematical Statistics, 34,* 199–205.

Arrow, K. J. (1959). "Rational Choice Functions and Orderings." *Economica, 26,* 121–7.

(1972). "Exposition of the Theory of Choice Under Conditions of Uncertainty." In *Decision and Organization,* ed. C. B. McGuire and R. Radner. Amsterdam: North Holland, 19–55.

Baumol, W. J. (1951). "The Neumann–Morgenstern Utility Index: An Ordinalist View." *Journal of Political Economy, 59,* 61–6.

Bellman, R. (1954). "The Theory of Dynamic Programming." *Bulletin of the American Mathematical Society, 60,* 503–15.

Blackorby, C., Nissen, D., Primont, D., and Russell, R. R. (1973). "Consistent Intertemporal Decision Making." *Review of Economic Studies, 40,* 239–48.

Bratman, M. E. (1987). *Intention, Plans, and Practical Reason.* Cambridge, Mass.: Harvard University Press.

Brewer, K. R. W. (1963). "Decisions under Uncertainty: Comment." *Quarterly Journal of Economics, 77,* 159–61.

Broome, J. (1988). "Rationality and the Sure-Thing Principle." Unpublished manuscript.

Buchanan, J., and Tullock, G. (1962). *The Calculus of Consent.* Ann Arbor: University of Michigan Press.

Butler, J. (1726, 2d ed., 1729). *Fifteen Sermons upon Human Nature.* London.

Campbell, R., and Sowden, L., eds. (1985). *Paradoxes of Rationality and Cooperation: Prisoner's Dilemma and Newcomb's Problem.* Vancouver: University of British Columbia Press.

Chernoff, H. (1949). "Rational Selection of Decision Functions." *Econometrica, 22,* 422–43.

Daniels, N. (1979). "Wide Reflective Equilibrium and Theory Acceptance in Ethics." *Journal of Philosophy, 76,* 256–82.

Davidson, D., McKinsey, J., and Suppes, P. (1955). "Outlines of a Formal Theory of Value, I." *Philosophy of Science, 22,* 60–80.

de Finetti, B. (1937). "La prévision: ses lois logiques, ses sources subjectives." *Annales de l'Institut Henri Poincaré, 7,* 1–68 (translated and reprinted in Kyburg and Smokler [1964]).

Demsetz, H. (1964). "Toward a Theory of Property Rights." *American Economic Review, 57,* 347–59.

Diamond, P., and Rothschild, M., eds. (1978). *Uncertainty in Economics.* New York: Academic Press.

Econometrie. (1953). Colloque internationaux au Centre national de la recherche scientifique, *40,* Paris.

Ellsberg, D. (1954). "Classic and Current Notions of 'Measurable Utility.' " *Economic Journal, 64,* 528–56.

——— (1961). "Risk, Ambiguity, and the Savage Axioms." *Quarterly Journal of Economics, 75,* 643–69 (reprinted in Gärdenfors and Sahlin [1988]).

Elster, J. (1979). *Ulysses and the Sirens: Studies in Rationality and Irrationality.* Cambridge University Press.

——— (1982). "Sour Grapes: Utilitarianism and the Genesis of Wants." In *Utilitarianism and Beyond,* ed. A. K. Sen and B. Williams. Cambridge University Press, pp. 219–38.

——— (1983). *Sour Grapes: Studies in the Subversion of Rationality.* Cambridge University Press.

Fellner, W. (1961). "Distortion of Subjective Probabilities as a Reaction to Uncertainty." *Quarterly Journal of Economics, 75,* 670–89.

——— (1963). "Slanted Subjective Probabilities and Randomization: Reply to Howard Raiffa and K. R. W. Brewer." *Quarterly Journal of Economics, 77,* 676–90.

Fishburn, P. (1981). "Subjective Expected Utility: A Review of Normative Theories." *Theory and Decision, 13,* 139–99.

——— (1982). *The Foundations of Expected Utility Theory.* Dordrecht: Reidel.

Friedman, M., and Savage, L. (1948). "The Utility Analysis of Choices Involving Risk." *Journal of Political Economy, 56,* 279–304.

——— (1952). "The Expected-Utility Hypothesis and the Measurability of Utility." *Journal of Political Economy, 60,* 463–74.

Gärdenfors, P., and Sahlin, N.-E., eds. (1988). *Decision, Probability, and Utility: Selected Readings.* Cambridge University Press.

Gauthier, D. (1984). "Afterthoughts." In *The Security Gamble,* ed. D. MacLean. Totowa: Rowman & Allanheld, pp. 159–61.

——— (1986). *Morals by Agreement.* Oxford: Clarendon Press.

Gibbard, A., and Harper, W. L. (1978). "Counterfactuals and Two Kinds of Expected Utility." In *Foundations and Applications of Decision Theory,* Vol. 1, ed. C. Hooker, J. Leach, and E. F. McClennen. Dordrecht: Reidel, pp. 125–62 (reprinted in Campbell and Sowden [1985] and Gärdenfors and Sahlin [1988]).

Green, J. (1987). " 'Making Book Against Oneself': The Independence Axiom and Non-Linear Utility Theory." *Quarterly Journal of Economics, 102,* 785–96.

Grether, D. M., and Plott, C. R. (1979). "Economic Theory of Choice and the Preference Reversal Phenomenon." *American Economic Review, 69,* 623–38.

Hammond, P. (1976). "Changing Tastes and Coherent Dynamic Choice." *Review of Economic Studies, 43,* 159–73.

(1977). "Dynamic Restrictions on Metastatic Choice." *Economica, 44,* 337–50.

(1982a). "Consequentialism and Rationality in Dynamic Choice Under Uncertainty." *Institute for Mathematical Studies in the Social Sciences, Economics Technical Report No. 387.* Stanford, Calif.: Stanford University.

(1982b). "Utilitarianism, Uncertainty, and Information." In *Utilitarianism and Beyond,* ed. A. K. Sen and B. Williams. Cambridge University Press, pp. 85–102.

(1988a). "Consequentialism and the Independence Axiom." In *Risk, Decision and Rationality,* ed. B. R. Munier. Dordrecht: Reidel, pp. 503–16.

(1988b). "Consequentialist Foundations for Expected Utility." *Theory and Decision, 25,* 25–78.

(1988c). "Orderly Decision Theory: A Comment on Professor Seidenfeld." *Economics and Philosophy, 4,* 292–7.

Hansson, B. (1975). "The Appropriateness of the Expected Utility Model." *Erkenntnis, 9,* 175–93.

Hare, R. M. (1952). *The Language of Morals.* New York: Oxford University Press.

Harsanyi, J. C. (1977). *Rational Behavior and Bargaining Equilibrium in Games and Social Situations.* Cambridge University Press.

(1978). "Bayesian Decision Theory and Utilitarian Ethics." *American Economic Review, 68,* 223–8.

(1982). "Morality and the Theory of Rational Behavior." In *Utilitarianism and Beyond,* ed. A. K. Sen and B. Williams. Cambridge University Press, pp. 39–62.

Herstein, I. N., and Milnor, J. W. (1953). "An Axiomatic Approach to Measurable Utility." *Econometrica, 21,* 291–7.

Herzberger, H. (1973). "Ordinal Preference and Rational Choice." *Econometrica, 41,* 187–237.

Hirschman, A. O. (1977). *The Passions and the Interests: Political Arguments for Capitalism Before Its Triumph.* Princeton, N.J.: Princeton University Press.

Hobbes, T. (1651). *The English Works of Thomas Hobbes,* ed. W. Molesworth. Vol. 3: *Leviathan,* London: Bohn, 1839.

Hooker, C., Leach, J., and McClennen, E. F. (1978). *Foundatons and Applications of Decision Theory,* 2 vols. Dordrecht: Reidel.

Howard, N. (1971). *The Paradoxes of Rationality.* Cambridge, Mass.: MIT Press.

Hume, D. (1739–40, Selby-Bigge ed., 1888). *A Treatise of Human Nature.* Oxford: Clarendon Press.

(1951, Selby-Bigge 3d ed., 1975). *Enquiries Concerning Human Understanding and Concerning the Principles of Morals,* Oxford: Clarendon Press.

Jeffrey, R. C. (1965). *The Logic of Decision.* New York: McGraw-Hill.

Johnsen, T. H., and Donaldson, J. B. (1985). "The Structure of Intertemporal Preferences Under Uncertainty and Time Consistent Plans." *Econometrica, 53,* 1451–8.

Kahneman, D., and Tversky, A. (1979). "Prospect Theory: An Analysis of Decision Under Risk." *Econometrica, 47,* 263–91 (reprinted in Gärdenfors and Sahlin [1988]).

Kahneman, D., Slovic, P., and Tversky, A. (1982). *Judgement Under Uncertainty: Heuristics and Biases.* Cambridge University Press.

Kavka, G. (1983). "The Toxin Puzzle." *Analysis, 43,* 33–6.

Kaysen, K. (1946–7). "A Revolution in Economic Theory?" *Review of Economic Studies, 14*(1), 1–15.

Kemeny, J. (1955). "Fair Bets and Inductive Probabilities." *Journal of Symbolic Logic, 20,* 263–73.

Krantz, D., Luce, R. D., Suppes, P., and Tversky, A. (1971). *Foundations of Measurement.* New York: Academic Press.

Kreps, D., and Porteus, E. (1978). "Temporal Resolution of Uncertainty and Dynamic Choice Theory." *Econometrica, 46,* 185–200.

(1979). "Temporal von Neumann–Morgenstern and Induced Preferences." *Journal of Economic Theory, 20,* 81–109.

Kyburg, H. E. (1961). *Probability and the Logic of Rational Belief.* Middletown, Conn.: Wesleyan University Press.

(1978). "Subjective Probability: Criticisms, Reflections, and Problems." *Journal of Philosophical Logic, 7,*157–80.

Kyburg, H. E., and Smokler, H., eds. (1964). *Studies in Subjective Probability.* New York: Wiley.

Lehmann, R. S. (1955). "On Confirmation and Rational Betting." *Journal of Symbolic Logic, 20,* 251–62.

Levi, I. (1974). "Indeterminate Probabilities." *Journal of Philosophy, 71,* 391–418 (reprinted in Hooker, Leach, and McClennen [1978], Vol. 1, and Gärdenfors and Sahlin [1988]).

(1980). *The Enterprise of Knowledge.* Cambridge, Mass.: MIT Press.

(1986a). "The Paradoxes of Allais and Ellsberg." *Economics and Philosophy, 2,* 23–53.

(1986b). *Hard Choices.* Cambridge University Press.

(1987). "The Demons of Decision," *The Monist, 70,* 193–211.

Lewis, C. I. (1946). *An Analysis of Knowledge and Valuation,* La Salle, Ill.: Open Court.

Lewis, D. (1981). "Why Ain'cha Rich?" *Nous, 5,* 377–80.

Loomes, G., and Sugden, R. (1982). "Regret Theory: An Alternative Theory of Rational Choice Under Uncertainty." *Economic Journal, 92,* 805–24.

(1984). "The Importance of What Might Have Been." In *Progress in Utility and Risk Theory,* ed. O. Hagen and F. Wenstop, Dordrecht: Reidel, pp. 219–35.

(1986). "Disappointment and Dynamic Consistency in Choice Under Uncertainty." *Review of Economic Studies, 53,* 271–82.

Luce, R. D., and Raiffa, H. (1957). *Games and Decisions.* New York: Wiley.

Luce, R. D., and Suppes, P. (1965). "Preference, Utility and Subjective Probability." In *Handbook of Mathematical Psychology,* Vol. 3, ed. R. D. Luce, R. R. Bush, and E. Galanter. New York: Wiley, pp. 191–243.

Lyon, P. (1980). *Preference Aggregation,* Ph. D. dissertation, Washington University.

Machina, M. (1981). " 'Rational' Decision Making versus 'Rational' Decision Modelling?" *Journal of Mathematical Psychology, 24,* 163–75.

(1982). " 'Expected Utility' Analysis without the Independence Axiom." *Econometrica, 50,* 277–323.

(1983). "The Economic Theory of Individual Behavior Toward Risk: Theory, Evidence, and New Directions." *Institute for Mathematical Studies in the Social Sciences, Economics Technical Report No. 433,* Stanford, Calif.: Stanford University.

(1989). "Dynamic Consistency and Non-expected Utility Models of Choice under Uncertainty." *Journal of Economic Theory, 27,* 1622–68.

MacCrimmon, K. R., and Larsson, S. (1979). "Utility Theory: Axioms versus

'Paradoxes.' " In *Expected Utility Hypothesis and the Allais Paradox*, ed.
    M. Allais and O. Hagen. Dordrecht: Reidel, pp. 333–409.
Malinvaud, E. (1952). "Note on von Neumann–Morgenstern's Strong Inde-
    pendence Axiom." *Econometrica, 20*, 679.
Manne, A. S. (1952). "The Strong Independence Assumption: Gasoline
    Blends and Probability Mixtures." *Econometrica, 20*, 665–8.
Markowitz, H. (1959). *Portfolio Selection: Efficient Diversification of Investments*.
    New Haven, Conn.: Yale University Press.
Marschak, J. (1951). "Why 'Should' Statisticians and Businessmen Maximize
    Moral Expectation?" In *Proceedings of the Second Berkeley Symposium on
    Mathematical Statistics and Probability*, ed. J. Neyman. Berkeley and Los
    Angeles: University of California Press, pp. 493–506.
    (1968). "Decision Making: Economic Aspects." *International Encyclopedia of
    the Social Sciences*, Vol. 4. New York: Macmillan and the Free Press, pp.
    42–55.
McClennen, E. F. (1972). "An Incompleteness Problem in Harsanyi's General
    Theory of Games and Certain Related Theories of Non-cooperative
    Games." *Theory and Decision, 2*, 314–41.
    (1975). "Some Formal Problems with the von Neumann and Morgenstern
    Theory of Two-Person, Zero-Sum Games, I: The Direct Proof." *Theory
    and Decision, 6*, 1–28.
    (1978). "The Minimax Theory and Expected-Utility Reasoning." In *Foun-
    dations and Applications of Decision Theory*, Vol. 1, ed. C. Hooker, J. Leach,
    and E. F. McClennen. Dordrecht: Reidel, pp. 337–67.
    (1981). "Constitutional Choice: Rawls vs. Harsanyi." In *Philosophical Prob-
    lems in Economics*, ed. J. Pitt. Dordrecht: Reidel, pp. 93–109.
    (1983). "Sure-Thing Doubts." In *Foundations of Utility and Risk Theory with
    Applications*, ed. B. P. Stigum and F. Wenstop, pp. 117–36 (reprinted,
    with a postscript, in Gärdenfors and Sahlin [1988]).
    (1985). "Prisoner's Dilemma and Resolute Choice." In *Paradoxes of Ratio-
    nality and Cooperation*, ed. R. Campbell and L. Sowden. Vancouver: Uni-
    versity of British Columbia Press, pp. 94–104.
    (1988a). "Ordering and Independence: A Comment on Professor Seiden-
    feld." *Economics and Philosophy, 4*, 298–308.
    (1988b). "Constrained Maximization and Resolute Choice." *Social Philosophy
    and Policy, 5*, 95–118.
    (1989). "Justice and the Problem of Stability." *Philosophy and Public Affairs,
    18*, 3–30.
Milnor, J. (1954). "Games Against Nature." In *Decision Processes*, ed. R. M.
    Thrall, C. H. Coombs, and R. L. Davis. New York: Wiley, pp. 49–60.
Nash, J. (1951). "Non-Cooperative Games." *Annals of Mathematics, 54*, 286–95.
    (1953). "Two-Person Cooperative Games." *Econometrica, 21*, 128–40.
Parfit, D. (1984). *Reasons and Persons*. Oxford: Clarendon Press.
Peleg, B., and Yaari, M. E. (1973). "On the Existence of a Consistent Course
    of Action When Tastes Are Changing." *Review of Economic Studies, 40*,
    391–401.
Pollack, R. A. (1968). "Consistent Planning." *Review of Economic Studies, 35*,
    201–8.
Pratt, J. W., Raiffa, H., and Schlaifer, R. (1964). "The Foundations of Deci-
    sions under Uncertainty: An Elementary Exposition." *Journal of the Amer-
    ican Statistical Association, 59*, 353–75.
Quine, W. V. O. (1951). "Two Dogmas of Empiricism." *Philosophical Review*,

60, 20–43 (reprinted, with minor revisions, in W. V. O. Quine, *From A Logical Point of View*, Cambridge, Mass.: Harvard University Press [1953]).

Raiffa, H. (1961). "Risk, Ambiguity, and the Savage Axioms: Comment." *Quarterly Journal of Economics, 75,* 690–4.

——— (1968). *Decision Analysis.* Reading, Mass.: Addison-Wesley.

Ramsey, F. P. (1931). "Truth and Probability." In *Foundations of Mathematics and Other Logical Essays,* ed. R. B. Braithwaite. London: Routledge & Kegan Paul, pp. 156–98 (reprinted in Kyburg and Smokler [1964] and Gärdenfors and Sahlin [1988]).

Rawls, J. (1951). "An Outline of a Decision Procedure for Ethics." *Philosophical Review, 60,* 177–97.

——— (1955). "Two Concepts of Rules." *Philosophical Review, 64,* 3–32.

——— (1971). *A Theory of Justice.* Cambridge, Mass.: Harvard University Press.

Rubin, H. (1949). "The Existence of Measurable Utility and Psychological Probability." Cowles Commission Discussion Paper, Statistics, No. 332.

Samuelson, P. (1950). "Probability and the Attempts to Measure Utility." In *The Collected Scientific Papers of Paul A. Samuelson,* Vol. 1, ed. J. E. Stiglitz. Cambridge, Mass.: MIT Press, 1966, pp. 117–26.

——— (1952). "Probability, Utility, and the Independence Axiom." *Econometrica, 20,* 670–8.

Savage, L. J. (1951). "The Theory of Statistical Decision." *Journal of American Statistics Association, 46,* 55–67.

——— (1954, 2d rev. ed., 1972). *The Foundations of Statistics.* New York: Dover.

Schelling, T. C. (1960). *The Strategy of Conflict.* Cambridge, Mass.: Harvard University Press.

——— (1978a). "Egonomics, or the Art of Self-Management." *American Economic Review: Papers and Proceedings, 68,* 290–4.

——— (1978b). *Micromotives and Macrobehavior.* New York: Norton.

——— (1984). *Choice and Consequence.* Cambridge, Mass.: Harvard University Press.

Schick, F. (1958). *Explication and Inductive Logic,* Ph.D. dissertation, Columbia University.

——— (1979). "Self-Knowledge, Uncertainty, and Choice." *British Journal for the Philosophy of Science, 30,* 235–52 (reprinted in Gärdenfors and Sahlin [1988]).

——— (1984). *Having Reasons: An Essay in Sociality.* Princeton, N.J.: Princeton University Press.

——— (1986). "Dutch Bookies and Money Pumps." *Journal of Philosophy, 83,* 112–19.

Schoemaker, P. J. H. (1980). *Experiments on Decision Under Risk: The Expected Utility Hypothesis.* Boston: Nijhoff.

Schotter, A. (1980). *The Economic Theory of Social Institutions.* Cambridge University Press.

Seidenfeld, T. (1988a). "Decision Theory without 'Independence' or without 'Ordering': What Is the Difference?" *Economics and Philosophy, 4,* 267–90.

——— (1988b). "Rejoinder." *Economics and Philosophy, 4,* 309–15.

Sen, A. K. (1970). *Collective Choice and Social Welfare.* San Francisco: Holden Day.

——— (1971). "Choice Functions and Revealed Preference." *Review of Economic Studies, 38,* 307–17 (reprinted in Sen [1982]).

(1973). "Behaviour and the Concept of Preference." *Economica, 40,* 241–259 (reprinted in Sen [1982]).

(1982). *Choice, Welfare and Measurement.* Oxford: Blackwell Publisher.

(1985). "Rationality and Uncertainty." *Theory and Decision, 18,* 109–27.

Shimony, A. (1955). "Coherence and the Axioms of Confirmation." *Journal of Symbolic Logic, 20,* 1–28.

Stigum, B. P., and Wenstop, F., eds. (1983). *Foundations of Utility and Risk Theory with Applications.* Dordrecht: Reidel.

Strotz, R. H. (1956). "Myopia and Inconsistency in Dynamic Utility Maximization." *Review of Economic Studies, 23,* 165–80.

Sugden, R. (1986). "Regret, Recrimination and Rationality." *Theory and Decision, 19,* 77–99.

Suzumura, K. (1976). "Rational Choice and Revealed Preference." *Review of Economic Studies, 43,* 149–58.

Thaler, R. H., and Shefrin, H. M. (1981). "An Economic Theory of Self-Control." *Journal of Political Economy, 89,* 392–406.

Timmons, M. (1987). "Foundationalism and the Structure of Ethical Justification." *Ethics, 97,* 595–609.

Tversky, A. (1975). "A Critique of Expected Utility Theory: Descriptive and Normative Considerations." *Erkenntnis, 9,* 163–73.

Tversky, A., and Kahneman, D. (1981). "The Framing of Decisions and the Psychology of Choice." *Science, 211,* 453–8.

Ullmann-Margalit, E. (1977). *The Emergence of Norms.* New York: Oxford University Press.

von Neumann, J., and Morgenstern, O. (1944, 3d ed., 1953). *Theory of Games and Economic Behavior.* New York: Wiley.

White, M. (1956). *Toward Reunion in Philosophy.* Cambridge, Mass.: Harvard University Press.

Yaari, M. E. (1977). "Endogenous Changes in Taste: A Philosophical Discussion." *Erkenntnis, 11,* 157–96.

(1985). "On the Role of 'Dutch Books' in the Theory of Choice Under Risk." 1985 Nancy L. Schwartz Memorial Lecture, J. L. Kellog Graduate School of Management, Northwestern University.

Author index

Subject index